CHRISTIAN ETHICS
AND THE
HUMAN PERSON

CHRISTIAN ETHICS
AND THE
HUMAN PERSON

Truth and Relativism
in Contemporary Moral Theology

PETER BRISTOW

GRACEWING

First published jointly in England in 2009 by
Maryvale Institute and Family Publications

This edition published in 2013
by
Gracewing
2 Southern Avenue
Leominster
Herefordshire HR6 0QF
United Kingdom
www.gracewing.co.uk

No part of this publication may be reproduced, stored in a
retrieval system, or transmitted in any form or by any means,
electronic, mechanical, photocopying, recording or otherwise,
without the written permission of the publisher.

The right of Peter Bristow to be identified
as the author of this work has been asserted in accordance
with the Copyright, Designs and Patents Act 1988.

© Peter Bristow 2009, 2013

ISBN 978 085244 814 4

Imprimatur
Monsignor Canon Mark Davies
Vicar General of the Diocese of Salford
12 March 2009

Nihil Obstat
Monsignor Richard Stork MSc STD
26 February 2009

Cover design by Bernardita Peña Hurtado

Contents

Preface 5

Foreword 8

I Fundamental Principles of Ethics

1. Ethics after Vatican II: Personalism and Renewal in an Age of Secularism 19
2. The Fundamental Elements and the distinctiveness of Rational Christian Ethics 44
3. The Anthropological basis of Ethics and Bio-Ethics 74
4. Contemporary Personalism: the Subjectivity and Self-determination of the Person 102
5. Natural Law protects the Goods and Rights of the Person ... 129
6. Freedom, Autonomy and Truth 156

II Controversy and Renewal

7. Moral Revisionism: Proportionalism and the Fundamental Option 182
8. Human Action and the Sources of Morality 208

III Biblical Ethics

9. The Biblical Foundations: Law and Evangelical Grace 224
10. The Pursuit of Virtue and the Sermon on the Mount 248

IV Special Questions: Gender, Contraception and the Renewal of Marriage

11. The Theology of the Body Discourses on the Human Person in Genesis 272
12. Sexuality, Gender and Feminism 294
13. Marriage and the Renewal of the Family 313
14. *Humanae Vitae*: A Test-Case for Christian Ethics 336

Conclusion: Morality and Evangelization 362

Bibliography 373

Index 380

*In gratitude to my mother
from whom I received my first lessons in
faith, love and human dignity*

PREFACE

The present work proposes to fulfil the contemporary need for an explanation of Catholic ethics as it has been renewed in the second half of the twentieth century by Vatican II, the *Catechism of the Catholic Church*, *Veritatis Splendor*, *Evangelium Vitae* and the theology which gave rise to it. It explains how this process consists in a return to the sources of Tradition and Scripture, as well as to the Thomistic-Aristotelian roots of natural law, freedom and reason, virtue ethics, happiness and the goods and final good of the person. At the same time renewal consists in taking account of the contemporary post-Enlightenment mentality with its concern for the human person, subjectivity, human rights, gender questions and freedom. This updating of moral theology has been essential to enable it to confront successfully today's questions concerning moral autonomy, sexual ethics and bio-technology, etc.

In addition to those already mentioned it deals with basic ethical principles and concepts such as the nature of personhood, the question of moral absolutes, the principle of double effect, the link between act and experience, conscience, the relation of faith and reason, and that between freedom and truth, which are of perennial interest, but are also at the heart of contemporary ethical debate. It applies these principles particularly to issues of sexual ethics, such as cohabitation, contraception and gender matters, as well as to bio-ethical issues of human fertilization and genetic research. The purpose is to explain the reasons behind the moral positions the Catholic Church holds in the light of today's developments.

A further purpose is to examine the vast ethical heritage left by Pope John Paul II whose aim was to present and explain ethics according to the needs of our time, and so it draws extensively on his personalism and considers his use of the phenomenological method. We have principally studied his contribution to the renewal of marriage and family life as it is found in *Familiaris*

Consortio, the *Theology of the Body* discourses and the *Letter to Families*. These bring out clearly the sanctity of human life and, indeed, of the body as an integral part of the person which has crucial consequences for understanding Christian ethics. It was also necessary to consider his writings prior to being Pope. He trained as a moral philosopher and theologian. While there is published work on this part of his life, little has so far been done to show the link between this and the renewal of moral teaching during his pontificate. It is a vast subject, but the present work intends to make an initial contribution.

This updating, together with the contribution of major ethical writers such as Pinckaers, Grisez, MacIntyre and others, equips Catholic ethics for the debate brought about by the bio-scientific and sexual revolutions. It also enables it to respond at a philosophical and theological level to the moral revisionism and proportionalism which have drifted away from Christian moral tradition as it is authoritatively taught in *Veritatis Splendor*.

Catholics need to know at the present time how to draw on the riches of their own Tradition to be able to confront the new issues of the twenty-first century, and explain that Tradition in the language of today. The Church has been going through a period of renewal of moral theology since Vatican II, but the multiplicity of, sometimes, discordant voices has left aspects of its teaching obscure, thereby necessitating that the Magisterium attend to 'sound doctrine' (2 Tim 4:3) so that the renewal may proceed according to a 'hermeneutic of continuity'[1].

The explanation of Catholic moral principles and the reasoning behind them also requires an investigation into the origins of contemporary secularism and relativism in order to be able to put over a more adequate Christian response. The Christian theologian, like the scribe of the Kingdom, must bring new things and old out of his storehouse (cf. Mt 13:52). Theology consists in the affirming of basic principles, but also in an ever deepening growth in the understanding of God's Word, using the tools of reason and philosophical analysis, in order to be able to throw new light on developing problems.

---

[1] See Benedict XVI, Discourse to the Roman Curia, 22-XII-2005.

PREFACE

The Faith of the Church has often received systematic treatment in handy and reader-friendly volumes. They bring out the coherence and consistency of Catholic teaching and thought by giving us an understanding of a particular doctrine and enabling us to grasp it more deeply by seeing its relationship to the whole spectrum of the Faith. Something similar is timely for Christian ethics so that the faithful and those who seek to understand Christian morality can see its unity and the force of its rationale in the face of constant criticism from secularism.

We also need to be able to appreciate not only the relation and harmony of faith and reason, but also the indispensable connection between faith and ethics bearing in mind that ethics is lived doctrine. That is to say, faith requires a determinate behaviour of its adherents and the assurance that a moral stance and growth in a Christian way of life is indispensable to a strong faith especially at a time when relativism eats away at the tenets of Christian customs. This is particularly pertinent when many Catholics cease to practise their faith, often, at least initially, due to problems of a moral nature, whether intellectual or practical.

We wish to show that the moral teaching of Christianity has a compelling attractiveness which enables the human person to live and grow according to human dignity, become more of a person and contribute meaningfully to the common good and the well-being of his, or her, neighbour and society in general. However, to paraphrase what Chesterton said about Christianity as a whole, very often it has not been tried and found wanting, but in our own time it has not been learnt properly in the first place. We wish to counteract this void by contributing to a wider and deeper understanding of Christian ethics.

I have many debts to pay; in the first place to my parents and my many teachers in philosophy and theology who guided my steps and laid the foundations for my grasp of ethics. I wish to express my thanks to Fr Richard Stork, Colin Harte, Tom D'Andrea and Russell D'Arcy who read all or part of the manuscript and made comments. Also to Petroc Willey and the staff at Maryvale Institute who have always been supportive and encouraging in this work.

FOREWORD

The history of Christian ethics during the first half-century following Vatican II has been characterized by development and renewal as well as by an unrelenting struggle with secularism and relativism. During this time the Church has endeavoured to engage more effectively with the world and communicate its message of salvation by shaping its presentation of Christian ethics to the needs of the times. This has involved retrieving sources from its own tradition that have been left in abeyance, as, for example, those which show the Evangelical Law and, especially, the virtues and the beatitudes of the Sermon on the Mount to be the fulfilment of the Old Law. It has also sought to put over moral theology in a more everyday and existential form, replacing the codified and manualistic practice of the earlier part of the last century with straightforward narrative writing, with a view to explaining its content rather than just proclaiming it, as law does. Greater attention has been given to the biblical basis of ethics, therefore, as well as to the philosophical underpinning of it and to a presentation more suited to contemporary language and experience.

The present work is not a study of personalism as such, but rather of Christian ethics in general with particular reference to the progress and problems of the last half-century. Hence the term 'personalism' is being used here to refer partly to the movement of that name but mainly to cover the truth and nature of the human person as it is communicated to us in Christian tradition as well as in Vatican II, especially *Gaudium et Spes,* and the pontificate of John Paul II. The recent Magisterium's abundant teaching on the subject reflects the modern age's concentration on anthropology and the Church's desire to carry out a new evangelization by dialoguing with the men and women of our times. Without an accurate anthropology, Christian teaching would not be able to deal adequately with the issues of sexual ethics, gender, marriage, homosexuality as well as the bio-ethical matters which have taken on so much importance in our time. In a word, Christian anthropology, which has always been an essential part of ethics, has become increasingly indispensable and has itself had to keep pace with new ethical questions, hence John Paul II's discourses on the theology of the body.

Our purpose is to treat of the main topics of Christian ethics and also ask why it often finds such infertile ground for its teaching in the West. Much of the general answer revolves around the issue of freedom, which for many stands alone as the value constituting their end and purpose and is conceived as a moral autonomy, giving them the right to define 'the meaning and mysteries of life' in a pragmatic way. The Church, however, counters that genuine freedom and moral conscience are guided by an objective truth and reason which rescue it from pure subjectivism. Hence, conscience needs to be formed, and informed, and to seek knowledge and counsel in order not to become detached from truth and reality. In the absence of such conditions, freedom tends to shape its own truth and the consequent many voices of subjective truth result in relativism.

The resolution of the confusion and disagreement over basic moral values depends on a right understanding of the goods of the person and also that freedom and behaviour should not become separated from the search for truth. This, in turn, raises the question of who, and what, man is, and of how he thinks of himself, that is, it requires a true anthropology which successfully identifies the unique dignity of each individual. The latter is expressed by the Christian tradition and also by the modern personalistic understanding of the human being which maintains that man must be treated as an end in himself and never as a mere means to an end, which the widely held utilitarian concept of the person allows. Not to treat a person for his or her own sake goes against the nature of personhood. A person is a rational thinking being able to formulate his own projects and aims and possessing the freedom to put them into practice. Human dignity places a person above abstract human nature and, in a certain sense, above the state and society which have a duty to uphold his fundamental rights which are sovereign. This is not to say that the individual does not also reciprocally have obligations to society in turn. Indeed, the very nature of society demands that the individual's objectives be good and in accordance with his dignity and that they do not threaten the rule of law and the peace and stability of the collective whole. In pursuing the roots of this dignity, whose consequences are so crucial, we will delve back into Christian tradition, as well as ponder the modern personalistic approach, which considers man's consciousness and experience of himself and of his freedom, and the goods and values that fulfil him or her.

John Paul II was aware that the patristic and medieval tradition concerning the person comes to us by way of the terminology of 'substance' and 'suppositum' which are words that have either changed their meaning in contemporary language or gone out of use. He, therefore, proposes a new definition of a person, as "an incarnate spirit, that is a soul that expresses itself in a body and a body informed by an immortal spirit."[1] And he goes on to illuminate the truth expressed by the metaphysical concept of 'substance' in a complementary way from our own experience and consciousness. Because a person is self-governing and self-determining, he must be affirmed for his own sake and therefore the person is unique and inviolable, and so are his basic goods which must not be transgressed. Here, then, is the basis for the natural law and those fundamental goods which cannot be overturned.

The response of the Magisterium, especially that of John Paul II, to the confusion and fall-out over *Humanae Vitae*, and its explanation of marriage and sexuality more generally, is not really comprehensible without an understanding of the subjectivity and internal life of the person. When people speak of the encyclical and indeed *Gaudium et Spes* as taking a more 'personalistic' approach to marriage and conjugal life, this is what they mean. Matters such as love, self-giving, emotion, desire, etc., can only be fully grasped by looking at the human subject and his own awareness of his internal life. Thus, it is necessary to consider the human being subjectively as well as objectively, since the whole truth about man includes both dimensions. The full explanation

---

[1] *Familiaris Consortio,* n. 11; and *Veritatis Splendor,* n. 50.

of the ethics of marriage and sexuality in these two documents is to be found in the discourses on the Theology of the Body which take the teaching of anthropology and subjectivity much further. We have therefore found it necessary to look at this anthropology both here and in the earlier writings of Karol Wojtyla in some detail and depth, to appreciate its bearing on the understanding of Christian sexual ethics in particular, but also more widely on the Church's moral teaching as a whole.

The Theology of the Body discourses offer an analysis of many fundamental questions stretching beyond contraception to the notion of sexuality and gender, marriage and spousal love, understood from a biblical and theological viewpoint. This is the first systematic attempt at a teaching of the theological meaning and purpose of the body which confirms it to be an integral part of the person and therefore also of the 'image of God'. It provides a foundation for a renewed understanding of the sanctity of human life and also of the human body. Naturally, it has many implications for the way the body is treated in sexual and bio-ethics, and specifically in the latter case, by requiring that it never be manipulated and used as a means to an end, even for supposed medical benefits, if it means harming and destroying embryonic human life. Given the topicality and importance of stem-cell research for the future progress of medicine it provides guidelines to distinguish between ethical and non-ethical practice in this area.

These discourses, therefore, express very pointedly the ways in which John Paul II brought a new dimension to ethics in conveying his teaching on subjectivity and thus the experience and consciousness of the person. For him action should never be separated from our consciousness and awareness of it. In this way he stresses that we are intimately involved in ethical decisions and behaviour and, therefore, morality should not be treated merely as a theoretical and formal subject, but as a practical and existential one, as Aristotle had already seen. He gives us an ethics of the first person and not just an abstract presentation of it from the third person point of view. He points out how the account of creation in the second chapter of Genesis is written from the point of view of Adam's subjectivity. In this respect, it goes further than a document like *Humanae Vitae* which is predominantly based on the deduction of conclusions from principles without the same emphasis on the existential and experiential aspect of morality, or the way we live and experience it, even though it made a start in this direction. Wojtyla's treatment of human love and married life in *Love and Responsibility* already fitted more into the latter category.

History testifies that difficulties and challenges for faith and morals are often the occasion for development in the understanding of them. In this regard, we cannot but notice how Pope John Paul's efforts to deal with the *Humanae Vitae* crisis and the threat to family life posed by widespread divorce and cohabitation have led to the deeper understanding of the aforesaid theology of the body, sexuality and marriage, and also insights beyond this into ecclesiology. Not only is the body, the Pope teaches, a sign of the person and an integral part of the personal dignity, but the 'one flesh' union of male and female also sheds light on the Great Mystery of Christ's, the Bridegroom's, love for us the Church, His Bride. He shows how we are not just talking about a linguistic metaphor, but of a life-giving force of grace which spouses and all of us share in, a point which must be borne in mind when people talk about the 'impossibility' of Christian morality in today's world. It goes without saying, of course, that the analogy also works the other way and that the union of Christ and the Church also sheds abundant light on the nature of marriage.

The encyclical *Humanae Vitae* provided a focal point for defining Christian ethics on marriage and sexuality, but also is often seen as a watershed, because of the dissent it produced within the Church and the consequent system of moral revisionism which opposed Catholic tradition on natural law. It should be remembered that while the discovery of the oral contraceptive was a prime cause of the so-called sexual revolution, it is not, of course, the only one and the phenomenon was due to a number of causes. Some ten years earlier, two events occurred in England; namely the Wolfenden Report on the de-penalization of homosexuality between consenting adults in private and the judicial declaration that the D.H. Lawrence novel, *Lady Chatterley's Lover*, was not obscene, ushered in a more permissive era regarding sexual customs. The ambiguous slogan, "a free society is a civilized society", was often used both to characterize and give impetus to the process. The late sixties were also the time when a resurgent and more radical feminism, known as 'Women's Lib' came to the fore, bringing gender into education and social life and generating new ethical questions which bore witness to a more militant secular ethics confronting many Christian principles. These developments, together with the bio-technological revolution, have defined the current ethical questions and have, in turn, influenced the choice of the principles and issues treated in the present work.

At the same time, Catholic ethics has also been refining the presentation of its own tradition regarding the natural law, freedom and the sources of morality, helped along by revisionist objections and the deficiencies of secular ethical theories. Natural law needed to be freed both from 'physicalistic' and 'biologistic' interpretations of it and, at the same time, from allegations that these represented the Church's teaching and tradition. The requirement, then, was for it to be accurately presented as based on reason in the light of a correct notion of the human person in his or her entirety, rather than simply on an abstract human nature. Freedom has suffered since the thirteenth century from a 'voluntaristic' current of interpretation which gives precedence to the will and separates it too much from reason and hence truth. This view departs from the classic definition of freedom by Peter Lombard as 'the power of reason and the power of will'[2] which is followed by Aquinas and the Thomistic tradition. Voluntarism has a clear link with legalism and relativism and also revisionism within the Church.

Crucial to the debate over relativism and dissent is a correct analysis of the moral act. Consequentialism, in particular, and much of secular ethics in general, leave out the moral object and reduce morality to the intention of the person doing it and, in addition, by concentrating on the results of the action, tend to convert the human action into a depersonalised event. Hence the

---

[2] "Liberum vero arbitrium est facultas rationis et voluntatis, qua bonum eligitur gratia assistente, vel malum eadem desistente" (Lombard, *Sent.* II, dist. 24, c. 3).

moral, or proximate object, of the act, needs to be fully understood and cannot be identified with the physical or natural object of an action. All of this work of restating fundamental ethical principles in the light of dissent and secularism was the work of *Veritatis Splendor*, where topics such as the natural law, freedom and the moral object were treated in an expanded and explanatory way to a far greater extent than hitherto by the Magisterium.

Given the impoverished and deficient level of moral analysis generated by proportionalist and consequentialist accounts, it is necessary to retrieve the full understanding of the moral act from Catholic tradition. This involves establishing the moral identity of the act and distinguishing it from the physical or natural identity, because the same physical action may have a different moral identity depending on other factors, as for example, the intention and circumstances surrounding taking, or donating, an organ for transplant. This paves the way for understanding the moral object. Though it may be a more pedestrian part of our narrative it is also decisive. Only thus are we able to apply natural law principles to the individual act and establish which actions are always wrong or intrinsically evil, because they transgress a moral absolute. Most secular ethical theories are unable to explain, or uphold, any actions to be wrong on all occasions. Indeed, we may go further and say that theories such as proportionalism and consequentialism are not strictly speaking moral theories at all since they describe a state of affairs rather than a relationship between the rational will and a good or evil object wherein morality resides. This relationship, in turn, affects the person for good or ill.

Renewal in Christian doctrine consists above all in faithfulness to apostolic teaching as well as the incorporation of new insights in continuity with the Tradition together with the effort to communicate it in a way which is comprehensible to the mentality of the times. In contrast to this, a so-called renewal which creates a break with the past and introduces novelties would not constitute genuine teaching and this type of dissent has been one of the trends in moral theology over the recent past. Frequently, dissent represents a compromise with the relativism and consensus morality of modern society and is based on inadequate philosophical premises, especially concerning the person, rationality and freedom, which is why an emphasis is needed on rational ethics. Side by side with this and partly in answer to it, genuine renewal and growth has been taking place in Christian ethics.

The renewal of ethical principles also contributes to the civilization of society as the Church's teaching has always done. A witness to this is its teaching on the dignity of the human person, the equal value of every human life, the right of freedom and other basic human rights, the value of marriage and the family both for the stability of society and for the protection of the fundamental rights of children to be born and brought up in the love of their parents and the warmth of the family home. It also furnishes us with an ethical response to the developments of bio-science and bio-technology by insisting on the inviolability of human life and the human person for there to be genuine developments in embryology, stem-cell and genetic research. This means in practice that such procedures are only moral if they benefit the individual human being, not simply mankind, because this could lead to individuals being used as a means an end. Similarly, Pope John Paul II was able to articulate Christian principles for matters of the present time such as gender issues, peace, justice and terrorism. With the end of the pontificate it is now possible to make a first appraisal of his ethical teaching which is such an integral part of the new evangelization.

The contribution of John Paul II is outstanding for its convincing response to modern relativism, based on his incisive account of human action and the resulting principle many times repeated that freedom cannot be separated from truth. This, in turn, depends on other perceptions, such as, that the full truth of the human act cannot be separated from experience by which the person is conscious of his own causality and responsibility. While the path of moral growth is known by reason, the practice of it belongs to the will and the right use of freedom, since the person empowers himself to act as the principal cause of his action and he is, therefore, responsible and accountable for it. Wojtyla in this way saw how behaviour and human action set up a relationship between freedom and truth. This was so, because a person's actions could not contribute to his fulfilment unless they went hand in hand with the truth of his personhood and the observance of a set of objective moral values, since it is by moral values alone that overall personal growth occurs. Without behaviour being based on a truthful judgement, freedom itself is diminished and the person is in danger of enslavement of one kind or another. For Wojtyla the person has a moral duty to attend to his own growth and fulfilment as a person and the root of this duty is his liberty.

John Paul II was an historic figure who foresaw the changes in presentation that were necessary in the Church's unchanging deposit of faith and morals to communicate it more successfully to the modern world. Personalism was only one plank of renewal. He was aware of the complexities and intricacies of dialoguing with contemporary thought while faithfully renewing Catholic tradition. He had to deal with a false and over hasty attempt at renewal, which we have called moral revisionism, and also known as 'proportionalism', which allied itself with a secular form of thought called consequentialism which was inadequate for expressing Catholic moral tradition. Consequently, at the same time as updating moral theology John Paul II had to pay attention to sound doctrine. Renewal had to go hand in hand with presenting a firmer basis for, and explanation of, the foundations of Catholic moral tradition. Any renewal had to be a hermeneutic of continuity with the past, that is to say, a reading of moral theology which was a homogenous and faithful development of tradition. Moral revisionism was a hermeneutic of discontinuity and represented a rupture with past doctrine. Newman, writing in the *Apologia*, said of the recently defined dogma of the Immaculate Conception that "it is a simple fact to say, that Catholics have not come to believe it because it is defined, but it was defined because they believed it".[3] In this he expresses the essence of Catholic development, that it is a deeper presentation of the original deposit.

In a passage of *Faith and Reason*, John Paul II summarizes the task of moral theology which serves as a very good outline of the following pages:

---

[3] Cardinal John Henry Newman, *Apologia pro Vita sua*, J.M. Dent & Son, Everyman's Library, 1955, p. 228.

Throughout the Encyclical (*Veritatis Splendor*) I under-scored clearly the fundamental role of truth in the moral field. In the case of the more pressing ethical problems, this truth demands of moral theology a careful enquiry rooted unambiguously in the word of God. In order to fulfil its mission, moral theology must turn to a philosophical ethics which looks to the truth of the good, to an ethics which is neither subjectivist nor utilitarian. Such an ethics implies and presupposes philosophical anthropology and a metaphysics of the good. Drawing on this organic vision, linked necessarily to Christian holiness and to the practice of the human and supernatural virtues, moral theology will be able to tackle the various problems in its competence, such as peace, social justice, the family, the defence of life and the natural environment, in a more appropriate and effective way.[4]

---

[4] Pope John Paul II, *Fides et Ratio*, n. 98.

PART I

FUNDAMENTAL PRINCIPLES OF ETHICS

I.

ETHICS AFTER VATICAN II: PERSONALISM AND RENEWAL IN AN AGE OF SECULARISM

From the earliest times the dignity of the human person has been one of the pillars of Christian moral doctrine. The very truth of man's condition requires him to live in accordance with it if he is to fulfil himself, and treat all other persons in the same way. Morality is known by reason in the context of the full truth of the human person and therefore requires as a pre-condition an adequate anthropology. Divergence of opinion on personhood and on the meaning of freedom and reason (also part of what we mean by anthropology) is invariably the underlying cause of the different and incompatible conclusions reached by Christian and secular ethics. Building on Christian revelation and tradition, which conveys the truth, not only about God, but also about man, and the emphasis given to the human person by Vatican II, John Paul II has taken forward philosophical and theological anthropology to a remarkable degree. It has enabled him to re-affirm and explain for our time the universal binding force of the natural moral law and underpin the existence of moral absolutes in the face of a growing relativism. He has also challenged the widespread culture of death by upholding the intrinsic and equal value of every human life from conception, and especially that of the weakest and most vulnerable, whether unborn, elderly or sick and suffering.

It was the original intention of the preparatory committee of Vatican II to produce a major document on morality. A draft schema *'De re morali'* was debated at the Council, but after receiving some trenchant criticism it did not succeed in being re-introduced.[1] Instead, the focus of attention shifted to the role of the Church in the modern world and the document produced was notable for the attention it devoted to the human person. The criticism made of the draft document indicated that it was too rationalistic and it called for a greater theologization of morality more firmly based around Scripture and the Person of Christ. However, events were to determine that anthropology and rational ethics would also play a major part in the renewal of the subject, and that the task would be accomplished by John Paul II following the Council. One document, *Optatum Totius*, incorporated the call for renewal, as mentioned above, and asked for a systematic scientific presentation of the subject which implies the application of rational ethics, and other documents laid considerable emphasis on anthropology.[2] Referring to human procreation, *Gaudium et Spes* noted that the solution should be based on 'human persons and their acts' and subsequently *Humanae Vitae*, dealing with the same subject, said the response required as a prerequisite 'a total vision of man' (n. 7).

In *Dignitatis Humanae*, the Council explicitly recognized that contemporary man was becoming increasingly conscious of his dignity and that he should be able to exercise his freedom and judgement without external constraints and in accordance with truth and duty.[3] In explaining its case, the decree summarizes Christian moral tradition: "It is in accordance with their dignity," it says, "that all men because they are persons ... are both impelled by their nature and bound by a moral obligation to seek the truth, especially religious truth." The responsibility arises from the free nature of persons which therefore makes them accountable and it goes on to ask that once they have found it they "should adhere to it and direct their whole lives in accordance with it".[4] The reason why it is especially true of religious and moral truth is because

---

[1] Servais Pinckaers, *Para Leer La Veritatis Splendor*, Rialp, Madrid, 1996, pp. 54-60; and 'Le retour de la Loi nouvelle en morale', in B. Hallensleben and G. Vergauwen eds, *Praedicando et docendo: Mélanges offerts au Père Liam Walsh*, Fribourg, 1998.
[2] Cf. Vatican II, *Optatum Totius*, Decree on the Training of Priests, n. 16.
[3] Vatican II, *Dignitatis Humanae*, n. 1.
[4] Ibid., n. 2.

"the highest norm of human life is the divine law itself – eternal, objective and universal by which God orders, directs and governs the whole world and the ways of the human community."[5] Man participates in it and can know it by his, or her, own reason, a reality which Christian tradition calls the natural law.

Consequently, it follows from this that for Christian tradition there is an objective moral law reflected in his conscience which man is called upon to recognize. As Christianity has always taught, it is not in its essentials a matter of opinion, or culturally relative, that is to say, different for different cultures. Today, precisely because of religious and ideological pluralism and the need for tolerance, many believe that ethical relativism is imperative. But in order to demonstrate the objectivity of morality, apart from Revelation, we need the 'full range of reason', or metaphysics. Only a philosophy which allows us to reach the essential nature of persons and things, and which provides us with a 'metaphysics of the good' and of man, can furnish the wherewithal for an objective morality, a point that will be more fully considered later. Suffice it to say for the moment that when he uses the phrase 'the transcendence of man' John Paul is referring, among other things, to the fact that the human mind is capable of attaining to a truth and knowledge of goodness which is universal and therefore rises above particular cultural visions and expressions and at the same time enriches all of them.

The anthropological teaching of *Gaudium et Spes*, and its influence on ethics, can be summarized by highlighting the stress it puts on two dimensions of the human being. Man, it says in a much quoted text, "is the only creature on earth which exists for its own sake" meaning that he is a self, an inviolable subject who, nevertheless, can only find true fulfilment and happiness by making a 'sincere gift of himself' to others".[6] The first characteristic of these is foundational for the intrinsic worth of the person and consequently for the basic goods of the natural law, and the second indicates the true nature of love and fulfillment and is of special importance for spousal love and family life. Ultimately, the

---

[5] Ibid., n. 3.
[6] *Gaudium et Spes*, n. 24.

dignity of the person consists in the fact that he exists for himself, in virtue of his self-determination, and cannot be an instrument of another, or used as a means to an end. This is the basis of the unique individuality of the person and the absolute respect due to him and his goods, and especially human life itself, and is the foundation of human rights. Nevertheless, selfhood cannot be divorced from a relationship of communion with others, which is also essential to the person, and therefore to his own fulfilment, and entails that he treat others according to the golden rule (cf. Mt 7:12), as he himself would be treated. The quality of the person as a gift for others finds it fullest expression in the communion of persons of marriage and family life. In other words, one is required to respect and love the other as a sovereign self, as another and a better self, and therefore also all his, or her, goods. The latter, which form the basis of the natural law, are discerned by human reason in the light of the nature of the human person.

The Council's concentration on anthropology turned out to be providential in another respect. Within the same timescale, moral teaching, and especially that of Pope John Paul II, has had the further task of responding to the ever-growing issues raised by the rapid progress of the bio-sciences and bio-technology. Personhood is at the center of the bio-ethical debate and society is divided over the definition of a person to the extent that often a distinction is made between human life and a person, as in the case of a foetus which is considered human, but not a person, by some sectors of secular morality.[7] For that reason it is most appropriate to go back and recover the Christian notion of personhood and to draw what is opportune from the modern movement of personalism. Christian ethics maintains the integrity of the person as a unity of body and soul while secular ethics tends to conceive him, or her, dualistically as a consciousness in a body, which, in turn, is treated as a biological organism, or a machine.[8] The result of this dualism is that the person is separated from the body, and therefore from his nature, as an embodied being. If the body is not an integral part of the subjectivity of the person, then it readily comes to be considered as less than

---

[7] See for example *The Warnock Report on Human Fertilization and Embryology*, n. 11.9.
[8] Cf. Council of Vienne, decree 1; and Vatican II, *Gaudium et Spes*, n. 16.

human, and it is easy to see how the body, and the person, become undervalued. If, in addition, personhood is reduced to consciousness then embryonic stem-cell research, the practice of freezing human embryos, and calls for the premature ending of suffering humanity with a so-called low quality of life, begin to grow. Human bodily life, on the contrary, gets its dignity and meaning from its union with the soul, and from being an integral part of personhood.

Dignity consists ultimately in that the human person is created "in the image and likeness of God", redeemed by Christ and called to communion with the divine life and thus eternal life. Christ is at the same time the 'creative Logos' which tells the Christian that the world is the expression of reason and truth.[9] Revelation teaches not only the divine mysteries, but echoes in certain places the human truths which the Greek philosophers had discovered, namely the existence of God, the immortality of the soul and human freedom, but which due to original sin are grasped by unaided reason with difficulty. A further example of this dual purpose is the statement of *Gaudium et Spes* that, "The mystery of man becomes clear only in the mystery of the Incarnate Word."[10] "Through the Incarnation God gave human life the dimension he intended man to have from his first beginning," wrote John Paul II.[11] Hence, the Church emphasizes the complementarity of faith and reason, because the former not only reveals mysteries but also confirms and deepens human truths while the latter helps theology to unveil some of the depths of Revelation. This follows the tradition of St Augustine whose two formulas expressed it as follows: 'believe in order to be able to understand' (*crede ut intellegas*) and 'understand in order to believe better' (*intellige ut credas*).[12] The Polish Pope was keen to restore the link between faith and reason and between anthropology and theology which had been broken by much of modern thought. He says in his second encyclical that the renewal of the link between anthropology and theology was perhaps the most important contribution of Vatican II.[13]

---

[9] Jn 1:1.
[10] Vatican Council II, *Gaudium et Spes*, n. 22.
[11] John Paul II, *Redemptor Hominis*, n. 1.
[12] St Augustine, *Sermones*, 43, 9.
[13] *Dives in Misericordia*, n. 1.

A word of warning is in order though, because it is worth emphasizing that we are presupposing a reason which can reach the truth, that is a philosophy of being. Just as the wheat grows with the chaff, but eventually has to be separated, so it is necessary to appreciate that not all systems of reason are compatible with Christian ethics. As is made clear in the encyclical *Faith and Reason*, what is required is a philosophy which allows reason its full range, namely to reach the truth. There are philosophies, however, which deny we can know 'human nature', for example, or that it has any enduring characteristics through the ages. This type of scepticism about truth leads to uncertainty and relativism about moral values. What ensues then is a morality of consensus, or consequences, which does not identify the moral good at all and, therefore, fails to fulfil the person. If one further asks how the questioning of basic ethical truths has arisen the answer lies in the influence of an over-secularised society, that is, one whose culture has become radically separated from Christian faith and moral customs. An aspect, as well as a cause of this division, is the gradual parting of the ways over recent centuries of faith and reason. The separation works to the detriment of both. Christianity teaches that both faith and reason seek the same moral truth according to their own paths. It must be borne in mind, however, that reason transmits it to us in a sketchy way whereas Revelation gives greater certainty and confidence and in this sense it guides reason.

Today's secular outlook is heavily influenced by the European cultural heritage marked by the Enlightenment, which consciously and deliberately cut off reason both from God and tradition in the name of rational autonomy and a supposed objectivity. Ironically, this weakened reason and separated it from such wisdom as past ages had achieved. In its place it put a rationality based exclusively on mathematical-empirical verifiability which can only pass judgement on facts not on philosophy and hence is incapable of founding even relativism. As historians put it, at this time the Age of Faith was followed by the Age of Reason which still characterizes our times. Contemporary society tends to value reason more for its usefulness in supplying economic and technological welfare and progress than for its more lofty function of true knowledge and wisdom. This explains the predominance since the nineteenth century and the continuing popularity of an ethical system, namely utilitarianism, and its offshoot consequentialism (of which more later), which calculates the benefits and harms of an action in order to determine what is ethically right and wrong.

If truth cannot be known by human reason, then everyone sees things from their own point of view with the consequence that all opinions are equally valid, even those that contradict one another, and none may be universally affirmed or censured. When applied to the moral order this relativism means that one is unable to draw a clear line between good and evil, or say that any actions are intrinsically and absolutely wrong. Uncertainty about reason's ability to reach moral truth usually ends up with freedom taking the lead role and shaping its own truth, which in turn, easily leads to behaviour being ruled by caprice and freedom descending into licence. This, however, yields contradictory rights and goods in society as a whole. The secular claim to abortion, embryonic stem-cell research and gay unions clashes with the rights of the unborn, parental and filial dignity and heterosexual marriage. We are witnesses to a looming battle between secular claims and the religious freedom to defend the right to life and traditional marriage.

In the separation between freedom, truth and goodness, Wojtyla saw the reasons for moral relativism and the source of many of the personal and social crises of the present time. All moral problems can be traced in one way or another to this separation. When freedom takes the place of reason and truth and usurps its guiding role then it easily descends into relativism bereft of the responsibility which truth imposes. This readily results in family breakdown and the social ills of binge-drinking, rape, etc. There is no common moral code, or public reason, which applies to the human being as a person, or common virtues by which he or she is fulfilled. Each one is his, or her, own lawmaker and hence there is no link between freedom, truth and goodness. There is no law other than positive law but it becomes clear that the latter itself must answer to a higher law. At Nuremberg the allies judged the Nazis on atrocious abuses of positive law but realized at the same time their own laws were based on positivism. This has led some to a greater appreciation of the necessity of natural law.

A Confrontation between two Systems of Ethics

Given the limitations modernity places on reason's ability to reach the truth it is not surprising that the secular world fails to comprehend some of the central Christian moral teachings. Indeed, we may even speak of a confrontation between two incompatible systems of ethics, Christian morality and secular morality. For confirmation of this, one only has to consider how the latter not only misunderstands, for example, the condemnation of contraception, but also alleges that the Church's stance leads to poverty and starvation, facilitates the transmission of AIDS, and wonders how it can possibly be for the benefit of mankind. In the same vein, it finds the Church uncompassionate in not permitting reproductive in vitro fertilization techniques to infertile couples, or the re-marriage of divorcees, or homosexual relations to gay people, or embryonic stem-cell research, etc.

Secular morality identifies these activities as 'goods' and 'rights' of the person thereby changing the traditional meaning of the words by 'free vote', overlooking the testimony of reason and natural law. Such a position is a very good example of the separation of freedom and truth. It can only be maintained on a particular view of freedom, one which is autonomous and independent, and ignores the truth of the person and marriage, or understands them with insufficient depth. Only thus can the secular world condemn the Catholic Church for its promotion of chastity and its prohibition of contraception and condoms, which keeps underdeveloped nations poor and furthers the spread of AIDS according to this mindset.

If, however, ethical relativism is taken to its logical conclusion it entails corollaries and consequences which no reasonable person wants to accept. Were it to be true, we could not say that such things as concentration camps, human torture and paedophilia were absolutely wrong. A society based on relativism can result in intolerable situations for its citizens, because pressure is increasingly exerted on people to conform in their public and professional activity to actions and situations which are contrary to the convictions of their moral conscience. So doctors and medical staff are under pressure to provide abortion and contraception prescriptions, and pharmacists to deliver on them. Politicians and lawyers can be under pressure from lobby groups and political correctness to enact, or act upon, such laws, or a host of others which grow relentlessly, for example, those relating to advance directives of euthanasia if one were to reach a state of mental incapacity, or experimentation on embryos and cloning.

Moral Revisionism and Ethical Relativism

Such presuppositions have also had their effect on Catholic thinkers in recent decades causing confusion concerning aspects of moral teaching which, until recently, produced dissent within the Church. These include the understanding of the natural law itself, the nature of the human act and the moral object, freedom, and the place of virtues and happiness within ethics. These were the issues *Veritatis Splendor* had in mind when it spoke about "certain fundamental truths of Catholic doctrine, which, in present circumstances, risk being distorted or denied." It went on: "It is no longer a matter of limited and occasional dissent, but of an overall and systematic calling into question of traditional moral doctrine on the basis of certain anthropological and ethical presuppositions."[14]

Early attempts at renewal misfired seriously because they lacked the features outlined by the Council, and departed from the moral tradition of the Church and the philosophy which underpins it. Faced with the great questions of the late twentieth century, like contraception, abortion, and bio-ethics, and unable to find the wherewithal for surmounting these in their limited arsenal, they wilted in the face of the modern world and compromised with secular morality. The result was moral revisionism and dissent within the Church which departed from the imperative to maintain unbroken continuity with Apostolic Tradition.

Ethical relativism makes moral norms dependent on the consequences and circumstances of actions precluding the possibility of moral absolutes. The moral revisionism associated with it compromises the Christian doctrine of sin in various ways. It opposes the universal application of the Commandments and

---

[14] John Paul II, *Veritatis Splendor*, n. 4.

the intrinsically evil acts they condemn. It changes the doctrine of mortal sin and replaces it with the 'fundamental option'. This ethical theory even imposes its own interpretation of the Bible by replacing the Commandments, which it calls categorical norms that permit exceptions, with transcendental norms which do not, but which refer to general attitudes rather than concrete acts.

Relativism in ethics makes every man his own judge in moral matters, and therefore, in the end, morality is a matter of opinion, and every moral view is equally acceptable. Thus, the link between conscience, or practical reason, and an objective moral law, or truth, has been broken. Once again such a position can only be maintained on the basis of an autonomous view of freedom and a weakened reason, which acts without responsibility for the truth, which it sees as unattainable. The so-called distinction between the transcendental and categorical level ultimately depends on a dualistic notion of the human person which will be discussed at greater length further on.

The Genuine Renewal of Morality

The challenge that secularism presents to Christian ethics serves as an important spur to the renewal of moral theology within the Church as desired by Vatican II. The false renewal of moral revisionism over the last forty years wrongly diagnosed what was needed and allowed itself to be over-influenced by secular morality, especially that variety known as consequentialism.

Genuine renewal in the area of moral theology did not really begin until twenty years after the end of Vatican II, although the guidelines were laid down at the Council. The latter encouraged a return to the sources of Scripture and the Fathers of the Church and asked that moral theology be more closely linked to other parts of theology, dogmatic and spiritual, so that its feasibility be more easily understood. This enables us to see the link between the moral subject and the person of Christ, the Holy Spirit, the sacraments, and the evangelical law. It also explains how the most characteristic of the Council's doctrines, the call to holiness, which is the purpose of Christian life for everybody, is to be carried out, since holiness is the full development of all the virtues. Finally, it asked that it be grounded more scientifically, which we may take to refer, in part, to the rational underpinning of morality which is more and more important as it becomes necessary to explain Christian ethics to a wider, increasingly more educated, audience. In this way, for example, it will be able to respond more successfully to the issues raised by the secular world, especially of sexual and bio-ethical matters.[15]

The renewal needed to bring about a deeper and broader appreciation of the subject than had hitherto been presented in the manuals, which concentrated too exclusively on laws and obligations. They left out the role of the virtues, happiness and the full explanation of the evangelical law, as exhibited in the Sermon on the Mount. They also treated freedom unsatisfactorily and dealt with grace only in dogmatic theology. Such an approach proved to be inadequate in facing the newly arising issues of the day beginning with contraception and continuing with the new bio-ethics. The renewal needed to show how the Commandments were not meant to be fulfilled simply externally and legalistically, but internally with the obedience of love and according to the truth and goods of the human person. Anyone familiar with the *Ethics* of Aristotle, and the moral theology of St Augustine and St Thomas Aquinas could not avoid seeing how much had to be recovered from these fundamental sources.

Our task then is to explain the principles of Christian ethics taking into account the foregoing presuppositions and clarifying as much as possible the confusion they have fallen into in some quarters and the reasons for it. The basic principles depend on moral truth, or natural law, which, as will become clear, depends on, and is embedded in, *practical* reason which contains and reflects the self-evident forms of human good which lead, via intermediate principles, to moral norms. Practical reason, while separate from speculative reason and metaphysics, has an organic relationship with them and thus with truth, as we saw. Conscience which is an act of practical reason or judgement, reflects and applies the principles of natural law and thus is not an autonomous and independent decision. In this way, the free act of behaviour

---
[15] Cf. Vatican II, *Optatem Totius*, n. 16.

based on this judgement is linked to the truth. Further ethical principles refer to the analysis of each act of freedom, the human act. The standard Catholic moral explanation of the human act has been turned on its head by the theory, already referred to, of consequentialism, that is, the view that the moral value of actions depends on their effects or consequences, as we will discover in some detail. The traditional Catholic moral analysis of an act, on the other hand, requires us to look at the moral object, intention and circumstances of the action which are known as the sources of morality.

Biblical Morality and the Newness of the Gospel

The progression of the law towards the virtues is the teaching of the Bible. Morality in the Old Testament is centred on the Commandments of Sinai, which are an essential part of God's Covenant with the people. The Israelites understand them in terms of external fulfilment, but the pedagogy of the Bible is to lead mankind to internalize the law, make it their own and fulfil it. This purpose is spelt out, above all, in the Sermon on the Mount and the Beatitudes, which typify the Evangelical Law. The latter, however, crucially, includes the presence of the Holy Spirit in the believer, with his gifts, and infused virtues, enabling and fostering compliance. The Holy Spirit enables the believer to live 'in Christ' and with Christ, sharing in the merits and power of his Redemption. This is why the moral teaching of the Gospel is not impossible, or utopian, and why it is always relevant. Virtue, as well as being a habit, is a power and so gives the strength to act. Though manifest in the New Testament, this had been hinted at, and foreseen, in the Old.

The goods and values known self-evidently to reason form the basis of the moral law, which is confirmed by the revelation of the Commandments. If it then be asked how the law can be fulfilled the answer begins here in these elements of the evangelical law. The virtues are both natural, that is, built up by repeated acts and habits, and supernatural, or infused by the Holy Spirit. Though the perfect fulfillment of the Commandments is not possible to fallen human nature by its own efforts, they are feasible through the work of the Holy Spirit, who fills the willing soul with his virtues, gifts and fruits. The third Person of the Trinity is Person-Love and it is the love of God, poured into the soul, which is the root and foundation of the holiness, or perfection in virtue, to which every person is called.

The pre-Vatican II treatment of moral theology typically revolved around the four topics of law, conscience, human acts and sin, thus failing to do justice to the decisive element of the evangelical law.[16] It led to a tendency to see morality in terms of obligations and prohibitions rather than in serving as a pointer to the meaning of one's whole life. 'Law' referred to the Commandments of the Old Testament without bringing out their fulfilment in the Gospel and the double precept of Love to which it calls us, and which is within our grasp, in virtue of the grace of Christ dwelling in us through the Holy Spirit. The separation of the treatise on justification from morality was one of the reasons for this oversight which has now been corrected. Another practical consequence of this approach was that it gave rise to a sort of 'double morality'. One was a 'minimum' level consisting in not transgressing the Decalogue which was expected of the laity, and the other was the way of 'perfection' addressed especially to religious. However, since the Council's principal teaching was a re-discovery of the universal call to holiness, teaching on ethics had to come into line with it. The Council itself did not achieve this required renewal of ethics, and the task was left to the *Catechism of the Catholic Church* and *Veritatis Splendor,* both of which clearly state that the fullness of Christian life and holiness is addressed to all the baptized.

The renewal of morality is inextricably bound up with the new evangelization which is proposed in order to communicate the Gospel with a new vigour and deeper understanding to our more educated times. Its task is, above all, to grasp the newness which the Gospel has always had. This new 'ethos', as it is called by John Paul II, is the shift from a morality based on an external law and works as found in the Old Testament, to the fulfilment of that same law in the 'heart', that is in the inner man. The deepened

---

[16] See Pinckaers, *Para Leer La Veritatis Splendor*, Rialp, Madrid, 1996, p. 16.

knowledge of the human person which is communicated by the theology of the body discourses and its personalist foundations, especially the study of subjectivity, that is, all that is interior in the human being, also has the purpose of putting over this truth more fully.

The real beginning of the renewal starts with the publication of the *Catechism of the Catholic Church* and *Veritatis Splendor*. The result is that we now have a morality which exhibits the above features and is based around the dignity of the person, a characteristic teaching of Vatican II, and a presentation of natural law which arises from, and protects, the goods of the person. It is thus able to analyse more fully the morality of human acts and point to those actions which radically contradict the true good of the human person. These are intrinsically evil acts, or moral absolutes, which ethical relativism is by definition incapable of upholding. Part of the reason is the absence once again of an adequate anthropology which we will therefore examine at some length.

The Contribution of Pope John Paul II: Personalism

A key part of the renewal has been growth in the study and teaching on the human person emanating from Vatican II and the major documents of John Paul II, the theology of the body discourses, *Veritatis Splendor* and *Evangelium Vitae*. The *Catechism of the Catholic Church* begins its ethical section with the dignity of the human person without meaning to imply that this is methodologically the best or only starting point, or that we deduce ethics from anthropology. It is rather pointing out that the full truth of the human being, that is the entire person, body and soul, is one of the essential presuppositions of ethics together with an understanding of human reason and freedom. The contemporary issues of bio-ethics and sexual ethics turn on how we understand the human person and human life. Confusion on this matter will decisively affect the outcome.

The growth of technology and medicine has thrown up a host of new issues. Increased life-expectancy brings with it ethical problems of patient treatment, care of the sick, elderly and terminally ill. Bio-technology has taken us to the point where the laboratory manufacture of life can take the place of parental love, and the scenario foreseen in *Brave New World* on the imaginative level has, to an extent, become a reality. Some of the more prominent ethical issues of the present time, such as in-vitro fertilization, embryonic stem-cell research, therapeutic cloning, and euthanasia and pain, raise questions about the place of bodily life within the dignity of the person. In most of these matters the majority secular opinion is taking a path opposed to Catholic teaching. Something similar might be said about sexual ethics, concerning cohabitation before marriage, divorce and the toleration of different sexual lifestyles.

In the light of these challenges one can see as providential Karol Wojtyla's use and development of the philosophy of personalism which had started at the beginning of the twentieth century very much as an attempt to uphold the intrinsic worth and inviolability of the human person against the pressures that threatened to crush him or her, especially state totalitarianism, and industrial, economic and technological power. If one of the purposes of ethics is to live according to our dignity, and ensure that technology is our servant and not our master, then the question is whether in some ways, it is not engulfing our humanity and taking over, by supplanting our dignity and leading to a certain de-humanization. In his first encyclical John Paul II wrote that the kingship and dominion of the human being over the visible world consists in "the priority of ethics over technology, in the primacy of the person over things, and in the superiority of spirit over matter."[17]

Just as at its inception personalism served as a valid instrument to protect the person from all that threatened his/her fundamental goods and rights, so it continues to do in our own time when the scope for doing so has widened considerably. It is an indispensable means for countering all forms of abuse and violence which instrumentalize human life, whether in the political sphere, the workplace, or the home, or by selective abortion, research on and destruction of embryos, euthanasia, human trafficking, cloning etc. It is used to show that all human life is of intrinsic

---

[17] *Redemptor Hominis*, n. 16.

and inviolable value from conception onwards as Christian tradition testifies.[18] It can be used to confront all forms of biotechnology which treat the human body as an object of use and experimentation and not part of personal dignity and therefore expendable thereby attacking the absolute and fundamental value of human life, because, as *Evangelium Vitae* tells us, "life is always a good" (n. 34).

Wojtyla notes that personalism is not primarily a theory of the person: "Its meaning is largely practical and ethical: it is concerned with the person as a subject and object of activity, as a subject of rights etc."[19] According to the Pope the human being can be known in his/her subjective and objective dimensions depending on whether the perspective is that of a third person observer, or one's own experience of oneself. The latter reveals the subjectivity of the person which, in turn, has a certain objective character since each person enjoys a corresponding subjectivity to which he can compare that of other beings. By speaking in this way he is taking the personal 'suppositum' and 'substance' of Christian tradition, developing it and updating it for our time, as we shall see when we consider the extent to which these realities can also be known subjectively as well.

The Polish Pope's personalism complements and completes the old Aristotelian conception of man as a rational animal. It contends that the being of a person comes out fully in his subjectivity, that is, in his self-consciousness and self-determination. The human being is a personal subject in body and soul such that the body is part of personhood and not an object which the person owns and uses. The organic unity is brought out by the expression, 'the body reveals the person' and its cognates, 'the body expresses, or makes visible the person'.[20] These phrases make abundantly clear that the body is an integral part of the person and reject any lingering platonic traces of it being the prison of the spirit, or a manichaeism which attributes evil to matter. Pope John Paul goes on to say that the body is the sacrament of the person in the wide

---

[18] John Paul II, *Evangelium Vitae*, n. 45.
[19] Karol Wojtyla, *Person and Community*, Selected Essays, Peter Lang, New York, 1993, p. 165.
[20] See John Paul II, General Audiences 14-XI-79 and 31-X-79.

sense of sacrament as being the outward sign of the internal life and meaning of the human being.

Wojtyla saw that traditional presentations of morality emphasized the object of the action and the person's intention but without developing and describing fully the role played by the acting subject. One of his guiding principles was that act cannot be separated from experience and therefore the description of a moral act must include the experience and consciousness of the subject acting. In addition, each action affects the whole person, hence the ethical question 'what shall I do?' includes the question 'What shall I become?' because every action contributes to making me the person I turn out to be morally speaking. Both questions presuppose an answer to the question 'who am I?' The values that each one aims at presuppose an understanding that he, or she, has of the meaning and purpose of their life. Classical ethics had asked what the good life consisted in and answered that it was an activity in accordance with virtue. Building on this, Christian tradition shows that the questions 'what shall I do?' and 'what shall I become?' are linked, because what I become is the result of the moral value of the actions performed. The person is destined to growth and the perfection of self through moral behaviour. Personhood is perfectible by means of moral values through the right use of freedom. Moral values, when good, lead one to become more and more mature and responsible, that is, to become more of a person. Hence, they affect the person *qua* person and not his technical, or professional ability, for example. Thus, the ultimate good is the human being's harmonious development, happiness and fulfilment.

Subjectivity confirms the spiritual faculties of intellect and will by their activity, that is, through the experience of self-consciousness and self-determination. In virtue of the spiritual dimension the person is not only unique in creation, but is also at the summit of it, or, in the words of St Thomas: the most perfect being in the world (*ens perfectissimum in totam naturam*).[21] A person, therefore, enjoys a unique individuality, since he has been 'left in

---

[21] Aquinas, ST, I, q. 29, a. 3.

the hand of his own counsel'[22] to provide and care for himself, and thanks to his spiritual powers of intellect and will has an ability to know the truth and attain self-mastery. For this reason, Christian tradition is opposed to what is called eco-centrism or biocentrism, according to which the moral and ontological difference between men and other living beings would be eliminated in favour of a biosphere of beings of undifferentiated value. The superior dignity of man would be replaced by an egalitarian 'dignity' accorded to all living beings.

John Paul II following the Council, then, accepted to a degree the shift to the human subject started by modern thought at the Renaissance. He accepts, in part and on certain conditions, the philosophy of consciousness which enables him to underline the subjectivity and inner life of the person. Side by side with this, the Holy Father, following *Gaudium et Spes*, has also highlighted the gift value of the person, namely that the latter is a being in relation. Thus the human being only realizes him, or herself, by giving not by taking, another important difference from the utilitarian self-interest theory. Finally, in describing the person as a being who possesses and governs himself, and is the principal agent of his activity and not the instrument of another, and thus is responsible and accountable for it, he takes forward our understanding of human freedom and action.

The statement of *Gaudium et Spes* that 'man must be affirmed for his own sake' though not in a selfish way, is better known than understood. If we take into account that a constitutive part of personhood is to give oneself and relate to others in a communion of persons, it is more readily comprehensible.[23] Karol Wojtyla further illuminates this statement by explaining that a human being has personal ends of his own, and enjoys self-determination and self-government and, hence, must not be treated as an instrument, but as an end in him, or herself, and never as a means to an end. He was therefore able to formulate his well known 'personalist principle' which lays down that when acting towards a human being he, or she, must never be treated

---

[22] Sir 15:14.
[23] Vatican II, *Gaudium et Spes*, n. 24.

as an object or thing, or manipulated for purposes of pleasure or gain, because the only adequate attitude to a person is love, and not use. The inspiration for this personalistic norm came from Kant's second formulation of the categorical imperative, although, as we shall see, the basis of it can equally be found in Aquinas. It emphasizes the crucial difference between persons and things and our behavioural attitudes towards the one and the other and indeed, according to Wojtyla, towards ourselves. This leads us to understand that the human person is inviolable and of intrinsic value in virtue of the dignity of the person which, in turn, is the foundation for the intrinsic value and obligatory nature of the basic goods of the natural law.

The expanded explanation of the subjectivity and unity of the human person enables him to convey the Christian understanding of gender. Sexuality applies to the whole person although it comes through the body, hence it is personal and not just biological. The entire person is male or female, not just the body. Through the body we can read the signs which reveal the purpose and meaning of sexual life and guide us in the way to treat the body in sexual matters. Here we see, for instance, that the male and female bodies are made for a communion of persons and for procreation. The dignity of the person and therefore the body require that the practice of sexuality be governed by the virtue of chastity and the accompanying virtues of modesty and self-mastery.

A hotly disputed question, of course, is when personhood begins and ends. The embryo is not a person, say those who would tamper with the boundaries at the beginning, or end of life, because it does not have consciousness and self-awareness. But it is only a dualistic position which defines a person by consciousness. Christian tradition says that it is already a human subject with its own genetic make-up, a unique individual enjoying equality with other members of the human family and a human life that is inviolable. If the body expresses the person, then that body is observable from the one cell stage (conception), albeit by microscope. We also find here the root of the Catholic doctrine regarding the modern developments of bio-technology such as IVF, embryonic stem-cell research, and cloning as well as the life issues of abortion and euthanasia and sexual ethics.

Theologically, we see in these aspects of personhood his character of being the 'image of God', and as such a bearer of rationality and freedom. Consequently, Pope John Paul is able to say "man appears in the visible world as the highest expression of the divine gift, because he bears within him the interior dimension of the gift and with it he brings into the world his particular likeness to God with which he transcends and dominates also his 'visibility' in the world."[24] Human existence is a gift which entails that it has been received. We enjoy autonomy, self-determination and self-possession, but we do not possess ourselves entirely with that *absolute* autonomy which people often bestow on themselves today. Hence, the gift value of a person is also a task bringing with it responsibilities to God, myself and others.

A deeper knowledge of the person, such as had been developed by Wojtyla's work as a professor of ethics, was undoubtedly of value when it came to dealing with the issues raised by the biotechnology revolution and by gender studies. We shall see that a deficient view, such as consciousness/body dualism, seriously undervalues bodily life by not making it an integral part of the person. Likewise, a utilitarian view tends to see the person as dominated by self-interest, which does not lend itself to an understanding of natural law. Similarly, faulty views of the human being are connected with mistaken notions of rationality and freedom. For example, one thinks of a rationality which is limited to scientific and pragmatic knowledge and is concerned with what works and can be the object of experimentation, thereby denying reason its full range. Or, we see many contemporary instances where freedom is merely identified with choice, or unbridled autonomy and is separated from truth.

Faith and Reason

The harmony between faith and reason entails that they both need each other. The very act of faith requires the assent of reason and it is an essential part of the definition of theology, namely, the study of Revelation by *reason* enlightened by faith. According to the encyclical *Fides et Ratio*, this operates on two

---

[24] John Paul II, General Audience 20-II-80, n. 3.

levels, namely, the *auditus fidei* and the *intellectus fidei*. With regard to the first, philosophy prepares the way for a correct 'hearing', or reception of Sacred Scripture, Sacred Tradition and Magisterium by its study of the structure of knowledge and the language necessary to communicate it. We do not find all the principles and details of moral life presented in an orderly way in Revelation, and therefore, as a coherent and coordinated moral system, rational ethics undertakes this task. As regards Tradition, very often the great masters of theology have taken their concepts from a philosophical school of thought about which reason must enlighten us if we are to acquire a proper comprehension of it. Hence, we find that moral theology relies, for example, on reason's concept of the dignity and the genuine goods and rights of the person, conscience and the natural law, a moral evaluation of human action, the nature of virtue and the end and purpose of life, and needs a good explanation of them.

The *intellectus fidei* seeks to enable theology to respond through speculative enquiry into a deeper understanding of faith and Revelation, often as a result of searching questions asked of it, in a disciplined and scientific way. It, therefore, renders service to Divine Truth by bringing out its "innate intelligibility, so logically consistent that it stands as an authentic body of knowledge."[25] This greater understanding of faith consists "not only in grasping the logical and conceptual structure of the propositions in which the Church's teaching is framed, but also, indeed primarily, in bringing to light the salvific meaning of these propositions for the individual and for humanity."[26] In Christian ethics today, in keeping with the teaching of Vatican II, there is a need to deal to a greater extent than hitherto with the morality of earthly realities and controversies without losing sight of the theology of ultimate truths, which corresponds to the teleological treatment of the subject and the salvific value of its content. Ethics, therefore, needs to relate to peoples' lives, and be explained in the light of present thinking and conditions, showing how it agrees with, or opposes it.

These considerations, which apply to theology as a whole, are

---

[25] John Paul II, *Fides et Ratio*, n. 66.
[26] Ibid.

especially relevant for the present subject as John Paul II noted in *Faith and Reason*.

> *Moral theology* has perhaps an even greater need of philosophy's contribution. In the New Testament, human life is much less governed by prescriptions than in the Old Testament. Life in the Spirit leads believers to a freedom and responsibility which surpasses the Law. Yet the Gospel and the Apostolic writings still set forth both general principles of Christian conduct and specific teachings and precepts. In order to apply these to the particular circumstances of individual and communal life, Christians must be able fully to engage their conscience and the power of their reason. In other words, moral theology requires a sound philosophical vision of human nature and society, as well as of the general principles of ethical decision-making.[27]

Reason also needs faith to have full confidence in its own powers and not fall into scepticism and relativism on the one hand, or over-reach itself with rationalism on the other, as it has tended to do since the separation of the two prior to the Enlightenment. An example, pertinent to ethics, is the way in which Revelation encourages philosophy to overcome the temptation to scepticism and an exclusive reliance on the principle of empirical viability. Metaphysics enables us to understand that the inherent goodness of the universe is crucial to the objectivity of ethics. The so-called anthropological turn to the person with Descartes which characterizes modern culture makes many think with Spinoza, that we confer value on the objects that we desire, when really it is the other way round. Things are not just good because the human person values them, or because we seek them, but we seek them and desire them because they are good and attractive. Here, we are helped by Revelation which tells us in Genesis (ch 1) that God saw that all that He had created was good. Metaphysics, in turn, explains that the world, and all that is in it, is good insofar as it exists, or has *esse*. Truth, being and goodness are interchangeable as the medievals taught. Evil is a privation of being. We can speak of the ontological goodness of the world around us from water and minerals through forests and vegetation to animals and mankind. All are good according

---

[27] Ibid., n. 68.

to their mode of being. Consequently, what exists has value and is desirable. All that is comes from God the supreme Good, whose name is, 'He Who Is'. And, therefore God, and not us, is the arbiter of good and evil.

However, 'good' is an analogical term in that, in its many uses, it is employed, partly in the same sense, and partly differently, and through all the various uses it will maintain some connection with the original meaning. Hence, the ethical 'good' is the product of practical reason, since the good sought is that of human action, behaviour and freedom. The moral good, then, is not simply a 'naturalistic' one but it is the fruit of the relation of freedom and the object it aims at. What starts as an ontological good becomes a moral one when it is sought after in a human action by the rational will of the acting subject. Nevertheless, not just any good will make the action morally upright since those who perform evil actions often claim to be doing 'good', as they see it, as consequentialists do in justifying abortion and euthanasia. Traditionally, moralists have distinguished between the just good (*bonum honestum*), the useful good (*bonum utile*) and the pleasurable good (*bonum delectabile*). John Paul II writes:

> When he acts, man chooses a certain good, which becomes the goal of his action. If the subject chooses a *bonum honestum*, his goal is conformed to the very essence of the object of his action and is therefore a just goal. When, on the other hand, the object of his choice is a *bonum utile*, the goal is the advantage to be gained from it for the subject. The question of the morality of the action remains open: only when the action bringing the advantage is just and the means used are just can the subject's goal also be said to be just.[28]

He goes on to say with regard to the *bonum delectabile* that the Aristotelian-Thomistic tradition always regarded a just good as productive of interior joy, but the utilitarians have interpreted it more in terms of advantage or pleasure.

Reason, therefore, in harmony with faith, enables Christians to understand their own tradition more deeply and also to communicate and dialogue with modern thought, but not accept it uncritically. A Christian does not countenance the modern

---

[28] John Paul II, *Memory and Identity*, Weidenfield and Nicholson, London, 2005, p. 39.

dualistic notion of the person, or its concept of rationality and freedom; he communicates that of Tradition, but in a language that can be more readily understood and its truth more fully opened up. He recognizes and emphasizes the universality of the human person *qua* person, of human rights and of the natural moral law, based on the indivisibility of truth.

Ethics and Different Cultures

Contemporary culture tends to claim that all views must be accommodated, but this does not mean that all are true, or equally valid, simply that some approximate more to the truth than others. Hence, a healthy pluralism in society is not an argument for relativism, since truth does not compromise genuine freedom, but guides it. If "all truths must be accommodated" means "all views are partially true and there is no ultimate truth", then this conflicts with Christ's statement that he came to bear witness to the truth.[29] Pluralism means that individuals and groups are at different stages in their journey to truth, but not that there is no destination for this journey, as relativism maintains. Only a freedom which chooses to ignore reason (and truth) can make itself a law unto itself, and claim the same for others, but this, by definition, is irrational, and not unnaturally leads to contradictions.

The Church teaches that a healthy variety of opinions does not entail an all-embracing pluralism which excludes a common truth, or the exclusivity of truth. In the relativistic circles of modern society, "a legitimate plurality of positions has yielded to an undifferentiated pluralism, based upon the assumption that all positions are equally valid, which is one of today's most widespread symptoms of lack of confidence in truth. Even certain conceptions of life coming from the East betray this lack of confidence, denying truth its exclusive character and assuming that truth reveals itself equally in different doctrines, even if they contradict one another."[30] The Church recognizes that there may be a plurality of opinions in any society and she defends the rights to religious freedom and individual conscience of all

---

[29] Cf. Jn 18:37.
[30] John Paul II, *Fides et Ratio*, nn. 9-10.

its citizens. She opposes, however, a pluralistic relativism which denies the capacity of the mind to attain truth and simply reminds mankind of the obligation to seek that truth, since the quest for the meaning of one's existence is a duty bound up with the nature of being a rational human person.

The Gospel, and thus Gospel morality, is not opposed to any culture nor is it identified with any one culture. A culture embodies, or expresses the truth, to a greater or lesser degree, but is not itself the truth. Rather, the Church and the Gospel appeal to, and depend upon, what is universal and transcendent in every culture. They raise up and purify those aspects of each culture which portray the constant features of human nature. If the Church enriches the different cultures it comes into contact with, it is also enriched by them. Christianity was born in the Greco-Roman culture, but that does not imply that this is its only cultural expression, but neither does it mean that the dogmas and moral truths of the Church expressed in the terms of that culture can be jettisoned, since this particular culture was especially and providentially apt as a vehicle for the first theological expression of the Faith. However, to dialogue with today's culture we must grasp the philosophies and patterns of thought that have brought it about. Hence, the need to emphasize the rational aspect of morality and for this reason we refer to the present study as Christian ethics rather than moral theology.

II.

FUNDAMENTAL ELEMENTS AND THE DISTINCTIVENESS OF RATIONAL CHRISTIAN ETHICS

The renewal of Christian morality finds its inspiration, as far as rational ethics is concerned, in the Aristotelian-Thomism of the classical age of philosophy and the high middle ages as well as in the way modern personalism has studied subjectivity and consciousness. The Aristotelian emphasis on happiness as the end of man, the virtues and the goods of the human person, contrasts sharply with the modern one-sided preoccupation with obligation, and its neglect of virtue and personal growth. Classical ethics is not so much concerned primarily with law, as with the good you ought to seek in order to be fulfilled as a person. Aquinas accepts this while at the same time showing that law has its place as pointing out the paths of human good and leading to the practice of virtue. An adequate study of the subjectivity of the person leads us away from subjectivism and establishes the objectivity of ethics. It helps us to see that ethics, properly speaking, as opposed to applied and meta-ethics, is done in the first person.

All of this coincides with the Scriptures and Tradition which speak of happiness as the subjective final good of man whose objective dimension is beatitude, or union with the supreme Good, or God. The desire for happiness is of divine origin, says the Catechism: "God has placed it in the human heart in order to draw man to the one who alone can fulfil it."[1] This is attained by individual human acts, the subject matter of ethics, and the attainment of virtues, as is indicated by the Beatitudes. Hence, we must ask ourselves what conditions rational ethics must satisfy if it is to qualify as Christian ethics and form a basis for the rational explanation of revealed morality and conversely which characteristics disqualify it. Particular attention will be paid to the unsuitable character of the widely influential theories of consequentialism.

One of Aristotle's major contributions to ethics, as is well known, is that it is done by that aspect of the intellect he calls *practical* reason. It is not simply about achieving theoretical knowledge and information which is the task of speculative reason, but rather about judgements which lead to behaviour and action. Wojtyla not only accepted this but he took it further. One of his principles was that act may not be separated from experience which he learnt from Kant's mistakes, but also it follows from his account of subjectivity and consciousness. Every act that we do is also accompanied by conscious awareness and, therefore, moral actions like other acts are not simply abstractions but lived experiences. This means ethics starts from experience and is rooted in it, both subjective and objective experience. The latter is the guarantee that our freedom remains united to truth.

Furthermore, subjectivity for Wojtyla is based on solitude and everybody knows the yearning of the human heart for communion with others. And yet no human communion or friendship, even the highest spousal union, fully satisfies the human heart. Only a value which transcends every human value, since man is the highest human value, can do that and this is the supreme Good, or God. The latter for Aquinas and Wojtyla far exceeds Aristotle's notion of the ultimate good for whom it was a final, but not efficient, cause and consisted in the rather abstract contemplation of it, while for the former it is communion with God, that is a personal and loving Being and Father. While for a Christian ethics is to live in communion with divine life in the midst of his ordinary actions, a lifestyle open to the whole of mankind, for

---

[1] CCC 1780.

Aristotle it was to be an upright member of the City-State with contemplation of truth as the highest activity.

Practical Reason, Truth and Goodness

Ethics, however, properly speaking is done in the first person and the starting point of rational ethics is our own moral experience. By this is meant the spontaneous activity and self-evident knowledge by which we know we should avoid certain actions such as cruelty, or lying, or theft, and practise others like being friendly and respectful to our neighbour, treat others as we would be treated and in general do good and avoid evil. So, for example, even a young child when told by its mother to eat food it doesn't like, feels like throwing it on the floor, but knows it is wrong to do so. Later on, having reached the age of reason, we know that telling a lie to excuse oneself, for example, is wrong. We have this knowledge thanks to what St Thomas called 'the habit of the first principles' or *synderesis*, which is intuitive to us although arising with experience. Though this information is usually very reliable it needs to be systematized and ordered rigorously, which is what we call the science of ethics. Although reliable in an everyday sense, pre-scientific moral experience is susceptible to the influence of educational, social, philosophical, anthropological and historical factors, which can deform its contents. One purpose of ethics is to correct errors, which can creep in in this way.

Aristotle saw decisively that the type of reason employed in ethics was not simply speculative reason, which has to do with ideas and theories, knowledge and first principles, but rather practical reason which deals with desires and actions, in a word, changeable matters. "Practical wisdom," says Aristotle, "is a rational faculty exercised for the attainment of truth in things that are humanly good and bad."[2] The area of practical wisdom covers variable and changeable matters, namely behaviour and things that are 'doable' as well as the making and creation of things which he calls 'art'. So it is that the medievals defined prudence as 'the right way of doing things' and art as 'the right way of making things'. He distinguishes this from 'science' where speculative reason belongs

---

[2] Aristotle, *Nichomachean Ethics*, Penguin, 1963, ed J.A.K. Thompson, p. 177.

and which depends on deductions from eternally valid premises, which clearly, for him, remain relatively stable once deduced.

The virtue of prudence (another name for practical reason) is central to the practice of ethics, and enjoys the singularity of being both an intellectual and moral virtue at the same time, as well as facilitating true judgement in practical matters. It enables us to understand higher, or first principles, and to judge correctly or judiciously about everyday matters in accordance with them. Furthermore, it commands the right action, because it makes the last practical judgement leading to it: "If wise deliberation reveals a prudent man, it must be correct deliberation about what serves an end. Prudence consists in a true conception of what serves that end."[3] Prudence, therefore, identifies the good and goods of the person, both those that serve as intermediate ends and means to other goods and finally the ultimate good. However, to judge correctly about the good one has to be a good person. The moral dimension of prudence enables one to have rectitude in the affections and in the will, that is, to live according to what is right and good, namely in accordance with virtue. You wouldn't put a fraudster in charge of your accounts and investments, or ask a hedonist about temperance. Without this type of practical wisdom one will not easily understand that the meaning of sex is to be part of self-giving spousal love and open to the fruitfulness of offspring and that it loses its correct meaning when used for other purposes. Nor will one appreciate that the intrinsic value and dignity of human life, which is inviolable, is present in the embryo and in the disabled and infirm elderly.

Prudence is more than knowledge of general principles, it also includes particulars. This accounts for the fact that men who know nothing of the theory of their subject often practise it better than those who do, says Aristotle. He goes on: "It is in fact experience rather than theory which gets results."[4] Since it is an acquired virtue as well as being infused it grows all the time with experience. While Scripture says, "the unspiritual man does not understand the things of God,"[5] by the same token, the amoral man will not

---

[3] Ibid., p. 184.
[4] Ibid., p. 180.
[5] 1 Cor 2:14.

understand moral virtue and truth. Socrates was wrong to think that virtue is mere knowledge of the truth, as we shall see further on. All the moral virtues require prudence because it combines correct moral reasoning and rectitude in the will and appetites, therefore making for virtuous action. It brings together truth and love in individual judgements as much as in first principles. This is why conscience is not only an act of prudence but always requires prudence to be correct. A non-prudent person, or one in whom the virtue is underdeveloped, will fall into erroneous judgements of conscience. Prudence has good counsel and right judgement and the order to act among its subordinate parts. It is in virtue of prudence that freedom remains firmly anchored to truth.

Practical reason runs parallel to speculative reason with a first principle on which it depends, similar to the principle of contradiction in speculative reason, and then followed by secondary common principles and more particular determinations of them. However, the good of practical reason is dependent on the speculative good, or, to put it another way, ethical concepts and categories assume a metaphysical foundation to be fully comprehensible. The philosophy which underlies Christian existence, and indeed Christian thought in general, is a philosophy of being or, more properly speaking, of existence. Things are true and good insofar as they exist, the greater the degree of existence the greater the truth and goodness. Being is true insofar as it is known by a mind, that is, being as known; goodness is being as desired by a rational will. The first thing known is that things are, or by contrast that they are not, and in this is rooted the principle of contradiction.

Aristotle, who famously starts his ethics with a discussion of the good and asserts that the good is 'that at which all things aim', quickly concludes that most goods such as wealth, honour, intellectual gifts, etc., can in their turn serve as means to others. He therefore asks whether there is a good which is sought for its own sake and is not a means to any other and concludes that such a one is happiness which is the final end and consists in the contemplation of truth.[6] Aquinas adapted this because he saw

---

[6] Aristotle, *Nichomachean Ethics*, bk 1, ch. 7.

that the final good must be beyond man and outside of the world, since man himself is the highest value in the world, and also that it concerned the whole man, including his emotions and external activity, not just reason. Aristotle goes on to ask if happiness consists in the *possession* of virtue or the *exercise* of it. He reasons that it must be the latter because a man gets a gold medal in the Olympic Games not because he looks handsome or registers a high degree of health but because of his performance. Goodness is concerned with, and comes about in, action. All of this, however, is the work of reason:

> For virtue preserves, while vice destroys, that *intuitive* perception of the true end of life which is the starting point in conduct ... In moral as in mathematical science the knowledge of the first principles is not reached by a *process* of reasoning. The good man has it in virtue of his goodness, whether innate or acquired by the habit of thinking rightly about the first principle.[7] (my italics)

If things are good insofar as they exist then participation in being is the same as participation in value and the metaphysical order is the foundation of the ethical order. The two orders are different although connected. Wojtyla puts his finger on it when he writes: "The basis of a being's real perfection ... should be sought in the order of existence whereas the good becomes an object of knowledge only from the point of view of essence – only essence is conceptualized."[8] When the good is known, what is in fact apprehended is an individual good, for example, one of the goods of the person. The universal good by contrast could be said to be, in Buttiglione's words, "the realization of values within existence".[9]

For Aquinas a thing is good insofar as it exists, or has being, so that being and goodness are convertible. He then goes on to refer to perfected being, understood as being which has fulfilled its potentialities. We are thus enabled to understand what Aristotle meant by saying that "the good is that at which all things aim, or desire" because, though one's very existence makes one already

---

[7] Ibid., bk 7, ch. 8.
[8] Karol Wojtyla, *Person and Community*, Selected Essays, Peter Lang, New York, 1993, p. 76.
[9] Buttiglione, *Karol Wojtyla, The Thought of the Man who became Pope John Paul II*, Eerdmans, Grand Rapids, Michigan, 1997, p. 76.

good, one is still destined to grow in goodness by the development of all one's powers and capacities. This occurs through freely choosing good actions throughout a lifetime which bring us closer to the source of goodness. All things seek the good insofar as they desire their own perfection according to their own specific capacities.[10] But since all created goods reflect the goodness of God as Creator, all creatures can be said to seek God insofar as they desire their own specific perfection. They desire to fulfil themselves, but how? By reason and knowledge, through actions directed to a specific end, bearing in mind that the good of man is to live in accordance with reason. Goodness, therefore, consists not only in a standard or measure, a set of rules, but comes through actions which perfect the powers of the person, giving rise to virtues through which one grows as a person.

One of the first things we must bear in mind when talking about goodness, as is obvious from the foregoing, is that the word 'good' is analogical, that is, it is predicated of different things partly in the same way and partly differently. 'Good' is applied in different ways, as for example when we speak of the human goods which are perfective of persons, or alternatively when we apply it to actions, or yet again when we apply it in a non-moral context to natural objects, e.g. a good computer, or a good game of cricket. There are different grades and degrees of goodness, but there is an underlying thread which unites them all. By moral goods we refer to those which are suitable for human beings and contribute to their fulfilment and flourishing. They are moral insofar as they relate to the overall good of the person. Hence, we will be concerned to understand more fully human persons and their actions.

Goodness can, therefore, be thought of as being or truth inasmuch as it is desirable. The good is, in fact, the truth under the aspect of desirability, that is to say, insofar as the good presented by the practical reason is sought after by the will. The mind is directed to the universal truth and the will to the universal good, because reason knows things in their universality (the abstracted essences of material things) and then also in their individuality. In any human act the reason presents truths, or goods, to the will, which

---

[10] Aquinas, ST, I, q. 5, aa. 4, 5.

are either accepted or rejected, hence the will chooses particular goods but in their universal dimension. So, reason does not create the law, or moral value, but it does discern it. If what are good or evil are acts of freedom, then the choices of the will are an essential feature of what we mean by moral, but the arbiter is reason.

By 'goods of the person' we mean those things which are the object and terminus of rationally directed activity and thus of desire and choice which when it is satisfied completes the act. A good is the object and end of a human moral act, which we are about to look at more closely, and which contributes to the overall well-being of the person. The fundamental goods of the person are the basis of the natural law. The question of which goods and in what measure they genuinely fulfil the person (called the *debitum*) is judged by practical reason, or prudence, according to the natural law and the virtues in the light of human dignity. For example, food and drink and rest and work are goods of the human person, but practical wisdom (i.e. virtue) must ensure that they are not used or practised to excess or defect.

In the light of this, it is worth noting how Wojtyla, following Scheler, uses the word 'value' and what its relation is with a good: "Roughly speaking one could say that [a good] is an object that in some way contains a source of value. Phenomenology allows us to speak only of a hierarchy of values and not of a hierarchy of goods."[11] Phenomenology is not metaphysics and does not go into the roots of goodness, it is content with our experience and consciousness of it to which it gives the name 'value'. Hence, ethics is man's fulfilment through the use of his freedom, that is, activity and behaviour, rather than just theoretical concurrence with an order of laws and rules and certainly not the contemplation and conceptualization of the good. Ethics is essentially a practical activity, as Aristotle observed.

Conscience according to Tradition

The aspect of consciousness which reflects the order of moral values is conscience. Contrary to popular opinion, conscience is not itself a faculty, but is rather an act of judgement of the practical intellect about the rightness or wrongness of a course of action.

---

[11] Wojtyla, *Person and Community*, op. cit., p. 90.

Normally it is used to mean the application of the general principles to a particular case, but it sometimes covers the apprehension of the general principles themselves which St Thomas refers to as *synderesis*. Conscience's task, in the words of *Veritatis Splendor*, is "to apply the universal knowledge of the good in a specific situation and thus express a judgement about the right conduct to be chosen here and now."[12] We call that act of judgement true conscience which is in accord with an objective order of goods. In this way conscience is said to be the proximate norm of morality. Practical reason, or prudence, is the correct context in which to speak of conscience, because the latter depends on the principles handed down by the former.

The judgement and decision of the deliberative will concerning an act of behaviour constitute freedom. But freedom cannot operate successfully without the criteria and formation given by knowledge of the moral law, the teaching of the Church, prudence and the taking of counsel. So freedom and moral law intersect in obedience to the truth via conscience, the proximate norm of morality. In order to bring freedom and conscience more in line with the truth, education in moral behaviour is essential and, depending on the degree of it and the effort made to acquire it, conscience will be culpably or inculpably ignorant.

Moral truth, or practical reason, is founded on the basic forms of human good which via intermediate principles become the first principles of natural law. Conscience is the individual reflection of these principles which are then applied to a particular case. It is here in conscience that we see the link between the act of freedom and truth, i.e. the truth of moral and practical reason. Conscience having deliberated and, perhaps taken counsel, makes a judgement about a particular course of action and this gives rise, via consent and command, to a decision of the will to go ahead with the action. To achieve a true conscience it is necessary that it be formed and informed with natural law principles, moral theology, the teaching of the Church, practical reason, study, consultation etc., and therefore it is not sufficient that it be 'sincere' and 'authentic', as is often suggested.

---

[12] *Veritatis Splendor*, n. 32.

The link with practical reason shows that conscience is not independent or autonomous and therefore is not creative of its own values, but is dependent on the truth of good and evil which is received by rational nature. This means that human reason shares in the eternal or creative reason, namely the 'Logos'. Glimmers of it are reflected in rational beings which we call the first principles of morality or natural law. *Veritatis Splendor* says that the dignity and authority of conscience "derive from the truth about moral good and evil, which it is called to listen to and express." [13] It argues, therefore against conscience as pure subjectivity, or one's own subjective opinion which we have seen so much of in post-modernity.

It follows that a certain or definite conscience is not necessarily a true one, because conscience itself is not an independent tribunal or source or creator of moral values. A certain conscience, as opposed to a true one, applies more to the psychological confidence with which it is held. In some contemporary thought says *Veritatis Splendor*, "the individual conscience is accorded the status of a supreme tribunal of moral judgement which hands down categorical and infallible decisions about good and evil. To the affirmation that one has a duty to follow one's conscience is unduly added the affirmation that one's moral judgement is true merely by the fact that it has its origin in the conscience. But in this way the inescapable claims of truth disappear, yielding their place to a criterion of sincerity, authenticity and 'being at peace with oneself', so much so that some have come to adopt a radically subjectivist conception of moral judgement."[14]

Conscience must be followed as long as it is a true, or inculpably ignorant, one, but not if the ignorance is blameworthy through wilful neglect of formation, or information, which it could reasonably easily acquire. It enjoys freedom not *from* the truth but *in* the truth. The Magisterium only brings to conscience those truths which it can achieve by its own formation. The Church's teaching should not therefore be seen as an external force pressurising you, but as helping and assisting you to a correct conscience. If one's conscience conflicts with the Magisterium

---

[13] Ibid., n. 60.
[14] Ibid., n. 32.

there may well be an error in first principles, or the reasoning process, or again in one's understanding of Catholic truth. We will look later at the way moral truths are taught by the Magisterium and the degrees of authority behind them.[15]

Voluntarism and legalism have dominated understandings of natural law and conscience since the late Middle Ages and both approaches tend to see conscience as obeying some authority outside, or beyond reason which would lead to a double truth. Rather ethical principles come from within, from our rational grasp of the first principles of natural law or moral norms. Of course this presupposes that human reason is a participation in eternal reason, that is, the 'Logos' or creative reason. But magisterial teaching is not something imposed on conscience but only guides and helps it in its deliberations.[16]

The very nature of conscience is to be free because it is the judgement of freedom about moral values. It is in their conscience that the moral autonomy of each person resides and in which their dignity consists. It is a moral autonomy which brings with it the responsibility of each one for their own decisions and for the actions based on them. If it is free it is responsible and because it is free it is accountable to the truth on which it depends. Only if it were independent would it not be accountable, except to oneself, but then it would run the risk of enslaving one to one's own passions, prejudices and licentiousness.

Human Action: the Voluntary and Free Act

The human person perfects him or herself through individual acts, and so ethics is about human acts from the point of view of good and evil, that is to say, it is about the ends and objects, which the rational will chooses and therefore it depends, in part, on a correct analysis of the human act. A desire or appetite follows an act of knowledge since one cannot desire what one does not know. If this is on the sensitive level it is called an emotion, or passion, and on the intellectual level, the will. The will is a rational

---

[15] See Bishop Anthony Fisher, 'Conscience and Authority', a paper presented at the conference organized by the Pontifical Academy for Life, *"The Christian Conscience in support of the Right to Life"* 3-III-07.
[16] Bishop Anthony Fisher, ibid.

appetite and covers what we mean by desire or intention. But it belongs to reason, and thus to persons, to identify the end which is the first principle in human acts, because there could be no act without the apprehension of the end. An action therefore comes about through an interplay between intellect and will. The will often chooses one of the goods presented to it by the reason, but it need not, because it can decide whether to accept what is presented to it, or not. Though it can prescind from reason, if it is to act correctly the will must act according to reason. According to Aquinas the will is only superior to the intellect when it is acting wrongly or not according to truth. This has great significance for freedom because it means that being free is not achieved by *any* choice or use of the will but by seeking the true good of the person, that is, those goods that are genuinely fulfilling and perfective of him or her.

A voluntary action is willed and not coerced, that is to say, is not the victim of force, ignorance, error or deceit. The so-called elicited act, (i.e. the ability to will or not to will), is always free whereas the commanded act, that is one in which the will acts through one of its faculties, is indeed susceptible of having its freedom curtailed. Voluntary acts include those which we sometimes find hard to do, or in different circumstances would not do, like some kinds of work, or having an operation. It may be hard, or I may not want to undergo an operation, but if that is what is necessary to regain health then I will do it. Similarly, the difficulty of temptation to concupiscence or sensuality does not stop one carrying out free actions. Passion is an irrational appetite, which the will either accepts or rejects in carrying out a human act and so either way it is free.

Christian tradition points out that an action has not one, but two ends or objects, namely the actual action which is done, which is called the proximate object and the original intention to do it, or that for the sake of which it is done. The two ends often coincide but may differ. For example a donor may initiate a laudable project to give aid to Africa for the relief of poverty and disease. With the passage of time he may realize that a portion of that money is going to the funding of condoms for AIDS patients, which, as a Catholic, he disagrees with. The moral object of the action has become wrong. Or, in another case a man may set out to pay no more than the necessary tax expected of him, a perfectly reasonable position as long as it is done truthfully and within the law since he is only avoiding taxes the law does not oblige him to pay. However, when it comes to putting into practice the project he does not declare the income he has received in cash, so falsifying what he earns and such a practice is usually known as tax evasion. The proximate object of his action has become wrong and with it the whole action.

In other words, the morality of an action is determined by the relationship of human freedom, that is rational deliberation, to a good or evil object. Bearing in mind the above, Aquinas tells us that three elements must be considered in determining the ethical value of an action, namely the moral object of the act, the intention of the agent and the circumstances in which it is done.[17] The latter do not normally change the morality of the action, but only increase or diminish its moral value, but they can lead to a re-description of the act as when one steals something from a sacred place and adds sacrilege to theft. For the action to be morally upright both the first two conditions must be good. As St Thomas' famous phrase puts it; an upright act requires all the parts to be good, but for it to be evil it is sufficient that one part be bad *(bonum ex integra causa, malum ex quoque defectu)*.[18]

The Link between Act and Experience

According to Wojtyla an action is not just something to be studied from a detached third person point of view, but must also take into account the personal experience of the action. He considers that it is vital not to separate act from experience, as Kant did, in the description of the human act. If the act is described simply in the third person objectively this leaves out the subjective experience and consciousness of it. The person is aware of the fact that he is the agent-subject and therefore that he is the efficient cause of the action. In other words, he experiences his freedom as self-determination, because he is aware that 'he can but he need not'

---

[17] Aquinas, ST, I-II, q. 18, aa. 2-4.
[18] Aquinas, *De Malo*, q. 2, a. 1, ad 3.

and the whole process is reflected in consciousness. Wojtyla, therefore, proposes that the subjective conscious experience needs to be brought into the description of an action if the full truth of the human act is to be adequately described.

Every human act includes an act of judgement of the intellect, and an act of decision of the will, which we call choice, as Aquinas had already noted. The union of act and experience situates ethics in its proper domain of human freedom and action. Experience connotes practical action and so ethical truth must be sought according to whether the human actions are in conformity with the true good of the person. The objective truth of actions is at issue, not simply the desires or satisfactions of the subject. For Wojtyla the link between act and experience ensures that a proper conception of subjectivity does not fall into subjectivism. Subjectivity for him is fully grounded in an openness of consciousness to the being of one's own person. Wojtyla's insistence on lived experience and the conscious experience of the act links up with Aristotle's notion of practical reason and ensures that it is maintained after Kant's betrayal of it.

The experience of subjectivity and of one's personal causality in the bringing about of an act fully underlines the human responsibility for one's actions and overcomes the danger of assimilating them to purely physical events. The power of self-determination, or freedom, not only leads to a change of affairs in the external world for which the subject must take responsibility, but also affects the character of the person him or herself. One cannot turn in action to an object without at the same time turning to oneself through whom the action is carried out. The action, in other words, is intransitive as well as transitive which means that the moral value of an action stays in the person and contributes to his growth, or otherwise if it is morally bad. So freedom is not just choice, but awareness of being the principal cause of an action and therefore responsible for it. One is aware of being self-governing and possessing oneself and hence one becomes responsible for not losing the self-dominion proper to the person. In this way modern personalism enriches our notion of the free act.

Emotions and Passions

For a proper understanding of action one must ask oneself what the motivating forces of human action are which drive a person to act in the first place and also the sequence of events involved. They are precisely the goods of the person known first of all on the sensitive level by the emotions and then on the rational level. These give rise to the goods and evils of the passions which, because they are the result of sense knowledge, are not yet moral, but become moral once they are accepted, or rejected by, reason and will. They are called passions because, until this moment, we are passive in regard to them. All conscious and reflective actions of the person are rational even though they might have begun on the sensitive level.

Although reason is the arbiter, the inclinations to action operate very powerfully also on the sensitive level where good and evil are likewise experienced. The passions or emotions are said to be 'movements of the sensitive appetite' which affect the whole composite and by which the person is inclined to, or repelled by, something felt to be good or evil.[19] So while a beautiful sunset may arouse feelings of joy and satisfaction, the experience of seeing a mugging in the street will conversely cause fear, the racing of the pulse and the desire to escape for one's own safety, and sorrow and sadness for the plight of the victim.

Passions and emotions, then, give rise to bodily changes in respect of which one is, in good part, passive, since they are in the irrational part of the soul. They manifestly belong to the sensitive appetite and not just to sense knowledge because they imply being drawn to some object, or person, or away from it.[20] The two forms of the sensitive appetite are the concupiscible and the irascible. The object of the first is good or evil taken absolutely, that is the pleasurable or the painful.[21] We have an instinctive inclination to the pleasurable and instinctively recoil away from pain. A pleasurable good gives rise to the emotion of love, a future good to desire and a possessed good to joy and delight; painful

---

[19] Aquinas, ST, I-II, q. 22, aa. 1-2.
[20] Ibid.
[21] Ibid. q. 23.

evil to hatred, a future evil to aversion and the presence of evil to sorrow and sadness.

At times, great difficulty is experienced in achieving good, or avoiding evil, and it is this arduous good which is the object of the irascible appetite. In respect of good or evil not yet obtained we speak of hope or despair, and of evil or good not yet present we feel fear or daring. With regard to the good obtained there is no irascible passion, but with present evil there is anger. Insofar as we merely feel these emotions we cannot be responsible, or blamed, for them. However, they are said to be voluntary either as commanded by the will, or not checked by it.[22]

Growth in Virtue and Dignity

The ethical vision of the Church and Aquinas sees a unity between a law-based morality and the virtue ethics which completes it. Without this unity it is easy to fall into legalism and casuistry. The latter tends to ask how far you can go or, what you can get away with. In treating goodness as simple conformity to law, and sometimes the letter of the law, it fails to appreciate that the law itself is based on the true goods and values which are meant to lead to the practice of virtue, in which true moral fulfilment consists. A virtue is a power for good in some aspect, or other, which is based on repeated acts of that good, e.g. self-control or temperance. The Christian ethical position requires that the Law of the Old Testament be internalised by the practice of virtue in the appetites and faculties of the person, especially the rational appetite of the will.

The very word 'ethics' comes from *'ethos'*, or habit, and 'morals' from *'mos, moris'*, custom. But, in fact, *'ethike'* means character, disposition of the affections, referring to the tendency to act in an accustomed way. So we already see from this that ethics is not merely about law, but about developing the right dispositions and habits of character, that is, it is about virtues. The human inclinations from which we know the goods, are the seeds of these habits and dispositions, which when frequently practised become virtues. Significantly, the Greek for virtue is *arête*, which means

---
[22] Aquinas, ST, I-II, q. 24.

excellence, capacity, ability or worth. 'Virtue' comes from *vir*, 'man', 'strength' referring to strength of character and will.

A habit implies a disposition in relation to a thing's nature, that is, to itself, or to its action. The subject of the habit may be a faculty, such as the mind or the will, or an appetite such as the concupiscible or the irascible. Virtue can apply to the emotional part of the soul only insofar as the passions or emotions come under the influence of reason, hence virtue is usually defined as "a good quality of the mind by which we live rightly, of which no one can make bad use".[23] That which is disposed, namely a faculty or a power of the soul, may be either well, or ill disposed, to itself or its act, which gives the habit an evaluative character.[24] When a faculty becomes habitually well disposed to its action we call it a virtue. A virtue is the perfection or excellence of a power or faculty whose end is to act and so a virtue is a 'good operative habit.'[25] Aristotle also passes on the well-known teaching that a virtue is a mean between two extremes of badness, either excess or deficiency, but looked at from the standard of right and wrong it is an extreme since once the good action is identified it must be taken towards excellence.[26] In this way the mind, for example, becomes, out of habit, well disposed to right judgement, or truth, or knowledge, or the determination to treat everyone fairly and give them their due, and so on. Habits build up character, so ethics, or morals, is about what one becomes through ingrained habits or virtues.

If a faculty, or appetite, improves and tends towards excellence through the quality of its actions, then, since the person is a unity, the same thing is going to happen to the whole human being. The entire human personality is shaped by his/her behaviour, predominantly of course by the intellect and will, but also, under their guidance, by the emotions and the senses. This follows from the fact that in every human act the whole person acts. Such a conclusion, as we shall see, however, cannot be derived from dualism. The human person realizes him or herself through action.

---

[23] Peter Lombard, *Sent.* II, dist. 27, citing Peter of Poitiers, *Sent.* III, ch. 2, quoted in Aquinas, I-II, q. 55, art 4.
[24] Aquinas, ST, I-II, q. 49, a. 3; cf. Aristotle, *Metaphysics*, V, 20.
[25] Ibid., I-II, q. 55, aa. 2-3.
[26] Aristotle, *Nichomachean Ethics*, II, 6.

A morally good life should lead to a happy and fulfilled life. So we see from experience the effects of self-control and temperance, but also conversely, those of self-indulgence, such as alcoholism, drugs or eating disorders, on the whole life of the person.

We are now in a better position to understand that moral values are those that affect the *whole* person for good, and help him or her to grow as a person. This Thomistic and Catholic view of the integral development of the person contrasts with consequentialism and proportionalism, which use a utilitarian principle, the benefit/harm analysis, to judge the rightness, or otherwise of an action. Such a principle is appropriate for the market place, or the world of technology, but it is not a moral principle, because it does not help the human being to grow as a person.

The Link between the Virtues, Freedom, Charity and other concepts of Ethics

Morally good human acts which are the basis of virtues fulfil a person in some particular area or other. They are incomplete steps on the journey to fulfilment and happiness. Aquinas often referred to Aristotle's point that a "virtue is that which makes the possessor good and his work good likewise."[27] It also make it possible for man to do good with greater facility. Virtue leads to, and teaches, love of the good. Virtues, therefore, are an important part of the ethical picture, but how do they fit into the other parts of it? The seeds of the virtues are the goods of the person, which are the basis of natural law and, in turn, are identified by practical reason. Every human act requires freedom, and the overall end of Christian (and indeed human) behaviour is love or charity. How then do all of these elements fit into the good, virtuous and happy life?

Freedom is connected with virtue since the latter is not simply a habit which is developed in a mechanical way. Our liberty is exercised in a double way in every act, both in the choice of a particular good or moral object and also the reason on account of which the choice is made. Every choice is either meritorious or blameworthy, and, if the former, contributes to the growth of

---

[27] Ibid.; cf. ST, I-II, q. 55, a. 3.

virtue in the subject. A virtue always has to do with goodness, but also to do with the degree of goodness. Aquinas follows Aristotle's definition: "The virtue of a thing is fixed by the highest degree of its power."[28] Freedom, then, is not just 'freedom of indifference', the ability to choose between opposites, but above all 'freedom for excellence' by which the agent chooses according to the good of the person and fosters a higher quality of that good.

Let us expand a little on this latter point. Freedom is not pure autonomous action creative of its own truth, but rather it is conditioned by the truth of its object. Our freedom, for example, is limited by the need to respect the equality of other persons, their goods and not to do them harm etc. It is not pure satisfaction of desire, but love for the true good of oneself and others and, therefore, is a self-giving love. Nor is it, either, pure indifference, or without constraint and direction, but finds its root in the orientation of reason to truth and the will to goodness which is, in turn, the basis of the first principle of practical reason, 'do good and avoid evil'. In the modern understanding, autonomy is frequently considered to be the greater the less restriction there is. However, given the rational will's orientation to truth and goodness, freedom is greater in the measure in which it is exercised in accordance with the true good of the person, and consequently the same may be said of happiness and fulfilment.

The study of subjectivity by Karol Wojtyla enables us to appreciate how ethics is done by each of us in our own lives in the first person, that is, by the acting person. When it is taught, of course, it is done in the third person. For a Christian, morality is neither simply rationalistic nor voluntaristic. An ethics of the first person, instead of starting with first principles and norms and deducing modes of action, begins with practical reason which identifies values which are actuated by freedom leading to virtuous acts. Similarly, on the theological level, Christ (and the Church) is not simply a law giver who hands down commands requiring a response of external actions, He is also a friend who attracts, strengthens and counsels us to attain the goods and virtues which make up the moral life. Charity understood as 'friendship with

---

[28] Aquinas, ST, I-II, q. 55, a. 3.

Christ' is 'the form of the virtues' in the teaching of Aquinas. Each virtue stands as an upright activity on its own, but the virtues as a whole are not complete without charity. According to St Bonaventure, "the moral virtues are a participation in the virtues of Christ, the origin, form and end of the moral life" whose task is to prepare the way for the divinisation of man.[29]

This charity and friendship with God by means of union with the Person of Christ is the end and fulfilment of Christian ethics. Fulfilment is attained by good works of virtue which gain merit. These are incomplete steps to the perfection of sharing in the divine life, and can only be completed and brought into unity by the grace of God, which raises them up to the divine level, or to increased union with it, in virtue of the merit which he himself has deigned to recognize in them. The initiative of God, by which he communicates supernatural grace and charity, ensures that the virtues of a Christian are not pursued in a selfish and 'naturalistic' way, because grace heals the effects of sin. It is required of a Christian that he make a gift of himself to Christ and others and therefore also to his commandments, as Our Lord's words to the Rich Young man, and his statement that he who wants to 'gain his life must lose it', indicate. In fact, the latter words are the basis for the Council's teaching that 'man only finds his true self by making a sincere gift of himself'.[30] This is the essence of love which binds all the other virtues together, leading the subject to love what is good and choose what is right which in turn leads to fulfilment and happiness.

For Aristotle, the last end and supreme good of man was the contemplation of truth. Aquinas accepted this, in part, because, clearly, ultimate human fulfilment is going to consist in the satisfaction of the highest human faculty, which is the intellect. However, he was also aware of its deficiencies. Fulfilment, for Aristotle, consists in an activity in accordance with virtue, or if there is more than one virtue in accordance with the best and most complete. It is much debated, therefore, whether for him the ultimate end consists in one virtue or a plurality of them. Aquinas,

---

[29] See Livio Melina, *Sharing Christ Virtues*, CUA Press, Washington, 2001, p. 58.
[30] *Gaudium et Spes*, n. 24.

for his part realized that ultimate fulfilment referred to the whole man and therefore comprehended the activity of the practical as well as speculative intellect and the will and the emotions. What is more, it was clear to him that the ultimate end and perfection of man is not attained in this world but beyond it and outside time. This is because no value on earth such as money, power or fame can satisfy man since he is the highest value. Or, to put it another way, man cannot achieve perfection in this life since he will always be a fallible creature, who awaits the grace of God to complete his sanctification which is given him in virtue of his merits and God's infinite mercy. That is to say, the sanctity which results in the beatific vision, is not possible in this life, or by human effort alone, and needs to be completed by the grace which Aquinas calls the *lumen gloriae.*

Happiness

The ends and objects man seeks in his actions, are steps on the way to the overall good of the person, referred to by the encyclical *Veritatis Splendor* as the meaning of life or as Aquinas says the '*veritas vitae*'.[31] However, happiness, or the personalistic good, should not be identified too exclusively with personal fulfilment, or a sort of psychological contentment and satisfaction with one's life, since this would make it difficult to distinguish between true and false happiness for want of an objective yardstick. For example, in this conception there is nothing to stop happiness being identified with a utilitarian type of pleasure. Here St Augustine comes to our aid when he says: "A happy man is one who has all he wants, and at the same time wants nothing bad."[32] The satisfaction of personal desire must be allied to uprightness in the will which seeks the genuine good and goods of the person. Aquinas, like Augustine, allows that there is a subjective side to happiness when he says: "To desire happiness is nothing other than

---

[31] Aquinas, ST, I, q. 16, a. 4, ad 3; II-II, q. 109, a. 2, ad 3, and a. 3, ad 3.
[32] St Augustine, *De Trinitate* XIII, 4, 7-9, 12 quoted in Livio Melina, 'Desire for Happiness and the Commandments in the First Chapter of Veritatis Splendor' in *Veritatis Splendor and the Renewal of Moral Theology*, eds DiNoia and Cessario, Scepter, New Jersey, 1999. I am indebted to this article for some of the ideas in this paragraph.

to desire the satisfaction of the will."[33] However, this subjective side needs to be completed with the classical objective sense of happiness as *eudaimonia,* or beatitude, which is part and parcel of it. Beatitude, therefore, has an objective meaning in virtue of the end to which it is directed, namely the last end or *summum bonum,* and the goods of the person which make it up, as well as a subjective one which corresponds to the activity of the subject. In this latter sense, happiness is said by Aquinas to be an action in accordance with virtue.[34] But the 'objective' and 'subjective' aspects are not opposed to each other but are rather two sides of the same reality looked at from different vantage points.

From this one can appreciate that concepts such as happiness and fulfilment carry with them a certain ambiguity and can be used in misleading ways. An example is the well-known statement in the American Constitution that every citizen has the right to 'life, liberty and the pursuit of happiness'. It would be more accurate to say that happiness ensues rather than is pursued, since it results from pursuing the true goods of the person, not just any good. Only by seeking a goal worthy of human dignity can there be rectitude in the will and without this there cannot be true fulfilment. At the same time Aquinas makes clear that earthly actions are only productive of imperfect happiness, and even then only as long as they are accompanied by virtue, but nevertheless they can be meritorious steps on the way to one's last end, or eternal life, in which perfect happiness alone exists.[35] They are imperfect realizations of the happiness, or beatitude that we seek.

All persons are orientated towards the Good, or *summum bonum,* in virtue of their rationality; they cannot help it, but they conceive it differently and its attainment depends on their freedom. This Good, however, is broken down and made up of the basic goods of the person, which are perfective of him, or her. They are discernible in accordance with the inclinations of the person to life, the generation of life, truth, and friendship, or social life, and it is here that a person in this life may choose against any one of these values. These are the basic goods of reason, which give

---

[33] Aquinas, ST, I-II, q. 5, a. 8.
[34] Ibid., q. 5, aa. 6-7.
[35] Ibid., q. 5, a. 5.

a moral character to human acts in virtue of their relationship to the final good whose normative character will depend on an accurate understanding of the dignity of the person (see chapter 3). They correspond to the truth of the person as discerned by reason, and form the basis of the moral law.

Consequently, the knowledge, right ordering and harmonizing of the human goods by reason, and the moral effort to pursue them throughout a lifetime, are necessary for human happiness. A series of supplementary goods depend on each fundamental good. The basic goods are all equally basic, but the supplementary goods are hierarchically ordered and have their due place in the scheme of things. If disorder enters in here it upsets the balance of a person's life and affects their happiness. So housing and nourishment and material well-being serve human life and not the other way round. The sensible goods depend on the fundamental ones and not vice versa. Pleasure is integral to human life, but even if at some point pain becomes a paramount consideration it cannot be deemed to override the good of life.

The relevance of this harmony to human happiness can be appreciated by considering some of the psycho-somatic disorders which take it away, such as drug addiction, alcoholism, eating disorders, anorexia and bulimia, lack of self-esteem etc. In these cases, lesser goods and concerns become more important and take up more of a person's energies than the basic goods themselves. The result is dysfunctionalism. Disharmony can also be seen in an avaricious person, either a thief or simply somebody who seeks happiness in purely material wealth. The lack of fulfilment shows in the fact that such a person is always seeking more, and tends to be insecure and dissatisfied with whatever he, or she, has. The very phenomenon of addiction and dissatisfaction with material things indicates that the human will ultimately seeks the transcendent good.

Different Systems of Ethics

Finally, it is worth considering why we find so much misunderstanding and opposition to Christian and Catholic morality. Part of the reason has to do with the different systems of rational ethics which underlie and influence theological ethics. If one looks at an elementary introduction today one is liable to see a series of different systems offered and explained which will normally include, Kantian deontological ethics, utilitarianism/consequentialism, and virtue ethics. Some acquaintance with them is therefore desirable, but since we are expounding here Thomistic-Aristotelian virtue ethics it will be sufficient to outline the other two systems briefly. This is not, however, to say that all virtue ethics are in line with Christian tradition. This will only be the case if the description of the virtues is informed by an account of the genuine human good. Only virtue ethics is compatible with Christian ethics and even then only on condition that it is linked with the natural law.

Kantian deontological Ethics. Deontological ethics refers to an ethical system based on duty and derives largely from Kant's philosophy. This alternative is often taken as equivalent to Christian ethics but it is not, because its Kantian basis does not allow reason its full range and the ability to reach objective truth. Furthermore, in making duty, or the categorical imperative, the foundation of practical reason it fails to appreciate that the ultimate flourishing of the human being results from seeking the true goods of the person which lead to the virtues, and law depends on these goods and not vice versa.

Only actions that are done out of pure duty can be good and this consequently excludes happiness, according to Kant, because it would introduce a selfish element into them. The will must be autonomous, in the sense that it is independent of external influences, and able to dictate its own norms. The categorical imperative states that an action is good when it can be universalised, by the subject, for all mankind. This appears to defend moral absolutes, but fails to do so, because the categorical imperative is formed by the acting agent without any guarantee of objectivity. John Paul II sees much merit in Kant's opposition to the utilitarian principles of pleasure and expediency and his emphasis on the obligatory character of ethics, but he criticizes him for falling short of the only objective basis for morality, namely the *bonum honestum*.[36] For Wojtyla, duty is based on the responsible

---

[36] For a development of this point see section 'The Truth and Value of the Person in Christian Tradition' below and John Paul II, *Memory and Identity*, Weidenfeld and Nicholson, p. 41.

freedom of the human person to seek the goods and practise the behaviour that lead to his or her fulfilment and happiness. This type of deontology would be compatible with Catholic ethics.

The tradition from which deontological ethics comes usually stresses the priority of the will over reason. This has the effect of making your moral code depend on freedom rather than reason; in the case of Ockham, who originated the idea, God's will, and in the case of Kant your own autonomous will. According to this, ethics depends on pure obligation and duty, either the all embracing will of God, or your duty to obey your own will stripped of all self-interest and leading to autonomous ethics in Kant's case. This is characterized by conformity to law and even casuistry, which has its place, but it overlooks the inclination to virtue and the call to happiness and love of God, characteristic of the Gospel and the Fathers of the Church. One can also see how this line of thought has led to giving priority and over-emphasis to autonomy and choice in moral questions when the religious background is taken away.

Utilitarianism. The ethical system of this name, which takes its origin from Jeremy Bentham and John Stuart Mill in the nineteenth century, determines what is right and wrong on the basis of the usefulness of an action to produce more pleasure than pain, or more benefits than harm. Many modern systems which claim to be moral, have a utilitarian, or consequentialist, criterion as their basis, which, in general, we may say, is a weighing of benefits over harm which accrue from the action. This gives you the useful and pragmatic good rather than the moral good, which rules out absolutes, and thus it is at the heart of contemporary relativism. It puts the accent on the action as event rather than on the choice of the deliberative will, which in morality is what is commended or reproved, and hence it concentrates on what works and is most convenient from an organizational point of view. But this is not what we mean by 'moral'. A utilitarian morality really assumes a utilitarian view of life. Life has to be made to work, as fairly as possible, with as little pain and suffering as possible etc. Emphasis is put on the 'quality of life' as opposed to the sanctity and inviolability of human life, to the workability of 'family life' rather than to the inviolability of the principle that it is directed to spousal love and the procreation and education of children. Utility, says John Paul II, is opposed to love.

According to the old-fashioned utilitarians it made no sense to calculate the effects of actions such as murder or theft, but only those whose morality was not already evident. Thus some early utilitarians saw certain actions as always wrong, but this was to change. The utilitarian principle may be expressed in two ways. One should always choose according to the principle or rule that will maximise the amount of good, on the whole, and in the long run (rule utilitarianism). Or, one should always choose the act which, as far as one can see, will produce the greatest amount of good in the long run (act utilitarianism).[37] Anscombe noted a change at the time of late nineteenth-century moralist Sidgwick who argued that all foreseen consequences were intended and therefore morally imputable. It locates morality in the relation of act to consequences, and nowadays this form of utilitarianism is referred to as consequentialism. It is not irrelevant to note that Anscombe considered the premise (of Sidgwick) to be incorrect, because some actions have side effects you foresee, but do not intend or desire in themselves, e.g. the hysterectomy operation which leads to sterility.

There are many problems with utilitarianism which have long been acknowledged. This is not the place to enter into them in any detail, suffice it to enumerate some of the principal difficulties: a) it is not possible to know and calculate all, or even many, of the consequences that might follow from any action; b) different goods and benefits are qualitatively different and hence cannot be quantified and compared, that is to say, they are incommensurate, e.g. how does one compare health with job satisfaction; c) the very name of utilitarianism tells us that we are speaking about the usefulness of an action to produce an effect which is happiness or pleasure, but what sort of pleasure? Is it sensual, emotional or intellectual or spiritual pleasure? Or, is it more akin to happiness, joy and satisfaction? How does one compare the joy of cycling with that of passing an exam? d) utilitarianism has no mechanism

---

[37] Cf. John Finnis, *Natural Law and Natural Rights*, Clarendon Press, Oxford, 1980, p. 112.

to ensure altruism. It gives us no criteria for whether to maximise our own happiness or that of everybody else first. The maxim, 'the greatest good of the greatest number' is too vague to indicate whether others should come before or after me;[38] e) the utilitarian principle encourages us to use our actions and choices as a means to an end for our own, or others', well-being. This is fine for deciding activities like going shopping. But what happens if we are dealing, not with things and objects, but with people? We can surely never 'use' them as a means to an end. In a word, the principle of utility gives us the useful good, or the pleasurable good, but it does not give us the just and true good, called by the ancients the *bonum honestum,* which equates to the moral good. The true moral good can only be known by reason working on the human inclinations and establishing the goods of the person. Notice the good is not the inclination itself or even the object of the inclination, but *reason's* perception of the good towards which it is directed.

Consequentialism, therefore, places the morality of an action not in the intrinsic good or evil of it, and not in the object of the action or indeed the intended object, but in the effects. It moves, therefore from a morality based on the object and intention of an act, to one based on the consequences of it. It is from this base that proportionalism, in other words, the theory that the right action is the one that has the highest proportion of good or beneficial effects and least harm, and hence moral revisionism, comes. A necessary consequence of it is that you cannot say any action is always or intrinsically wrong, but only better or worse than others. Hence if we ask, whether you can kill seven people to save a hundred, consequentialism does not seem to be able to deny it.

It is, therefore, opposed to a natural law morality which counts some actions as always wrong. As Aristotle famously said, the

> choice of mean is not possible in every action or every feeling. The very names of some have an immediate connotation of evil. Such are malice, shamelessness, envy among feelings, and among actions adultery, theft, murder. All these, and more like them, have a bad name as being evil in themselves; it is not merely

---

[38] See Finnis, op. cit., pp. 115-16.

the excess, or deficiency, of them that we censure. In their case, then, it is impossible to act rightly; whatever we do is wrong. Nor do circumstances make any difference to the rightness or wrongness of them. When a man commits adultery there is no point in asking whether it is with the right woman, or at the right time, or in the right way, for to do anything like that is simply wrong.[39]

Just as they cannot uphold moral absolutes, so utilitarianism and its surrogates also fail as a basis for upholding the universal and inviolable rights of every individual such as those to life and religious and moral freedom. If the civil law is not founded on the fundamental moral principles, then it runs the risk of falling into the hands of the most powerful individual or group, be it dictator, or parliamentary majority. Laws should respect the goods and rights that belong to the individual *per se* by reason of his or her inherent dignity, but these rights are not guaranteed by laws that are based on ethical relativism.

The Human Act in Secular Morality

Most versions of secular morality (of the consequentialist variety), therefore, analyse the human act in a completely different way from Aquinas and Christian tradition. The good is not the object of the action, it is claimed, but the balance of the consequences of it. All actions are neutral, or pre-moral, until we have calculated the consequences of doing them. For the followers of this theory it is the effects which are right or wrong, not the act. Hence, we are not talking here of an act which is, or is not, in line with objective moral norms, but we are in the process of constructing the ethical values. Yet it is surely necessary for the morality of an action to be known before it is begun, otherwise there cannot be true freedom to choose and without free action the question of morality does not arise.

One cannot understand what moral actions are, without an understanding of how human freedom works and affects the whole person and therefore his, or her, moral maturity and growth and development which each action either adds to, or takes away from. The consequences of not getting this right are catastrophic

---

[39] Aristotle, *Nichomachean Ethics*, bk 2, ch. 6.

for morality, since to be moral an action must be 'a freely chosen kind of behaviour', that is, carried out with reason and will, and which is therefore accountable and responsible.[40] Human action for utilitarians ends up ceasing to be human and personal, becoming more like a robotic act, or the action of a machine, and such actions cannot be moral.

It must be borne in mind that utilitarians are also dualists, for the most part, who hold that the person is composed of two separate principles of body and soul where the mind works on the body by means of a sort of physical causality and hence a human action is more like a series of causal events than a personal action, especially when the effects are also included. For them the body is a kind of mechanical instrument of the mind and will, which makes the action more like an impersonal event since the whole person is not involved as a unity and the action fails to leave its mark on the agent-subject. Dualists, therefore, are liable to underestimate the voluntary and personal aspects of action, which are central to their moral value. The role of the will in the terminus of the action is played down, to the point where the moral object is lost sight of, and the circumstances are played up. In the measure in which an action ceases to be understood as the result of rational deliberation, and is described more in mechanical terms, it succumbs to a 'naturalistic' description and in that measure it ceases to be moral. Not surprisingly, the dualist premises lead some to end up claiming that in certain cases the morality of the action is separate from the physical accomplishment of it, as when 'hard case' abortions or euthanasia are 'justified' by revisionists.

Hence, consequentialism does not see ethics in terms of the moral development of the person or their growth in virtue, since it does not see actions leading to good habits, and in the longer term, virtues. It is more concerned with a supposed state of affairs in the world than with personal goodness. To that extent, it is a prescription for social ethics, or even social engineering, rather than an individual morality, but even this is insufficient because the former should be based on the latter, since all ethics starts off primarily with individual behaviour and should defend

---

[40] Cf. *Veritatis Splendor*, n. 78.

fundamental human rights, based on a clear concept of the basic goods of the person which is lacking in consequentialism. Ethics, on this account, is not so much about living well as about increasing the amount of goodness in the world. Good behaviour is not seen as contributing to the moral growth and maturity of the individual but to the general fund of human well-being. If persons do not carry out human acts but causal events and, especially if they do not know all the consequences of them, then they feel more distant from responsibility for them.

In contrast, the anthropology of tradition sees a human act as a unified totality resulting from the freedom of the whole person, on whom it also leaves its mark contributing to the moral character, and requiring the accountability of the agent for his or her actions. Since the Christian tradition, and particularly Aquinas, has seen human action from the ethical point of view, as consisting in behaving in conformity with the inherent goodness of the object chosen, allied to rectitude of intention, both of which proceed from a deliberative will, consequentialism which lacks these characteristics will not qualify, by itself, as morality.[41] We, therefore, need a more thorough study of anthropology, or vision of the full truth of the human person and his freedom and personal goods, before returning to a definitive analysis of human action.

---

[41] See ST, I-II, q. 1, a. 1; see chapter 8 below.

III.

THE ANTHROPOLOGICAL BASIS OF ETHICS AND BIO-ETHICS

Peoples' moral convictions tend to be strongly influenced by their understanding of the meaning of human life and this in turn has a good deal to do with their conception of the human person. Two contrasting and conflicting conceptions, namely, the Christian and the secular, predominate today which affect the ethical standpoint we take on current moral issues. In this sense it is imperative to consider anthropology in some detail and particularly to look at Christian teaching on the person through the ages, in order to understand more fully the reasoning behind its moral stance and the consistency of it. This will afford us more insight into why it comes into conflict so often at present with those who assume a secular anthropology. Furthermore, we will also discover certain drawbacks appearing from time to time in the explanation of Christian anthropology, which need to be ironed out for it to serve as a satisfactory basis of its moral doctrine, and see the avenues of development which Karol Wojtyla / John Paul II pursued in order to present a more adequate anthropology for the issues of our age.

At the root of the separation between Christian ethics and much secular thought are two distinct views of the person, an older one arising out of the Trinitarian controversies of the fourth and fifth centuries, and a more recent one deriving from the Cartesian and Lockean philosophies of modern times. The more recent one does not have the completeness of the earlier one and hence fails to express the full truth of the person. The older one, however has encountered problems of incomprehensibility for the modern mentality which need attention. Pope John Paul was fully aware that the well known expression "individual substance (subject) of a rational nature", inherited from Boethius and accepted by Aquinas (with additions), suffered from the change in meaning over time that the word 'substance' had undergone and needed updating so as to be understood and enter into dialogue with modern thought. For this reason he was to give a more contemporary definition, more comprehensible to today's mentality, but without in any way detracting from the age old meaning of it, namely that a person is, "an incarnate spirit, that is a soul that expresses itself in a body and a body informed by an immortal spirit."[1]

With the above Boethian definition the tradition had wished to express three things: i) that a person exists in and by him or herself and not in another, i.e. he or she is an individual subsistent being in Aquinas's words; ii) that a person is a unity of body and soul; iii) that a person is distinguished from animals, things and objects by rationality and freedom. We will now examine these one by one. To say that a person is a substance or subject existing in himself means that he has his life and identity from himself and not as part of another, in the way, for example, that the life of the liver comes from being part of the body and the branch from being part of the tree etc. Furthermore, the substance is a living organism which maintains its identity through change. The different organs of the body exist for the good of the whole and contribute to the overall well-being of the person. Substances are to be distinguished from mechanical things, such as cars and machines, which are artificial constructions rather than living organisms and the parts are prior to the whole.

More specifically, Aquinas teaches that the unifier and life giver which makes a human being a living organism is the soul of the person. The body, or matter, is eminently suited to unite with the soul to produce a living human being. The soul is the principle of life and unity of the soul/body composite which unites the

---

[1] *Familiaris Consortio*, n. 11.

different organs and parts that make it up, and, in turn, works through the organs and senses of the body to produce unitary actions. Death is precisely the separation of the soul from the rest of the composite which results in the cessation of bodily life and the disintegration of its organs. Thirdly, the human soul is characterized by the faculties of freedom and reason which are capable of actions such as abstract thought, complex reasoning and self-reflection which surpass the possibilities of material organs and are therefore spiritual in nature. The human soul is thus intrinsically independent of matter, since the spiritual faculties function through material organs in this life but without them after death, though the separation is not permanent and the unity of body and soul will be restored when the soul is united to the glorified body. The soul of the animal in contrast is fundamentally bound up with the sense organs and thus dies with the body on which it is intrinsically dependent.

Animals can be said to have knowledge, and especially in the case of the chimpanzees and dolphins, a rudimentary power to reason, but there is no evidence that they know that they know, that is, that they have self-reflection and consciousness. The differences are summed up by the absence of any developed form of language by animals. While acknowledging that persons share the title of subject with non-humans, Wojtyla points out that a person must be distinguished from the latter in virtue of his or her spiritual faculties of intellect and will by which a human subject enjoys self-consciousness and self-determination. He concedes that at times a person can also be an object, e.g. an object of knowledge, but never a *mere* object which can be instrumentalized, and the emphasis on subjectivity guards against this danger. [2]

The above comments, then, serve to explain the terminology of Christian tradition, which in contrast to much secular dualism, sees man as a unity, that is, one rational substance of body and soul, where the soul is the life-giving and integrating principle and, for this reason, is said to be the 'form of the body' (*'forma corporis'*). He or she is a *substantial* unity (*'de corpore et anima una'* the Church teaches), not simply an accidental aggregate,

---

[2] K. Wojtyla, *Love and Responsibility*, Collins, London, 1981, p. 26.

separable at death, but never entirely separate, and working together in life as one human person.[3] Because of the unitary nature of human action, all acts which are done consciously and freely are personal in the sense that the whole person acts. None of his, or her, actions is simply biological unless they are unwilled physiological occurrences. Aristotle spoke of three levels of soul, vegetative, sensitive and rational, corresponding to the three levels of life and self-motion. In the human being, however, there is only one rational soul carrying out three functions.

Though the deficiencies of the Cartesian account of the person have become obvious in the light of the modern problems of sexual and bio-ethics, a true anthropology is crucial to other fundamental aspects of ethics. Without a firm grasp of the truth and unity of the person, it is impossible to give a coherent account of the unified working of mind and body in human action, a problem that goes back to Descartes himself. Nor can one formulate accurately the goods of the person which form the basis of natural law. A correct understanding of sexuality and gender matters depends on seeing the person as a unified totality. Finally, a dualistic account is unable to establish the intrinsic worth of the person as an end in him or herself who must always be treated with absolute respect. The existence of moral absolutes depends on this premise and will fail without it. It will be the concern of the succeeding chapters to demonstrate these contentions after looking in some detail at the origin and nature of the two accounts of personhood.

The Truth and Value of the Person in Christian Tradition

Christian Tradition had developed its notion of the person while working out its understanding of the theology of the Trinity and the Incarnation, one of whose fruits is the above mentioned Boethian definition of a human being. Aquinas noted an ambiguity in the notion of substance as inherited from Aristotle who referred to it, on the one hand, as the individualized subject (*hypostasis* or *substantia*) within the genus, and on the other, as the universal essence or nature of the genus itself (*ousia* or *essentia*). This meant that the Boethian definition can apply to

---

[3] Council of Vienne, 1311.

a human nature, as well as to a person, depending on how you understand substance. From a theological point of view after Chalcedon *hypostasis* or *substantia* came to mean person and *ousia* or *essentia*, essence or nature. Aquinas for his part succeeds in bringing out the difference philosophically by describing the person as a 'subsistent being' (*suppositum*), or 'thing', separated from others of rational nature which adds concrete existence to the notion of substance. A supposit (*suppositum*), or subsistence, then, is the existing subject in which the essence, or nature is, so to speak, contained.

Aquinas saw the crucial importance of distinguishing conceptually between person and nature, between the existential and essential level, while acknowledging that in reality they exist together. The person is to be distinguished from a nature in that he/she is a concretely existing individual who is the bearer of a nature. The nature is not opposed to the person, or freedom, but is part of it, as the Boethian definition makes clear. The nature of a human being then is a *rational* nature and so are all of his or her conscious activities. Many consequences follow from ignoring this, among them the misunderstanding of the notion of human nature, treating it as somehow identical with material nature, or below the person, at a time when many ethical questions have to do with the meaning of human life. The confusion leads some authors to suggest the moral good is deduced from human nature, rather than known in accordance with the nature of the singular human person (of which more later), or others to say there is no such thing as human nature. It tends then to be replaced by a concept of absolute autonomy, or freedom, which is not in accord with the human rational nature of the person.

However, the most important difference between human nature and person is that the person transcends even human nature. A person is more than just a member of a species, because the concretely existing human person is unique and unrepeatable since he possesses his own 'act of being' to a much greater extent and in a completely different way from any other material creature. The consequence is that the person is a being who enjoys self-possession, self-mastery and self-determination. This is the root of the superiority which a human being enjoys over the rest of the universe and in turn of the inviolability of the person and his fundamental goods and rights. It is for this reason that we call the person a transcendent being, because he or she literally rises above the rest of creation. From a scriptural point of view the foundation for this is his or her condition of being the 'image of God'. Hence the human being has a trace of God within, or perhaps we might say a capacity for God waiting to be fulfilled. If man is the highest being, nothing within creation will fulfil him.

On the level of reason, we owe this insight to the notion of the 'incommunicability' of the person used by the Roman law and continued by Richard of St Victor. All reputable legal systems since the Romans have afforded protection to the person and his or her fundamental goods based on it. They expressed it in the well-known principle: *Persona est sui iuris et incommunicabilis ad alteri* ('a person belongs to himself and is incommunicable to another'). The Roman law considered a person belonged to himself, was his own property, and his rights were laid down in terms of personal property rights. He acts on his own account and disposes of himself in virtue of his dominion over his acts. Thus a person exists in himself, and for his own sake as a self-determining being, and is more fully intransferable than inanimate things and irrational beings. For this reason a person is inalienable (cannot be transferred to another owner), and indefeasible (cannot be forfeited or annulled), and inviolable (his basic rights cannot be violated).

Richard of St Victor was unhappy with the substantialist definition of a person because he saw that it could not be applied to the persons of the Trinity, since each person then would be a substance and God is three Persons in *one substance*. He found an alternative definition in the Fathers, which was existentialist rather than essentialist, namely, 'an incommunicable existence of spiritual nature' (*spiritualis naturae incommunicabilis existentia*) which could apply both to God and man. The existentialist definition brings out the unique individuality of spiritual beings, based on the fact that they possess their own act of being, but only God is completely incommunicable. Richard saw that uniqueness and individuality derive from existential incommunicability and not simply from substantiality and spirituality. His discovery also alerted Aquinas to the deficiencies of the Boethian definition. Richard defined God as 'an incommunicable existence of divine nature', but he did not apply the consequences of his discovery to the human person which had to await the anthropological research of the twentieth century. This means that a person becomes 'an incommunicable existence of rational nature' showing thereby the similarity to God as well as the difference.[4]

While a person shares some of his being with others there is a core which is his own arising with freedom. The characteristics of incommunicability are based on the fact that each person is master of himself in virtue of enjoying self-determination because nobody can will for him. The person adds concrete existence to human nature, at the same time as he includes all the characteristics of this nature in himself as subject. He or she is, therefore, not only an existent subject, but a unique and unrepeatable one which does not stop him or her relating to others, but is, in fact the means for it to happen, as we shall see. The concretely existing human person surpasses the common nature and is more than the sum of his parts because he belongs to himself and exists for his own sake.[5] A person is a whole in him or herself, an independent self, residing in an existent subject, whereas a nature is part of the common human nature proper to all persons. As Livio Melina has written: "If a human being is but the replaceable exemplar of a specific nature, if he is simply the realization of a species, then nature and species are more valuable than the individual, and the individual human being can be subordinated and possibly sacrificed to the general well-being of the species."[6] Hence the individual human person transcends even the universal category of mankind which is why, for example, individual embryos cannot be expended to provide knowledge, or spare parts, for present or future humanitarian needs.

In virtue of his unique dignity, the person surpasses all other worldly creatures which in turn means that he, or she, cannot be subordinated to any other earthly being. In Wojtyla's language the

---

[4] Richard of St Victor, *De Trinitate*, IV, 23, *La Trinité*, Gaston Salet, S.J., ed., Coll. Sources Chrétiennes, 63, Paris, 1959, pp. 282, 284..
[5] Cf. Livio Melina, *Sharing in Christ's Virtues*, Catholic University Press, Washington, 2001, pp. 70-71.
[6] Ibid., p. 70.

person transcends all other material beings, a fact which accounts for St Thomas' description of him as the most perfect being in the world (*ens perfectissimum in totam naturam*). An echo of this is found in the Gospel phrase, "What does it profit a man if he gain the whole world and suffer the loss of his own soul?" Such a being is an end in himself in the sense that he does not act as a mere means, or instrument, of another. This is rooted in his dignity as a person, that is to say, in incommunicability and freedom and is the basis of his fundamental human rights and the reason why a person merits absolute respect and may not be treated as a means of pleasure, be manipulated by power, used as an object etc. Every person is a self in the sense that he belongs to himself and is intransferable to another.

Aquinas had already explained that a person exists and acts for his own sake in the *Summa contra Gentiles*, using, of course, the concepts and terminology of the time. He saw that a being which has dominion over its own actions and is the principal agent of its activity, acts by itself and for its own sake and not as an instrument of another. That which acts only when it is moved by another is like an instrument and an instrument is required, not for its own sake, but so that the principal agent may use it. Hence the action of instruments has the principal agent as its end, whereas the action directed by a principal agent, is done for its own sake. These arguments are based on the fact that God governs all creatures according to their condition, whether as free, rational and principal agents of their actions, or as instruments guided by instinct and the law of nature for the sake of the principal agents: "Accordingly, intellectual creatures are ruled by God as though He cared for them for their own sake, while other creatures are ruled as being directed to rational creatures."[7]

The foundation for Wojtyla's formulation of his personalistic principle is, therefore, firmly rooted in tradition. He states it in this way: "Whenever a person is the object of your activity you must not treat that person as only a means to an end, as an instrument but must allow for the fact that he or she too has, or

---

[7] Cf. *Summa contra Gentiles*, nn. 112-3.

at least should have, distinct personal ends."[8] He continues, "This principle thus formulated, lies at the basis of all human freedoms, properly understood, and especially freedom of conscience."[9] Later on when as John Paul II he issued an encyclical defending the reality of some intrinsically evil acts, or moral absolutes, against relativism, he ultimately founded them on the dignity of the person and specifically on this principle. The fundamental goods of the person to truth, life, friendship etc., are inviolable because of their relationship to the good of the person whose truth and transcendent dignity must be protected. The personalistic principle is rooted in the philosophy of being and not in the philosophy of consciousness as we will see when we make a fuller analysis of it. If it were not, it would continue to be subjectivist and not objective.

John Paul II credits Kant's second version of the categorical imperative with being the inspiration for the formula and even states that "Kant could be said to have laid the foundations for modern personalist ethics."[10] However, he recognizes Kant as an ally only in the sense that Kant opposes utilitarian pleasure ethics with an emphasis on duty and also because he identifies the person as the source of obligation. This second version states: "So act as to treat humanity, whether in thine own person or in that of any other, in every case as an end withal, never as means only."[11] However, John Paul cannot sign up to many aspects of Kant's system or the system as a whole, because of its anti-metaphysical character and non-realist epistemology. The German philosopher's thought is based on the 'a priori forms' of the mind and hence is subjectivist, which is why it cannot return to the tradition of the *bona honesta*. Karol Wojtyla writes that when man makes a choice,

> he does so in the light of a criterion which may be objective goodness or it may be utilitarian advantage. With the ethics of the categorical imperative Kant rightly emphasized the obligatory character of man's moral choices. At the same time, however, he distanced himself from the only truly objective criterion for those choices: he underlined the subjective

---
[8] *Love and Responsibility*, op. cit., p. 23.
[9] Ibid.
[10] John Paul II, *Memory and Identity*, Weidenfeld & Nicholson, London, 2005, p. 41.
[11] Immanuel Kant, *Fundamental Principles of the Metaphysic of Ethics*, tr. T.K. Abbott, Longmans, London, 1962, p. 56.

obligation, but overlooked what lies at the foundation of morals, that is the *bonum honestum*."[12]

The Pope also added at this point a distinctive feature of Kant's thought which he found favourable: "As for the *bonum delectabile*, in the sense in which it is understood by the Anglo-Saxon utilitarians, Kant essentially excluded it from the realm of morals.[13]

The ethics of John Paul II has been seen as a synthesis between the teleology of natural law and deontology of Kant, but this is going too far.[14] More than creating a synthesis between these two philosophies he is using duty ethics to pinpoint the fact that the obligatory element in natural law ethics is the dignity of the person, whose goods the natural law exists to protect.[15] Beyond this he sees a number of deficiencies even in Kant's second version of the categorical imperative. In the first place, the German philosopher sees the person as rationality thus leaving the body out of the definition and following the Cartesian dualistic tradition. Also, Karol Wojtyla had formulated the personalist norm as a secular version of the Gospel commandment of love of neighbour and therefore it was necessary to add to the Kantian formula ('always treat the person as an end and never as a means') the more positive aspect of the affirmation of a person as a person and hence the only adequate attitude to a person is one of love. Perhaps it is more accurate to see Wojtyla's espousal of this aspect of Kant as a starting point for dialogue with modern thought.

It was by underlining the rich singularity and uniqueness of each person that Aquinas surpassed the Boethian definition. The natural law is known by reason in conjunction with the 'nature of the human person' which is very different from saying it is known from human nature.[16] The concretely existing person has a moral value in the way that the common nature on its own does not which has implications for the relation between the dignity of the person and natural law. It is not difficult to see from this why the natural law is known by reason *in the light of the dignity of the human person*

---

[12] John Paul II, op. cit., pp. 41-2.
[13] Ibid., p. 42.
[14] Richard Spinello, *The Genius of John Paul II*, Sheed and Ward, Chicago, 2007, p. 104.
[15] Cf. *Veritatis Splendor*, n. 50.
[16] Ibid.

(cf. *Veritatis Splendor* n. 48), because the former refers to the goods of the *whole* person, not the physical or biological inclinations only. Further, this is going to be the basis for the affirmation that certain acts against the person and his or her goods are intrinsically evil. Such conclusions could never be derived from human nature alone, because it does not give us the full truth about man. Furthermore, this central characteristic of Christian anthropology and ethics, of the transcendence of the human being over all other material creatures, is opposed increasingly today by currents of thought which question the unique centrality and superiority of the person and want either to replace it in some cases, or make it all of a piece with animal rights. There are not lacking philosophies that argue some animals have more right to life, and not to suffer, than some humans with a very low quality of life.[17] Equally opposed are those who place the environment and ecological concerns at the centre of ethics, arguing that the condition of the planet for future human beings is more important than the well being of today's inhabitants. Such arguments, in their radical form of seeming to be willing to barter the lives and goods of some human beings for others, have overlooked, or failed to understand, the *unique* individuality and dignity of *every* human person.

Much depends on demonstrating the intrinsic worth and inviolability of the person, especially in the light of the challenges of the bio-ethical and sexual revolutions. A contemporary author, writing from a secular point of view, demonstrates the common ground and timelessness that can exist in this matter:

> Philosophers reject the idea that human life is sacred mainly because they believe that sanctity is a superstitious and outmoded concept. They reason that nothing can be holy, nothing can be sacred, because there are no gods. But sacred can simply mean inviolable, indefeasible, to be protected, to be safeguarded ... The primary notion of the sacred is that there are things which should be protected in all or most circumstances and for their own sakes, things which are both intrinsically valuable and highly valuable.[18]

---

[17] E.g. Peter Singer and Helen Kuhse, 'On Letting Handicapped Infants Die', in *The Right Thing to do: Basic Readings in Moral Philosophy*, ed. James Rachels, Random House, New York, 1989.

[18] J. Teichman, *Social Ethics*, Blackwell, Oxford, 1999, pp. 17-19.

Person as Consciousness

Before proceeding with further ethical consequences which result from pinpointing the intrinsic worth of the person, it is necessary to look at the second more recent understanding of the human person. It will help us to see the legacy and obstacles which the Cartesian-inspired philosophy of dualism has left for dealing with some of today's principal moral problems. Underlying the different positions of the Church and secular morality are "certain anthropological and ethical assumptions", says *Veritatis Splendor*.[19] Confusion on matters of anthropology will decisively affect the outcome of moral evaluation. Much of what was valuable in the Christian heritage was lost and today is waiting to be retrieved. When this is done the modern approach enables us to enrich our understanding of the person, as we shall see.

According to Descartes, man is a personal consciousness linked to a body and this tradition has been the dominant one in modern times since then. It is easy enough to see how Descartes arrives at this notion given his premises. In search of certainty and an indubitable starting point, he sets out to doubt all previously received knowledge. In doing this he finds there is one thing that he cannot doubt, namely that he is a thinking being, and so if he is thinking he must exist, a truth immortalised in the famous '*cogito ergo sum*'. This had the disadvantage of making subjective thought and consciousness the source of all knowledge and at the same time radically separating thought, or the spiritual world, from matter and what he called extension. This dualism of Descartes was cemented by making thought and extension two separate substances of all that is, thinking substance and corporeal substance. This was based on his definition of substance as, "nothing else than a thing which so exists that it needs no other thing in order to exist."[20] Within the two circumscriptions, of thought and extension, very different laws of mind and physical matter operated making it impossible to see how the two could combine in the human being let alone in the world at large.

---

[19] John Paul II, *Veritatis Splendor*, n. 4.
[20] Descartes, *Principles of Philosophy*, 1, 51 in Descartes, *Key Philosophical Writings*, Wordsworth Editions, Ltd. London, 1997, p. 296.

The trend continued in the philosophy of John Locke. He defines 'person' as "a thinking intelligent being, that has reason and reflection, and can consider itself as itself, the same thinking thing, in different times and places." It achieves this "only by that consciousness" which always accompanies thinking "and it is that which makes every one to be what he calls self."[21] The metaphysical definition is replaced by a psychological one and the body is left out of the conception of a person altogether. Locke held on to the idea of substance as a support for qualities, but weakened it by treating it as an unknowable supposition or hypothesis, thereby preparing the way for its abolition by Hume. For the latter, a person is "a succession of perceptions."[22] There is no subject and no self, and personal identity simply becomes a succession of mental states and the recollected memory of them. Locke and Hume substitute the being of a person rooted in substance for the activity of consciousness. There is a primacy here of action over being.

Certainly one sees the influence of the Lockean/Humean view of the human person as consciousness widely represented at the present day. The result is that the timing of the beginning and end of life is considered an open issue, the boundaries are blurred. It has led many to believe that a person is a person, when, and as long as, they are capable of conscious activity. This, of course, makes the issue all the more uncertain inasmuch as the question as to whether, or not, there is consciousness, is a somewhat subjective matter. It is also contradictory because it would not occur to anyone to question the personhood of those who are asleep, or in a coma, while it is questioned, by some, in the case of those in the so-called 'persistent vegetative state',[23] although some, but not most, begin the debate at this point. Clarity is only possible on the basis that the human being is a substance of intellectual nature, because the dignity of a person is rooted in what one is, not in what one does, or what abilities or faculties one can exercise. Also

---

[21] John Locke, *An Essay concerning Human Understanding*, II, 27, 9, ed. Peter H. Nidditch, Clarendon Press, Oxford, 1979, p. 246.
[22] David Hume, *A Treatise of Human Nature*, 1, 4, 6, ed. Ernest C. Mossner, Penguin books, London, 1985, p. 309.
[23] For example, by Sir Stephen Brown, President of the Family Division in the Tony Bland case (1992-3) where he authorized the withdrawal of nutrition on the grounds that Tony Bland's spirit had left his body which had become a 'shell'.

this latter view discriminates, perhaps unwittingly, against the weakest and most vulnerable.

The result was that the person gradually came to be identified with consciousness *per se*. Karol Wojtyla calls it "a kind of hypostatization of consciousness. Consciousness becomes an independent subject of activity and indirectly of existence, occurring somehow alongside the body, which is a material structure subject to the laws of nature, to natural determinism."[24] A similar thing happens to freedom which is conceived as total independence. Freedom as a property of the person, or an attribute of the rational will, is completely lost sight of. Human freedom must be inscribed in a subject and circumscribed by the nature of the person. Rather than say the person is consciousness we should say the person has or possesses consciousness or freedom.

Dualism changes the nature of human bodily life and with it damages the person's dignity. For this line of thought the soul and the body are separate and even in opposition, such that spirit and freedom dominate the body, and therefore manipulate it, and treat it as an object, whereby the bodily aspect of the subjectivity and dignity of the person is lost sight of. This affects the dignity of procreation and of suffering and elderly humanity, with a tendency to make all these processes more inhuman in the measure in which the predominance of technology leads us to treat the body more like an object, or consumer item. The result is that we are

> facing the challenge of a *new Manichaeism*, in which body and spirit are put in radical opposition; the body does not receive life from the spirit, and the spirit does not give life to the body. Man thus *ceases to live as a person and a subject*. Regardless of all intentions and declarations to the contrary, he becomes merely an *object*. This neo-Manichaean culture has led, for example, to human sexuality being regarded as an area *for* manipulation and exploitation ...[25]

By separating the person from his embodied nature, the anthropology associated with the new bio-technology fails to give us a full definition of the truth of the person. And by treating humans as a means to an end in embryonic stem-cell research

---

[24] Karol Wojtyla, *Person and Community*, Peter Lang, New York, 1993, p. 169.
[25] Pope John Paul II, *Letter to Families*, 1994, n. 19

it fails to respect the person, first as a subject, and even more as a subject of intrinsic worth and dignity. The result is that IVF and the successor techniques are dehumanizing because they set up technology over and above our nature as intelligent and loving, procreative beings. In cases where babies are conceived with anonymous donor sperm we are paying insufficient attention to the importance of the genealogy and genetic identity of the person and the effect this can have on the individual and future generations. The contemporary issues of bio-ethics and sexual ethics, therefore, turn on how we understand the human person and human life. If the latter is an intrinsic good then it deserves absolute respect and it is wrong to take it away, or endanger it, even for purposes of research, or if it is your own life.

John Paul II, as Pope, refers to this line of thought which so influences our times in the following way:

> It is typical of rationalism [he is thinking of its Cartesian origins] to make a radical contrast between spirit and body, between body and spirit. But man is a person in the unity of his body and spirit.[26] The body can never be reduced to mere matter: it is a *spiritualised body*, just as man's spirit is so closely united to the body that he can be described as *an embodied spirit*. The richest source for knowledge of the body is the Word made flesh. *Christ reveals man to himself*.[27] In a certain sense this statement of the Second Vatican Council is the reply, so long awaited, which the Church has given to modern rationalism.[28]

The latter, however, is not willing to admit that the full truth about man has been revealed in Christ. In particular it does not accept the "great mystery" of spousal love according to which the Divine Bridegroom is the unique source of love of mankind. Once this is lost all that is left is the temporal dimension of life and earthly life becomes nothing more than a battle for existence.[29] Christ then, not only brings us the truth about man, but He is the source and objective of all moral life and therefore of the true fulfilment and happiness of the human person. "Indeed to forget God is to

---

[26] Cf. *Gaudium et Spes*, n. 14.
[27] Ibid., n. 22.
[28] *Letter to Families*, op. cit., n. 19.
[29] Ibid.

cast the creature into shadow", says Vatican II.[30] Thus if God is neglected we cannot really defend the dignity of man and hence from this follow all the manipulations of human life and sexuality we are witnesses to today.

Equally, the dignity which the body enjoys as part of the person, enables us to read the signs which reveal the purpose and meaning of sexual life and guide us in the way to treat the body in sexual matters. Without an appreciation of the full truth about man, it is not possible to understand adequately the dual nature of the human person as male and female and the fundamental reason for it and meaning of it, that is of love and the 'one flesh' communion of persons and the lofty vocation every married person has received, which St Paul calls 'the great mystery' and which the teaching of the pontificate of John Paul II has shed so much light on. We need to establish that the whole embodied person is a subject of intrinsic worth and hence is deserving of absolute respect and love, and must never be treated as an object of use or manipulation for reasons of domination or pleasure or power. This is called in religious terminology the sanctity of life, but it can also be expressed in secular terms, which will underline the fact that the basic moral imperatives apply across the board.

The Consequences for Ethics

The person must always be treated as an end in him, or herself, and never as a means to an end or manipulated as an object for someone else's satisfaction. This absolute respect, which must be shown for the person, and indeed, which the person must show for his, or her, own self is the basis of the true good of the person which must always be acknowledged, as must, by extension, the basic goods which make it up. As *Veritatis Splendor* says:

> And since the human person cannot be reduced to a freedom which is self-designing, but entails a particular spiritual and bodily structure, the primordial moral requirement of loving and respecting the person as an end and never as a mere means also implies, by its very nature, respect for certain fundamental goods, without which one would fall into relativism and arbitrariness.[31]

---

[30] *Gaudium et Spes*, n. 36.
[31] John Paul II, *Veritatis Splendor*, n. 48.

If the concrete human person rises above even human nature as a whole, then the good of the person can only consist in communion with a being and good above him which is his last end, or God, as *Veritatis Splendor* teaches.[32] Or, to put it another way, if the human being is the highest value on earth then no purely human or material value will fulfil him or her. The good of the person *qua* person "which is the person himself and his perfection"[33], surpasses the basic goods of the person of which it is made up, and which are known in accordance with the natural inclinations. The basic goods get their normative value from their link with the good of the person. The latter, which is the completion through individual actions of the potential of the whole person, is linked to the last end of the human being. In this sense, the good of the person may not be transgressed or taken away from him. For this reason the inviolability of human life, for example, is due, not simply to the inclination to preserve one's life, but to the value and dignity of the person as such.[34]

Because the human person has a unique value which cannot be taken away from him or her, each individual is called to become what they are and live according to their dignity. This happens by building up the goods of the person, or personal goods, by individual actions. The person is fulfilled in action. Such is the moral life but it is directed to and gets its morality from the union of individual acts with the good of the person. In other words, an action to be morally good must be compatible with the good of the person, or his last end in God. As *Veritatis Splendor* teaches:

> The primary and decisive element for moral judgement is the object of the human act, which establishes whether it is *capable of being ordered to the good and ultimate end, which is God.* This capability is grasped by reason in the very being of man considered in his integral truth and therefore in his natural inclinations, his motivations and his finalities, which always have a spiritual dimension.[35]

Just as the person in virtue of his, or her, dignity is unique and

---

[32] Ibid., nn. 78-9.
[33] Ibid., n. 79.
[34] Cf. ibid., n. 50.
[35] Ibid., n. 79.

inviolable, so also is the good of the person and the basic goods of which it is made up.[36]

Some Practical Applications of the Intrinsic worth of the Person

Since persons are unique and unrepeatable, they are not specimens, or samples, or repeat issues of human nature, in the way that postage stamps are simply specimens of the original model.[37] It is true that animals are also unique, but we are perfectly happy to accept that animals can be possessed and kept as pets, and they do not enjoy the self-possession of a person. The uniqueness of a human being, then, is of a higher value and of a different category from that of an animal. The latter is an exemplar of the species which in the case of animals is superior to the individual. We would not regard animals as ends in themselves, acting on their own account. Although they must not be wantonly killed or harmed, animals may be used for the reasonable needs of the human community. Though some authors today speak of the intrinsic worth of animals, these do not possess the absolute respect due to persons in virtue of the latter's spirituality and incommunicability which most people understand must never be transgressed. Animals do not know that they know, for example. So, human life, bodily integrity and the human rights flowing from that life, must never be trampled on, but we would not say that of animals.

Each person is a whole and not simply a mere part of a greater organism, but an open whole (open to others) and not a closed whole. His unique dignity and unrepeatability together with his superiority over the natural world are due to his spiritual faculties and incommunicability, which bear testimony to this. In view of this, each individual person is above the society of mankind, it is ordered to him rather than he to it. Again, this is the reverse of the animal world where each animal exists for the species and not the other way round. Consequently, a person cannot be used as a pawn

---

[36] Cf. ibid., n. 50.
[37] Cf. John F. Crosby, *The Selfhood of the Human Person*, Catholic University of America Press, Washington D.C., 1996, ch. 1, sections 1 & 2, for this and some of the thoughts in the following paragraphs of this section.

for the good of the community or State. So, for example, everyone would agree that an innocent man should never be framed to satisfy a community's thirst for justice. He cannot be used as slave labour in a State's war effort, in the way that the Nazis did, or manipulated to satisfy a company's drive for business success, or taken as a hostage and used as a bargaining chip. The State, or community, exist for the sake of the person's dignity and not the other way round, although the individual also has reciprocal duties to the common good of the State. In one sense, as we shall see, man is part of the community and brotherhood of mankind towards which he has duties, but from the point of view of his dignity he is a whole with inviolable rights which every State has the duty to acknowledge.

The person including the body is an acting subject to be distinguished from things and objects. When another person is not perceived as a gift, or a being of intrinsic worth but as an object to be possessed and enjoyed, or manipulated and experimented with in the laboratory, then their sexuality and/or dignity suffer. The body and sexuality of the other are not seen as a sign, or expression, of their personal subjectivity. The person is then reduced from a subject to an object. The other is not now loved, or respected in themselves, or for themselves, but is reduced to the level of an object to be used. Our Lord condemned adultery in the heart which occurs in thought, or attitude, before it occurs in an external act.

Furthermore, the intrinsic value of a human being depends on him, or her, being the subject of spiritual properties and the unique dignity of each person, not on the exercise of those properties, just as a baby or a comatose person has rational powers they cannot use for the moment. One must distinguish between the power and the exercise of a faculty. The baby enjoys the power of thought but insufficient neurological development impedes the activity for the moment. Into this category, also, fit the foetus, the PVS patient and the mentally disabled etc. It should be clear that rationality is a capacity of the soul working through an organ of the body which can be hampered by insufficient biological development, or physiological damage. The power, as distinct from its exercise, or the consciousness of it, gives human life its intrinsic value. This is one of the reasons why Catholic morality considers a full human being to be present from conception, because it is a human being with potential which still has to be developed. And by the same token, why Catholic morality rejects IVF, embryo research, cloning and the freezing of embryos etc., since they involve the destruction of a human life of intrinsic worth, and/or the unwarranted manipulation of one human being by another.

In contrast to this, one cannot help note the incongruity of what might be called the 'official' position in Great Britain, since it is the argument of the Warnock Report, which was accepted by Parliament. Mary Warnock concedes the humanity of the 'conceptus' in an Introduction to the published account of her Report, but then refuses to draw the conclusion that it should be treated as a human person. She writes: "According to the majority view, the question was not ... whether the embryo was alive and human, or whether if implanted, it might eventually become a full human being. We conceded all these things were true. We nevertheless argued that in practical terms ... it (the embryo) unlike a *full human being* (my italics) might legitimately be used as a means to an end that was good for other humans, both now and in the future."[38] We are thus faced with a view that makes a distinction between a human being and a person in the full sense of the word.

False Personalism

The goods and rights of persons are based on their intrinsic worth, the fact that they are ends in themselves and not merely means and objects, but this in turn for John Paul II depends on the unity of the human being. For contemporary thought these goods and rights tend to have their origin in a supposed autonomy of the person which depends on the dualistic argument that consciousness and autonomy dominate the forces of nature which is how the body is conceived. But the body cannot be identified with the physical material world without further ado. It is rather part of the personal subject and so participates in the dignity of the person and the sanctity of life and thus must be treated with

---

[38] Mary Warnock, *A Question of Life*, Basil Blackwell, Oxford, 1985, see Introduction.

the same respect as the person as a whole. Nor can autonomy be understood as a subject, unlimited in scope, but as an attribute of the personal subject. The protagonist of moral action, and also the object of it, is the human being understood in all his personal subjectivity, that is, in the unity of his body and soul and as the subject of his own actions.

Self-determination, then, does not mean total independence, or unfettered autonomy, since a person must conduct him or herself according to the truth of his, or her, nature as a created being. He, or she, shares in the freedom and rationality of God and is not the origin of them. There is a false personalism which puts autonomy and reason outside of God such that man must impose his own reason and law on the visible world, in the way he sees fit. It fails to see that reason, autonomy and moral law have their origin in God. Hence, personal rational liberty is not totally independent and autonomous, but subject to the truth of the creaturely condition of the human person.

The above-mentioned false personalism takes the view that concentration on the person means to emphasize individual autonomy and responsibility as uppermost in ethical theories, at the expense of rules received from universal moral principles, authority etc.[39] For example, this position would favour the use of contraception among the poor, or the use of condoms among AIDS victims, or IVF to the infertile. This is an example of a confused understanding of personal dignity and inviolability, which certainly includes rational autonomy, but autonomy alone is not exhaustive of what it is to be a person, since human dignity includes the unity of the whole person including the body. It also fails to appreciate that the goods and values, which found the moral law, have the same inviolability as the person.

It depends on a personalism which is based on dualism where the person is identified with consciousness. A variant of this position is to make a distinction between goods *of* the person and goods *for* the person, the first being goods of which one is consciously aware such as love, freedom, enjoyment, and the second, goods *for* the person, are so called biological goods such as sex and procreation.

---

[39] L. Hogan, *Confronting the Truth*, Darton, Longman & Todd, London, 2001.

The latter, goods *for* the person, may then be used and manipulated as one's unfettered autonomy sees fit. In other words, rational autonomy must impose itself and dominate biological nature. This, however, ignores the ethical significance of the body, and the fact that natural laws are to be discerned by reason from the human person as a spirit/body unity and only emphasises further the importance of an adequate anthropology for ethics.

The Pope sees serious ethical dangers in a culture which has moved away from a clear understanding of the unity of the person. He writes:

> The separation of soul and body in man has led to a growing tendency to consider the human body, not in accordance with the categories of its specific likeness to God, but rather on the basis of its similarity with all other bodies present in the world of nature, bodies which man uses as raw material in his efforts to produce goods for consumption. But everyone can immediately realize what enormous dangers lurk behind the application of such criteria to man. When the human body considered apart from spirit and thought, comes to be used as *raw material* in the same way that the bodies of animals are used – and this actually occurs for example in the experimentation on embryos and foetuses – we will inevitably arrive at a dreadful ethical defeat.[40]

The Person as Gift and Relation

The first insight into why the individuality and uniqueness of the person are not opposed to his or her social nature and ability to relate to others, must be credited to Richard of St Victor, as mentioned previously. He introduced the notion of incommunicability into the definition of God (and therefore of a person); describing him as "an incommunicable existence of divine nature". But he saw, quite ingeniously, that incommunicability did not lead God to be closed in on Himself, but on the contrary it was the basis of outgoingness and self-giving to others. This was later to be decisive for our understanding of a person. Working on the notion that 'God is love' he realized that communion and the inter-relation of persons was essential to his being.

---

[40] John Paul II, *Letter to Families*, n. 19.

Etymologically, 'existence' comes from 'ex-sistere' (to step outside of), which leads him to think that a person can only be himself if he is at the same time related to others. Relationship and gift to another thus become part of what it is to be a person.

Richard, however, did not get beyond applying this notion to God; it was to be left to our own time to draw the conclusions for anthropology and ethics. This leads on to a better understanding of a person as interdependent and relational, that is, a person can make themselves a gift for others and enter into communion with them. The root of his incommunicability – his free, rational and spiritual nature – is at the same time the root of his ability to reach out and form a union of friendship, dialogue and love with other persons. This relational quality is an essential part of a person's nature. As Maritain put it, a person is an intransferable whole, but an open whole not a whole closed in on itself.[41] This Law of the Gift as it is presently denominated requires further elucidation.

The well known statement of *Gaudium et Spes* confirms that persons exist for their own sake and yet they only fulfil themselves by making a gift of themselves to others.[42] The first of these means that man exists in his own right, as an end in himself and is of intrinsic worth, and may never be treated as a means to an end, or manipulated etc. Only if a person possesses himself and strives to be master of himself can he give himself to others, sincerely and generously. Nobody can genuinely give what he doesn't possess. This is a first step, but it doesn't get to the root of the dilemma. To say man exists with and for others still seems to be at variance with saying he exists for his own sake. Is there not a contradiction here? Can he both make a gift of himself to others and exist in his own right?

The reason for the gift-value of the person is rooted in the spirituality by which the human being, in Aristotle's phrase, "is in a certain sense all things." He can reach all things and dominate the world by knowledge and thus transcend it. He can make it an object of his love and affections, of his industry and service etc., though he should not make things like knowledge and power

---

[41] See Jacques Maritain, *The Rights of Man*, Geoffrey Bles, Centenary Press, 1944.
[42] Vatican II, *Gaudium et Spes*, n. 24.

the object of his total affection. These are not worthy of him because he has a value beyond any object or thing. In any case, the ability to relate to other persons is of a different order from one's relations to things for the simple reason that persons can relate back, or reciprocate. This reciprocity is admissible of degrees. It is greatest with God and, on earth, with one's spouse and family, followed by friends, neighbours, professional colleagues etc. Such a relationship is reduced by neurological injury such as brain damage. It is precisely because man is his own master, and in control of his own acts, that he can direct those acts to care for and take an interest in others. Man does not exist for his own sake in a selfish way, but precisely in the sense that he has been given the self-determination under God to dominate his actions, emotions and impulses and lead them to what is true and good.

Thus the uniqueness of the human subject does not stop him or her relating to others. The person does not transcend other persons but is open to them, he communicates himself to them, he is able to love and be loved by them. Because of this relational value the person is made for a communion of persons and therefore for love. The full realization of the human being comes about in love for others, first for God and then our neighbour. In this relationship other persons must be affirmed for themselves as ends and not as means and in turn the subject, to fulfil himself, must make a gift of himself. At the same time as existing for his own sake, the human being only grows and develops as a person by living as a gift for others. As a result, a constituent part of the nature of a person is to exist in communion with others and therefore to relate to them and give himself to them in friendship, communication and love. The highest level of self-giving is communion with God and the highest on a human level is in marriage between male and female which is expressed through the body. The latter is made for this, a fact which John Paul II calls the 'nuptial meaning of the body'.

Persons are therefore inter-dependent characters meant to relate to one another. We all need others for the basic necessities of life, physical, psychological, intellectual and spiritual. "No man is an island alone of himself, each one is part of the whole," but, we should add, without losing his own individuality. Man has the capacity to communicate himself to others by knowledge, language, friendship, love and the whole range of his talents and skills. He is thus a gift for others (as they are for him) and his fulfilment depends on the degree of his self-giving. Not only, then, are the family and society natural institutions, but the former is the basic cell and foundation of the latter.

The relational dimension of the person is the basis of his ability to form friendships, to socialize and form communities, and above all for men and women to marry and form families. As the philosophers of dialogue put it, man's existence is one of I-thou and I-we and on a different level I-it. "Being a person in the image and likeness of God thus involves existing in a relationship, in relation to the other 'I'."[43] A firm grasp of the person as relation and 'gift' will be of the utmost importance when we come to study special questions within sexual ethics and, in particular, marriage and its adversaries such as cohabitation, adultery etc., whether there is a 'right' to children, contraception and so on. Underlying these issues is the nature of love, conjugal love and parental love, and the fact that a constituent dimension of a person is to be a gift for others will be a key factor in the understanding of love as the gift of self. But first we must become familiar with the riches which contemporary personalism has added to our traditional knowledge of the person.

Just as for Aquinas the person is known by his actions so for Wojtyla, but the latter also develops the subjective actions much more and especially the conscious experience of them which Aquinas hardly deals with. Wojtyla finds that our conscious experience of knowing and loving, for example, confirms what ontology has already said about them and builds on it. Nevertheless this phenomenological knowledge can only complement our metaphysical knowledge, it can never take its place.

For Wojtyla, therefore, St Thomas' anthropology is above all objectivist, given there is little development of the subjectivity of the person and of personal experience. He writes: "We can see how very objectivist St Thomas' view of the person is. It almost seems as though there is no room in it for an analysis of consciousness and self-consciousness as totally unique manifestations of the

---

[43] John Paul II, *Mulieris Dignitatem*, n. 7.

person as subject..." Aquinas acknowledges the latter but he gives no time to analysing them in the way that modern philosophy is interested in. The person's subjectivity is presented in a most objective way. "He shows us the particular faculties, both spiritual and sensory, thanks to which the whole human consciousness and self-consciousness – the human personality in a psychological and moral sense – takes shape, but that is where he stops. Thus St Thomas gives us an excellent view of the objective existence and activity of the person, but it would be difficult to speak in his view of the lived experience of the person." [44]

While accepting the enduring value of the Boethian definition and its modification by Aquinas, Wojtyla was alert to its deficiencies and drawbacks especially for the times we live in. Although this is to jump ahead a bit, because we will consider Wojtyla's expanded understanding of the human person fully in the rest of this chapter and the next, it is necessary to introduce at this stage his notion of the structure of personal subjectivity into our narrative because it gives our contemporaries an alternative understanding of what is meant by the human *suppositum*, or *substantia*, or subject. He was aware that these concepts have dropped out of our language or changed their use in it and consequently do not convey the original meaning.

Wojtyla considered that the Thomistic concept of the person leaves something to be desired by tending to reduce the person to an object in the world by not doing justice to the subjectivity and internal life of the human being. The future Pope proposed to rectify this by reflecting on the activity, the experience and consciousness of the person and working back to what this tells us about man. Human actions, intellectual, emotional and bodily and the inner happenings disclose to us the rich internal life of the person and the lived experience which makes each one unique and unrepeatable. Through consciousness, which reflects the inner acts and happenings, we are all in touch with what we call 'the self'. This 'self' is not reducible to consciousness or identical with it but is mediated through it. However, 'the self' is none other than the *suppositum* or subject, but known in a different way because

---

[44] Ibid., pp. 170-1.

it is apprehended at the level of conscious experience rather than at the metaphysical level.

Through my conscious experience I am aware of my thoughts and judgements, my freedom, my joy and sorrow, my laughter, etc., and so I am aware of my rational, emotional and bodily actions as part of me. This reveals how the different dimensions of the self are all parts of the one person, that is, of the subjectivity of the person. In this way, I know the concrete human self, and am thus able to know in a general way other selves. We have here undoubtedly a further and deeper understanding both of the human subject and of the unity of the person. Through this analysis we are also able to grasp what Wojtyla means by phrases like 'the body expresses the person' and 'the body in the structure of personal subjectivity'.[45] We will leave for later a consideration of 'the structure of self-determination' which, apart from the light it throws on freedom, is perhaps the principal confirmation of the nature of personal dignity and subjectivity and therefore of the intrinsic worth and inviolability of the person. Although the latter is of decisive value for ethics, this knowledge has already been reached by tradition which at present we are concerned with expounding.

As Pope, John Paul II defined man as, "an incarnate spirit, that is a soul that expresses itself in a body and a body informed by an immortal spirit."[46] The body, then, enters into the dignity of the person and also into its condition of the 'image of God'. It is the visible expression of the person and an integral part of the human being but not the whole of it. The rational soul invests the body with human corporality, *human* genes and chromosomes. This entails that the matter of the body cannot be identified with the matter of the natural world without more ado; it is rather the matter of a 'spiritualised body'.[47] Contemporary thought would say the soul and the body constitute a 'self' manifested in actions, speech, laughter, pain etc.

Nevertheless, before continuing it is worth saying a word about the historical significance for both philosophy and

---

[45] See General Audience 9-I-80 and other discourses in this series.
[46] John Paul II, *Familiaris Consortio*, n. 11.
[47] John Paul II, *Letter to Families*, n. 19.

theology which Wojtyla's work signifies. The objective nature of the person was overstressed by the tradition to counteract the danger of subjectivism. Wojtyla is well aware of the peril of subjectivism which leads to idealism and the Hegelian notion of truth and knowledge as 'pure consciousness', on the one hand, and relativism on the other. But he also sees the need to overcome the old antinomies and he considers that the route to doing this is by an analysis of lived experience, ironically the very thing which caused the opposition in the first place, which guarantees the link to reality and truth and at the same time includes consciousness. These insights are epoch making because for years Catholic tradition has opposed the philosophy of consciousness, rightly because of its dualism and epistemological idealism, but in doing so has tended to throw the baby out with the bathwater and overlooked valid insights of consciousness and experience. Wojtyla is keen to build a bridge and show how, on certain conditions, there need not be opposition but complementarity since the Thomistic-Aristotelian position maintains its validity but needs completion. The development of the notion of personal subjectivity is characteristic of the philosophy of personalism and of what we mean by the personalistic understanding of the human being.

IV.

CONTEMPORARY PERSONALISM: THE SUBJECTIVITY AND SELF-DETERMINATION OF THE PERSON

Among the requirements of a renewed Christian ethics is its ability to dialogue with today's mentality. To achieve this, not only do we have to put over objective truth, but also pay attention to the way people experience it and in this respect Wojtyla's study of subjectivity makes a decisive contribution to the updating both of Christian ethics and the perennial philosophy. Wojtyla's purpose was to develop the subjective experience of the person and create a synthesis between ontology and phenomenology understood in his sense. *Love and Responsibility* provides a model for the integration of these two modes of thought, the philosophy of being and the philosophy of consciousness and values as derived from his critique of Scheler. We find in this presentation such notions as subjectivity, intersubjectivity, values, lived experience and consciousness, which are found regularly in the discourses on the theology of the body.

The personalistic understanding of man as a self-experiencing subject is the complement, not the antithesis, of what Wojtyla calls the cosmological understanding of traditional Aristotelianism and metaphysics. By experiencing his own acts and inner happenings, the person experiences his own subjectivity. The subjectivity "refers to everything in the human being that is internal and invisible, whereby each human being is an eye witness of its own self."[1] However, by subjectivity we do not mean that the person knows the contents of consciousness by a process of introspection. Rather it is by awareness and reflective awareness of the actions he carries out. So our subjective knowledge follows the age-old principle of 'action follows being' such that from our actions we are able to know our inner selves.

Wojtyla comments that the Aristotelian description of man as a 'rational animal', taken on its own, is in danger of reducing man to the world. This can happen if we treat man as just another object in the world and leave underdeveloped his inner life, that is all the aspects of his spirituality and rationality, not least his own personal experience of them. As well as knowing others, man also knows himself through his own consciousness and self-consciousness of his actions and inner happenings. One of the effects of rationality is that he can make sense of his thoughts, words and actions and give meaning to his activity in the world. As well as viewing man in an objective way, from an external point of view as an object of knowledge, we also have another way through our own consciousness and self-consciousness. We are subjects of our own activity and experience it directly. Furthermore we can also make our experience an object of knowledge.

We saw in the last chapter that an underlying defect in contemporary anthropological theories was the absence of a coherent subject of activity which gives unity to the human *suppositum*. The Christian personalism of Karol Wojtyla has found a complementary way of verifying the selfhood of the person as a personal subject through experience, that is to say, the human being's personal experience of him or herself. In knowing oneself, therefore, through one's inner awareness of the self, one is able to arrive at the self-same subject, or human *suppositum*, known in a different way by metaphysics, which, therefore, becomes a confirmation of it. Just as the 'outer reality' of the person can be known in the traditional way so the 'inner reality' can be known by experience, or as Wojtyla calls, it 'reflexive consciousness.' Both the subjective and objective are the same reality but looked at from different points of view.

---

[1] Wojtyla, *Person and Community*, 'Subjectivity and the Irreducible', op. cit., p. 214.

Naturally, also, the phenomenological approach to the person is different and, indeed, diametrically opposed to a phenomenalist understanding. The latter tends to conceive a person in terms of a succession of ideas, images and memories, without paying sufficient attention to the underlying identity, or substratum, which alone can explain the unity of this succession of sensations and experiences.

The Phenomenological Approach

The study of the person by means of experience and the consciousness of self does not give us a metaphysical understanding but rather a phenomenological one insofar as we bracket and circumscribe our study to what lived experience and consciousness tell us. But it does complement a full metaphysical understanding where we look at man not simply from the point of view of his subjective consciousness, but as an objective spiritual/material being. By the phenomenological method we *experience* the unity of soul and body, our autonomy (self-determination and self-governance), and our capacity to make a gift of ourselves. It is only in metaphysics which goes beyond empirical experience to get to the core of things that we get a fully rounded understanding of the meaning of these concepts. But, as we shall see, the two spheres are irreducible to each other.

The phenomenological method is very much in tune with the modern approach to knowledge, in the sense that it is based on empirical experience. The name comes from the Greek word to appear (*phainesthai, phainomenon*), and its purpose is to let reality appear to our gaze by studying it as it manifests itself in our consciousness. Karol Wojtyla is interested in the way in which actions manifest the person and the way the body expresses the person. In general, therefore, the principle is that the outer or visible reveals the inner or invisible, understood as the parts of which the subject is made up.

In carrying through this project Karol Wojtyla employs phenomenology in a somewhat critical way. Without accepting the system as such he makes use of the methodology which can be a powerful tool, particularly its use of 'bracketing' which sets aside and studies a particular area, so as to look at the whole through that aspect. He does not accept the thoroughgoing idealism of the Husserlian version of this philosophy, which holds that consciousness only grasps ideal, or intentional, objects, that is those that are only in the mind. It holds that consciousness is always cognitional, which Wojtyla denies, and he even contends that it is not primarily cognitional. Hence, the insistence that one type of consciousness, known as reflexive, comes directly into contact with reality and not by means of cognition. Here 'cognitional' means the same as 'intentional' in phenomenology, which signifies that we know real objects through intermediary ideas rather than directly, a position the Thomistic philosophy rejects as idealism.

This point can only be established on certain conditions. In order to do so, Wojtyla makes a distinction between 'reflective consciousness' and 'reflexive consciousness'. The distinction depends on the fact that not all consciousness is cognitional or 'intentional', in the way that mainstream phenomenologists would maintain. Reflective consciousness would be the knowledge you have of yourself as a result of reflecting consciously on yourself and your activity, that is to say, your feelings, your emotions, your body as well as your actions. Reflective consciousness should not be confused with introspection; it is rather the turning back on manifested actions and experiences of oneself. Reflexive consciousness, on the other hand, is direct awareness of the reality of the ego, that is, of oneself as an acting subject. As Wojtyla puts it: "We then discern clearly that it is one thing to *be* the subject, another to *be cognized* (that is, objectivized) as the subject, and a still different thing to *experience* one's self as the subject of one's own acts and experiences."[2] A distinction is drawn between cognition and self-consciousness or experience of oneself. This can be turned into knowledge by objectifying it, but in the first instance consciousness is not cognitional or 'intentional' (as phenomenological terminology has it), but rather simply the awareness that accompanies not only cognition but also the other acts of the self. He wants to maintain consciousness as open to the

---

[2] Karol Wojtyla, *The Acting Person*, D. Reidel Publishing Company, Dordrecht, Holland, London and Boston, 1979, p. 44.

direct experience of reality which it will not be if it is identified with cognition.

This distinction between self-knowledge and consciousness separates his account of subjectivity from subjectivism and relativism. Subjectivism separates experience from action and eliminates, or ignores, the experience of one's own responsibility and causality in relation to the action and therefore it considers that values automatically create themselves in conscience when the action takes place.[3] Hence, values are not derived from objective reality. In contrast, according to Wojtyla, being is experienced in act by non-cognitional self-knowledge, since act and experience can never be separated. On the one hand, self-knowledge communicates the experience of being the efficient cause of the action, and, on the other, consciouness reflects it. In this way, Wojtyla is able to give a realist foundation to subjective experience, because for him, unlike for post-Cartesian thinkers, consciousness does not found being but reflects it. Being precedes consciousness, not vice versa.

As a result, Wojtyla is able to make the gigantic step of welcoming the modern phenomenon of subjective consciousness, because only with it do we describe the human experience of action in a complete way. But he does it without denying the being and reality of his knowledge of himself and the external world. He rejects both the notion that there can be a knowledge which does not take account of the act of consciousness and also that there can be consciousness that does not reflect a true knowledge of reality. Neither the one, nor the other, would accurately describe the full act of knowing. He is proposing here a fusion between the insights of classical philosophy and a remodelled form of the modern philosophy of consciousness.

The Unity of the Person is revealed in Action

The unity of the person is revealed in action because action includes all aspects of the person, e.g., body, organs, emotions, as well as rational will. Action and the body are what appear and

---

[3] Cf. Rocco Buttiglione, *Karol Wojtyla, The Thought of he Man who Became Pope John Paul II*, Eerdmans Publishing Company, Grand Rapids, Michigan, p. 134.

they make manifest what is invisible in the rest of the person. This is the thesis of Wojtyla's *The Acting Person*. "For our position is that action serves as a particular moment of apprehending – that is experiencing – the person."[4]

Instead of beginning with a theoretical definition of the person and going on to action, he starts the other way round. He starts with what is visible (outer) and asks what it reveals about what is invisible (inner). When he comes to consider the body, given the fact of psycho-somatic unity which comes out in action, he follows the same procedure. He asks what does the body reveal about the person, and the action of the person? If the inner and the outer are a unity we can say the body is an expression of the person and reveals the person: "Action gives us the best insight into the inherent essence of the person and allows us to understand the person most fully."[5]

The consciousness of the body comes through the direct experience we have of the body by means of feelings, emotions, joys, sadness and many other states. It is also the case that self-governance and self-possession which follow from self-determination, that is the action of the will and the intellect, express themselves through the body. The reason why all this doesn't take the place of the traditional metaphysics (i.e. the philosophy of being) of the person who then acts, is not only that it looks at the same phenomenon the other way round – metaphysics also does that – but it does so through reflexive consciousness and self-consciousness. Our study of the person is bracketed and confined to direct subjective awareness *only*.

A further example of the method of 'bracketing' can also be pointed out. Wojtyla is looking at the person *only* from the point of view of its expression by the body. We can say that what we finish up with is a greater knowledge of the so-called interiority of the person, understood as the parts of which he, or she, is made up. The body as the outer visible expression of the person becomes the territory and means for the manifestation of the powers of the soul, intellect, freedom and senses, and therefore it builds on the traditional approach.[6] It should be noted that the traditional approach itself

---

[4] Karol Wojtyla, *The Acting Person*, op. cit., p. 10.
[5] Ibid., p. 11.
[6] Ibid., p. 205.

apprehended the powers by their acts, but without developing it to the same degree by applying it to the whole person.

Wojtyla's personalism, then, contends that the truth of the person can be known through subjective experience and consciousness and also by working back from the actions to the being of the person. We are subjects of our own activity and know it directly. We must not reduce the being of the person to consciousness, but neither must we separate it from consciousness as if through consciousness one cannot experience oneself. It tells you much more about the dignity of the person than the Aristotelian approach could on its own.

Thomists have always argued that 'action follows being' and therefore one can know something or someone by their actions, but contemporary personalism makes the further point that we can know *ourselves* by awareness and consciousness of our own actions. This experience confirms the unity of the person. It tells us that the body is not just a biological organism, but an integral part of the dignity of the person. Man is a personal subject both in his body and soul such that his body is part of his personhood and his dignity and is not an object which the soul owns and uses.

In the beginning, in the early part of the twentieth century, personalism was used to assert the superiority of the person over the State and especially over all forms of totalitarianism which crushed him and some of his fundamental rights. Today it is an indispensable means of countering all forms of abuse which instrumentalize the human body and human life, such as sexual abuse, or bio-technology, which treat the human body as an object of use or experimentation and not part of man's dignity and, therefore, expendable. It is used to show that all human life is of intrinsic and inviolable value.

The Structure of Self-Determination and the Subjectivity of the Person

Just as my personal experience of consciousness and self-consciousness discloses my rationality, so the experience of my actions reveals my power of self-determination. Wojtyla distinguishes between my actions and what 'happens' in me. The latter consist of the data of sense knowledge, our physiology and emotions which are not rational, and hence over which we have less than complete control. They were known traditionally as 'acts of man'. Of the action, I am the principal efficient cause, whereas of what happens in me I am the passive recipient. Nevertheless, they are integrated into the "I", or the subject of the actions. In other words, the freedom of the subject rooted in will and intellect integrates and directs the acts of man. However, the power of self-determination comes not only through the action of the will, but through the actions of the whole person by means of the will. This power to give rise to actions and control of his own self is what freedom essentially consists in. That is to say, it includes much more than just the power of choice.[7]

The difference between what happens in me and all actions of the form 'I act', i.e., those in which I am the subject of the actions, points to an element in the latter which clearly distinguishes it from the former, and this is what we call self-determination. In the latter, the subject experiences the empowering or efficacy of the self to perform the action, or in other words, the person realizes he or she is the efficient cause of it which is not the case in what happens in me. This experience is, in turn, intimately connected with a sense of responsibility because I know I am accountable for that of which I am the principal agent. Through my freedom I am able to carry through the action which is what Wojtyla means by 'efficacy'.

A free human act is not just directed towards an end or object, but also directed inwardly towards oneself. I become an object for myself and determine not only my direction to an object, but also to myself. The affirmation that the subject turns to himself in carrying

---

[7] All the potencies of man are integrated by the "I" or the subject in the free act. This is what Wojtyla means by saying that freedom transcends the natural inclinations in action. This transcendence, however is different from the usual use of transcendence in phenomenology which refers to knowledge and will going out to an external object, that is horizontal transcendence. But he also refers to a vertical trancendence which goes inwards to the ontological core of the person, to his rational essence where the highest faculties reach the deepest values. The person, then, is not only the place where value manifests itself, but "it is also an autonomous subjectivity which is at the source of action and makes free decisions by orienting the different events which take place in it and by giving or denying his own assent to them. To say that man is free therefore implies the affirmation that he empowers his own subject." Buttiglione, op. cit., p. 145.

out an action needs some explanation. The external causal relation of freedom to the object desired is not the only one, there is also a causal relationship to the subject of the act who is consciously aware of carrying out the action. And it is through this awareness, or what Wojtyla calls reflexive consciousness, that he turns to himself and that the action is causally linked to the subject. Consequently, through one's acts one makes oneself to be the person that one becomes. My actions can be divided into the general experience of the human being and the experience of morality. In turning towards an object I also turn to myself and so in devoting myself to tennis I become a tennis player, hopefully getting better the more I practise. But where moral values are concerned one becomes by means of the relevant actions a better or worse person.

The goods and values which appear to man's consciousness, then, are not only physical or spiritual, but also have a moral dimension. This is what we mean when we talk about moral conscience, which, as well as having an intellectual element to apprehend true goods, also has a reflective dimension. Not only do we affirm some value or disvalue, but we are also conscious of taking it into ourselves reflexively and identifying ourselves with it and thus determining ourselves by it. In this way, we either grow in the value of friendship, for example, by acts of kindness to another, or we become a thief by taking his property etc. Wojtyla writes: "In turning towards ... ends, objects and values, however, I cannot help but also in my conscious activity turn towards myself as an end, for I cannot relate to different objects of activity and choose different values without thereby determining myself ... and my own value."[8]

The person knows himself to be the cause of his actions and hence, the subject of them, by self-knowledge, that is direct awareness, and the whole process is reflected in consciousness. An analysis of this process leads to further important conclusions about the constitution of the self and the subject. A corollary of self-determination is that the person must govern himself, and to do this, in turn, he must possess himself and be possessed by himself, otherwise he would not be the principal cause of the

---

[8] Wojtyla, *Person and Community*, op. cit., p. 230.

action. If self-government and self-possession form part of the truth of the human person then ethical consequences follow. A human being may not be possessed, or used, or manipulated by other persons on any pretext, or occasion. Kant's second formulation of the categorical imperative was, therefore, correct: 'Always treat a person as an end in himself and never as a means'.

It is in acts of self-determination that the constitution of the self is fully revealed. The acting person is aware of his own 'self' as the subject of what is being brought about. This self is identical from the viewpoint of phenomenological experience with what is called on the level of metaphysical knowledge the human *suppositum*, because the self is not just self-consciousness but self-possession and governance proper to the human *suppositum*. The self and the *suppositum* are, therefore, the same reality but arrived at in different ways. And furthermore, the knowledge of self-government and self-possession are simply, on the level of conscious experience, what the ancients and the philosophy of being called 'incommunicablity'. However, it is only by means of the former that one has *direct* experience of the self and its properties.

To experience the self as the subject of an action confirms that one exists in oneself as a metaphysical subject, though this is known on a different level. It clearly discloses that before and after the action one is an independent subject who exists by himself, though at this point we are making a statement of metaphysics, which can be corroborated by experience. The latter confirms what metaphysical analysis had already established about the person being an *individual subject of rational nature*, and incommunicable and intransferable etc., but it gives us a lot more explanation of what is meant by these concepts. Through conscious experience one becomes more aware of the richness of one's personal subjectivity and the experiential route is likely to be more comprehensible and persuasive to the contemporary mind. It is an example of the Church's commitment stated at Vatican II to express Catholic tradition in a more accessible way.

The analysis also throws a lot of light on all the elements of the free act and, indeed, on why the will is free. To will is always to will something, but the object willed is a necessary, but not a sufficient, condition of willing, since the subject willing is equally, and indeed more, important. What I need, or find attractive, is not necessarily what I want, or know I should have, because it is not likely to be of value to me. However, I am also aware that I can choose any of the alternatives, because I have experience of having done so in the past. The willed object, then, is crucial because of the effect it has on the acting subject. One recalls here Pope John Paul II's point in *Veritatis Splendor* that in order to understand the moral object it is necessary to put oneself in the position of the acting person, since it is from the subject that acts and intentions arise.[9]

Self-determination is not absolute in man, in that while man is autonomous he is so only under the universal autonomy of God. Nevertheless, within these limits, man as the 'image of God' enjoys a genuine autonomy which gives him the power to make of himself what he will by his conscious and free acts. Autonomy means, however, not only that man has rights, but also that his perfection and fulfilment depends in no small part on his own freedom. As Eleanor Roosevelt said, "No one can hurt you without your consent", or in the words of Gandhi, "they cannot take away our self-respect if we do not give it to them".[10] So, given that God grants us the means to achieve it, our potential for self-development, fulfilment, and sanctity is in our own hands.

Hence, based on the reflexive awareness of his own selfhood, i.e. by the access he has to his own being by subjective consciousness, the human person is aware, to a greater or lesser extent, of the values which are in accord with the truth of his human dignity. This will depend, in some measure, on his moral education and upbringing, but only actions done in agreement with the truth about the person can contribute to his growth.

Subjective Knowledge of the Self is Irreducible

More needs to be said about the relation and difference between knowledge of the self by reflexive awareness and the objective knowledge that comes from the traditional cosmological approach, as Wojtyla calls it. As noted, our knowledge of our own subjectivity

---

[9] John Paul II, *Veritatis Splendor*, n. 78.
[10] Stephen Covey, *The Seven Habits of Highly Effective People*, Simon & Shuster, London, 1992, p. 72.

reveals to us the same subject or substance that is given to us in the tradition which follows the Boethian definition; however, it comes in a different way and reveals a much richer content. The difference is that the knowledge of subjective consciousness is not reducible to an abstract knowledge which gives us a definition by genus and specific difference, as in cosmological knowledge, since it is knowledge of lived experience which cannot be reduced further. That which comes by means of reflexive consciousness is no less knowledge than the traditional objective form of knowing, but it is knowledge by a different method which *reveals* or *discloses* the self to us. This does not make it any the less informative; on the contrary, it discloses the subjectivity of the self much more fully and richly than the traditional avenue does. Rather than being opposed to each other these two epistemological approaches are complementary, the one is called by Wojtyla cosmological and the other is personalistic. He also explains why the two pathways are irreducible to one another: "We cannot complete this picture through reduction alone; we also cannot remain within the irreducible alone (for then we would be unable to get beyond the pure self)."[11]

Irreducible self-conscious experience discloses my personal structure of self-determination "through which I discover my self as that through which I possess myself and govern myself."[12] The importance of this knowledge is that it reveals to us in much more depth the uniqueness and individuality of the personal subject since it focuses on the interior happenings and the day to day biography of the human person. In contrast, the traditional and objective method tends to emphasize the human nature without always reaching the person in his richness and singularity. This focus helps us to understand each person more fully as a sovereign self who transcends and goes beyond the common nature of humanity. "*In my lived experience of self-possession and self-governance, I experience that I am a person and that I am a subject*" and it tells us a great deal about the inner workings of that person.[13] Wojtyla suggests that in reducing the human being

---

[11] Karol Wojtyla, *Person and Community*, op. cit., p. 214.
[12] Cf. ibid.
[13] Ibid.

to the abstract definition, 'rational animal', one leaves out what is most human, namely the *personal* aspect of his existence known fully only by conscious self-knowledge.

Knowledge of our subjectivity from lived experience, then, tells us a great deal more about human dignity than metaphysical knowledge alone, although both sources of information are complementary and necessary. However, in enlightening us with regard to the sovereignty and inviolability of each person by demonstrating, beyond doubt, the superiority of each one over the abstract category of human nature, it brings out the moral value and identity of each person which has vital implications for ethics. Each person is more than just a member of the human species, or just an exemplar of human nature. If they were not more, it would be enough to safeguard human nature and replace each individual with another to do this. However, we rightly recoil from such a view, because each individual is irreplaceable over and above human nature, and each one is a sovereign self who exists for his own sake and must be treated as such. Hence, the full understanding of the human person obtained by these two forms of enquiry, especially by reflexive consciousness, shows us the moral value of personhood and has clear ethical consequences, because it means that the intrinsic, and in some ways absolute, value of the person may not be transgressed on any occasion. It thus forms the basis of human rights and moral absolutes.

Knowledge of the Body and its Integration in the Person

Further decisive moral implications follow from the Christian position that the human body is an integral part of the human person and so shares fully in its dignity. This is foreign to all forms of dualism which see the human body as an adjunct appendage of the soul or spirit, which alone is the real seat of the person just as much as it is to a materialistic or behaviourist concept of man which sees no role for the spiritual dimension. Nevertheless, while man is a unity he is also a compound of body/soul, or matter/form so how are we to understand these two aspects more deeply? John Paul II writes, "the body can never be reduced to mere matter: it is a *spiritualized* body, just as man's spirit is so closely united to the body that he can be described as an *embodied spirit*."[14] The personalism of the Pope develops this unity in duality of the person, so crucial to modern ethical issues, such as abortion or embryonic stem-cell research, with a complementary account.

When we say that man is a personal subject we mean that the actions which proceed from the different parts of the human being – will, mind, emotion, body – are all actions of the person. They are not simply spiritual, intellectual or physical actions, but personal and human ones. The way we use language bears out this contention that our different actions are integrated into personal action. We do not usually say my mind thinks or my will desires, but I think or I desire. Man acts as a unity. This is what we mean by self-government, that is, the person governs and directs the body with its emotions, senses and movements, integrating them all into actions of the person, that is, if the body lets it, or if the person has attained sufficient self-control and dominion. This, in turn, occurs in virtue of self-possession because the person possesses his or her act of being. However, the integration of the body into the person is not automatic because of freedom. Integration can also be understood in opposition to the disintegration that can befall the person through mental illness, old age or moral decline.

The human body for Wojtyla is endowed with what he calls an interiority and an exteriority, the latter referring simply to the shape, harmony, movements etc. Here he is referring to the unity of the bodily *members* in action and the way the person manifests himself through them. The inwardness of the body refers to the diversity and coordination of the bodily *organs*, that is, the way in which the body functions as an organism according to the laws of nature. In between the corporeal level and the spiritual faculties of intellect and will we find the psyche in its first manifestation at the level of the feelings, instincts, emotions etc. These are not themselves corporeal but they show a measure of dependence on the body in that they are conditioned by it. For instance, the eye may not function, or feeling may not happen, if there is bodily pathology. But the conditioning, both ways, psyche to body and vice versa, shows the interrelation as well as the difference between

---

[14] John Paul II, *Letter to Families*, n. 19.

the two spheres and this is what Wojtyla means by psycho-somatic integration, which is another word for unity.

Human activity, therefore, presupposes the integration, or unification of the body and of the psyche. Action also presupposes the openness of the psycho-somatic subjectivity to the person's self-government, which is rooted in rational self-determination. At this point we are at the boundary between the soul and the body which is a metaphysical issue, in that we cannot have direct experience of the soul, and hence it is not reached by phenomenological analysis. However, we do have experience of it indirectly through its actions on which our metaphysical knowledge is based. Nevertheless, what concerns us here from the ethical point of view is that the continued and habitual integration of the person, that is, between the body, the psyche and the self-government of the person is a virtue. This is a reference to the self-control and dominion the spiritual faculties need to acquire over the passions and bodily impulses for virtuous action, as in the virtue of temperance or self-control.[15] The Catechism in its treatment of chastity speaks of the need to achieve the integrity of the person, meaning the self-mastery that needs to be acquired over the sexual impulse so that it is directed to genuine spousal love and the begetting of human life. Married love requires, in addition, the integrality of the gift of self to one's spouse, just as celibacy means total self-giving to the service of God and the Kingdom of Heaven.[16]

By reflective consciousness we are able to objectify the actions of our body and therefore know and study the body in the way we have just described. Through reflexive self-consciousness we are able to know our own body in the sense that we have direct experience and awareness of its activities. I experience my bodily activities as part of me, as part of my personal being. That is why I usually say, "*I* see an eagle" rather than "my eyes see an eagle", or "I smell a rat", not "my nose smells a rat", or "I hear music" not "my ears hear music" and so on. In other words, we are in the habit of attributing the activity of our senses to the activity of the

---

[15] Cf. *The Acting Person*, op. cit., ch. 5; and Buttiglione, op. cit., p. 160.
[16] See CCC 2338-2347.

whole self and not simply to the senses as if they were in some way detached from the personal self. We experience the body and its senses and emotions, and so on, as an integral part of ourselves.

We are now in a better position to understand what Karol Wojtyla means when he says that 'the body expresses the person' or 'the body makes the person visible'. He means that the integration of the person in action, which takes place in the body, expresses and makes the person visible. Therefore the body is a visible, and integral, part of the personal structure of human subjectivity which also has an invisible dimension. This language makes it quite clear from the outset that the person is a unity of spirit and matter, body and soul etc. Indeed, so much are the two dimensions integrated as two principles of being of the same person that the human body is spiritualised matter: it is made up of *human* matter, DNA, genes and chromosomes and cannot simply be lumped together with the atoms and molecules of the material world.

In this way personalism confronts dualism which identifies the person with thought and spirit, and the body with biology. Here we have the source of many present day difficulties in sexual and bio-ethics. For much contemporary thought, which derives from dualism, personhood is identified with consciousness, or self-awareness, while the body is mere matter over which one has complete autonomy and control, because the body is not an integral part of the person but rather like a suit of clothes which one has and uses. As John Paul II puts it: "Using such a one sided knowledge [of the body as biology] ... it is not difficult to arrive at treating the body ... as an object of manipulations. In this case man ceases to identify himself with his own body, because it is deprived of the meaning and dignity deriving from the fact that this body is proper to the person."[17] Personalism is the philosophical basis of the Pope's theology of the body which underpins the unity of the person as an embodied spirit, as for example, when he says that the "body reveals the living soul such as man became when God breathed life into him" (Gen 2:7).[18]

These expressions bear a certain resemblance to Wittgenstein's

---

[17] John Paul II, General Audience 8-IV-81
[18] John Paul II, General Audience 9-I-80.

view that the best picture of the human soul is the human body. What Wojtyla is saying here is that a person is an animated body. The soul is the principle of life and activity of the human being endowed with the faculties of reason and freedom. It also acts through faculties dependent on matter, such as the procreative, vegetative, nutritive and locomotive, as well as the faculties of the five senses and the common sense. Human activity proceeds from the soul and works through the bodily organs showing how the spiritual aspect of the person is eminently suited to uniting with the corporeal as a substantial whole.

The Internal Process of the Human Act: Freedom and Truth

Phenomenological analysis is well placed to give an illuminating account of the internal process of the human and moral act as it occurs in subjective experience. Wojtyla was opposed to separating act from experience, and defining 'act' in a wholly abstract way, because being, and therefore truth, is experienced in act and ignoring this led to the Kantian errors which give rise to purely formal ethical principles. Every act is a human experience and, provided this is borne in mind, the link can be maintained between freedom and truth, because truth is the correspondence between the intellect and reality (*adequatio rei et intellectus*). If we leave out experience we are in danger of forgetting about reality, be it empirical, moral or intellectual reality: "Neither a pure knowledge which prescinds from the act of consciousness, nor a consciousness which does not reflect the cognitive element of reality and of man, can lead to a full understanding of human acting."[19] The process of the act which is known by direct self-awareness can be described from the objective point of view, but is also mirrored in consciousness and is, therefore, confirmed from the angle of subjective experience.

We know that the will is a power which is shown, not only in the power of choice, but also in the fact that the human subject is the cause of his, or her, own actions. The act of will also implies knowledge both of the object and of oneself. The

---

[19] Buttiglione, op. cit., p. 141.

will is a rational appetite and is attracted to objects which are called 'goods' for that reason. It is self-determination and not indetermination. Knowledge is a condition of willing and desiring. Reason has truth as its object, while good is the object of the will, as Aquinas would say, and only by reason can one know the truth of things and direct one's actions. One cannot will without willing something which we call the object, but one cannot turn towards an object without turning towards oneself as the agent of the action. The object cannot be willed without being willed as a good, since good or value are the object of the will and accompany all choice, and therefore, one cannot will a good without willing one's own good.

Wojtyla often uses the words 'good' and 'value' together, or he uses them interchangeably. There is, however, a certain difference as well as similarity between them. Value is the good as it is experienced in subjective consciousness and awareness and therefore the good is the objective basis founded on the natural law for our experience of value. To put it briefly, a value is the subjective experience of a good. To be of moral value the good must be a true good, that is based on the natural law in conformity with the truth and dignity of the person. In *Faith and Reason* John Paul II says, "there are signs of widespread distrust of universal and absolute statements, especially among those who think that truth is born of consensus and not of a consonance between intellect and objective reality."[20]

When consciousness, which makes us aware of, and *reflects*, objects of thought, is applied to the moral area, we call it moral consciousness which is equivalent to what we have called from time immemorial, conscience. The job of conscience (used in a way which includes *synderesis*, or knowledge of first principles) is to *reflect* the natural law inside us. In this way, the law of right and wrong, i.e. ethical principles, is interiorised, it is written on the heart. It wells up inside us. But this interiorization of moral values does not make them subjective. The subject does not invent them, because to be genuine they must respond to the truth, that is to say, they must *reflect* accurately the natural law which is common

---

[20] John Paul II, *Fides et Ratio*, n. 56.

to all, to the person as person. The philosophy of consciousness approach to morality, therefore, clears up an ambiguity which is frequently associated with conscience (considered as *synderesis*), namely that it is autonomous and independently determines moral norms. The reality is rather different, because it mirrors and reflects norms which are already there and through formation and information, in Wojtyla's phrase, should be 'read in truth'.

Consequently, reason has to make a judgement about the truth of an object or value based on the evidence and counsel given to it. On this basis the will makes its decision and gives its consent. The will intends an object or goal, but it is only to the extent that the judgement of the truth of the object is made that the intending becomes a real intention and an act of the will is made. This accounts for the fact that we sometimes say, 'I'm thinking of doing this or that' without getting as far as putting it into practice. In this sense, thinking is less active than knowing. By judgement man assumes his responsibility for the truth and the decision of the will usually follows the judgement, though it may not do so. Let us consider this in somewhat more detail.

The will is directed to an object outside itself, but cognition knows its object intentionally, that is conceptually in the mind. By judgement thought engages with reality and a statement is made about the truth in continuity with Aquinas' definition of it as *adequatio intellectus et rei*.[21] In this way thinking culminates in judgement and judgement in action by means of a choice of the will. Truth is a presupposition of judgement and decision in that the subject, by linking subject and predicate to affirm or deny a state of affairs, assumes responsibility for the truth of the affirmation. Thus, all deliberative actions involve a value judgement and so in each action the person also fulfils himself, or otherwise, because the value of the action remains in him. One fulfils oneself by acknowledging the truth about the good and putting it into practice. In this sense, freedom depends on a judgement of truth. As Buttiglione puts it: "Anthropology, therefore, contains the foundations of ethics for it conceives of human beings as responsible subjects of their actions which are

---

[21] Aquinas, *De Veritate*, 1, 1.

realized through themselves."²²

The test comes in action when a moral judgement is put into effect. The person transcends himself in action in the sense that one of the effects of the action is in the subject acting. The efficient causality is both outward towards an object, called by Wojtyla *horizontal* transcendence, and inward towards the agent, which he calls *vertical*. By his actions, therefore, a person makes himself to be what he becomes. The subject grows as a person if the action is realized in truth, or alternatively with a false moral action he damages his dignity as a person. Wojtyla stresses that there is a duty for the person to fulfil and realize himself as a person, and act according to the truth and goodness to which he tends, the principle on which all other duties, including the duty to serve others, is based. Buttiglione writes, "normative objective order and individual conscience meet in the truth which founds and justifies both. When value is acknowledged in conscience, and becomes in this way an experience of the subject, obligation arises."²³

This, in turn, enables us to pass judgement on the famous objection to the derivation and certainty of moral principles repeated in empirical philosophy and deriving from Hume, that you cannot get an 'ought' from an 'is', or as Weber puts it, you cannot derives values from facts. We are led to believe there is an inseparable gulf, an impasse, between these two orders, that is the descriptive and the normative order. But according to Buttiglione, the first and one of most authoritative commentators on Wojtyla's thought, the source of moral obligation is to be found in man himself if we understand him rightly. He believes that the separation between the natural and the moral orders can be overcome if we understand "the structure of the person and the action which would bring to light the general obligation towards the truth and the good which constitutes the kernel of human freedom ... There is a human obligation to bring the good into reality ... since his self-realization as a man is at stake."²⁴ If one realizes oneself through the performance of good actions then one has a duty to do them, because the fulfilment of self is

---

[22] Buttiglione, op. cit., p. 449.
[23] Buttiglione, op. cit., p. 152.
[24] See Buttiglione, op. cit., p. 151.

the foundation of all duties. One fulfils oneself as a person not only by acknowledging the truth, but by living according to it which leads the person along the path of fulfilment, happiness and genuine freedom.

In order to clarify this we need to recall the analysis we have already made. All action falls under the heading of practical reason, but, as we saw, practical reason is twofold in that it refers both to the 'right way of making things' and 'the right way of acting'. The former refers to 'naturalistic' action, namely whether an architect builds useful and beautiful buildings, or a nurse brings people back to health where this is possible, that is to say, whether they do a good job. However, the human being is also a moral person and in everything he does one can ask whether he has acted in a morally good or bad way, that is to say, has he acted rightly according to an objective order of good and evil. His freedom constitutes him as a moral person and it brings with it the responsibility to act in a morally upright way. There is no passage here from the naturalistic to the moral: both dimensions are found in all human behaviour. Subjectively, man becomes a moral creature in virtue of the freedom he has to act which brings with it the responsibility to act according to truth and goodness, which in practice can be tested by whether the object and intention of his action corresponds to an objective moral order which is reflected in man's moral consciousness, or conscience. Confusion can arise, however, because the object of an act can be seen purely as a 'naturalistic' or physical object, such as the picture painted by an artist, the profit made by a business man or the feature article written by a journalist. All of these can be judged better or worse according to the standards of the profession and public opinion, but in addition every action has a moral dimension as well as a 'natural' one in virtue of man's freedom and responsibility for seeking true goodness in each action. As Wojtyla taught, in the words of Buttiglione: "The root of duty is freedom, which constitutes the person as responsible for his action."[25] This distinction between the moral object and the natural, physical or biologistic object of behaviour is one of

---

[25] Ibid.

the most debated questions in contemporary ethics and we will devote a whole chapter to it later.

Some Moral Consequences of the Person as Gift

The relational character of the human being is rooted in his or her spiritual nature, its knowledge and will, as we have noted. In virtue of these capacities it is able to go out of itself and unite with others by knowledge, friendship, social life, love etc. He is able to bond with another in an I-thou relationship, and with others in an I-we one. The capacity of man and woman to unite in marriage falls into this gift category of human existence. The Pope uses the expression 'nuptial meaning of the body' to express the ability of a person to give themselves to another. This refers to the capacity of the person to give themself to another, or to others, and indeed to God in a disinterested and selfless way, out of love for the other, that is for the good of the other.

Again, the categories of self-possession and self-governance point to the ability of the person to make a gift of him/herself. An understanding of the person in terms of gift, as in Vatican II, points to a constitutive aspect of personhood and reveals more deeply the nature of personal self-determination. If I determine myself then this implies that I possess and govern myself. I belong to myself and am the master of my acts. It is the capacity of self-possession which is the key to solving the apparent riddle that man is wanted 'for his own sake' and yet can only fulfil himself by becoming a gift for others, because only if one determines and governs oneself can one become a gift for others.[26]

> The lived experience of my own *I* ... is determined ... not only by self-consciousness, but also, and to a far greater degree, by the self-possession conditioned by self-consciousness. Self-possession is connected more with the will than with knowledge. I possess my self not so much by knowing myself as by determining myself. Self-possession brings to light both my full subjectivity and the objective unity that exists between my activities and the being that I am as the subject of those activities.[27]

---

[26] See Pope John Paul II, *Letter to Families*, n. 11.
[27] Karol Wojtyla, 'Participation or Alienation?' in idem, *Person and Community*, op.

Here is the basis for the *I-other* relationship because it starts by my becoming acquainted with the humanity of another, but is realized by experiencing the other as a person. I cannot experience the self of another as I experience my own self because that is intransferable; however, in friendship I come as close as possible to experiencing the *I* of another as that of a human person. Love, which is to want the good for others, is born of this capacity and since the will is directed towards the universal good this overcomes our inborn tendency to selfishness. However, love for others and relationship does not exist so much as an accomplished fact, as a potentiality to be realized. It requires a certain impulse to start it and consists not only in external relationship, but more in entering into the interior of the other person. It is a task to be accomplished, as the Gospels' commandment of love, of which this is an analysis, clearly teaches.[28] Self-dominion and self-giving, both necessary to live according to human dignity, are, of course, susceptible of growth by means of the cultivation of the habits and virtues of the moral life.

The human person may never be treated as an object of use, pleasure or manipulation, as we have consistently said. Clearly, a first reason is that he, or she, is an autonomous subject wanted by God 'for his own sake' and therefore an end in himself who may not be treated as a means to an end by others. This is because man belongs to himself, he is *sui iuris* as the classical tradition expressed it, a reality with which he is also acquainted by the lived experience of self-possession as described above and which brings with it rights and duties. But since he is equal to others and made for communion with them and knows them as persons, he must in turn treat others in the same way also, that is, he must look on them as other selves.

The modern personalist philosophers speak of the mutuality, complementarity and reciprocity which personal relationships have. So the relationship between persons is reciprocal in a way that a relationship with animals or things is not, in that human beings can relate back with language, friendship, love etc. The relationship between men and women is complementary,

---

cit., p. 202.
[28] Cf. ibid., pp. 202-3.

physiologically and psycho-somatically in general terms. Relatives and doctors seek a minimum reciprocity with 'PVS' patients, because of past memories and later on if there is the sightest sign of activity like eye movement. A reciprocity may also be sought between mother and child in pregnancy. Complementarity and mutuality exist not only between male and female, but between teacher and student, boss and employee etc., based on the different talents and capacities brought to bear in any community of persons; be it work, family or society.

In this life this kind of self-gift is far from perfect, tinged as it is with selfishness, concupiscence and sin. Yet man is called to tend to that perfection in love of God, and of spouse for those in the married state. We know that in the state of original innocence man enjoyed this privilege and is destined to regain it through the Redemption. The Pope refers to this state as the 'freedom of the gift', that is to say, man free of concupiscence (the tendency to sin) and the disorder of the passions. It is interesting that freedom is defined in this sense of being detached and distanced from evil.

Historicity and Transcendence of the Person

The person transcends the world of material things both in the sense of being superior to the rest of the visible world in virtue of possessing intellect and will, and also in the sense of going beyond them by the exercise of these faculties, namely by knowledge and love. We have seen at some length how the person surpasses other creatures by possessing self-determination. The process is perfected by reaching God, or one's last end, but is also carried out by loving one's neighbour and one's work for the sake of God, etc. Man is also an historical being and so his last end and eternity are secured through a gradual process of this worldly activity exercising knowledge and love above all in fulfilling his duties to God, his family, his neighbour and his work. Transcendence is used in many ways in philosophy, but always expresses a going beyond or rising above. In metaphysics the 'transcendentals', namely, being, truth, unity, etc., surpass the categories of being. But in anthropology the different actions by which man transcends himself and the world around him have a single source: his spiritual nature. As Wojtyla puts it: "Transcendence is the spirituality of the human being revealing itself."[29]

The ability of the person to make a gift of him, or herself, is connected with the transcendence of the person. He fulfils himself by his actions, knowing, willing, loving etc., vertically towards himself and horizontally towards objects. Here we must recall that in performing an action, which if fully human will be moral, a person turns not only to the object, but also to himself such that each action has an effect on what the person becomes. Wojtyla called this vertical transcendence. Transcendence then for man signifies a rising above or a going beyond and coming out of oneself, insofar as this is revealed in human existence, activity and experience. The capacity for the gift of self shows the person not to be a being closed in on him or herself, but one open to reality and it is precisely through this transcendence that he fulfils himself.

Man is an historical being, since by means of his freedom he is the author and subject of history and his own personal biography. History can only exist if there is a permanent subject of it, otherwise there would simply be a non-historic succession of episodes. To call the human being historical does not mean that he changes substantially, since the changes can only be accidental if he is a permanent subject, but nor does it imply that he is unaffected by historical change since the accidents are modes of being of the substance itself. However, the biographical journey of man brought about by freedom – which we call history – is wholly different from that of irrational creatures – which we might call *evolution*.[30]

Due to human self-determination, the history of each person is not a necessary process governed by fixed laws. Man or woman themselves are the authors of it. God, then, is not the subject of history, but rather its Author as the first cause of the being and action of each person including their freedom. Historicity signifies that man, presupposing the divine primary causality, creates himself and makes himself to be what he becomes by his free actions and choices, not in an absolute sense, but in the moral order. The making of himself, therefore, refers to what man

---

[29] Karol Wojtyla, *Person and Community*, op. cit., p. 233.
[30] Fernando Ocariz, 'Dignidad Persona, Trascendencia e Historicidad del Hombre' in idem, *Naturaleza, Gracia y Gloria*, Eunsa, Pamplona, 1999, p. 55.

can and ought to become freely in order to reach goodness and fulfilment. The latter refers to the moral order as the only one that affects man in his totality, that is, the whole person.[31]

The transcendence of the person is shown also by his dominion over the visible world, a principal aspect of which is work. St Josemaria Escriva teaches that, "all work bears witness to the dignity of man, to his dominion over creation ... [and] is a means to aiding in the progress of society ... and in the progress of all humanity."[32] Work, then, has an ethical and spiritual dimension as long as man does not limit it to its worldly and material dimension. Its transcendence is prolonged in a higher supernatural transcendence, "since Christ took it into his hands, work has become for us a redeemed and redemptive reality. Not only is it the background of man's life, it is a means and path of holiness. It is something to be sanctified and something which sanctifies."[33] We are reminded "that the dignity of work is based on Love. Man's great privilege is to be able to love and transcend what is fleeting and ephemeral."[34] John Paul II wrote in his first encyclical, *Redemptor Hominis*, "The essential meaning of this 'kingship' and 'dominion' of man over the visible world, which the Creator himself gave man for his task, consists in the priority of ethics over technology, in the primacy of the person over things, and in the superiority of spirit over matter."[35]

The observance of moral values, then, testifies to the transcendence of the person. The latter is a transcendence in history, since by shaping his own biography man transcends the visible world and at the same time, with the help of divine grace, he 'creates' himself and journeys towards his eternal goal. That is to say, as the classical tradition has always taught, all human decisions, which are conscious and free, constitute moral acts and hence all lead towards our final destiny or away from it. Decisions of conscience responsibly arrived at reveal us to be persons who are fulfilled by going beyond ourselves to values accepted in truth.

---

[31] Ibid., pp. 55-6.
[32] St Josemaria Escriva, *Christ is Passing by*, Scepter, n. 47.
[33] Ibid..
[34] Ibid., n. 48.
[35] John Paul II, *Redemptor Hominis*, n. 16.

According to Edith Stein, whose influence on the young Wojtyla was considerable, the desire that we have to be complete persons testifies to the transcendence of human beings. She writes of the moral and religious vocation of all human beings as follows:

> The human person is more precious than all objective values. All truth is discerned by persons; all beauty is beheld and measured by persons. All objective values exist in this sense for persons. And behind all things of value to be found in the world stands the *person of the Creator* who as prefigurement, encloses all earthly values in himself and transmits them. In the area of our common experience, the human being is the highest among creation since his personality is created in the image of God. It is the *whole person* about whom we are speaking: that human being in whom God's image is developed most purely, in which the gifts which the Creator has bestowed do not wither but bloom, and in whom the faculties are balanced in conformity to God's image and God's will – the will led by intellect, and the lower faculties bridled by intellect and will ... Each human being is called naturally to this total humanity, and the desire for it lives in each one of us.[36]

Wojtyla's personalism has a number of advantages for a deeper presentation of Christian ethics. It enables him to present ethics from the first person point of view, that is, from the angle of the acting person which complements the traditional third person presentation, thereby ensuring that it is seen as a practical subject and not just an abstract pursuit. It maintains the link between act and experience. It makes it possible for him to exhibit fully the new ethos of the Gospel according to which the laws and precepts of the Old Testament are fulfilled in the heart, that is, in the interior of man as virtues according to Our Lord's teaching in the Sermon on the Mount. It also enables him to give an alternative way of understanding what is meant by the metaphysical concept of substance and an updated definition of a person.

---

[36] See Edith Stein, *Collected Works*, vol. II, p. 256.

V.

NATURAL LAW PROTECTS THE GOODS AND RIGHTS OF THE PERSON

Natural law is a system of practical reason based on the goods of the person laying down human duties, which, in turn, protects the same goods and the human rights which flow from them. Its principles are known by reason in accordance with a true knowledge of the dignity of the person as a unity of spirit and body. Hence, they cannot be thought of as goods and norms on the biological level only. Rather, they are part of the rational order whereby man is called to regulate and direct his life. The establishment of the inviolable dignity of the human person is the basis for the absolute respect that must also be accorded to his or her fundamental goods. If the person must be affirmed for his or her own sake, so also must they. Given that the nature of the person is universal, so also are the goods known in accordance with it, and therefore, they apply across the board. Today, with greater globalisation and international contact, we are able to see more clearly that basic natural law principles apply to everyone because of their common humanity. Thus war crimes are tried by international law beyond national boundaries, because they are acts against natural justice and the fundamental rights of persons and their bodily integrity, irrespective of whether they are forbidden by a particular positive law or not.

Positive law, therefore, is based on natural law and not the other way round and natural law is part of the eternal law of God insofar as it is known by human reason and applies to, and directs, man's behaviour. So by natural law we refer to an unwritten law whose first principles are inscribed on the heart and mind, that is to say, in the interior of man, called by Aquinas 'synderisis' as was mentioned above. The basic goods are discerned from the inclinations we all have to the preservation and transmission of life, to truth, and friendship, the development of the material world and to beauty.[1] They are not innate, but arise in our rational consciousness on the occasion of experience and knowledge of the world. They form part of our subjectivity, but are not purely subjective, indeed they are universal because known in the subjectivity of every person. All reasonable people agree it is wrong to be cruel, or unfair and discriminatory, or tell lies, or kill others such as innocent non-combatants, or commit rape and so on.

Aquinas's well-known definition tells us the natural law is "the participation of the eternal law in the rational creature",[2] and these together with positive law, which is enacted within them, form the three types of law known to reason outside of revealed law. By the eternal law he means the plan of God's wisdom for the functioning of the universe, and so man shares in God's reason and autonomy, though as a secondary cause, not primary. Far from being put down or oppressed by natural law, man is raised up by participating in an attribute of divine life. It gets its name from the fact that it refers to what is specific to human nature, which is reason, and hence by natural law we mean more specifically the law of human reason, or the natural rational law. The natural law does not just refer to the physical and biological patterns empirically observable in the universe, or in the human person, but to the *rational* meaning of them. Though the human goods are known by means of our personal inclinations, it is neither the inclinations themselves, nor even the objects of these inclinations which would still be 'naturalistic' goods, but rather the goods and values, which reason discerns in them as referring to the whole person, which form the basis of natural law.

---

[1] Cf. *Veritatis Splendor*, n. 51.
[2] Aquinas, ST, I-II, q. 91, a. 2.

Its foundation in reason is also acknowledged by the pagan philosophers. The notion arises with the early Greek thinkers who use it to refer to the unity and order of the cosmos. The same idea is taken up and developed by Plato whose well-known theory of Forms, or Ideas, finds the essences of all earthly realities, and especially of such virtues as justice, temperance, courage, wisdom and so on, in these celestial exemplars and causes. With Aristotle and the Stoics and especially Cicero, the natural law finds its foundation in reason more than in cosmic unity. Rather than a change in meaning this is a deepening of the notion because the order and meaning of the universe, and of human life and behaviour, is reflected in reason. The shift here is from a predominantly physical and material understanding of order to an intelligent and rational grasp of it. The human mind is able to grasp that intelligent plan, or wisdom, and the good, or goal, to which it tends, as well as other intermediate ends and goods.

St Paul refers to it in his Letter to the Romans where he says: "When Gentiles who have not the law do by nature what the law requires, they are a law to themselves, even though they do not have the law. They show that what the law requires is written on their hearts, while their conscience also bears witness …"[3] According to Cardinal Ratzinger this is identical with 'nature' as used by the Stoics transformed by the theology of creation.[4] The latter helps Christians to discern an intelligent design in the universe, but St Paul had earlier emphasized the gentiles' ability to know God by reason alone from the created universe.[5] And in the Book of Sirach we read: "He filled them with knowledge and understanding and showed them good and evil."[6]

If, by contrast, a man or woman of today assumes the universe to be without meaning or order, and considers that it simply results from chance, coincidence, or luck, then such a mind will be unlikely to grasp natural law. That this was not the perception of many of the ancients is shown by the following words of one of the Stoic teaching's most eloquent exponents, Cicero, himself

---

[3] Rom 2:14-15.
[4] Ratzinger, Joseph, *Truth and Tolerance*, Ignatius Press, 2004, p. 239.
[5] Cf. Rom 1:20.
[6] Sir 17:17.

a non-Christian:

> True law is right reason in agreement with nature *("recta ratio naturae congruens")*; it is of universal application, unchanging and everlasting; it summons to duty by its commands, and averts from wrongdoing by its prohibitions. And it does not lay its commands or prohibitions upon good men in vain, though neither have any effect on the wicked. It is a sin to try to alter this law, nor is it allowable to attempt to repeal any part of it, and it is impossible to abolish it entirely.[7]

Modern doubts about natural law arise from the weakening of human reason, due originally, though not entirely, to Descartes' system of methodic doubt with its rejection of all authority and tradition. In the process it has also lost the notion of human nature to the point where Sartre can say there is no such thing. Other less radical thinkers are unable to agree on a common definition of the person. This is what happens once human nature, or the person, is understood as consciousness or as, for example, Sartre suggested, freedom. As was discussed previously, the human person must be recognized as a unity of mind and body which alone gives you an objective definition. Descartes explicitly doubted the body and went on to argue that, if I am doubting, I must be thinking. But that does not make thinking the essence of human nature. It is part of the core of it but not all of it. This is an instance of the modern narrowing of reason, but a rather important one as far as natural law is concerned, because to establish universal laws one needs the full powers of human reason in accordance with the whole truth of the human person.

The morality of the Gospel and the Church is a unified whole within which the dignity of the person occupies a pivotal position. Our knowledge of the different forms of human good, including and beyond the first principles, is known by reason and assisted by an understanding of the nature and truth of the human person. The goods of the person, in turn, require virtues and rules for their full moral development. If you take away the virtues, the rules or laws remain as dry and arbitrary decrees exposing one to a legalistic

---

[7] Cicero, (Marcus Tullius), *The Republic*, (or *De Republica*), Bk III, XXII, 33, Loeb Library ed., 1928, Harvard University Press, Cambridge Mass., p. 211.

view of ethics.[8] Furthermore, the natural law, even though it is known by reason, includes a knowledge of God, because the love, worship and service of God are one of its precepts, even though for the rational thinker this may be a conclusion rather than starting point.

If you take away the natural law basis of right and wrong together with the pleasure in judging and acting rightly and the remorse in judging and acting wrongly, then all that is left is the individual experience of pleasure and pain.[9] It is then but a small step to identifying good and evil solely in terms of pleasure and pain, i.e. utilitarianism. A natural law ethics establishes a moral order beyond the individual, which, though reflected in him, is not created by him. In other words, conscience reflects the moral order, but like freedom does not take its place, since both are subject to an objective truth. This is connected to the right order between reason and will, which is reflected in John Paul II's frequent insistence on the non-separation of freedom and truth. Without the continued assistance of truth it is very easy for reason and conscience to seek their own good, but not that of God or others.

The Scope of Reason

St Thomas likens reason's sense of right and wrong to a light, which is the imprint of the divine light in us. Light is not itself the reality seen, but it draws back the veil of darkness to enable you to see what is there; it uncovers what is hidden. The moral goods and principles are discovered rather than invented or created. It echoes the tradition of Plato, who likened the idea of the Good, the knowledge of truth, to the sun, and of Aristotle who saw "something divine" in the intellect, our "true self", "our best and noblest part".[10] It drives the darkness of ignorance and error from the mind, and if in some cases it fails to do this, it is not due to any defect in the light but to self-love and corrupt customs in us. Classical Greek philosophy, therefore, sees in man's intellect/

---

[8] Cf. Alasdair MacIntyre, *Three Rival Versions of Moral Enquiry*, Duckworth, London, 1990, p. 139.
[9] Cf. ibid., p. 138.
[10] Aristotle, *Nichomachean Ethics*, op. cit., Bk 10, ch. 7, p. 305.

reason an unerring power of attaining truth. It was no accident that the rise of Christianity coincided with the aftermath of the Greek discoveries and made some of them its own. Thus Aquinas was to say that if the power of reason is not hindered by the will and disordered sensitive passions, it correctly reveals the truth to man and enables him to strive for the good. The human intellect does not simply think, reason and conclude, it contains and discovers truth, due to its participation in the divine truth, because of the divine image characteristic of all human beings rooted principally in the intellect and the will.

The human intellect has two functions, one of which concerns those things which are naturally and spontaneously known, and the other is its ability to find out, to discover what is hidden, to proceed from the known to the unknown by discursive reasoning. The most common principles contain knowledge from which reason by experience and learning can derive further principles, so that, for example, from the good of life it can conclude to the need for food, shelter and health. Of this we will see more below when we come to the secondary and tertiary principles. The two functions bear some resemblance to the two words used by the Greeks for the mind, namely 'nous' (intellect) and 'logos' (reason), though they are not identical with it. Intellect and reason are fundamentally one and the same, but can be used to refer to the different aspects of reason, the one more intuitive and the other, discursive. The latter finds out more, it judges and decides on truth and discovers what is still unknown in the principles.[11]

Aquinas says that, "Law is a rule and measure of acts, by which man is induced to act, or restrained from acting; for *lex* (law) is derived from *ligare* (to bind), because it obliges one to act. Now the rule and measure of human acts is the reason ... for it belongs to reason to direct to the end which is the first principle in all matters of action."[12] He says law may be a rule and measure in two ways, first as a norm and standard which directs to the end and, secondly, we may speak of a 'law' in that which is ruled and measured. When we apply this latter to the inclinations and

---

[11] Cf. Martin Rhonheimer, *Natural Law and Practical Reason*, Fordham University Press, New York, ch. 6, pp. 257-274.
[12] Aquinas, ST, I-II, q. 90, a. 1.

strivings in man in his present condition we see why St Paul speaks of another law in his members.[13] The fact that man has reason already constitutes a hierarchy of powers within him, since it places the strivings and inclinations of man, such as the will and the sensitive emotions, in subordination to it and under its rule. It orders them and leads them to their true end. Aristotle taught, based on the intellect as man's highest faculty, that a man's goal, or the meaning of his life, is going to be an activity in conjunction with virtue consisting in the contemplation and love of truth.

Reason is also a rule and measure, or standard of human behaviour, when it is applied through practical reason to human acts on the particular and contingent level. This is the activity of prudence we have looked at. The normative and measuring activity of reason due to its 'telos' character, may be summarized in the following way. First, it is the 'telos', or end and goal of human life in general, in that it reveals the meaning and purpose of life as an activity associated with virtue which consists in the knowledge and love of truth. The intellect is the light of the will which can only strive after what is presented to it by the reason both in universal principles and in particular acts. Secondly, it is normative because the reason orders the powers of the soul, when it is allowed to and not obstructed or blinded by the passions. Thirdly, reason becomes part of the rationally ordered appetitive powers through the growth of the moral virtues which then assist it in making further practical judgements.[14] For this reason Aquinas often speaks of rational human nature.

Nevertheless, it remains the case that natural law, by whatever path it is known, is participated and not autonomous knowledge. In the *Summa Theologica*, Aquinas twice quotes psalm IV which says as follows, "Who shows us what is good? The light of your countenance, Lord, is signed upon us".[15] The human reason is a rule of moral behaviour because of its participation in the divine reason. As Leo XIII wrote,

> this prescription of human reason could not have the force of law unless it were the voice and interpreter of some higher

---

[13] Rom 7:3.
[14] Cf. Rhonheimer, op. cit., p. 318.
[15] Aquinas, ST, I-II, q. 19, a. 4; q. 91, a. 2.

reason to which our spirit and freedom must be subject ... Now all of this, clearly, could not exist in man if, as his own supreme legislator he gave himself the rule of his own actions ... it follows that the natural law is *itself the eternal law*, implanted in beings endowed with reason, and inclining them towards their right action and end; it is none other than the Creator and Ruler of the universe.[16]

The Goods of the Human Person

With this preamble let us proceed to a more orderly presentation of the goods and principles. By the goods of the person we mean those things which are the object and terminus of rational desire, inclination or passion such as housing, employment or love. We have already seen that the end of rationally directed actions is called a good. Furthermore, the objects of all these activities are also known as 'goods' because they fulfil and partially contribute to the overall well-being of the person. These goods, which are the basis of natural law, are discerned by reason in the light of the truth of the human person. In order that they genuinely fulfil the person they must be true goods and sought after in the right measure. For example, food and drink are personal goods but practical wisdom, that is virtue, must ensure that they are not pursued to excess or indeed, on the contrary, neglected. The language of goods shows us that with natural law we are not talking about the physical and biological patterns in nature, but about the goods and values of the whole rational person, body and soul, which can only be grasped by reason.

Rational reflection leads us back to the most general and universal principles of behaviour, which form the first principles of practical reason, or natural law, which are said to be self-evident and indemonstrable.[17] This does not mean that everybody knows them perfectly, but rather they are self-evident in themselves (because the predicate is contained in the subject) and also to the wise and knowledgeable, that is those who know what the terms mean. The first principle of practical reason, 'the good is to be done and evil avoided', is based on the fact that the good

---

[16] Pope Leo XIII, *Libertas Praestantissimum*, June, 1888; cf. *Veritatis Splendor*, n. 44
[17] Aquinas, ST, I-II, q. 94, a. 2.

is the universal object of the will, according to the Aristotelian expression 'the good is that at which all things aim'.[18] Aquinas describes it as a 'precept of law' which follows from the principle of practical reason that the good is desired.[19] It is the perception of a good by a subject, whether it is in reality so or not, which causes a person to act. The principle may be expressed in different ways in different systems, and as we shall see Aquinas was to give it a fuller definition in the light of the background of Revelation which Aristotle's system had not had the benefit of.

The primary precepts of the natural law are based on the personal goods, which form the content of this first principle. These basic goods are known from the fundamental inclinations of the human person, which are also self-evident, albeit after reflection. The inclinations are as follows: a) those which we share with all other living beings, viz. to preserve life; and with other animals, namely to procreate life and educate and care for offspring; b) those which are proper to the rational being such as social life and friendship, not offending those with whom one has to live and so on; and truth since the purpose of reason is to know the truth and especially the truth of God.[20] These inclinations are then grasped by *reason* as leading to basic goods of the person, and then translated into precepts or laws (following the principle of Aquinas mentioned in the next paragraph) such as 'preserve and respect human life', 'treat your neighbour justly', 'seek the truth' and so on. These primary precepts still do not indicate any specific types of action. This comes with the experience and learning which enables reason and prudence to 'discover' their application to ordinary human activity of which we will see examples further on. The result is the emergence of secondary precepts close in content to the Ten Commandments.[21]

In what sense are the primary and secondary principles also precepts? Aquinas holds that wherever we find something moving

---

[18] Aristotle, *Ethics*, op. cit., I, 1.
[19] See Aquinas, ST, I-II, q. 94, a. 2, "Et ideo primum principium in ratione practica est quod fundatur supra rationem boni, quae est, quae est bonum est quod omnia appetunt. Hoc est ergo primum praeceptum legis, quod bonum est faciendum et prosequendum, et malum vitandum."
[20] Cf. ibid.
[21] Cf. ST, I-II, q. 100, a. 3.

towards an end we find a precept or law and this is true not only of the precepts of law, which tend to justice, but also of the natural inclinations which tend to personal goods such as food, progeny, shelter etc.[22] For this reason he speaks of the principles of the practical reason as precepts, but the obligation comes not only from the law, but from the goods of the person that the law points to. And the goods depend on truth. The purpose of the law is to lead to virtue, and the goods and inclinations of the person are the seeds of the virtues. The law is based on the goods which fulfil a person and not the goods on the law. So if the law is seen in this way it will not be perceived as burdensome and restrictive, but as leading to true personal fulfilment.

The precepts of the natural law are universal and immutable, but the more they are subject to particular conditions the more mutable they become. St Thomas teaches that the secondary precepts of the law are moral absolutes in 'the majority of cases' (*ut in pluribus*).[23] (We will examine this statement more fully below.) Many other secondary and remote goods are particular determinations of the precepts of the natural law. "It is from the precepts of natural law, as from general and indemonstrable principles that the human reason needs to proceed to more particular determinations of certain matters", says St Thomas.[24] We will see why if we look at some of these goods, which depend more on contingencies, such as the good of universal education which depends on the degree of human development achieved in a particular place.

So the things that sustain life and flow from it are such goods as health, housing, medical attention, food and nourishment, all of which are available in differing degrees around the world. Some goods like holidays are a combination of goods, in this case partly knowledge and partly the intellectual/sensible good of relaxation of mind and body. Or house decoration is partly the basic good of beauty and partly the sensible good of comfort. All these goods, even those which have a strong biological and corporal element,

---

[22] Aquinas, ST, I-II, q. 5, a. 5, ad 1; q. 95, a. 1c; Quodl., VII, a.1. See Kevin L Flannery, *Acts Amid Precepts*, T & T Clark, Edinburgh, 2001, p. 28.
[23] Aquinas, ST, I-II, q. 94, a. 4.
[24] Aquinas, ST, I-II, q. 92, a. 3.

are grasped and pursued by human beings on the level which is specific to human nature, that is the rational level.

The civil law falls into the category of particular determinations of the general precepts of natural law. Hence it enacts laws to protect values such as life itself, the good name and physical well-being and security of the person, together with property, truthfulness and public order in society. Laws passed by purely human authorities or governments are known as positive laws, many of which are within the natural law but not all. If lawmakers consider they have an autonomous authority to pass laws which issues from themselves alone, they are pursuing positivism which eventually exposes them to stray from the truth, as we see with much of today's anti-life legislation. Attempts by legislators to pass laws contrary to natural law are invalid as laws, and hence such 'legislation' is without binding force.[25]

These goods apply to a person as a rational animal, that is, as a unity of body and soul, and so all have a rational and bodily aspect to them. Though man shares some of these tendencies with the animal world, in him the tendencies are all rational due to the unity of body and soul. The body is part of human dignity and therefore shares in the sanctity and inviolability of all human life. When we say that a person tends to the true and the good we have to remember that a being is good insofar as it exists and therefore it tends to the fullness of its own existence and, indeed, to the preservation of it. Here is the origin of the instinct of self-preservation. If the will tends to the good, i.e. being insofar as it is desirable, the mind tends to truth, that is, being insofar as it is intelligible. At the root of natural law, then, is a philosophy of being.

The goods that follow from the inclinations presuppose the anthropological knowledge we have established, and, taking all that into account, are grasped by reason. Our knowledge of the person has taught us that the purpose of his intellect is to seek and attain the truth and especially the truth about God, the meaning of life and the goods of the person. It is capable of grasping that the object of the inclination to self-preservation is based on the

---

[25] Aquinas, ST, I-II, q. 93, a. 3, ad 2.

intrinsic worth of every human life, including one's own, and therefore is aware of the absolute respect that must be shown for the sanctity of life of every human being. The social inclination presupposes we know that man is a being open to others called to communion and relationship with others and in loving them also fulfils him or herself. Reason also grasps that the object of the tendency to friendship and sociability is to love others for their own sake, not as a means to an end.

The capacity for sexuality indicates that the body has a 'spousal meaning', which signifies that it is meant for love, and since it is the product of love it is destined to pass it on by that special form of friendship, which is marriage. This determines the direction that Christian morality takes on matters of sexual ethics. Sexuality has two inter-related meanings, both of which include love, namely, the generation and raising of children and the communion of man and wife. Marriage, then, is a loving union of persons, not just of bodies, but of 'one flesh', which is procreative in type and unconditional. This is the basis, not only of the sixth commandment, which prohibits the indulgence of sexuality for other or lesser purposes, but also of the fourth which regulates the relations between parents and children and vice versa.

The preservation of life is a basic instinct which is not just passive but active. It includes the quest for all the supplementary goods which make it possible, such as health, food, housing, clothing, etc. It refers to spiritual life as well as physical and denotes a natural and healthy love of self which is antithetical to selfishness. It underlies all our actions which are directed to our genuine improvement, and provides the yardstick for the love of others and the Golden Rule, ('treat others as you would have them treat you'). In turn, it is the foundation for the fifth commandment, 'do not kill', which refers not only to all other human beings but also to ourselves.

Natural Law and the Commandments

It is because of the sketchy hold we have on the principles of natural law that they are also revealed in the Commandments, even though their content can be known by unaided reason given the right conditions.²⁶ Natural law is really about upholding the goods of the person, our own and others. Because of the closeness of the precepts of the natural law to the Decalogue, Aquinas says a little reflection tells us that the first and common principles of the former are the love of God and neighbour. These include within them as proximate conclusions the principle that one should do evil to no man, known as the principle of non-maleficence,²⁷ and the principle of equality,²⁸ which places many conditions on the way persons may be treated. From this it can be seen that the first principles, love of God and neighbour, cover the basic goods enumerated above. Although these principles are not in the Decalogue, they are related to it as general principles to specific precepts. From the first principles follow more particular determinations, which are the specific and secondary precepts of the law, natural and revealed.

A man is required by the natural law and the Decalogue to behave well both in particular and in general; in particular, to those to whom he is indebted, such as his parents, and he repays the debts by honouring them. In general, he behaves correctly by doing harm to no one in deed, word, or thought. By deed, harm can be done to one's neighbour in his personal existence and this is forbidden by the words, *do not kill;* to those closely united to him, as to the propagation of offspring outside marriage which is prohibited by the words, *do not commit adultery*, and sometimes harm is done to the person's possessions, so theft is forbidden. Harm done by word is forbidden when it is said, *do not bear false witness against your neighbour,* and by thought when it says, *do not covet.*²⁹ These are known easily by reason to everybody, but there are further precepts of natural law known only to all by the testimony of wise men, as for example, the precept that one should honour and respect the elderly.³⁰

For this reason, Pope John Paul referring to the commandments of the second tablet of the Decalogue, concerning the love

---

[26] Cf. Rom 2:14.
[27] Aquinas, ST, I-II, q. 100, aa. 1, 3, 5; and II-II, q. 72, a. 1.
[28] Ibid., II-II, q. 58, a. 1.
[29] Cf. ibid., I-II, q. 100, a. 5.
[30] Cf. Lev 19:32.

of neighbour, says we find here a "precise expression of the singular dignity of the human person" and that, "[t]he different commandments of the Decalogue are really only so many reflections of the one commandment about the good of the person, at the level of the many different goods which characterize his identity as a spiritual and bodily being in relationship with God, with his neighbour and with the material world."[31] An important distinction is made here between the 'good of the person' meaning "the good which is the person himself and his perfection"[32] and the 'goods of the person', which are the particular goods which make it up. So the latter, or the basic goods, are reflections of the supreme good in a particular area, or participations in it.

In other words, it may be said that the precepts of the Decalogue are fundamental participations in the supreme good of loving God and neighbour. They are related as conclusions to principles, whether at the level of faith, or reason. Now those precepts which apply to our neighbour pick out the goods which benefit the true humanity of the individual, and protect him, and, by contrast, forbid the evils which harm it. The Pope goes on: "'You shall not murder; you shall not commit adultery; you shall not steal; you shall not bear false witness' are moral rules formulated in terms of prohibitions. These negative precepts express with particular force the ever urgent need to protect human life, the communion of persons in marriage, private property, truthfulness and people's good name."[33] These coincide with the basic goods founded on the human inclinations known by reason.

It is not, therefore, possible to love the person without upholding all the goods which go towards his integral fulfilment as a human being and, by implication, defending all the rights which flow from these. Hence, freely chosen acts, which damage, or fail to uphold, these basic goods which are perfective of human persons, are wrong, because they harm a good of a person of intrinsic worth and dignity.[34] And indeed we harm ourselves, because as

---

[31] John Paul II, *Veritatis Splendor*, n. 13.
[32] *Veritatis Splendor*, n. 79.
[33] *Veritatis Splendor*, n. 13.
[34] Cf. William May, *Catholic Bioethics and the Gift of Human Life*, Our Sunday Visitor, Huntingdon, Indiana, 2000, p. 57.

St Thomas observed, "God is offended by us only because we act contrary to our own good."[35]

Nor would it be possible to act in this way without at the same time failing to love God, because the love of God implies the love of neighbour.[36] The Pope emphasizes the love of neighbour because these are the goods mentioned by Jesus to the young man, but he also stresses the inseparable unity between it and the love of God, as instanced by Jesus' answer to the teacher of the Law who asked a similar question.[37] The reason why the other precepts in the Decalogue are phrased mainly in the negative is because they tell us the minimum level below which we must not fall if we are not to offend and harm our neighbour seriously.

These precepts tell us that such actions radically contradict the fundamental goods of the human person and so are always wrong in virtue of their object. This moral object is not compatible with the supreme good of the person and the other goods of human existence and, therefore, is incompatible with the goodness of the will of the acting person. Here, we pinpoint one of the major themes of *Veritatis Splendor*, which says, "reason attests that there are objects of the human act which are by their nature 'incapable of being ordered to God,' because they radically contradict the good of the person made in his image."[38] The theme of the good of the person made up of the personal basic goods runs through the encyclical and applies both at the level of reason and of Revelation, and by means of them we see that rational truth and the Christian Commandments, and Christian moral doctrine as a whole, uphold and protect the dignity of the person and his genuine freedom.

The Correct Understanding of Natural Law is not Naturalism or Physicalism

The natural law, which is based on the inclinations and basic goods of the man is a rational plan of action and cannot be understood (and never was understood) as a biological system. The revisionists have accused it of presenting biological laws as moral laws and

---

[35] Aquinas, *Summa Contra Gentiles*, 3.122.
[36] 1 Jn 4:20.
[37] Lk 10:28.
[38] John Paul II, *Veritatis Splendor*, n. 80.

thus claiming a universality and immutability, which biological laws cannot have, given that more and more facts can always be discovered about biology, which means that its laws are constantly subject to revision. The goods which accrue by this means would be pre-moral, physical or ontic goods, they say. If, however, the natural law is not biological or physical but rational, then these objections go by the board.

According to the biologistic understanding of the natural law, various forms of sexual behaviour were deemed to be immoral, including contraception. The revisionists then go on to argue, that freedom must determine the meaning of man's behaviour, it must dominate and direct the physical side of his nature. They formulate a theory, which assumes a dualism in man of mind and matter, and not a harmonious unity whereby the mind works through the body in the way described above. The result is that freedom, which is part of personal consciousness, must impose itself on the biology of the body, and hence on sexuality and 'assume' it into the human sphere. Such a step is unnecessary, of course, if the body and sexuality are already an integral part of the person.

A key argument of the revisionists' position is that man's rational and free dominion over physical nature gives him the authority to use contraception, rather in the same way that we use drugs and medicine. An argument such as this was employed by the Majority Report presented to Paul VI on contraception which said, "in the matter at hand, there is a certain change in the mind of contemporary man. He feels that he is more conformed to his rational nature, created by God with liberty and responsibility, when he uses his skill to intervene in the biological processes of nature so that he can achieve the ends of the institution of matrimony in the conditions of actual life, than if he would abandon himself to chance."[39] And Jack Dominian comments: "The traditional teaching on sexual matters depended on a view of sexuality which was biologically based and was largely concerned with reproduction. In Western society and many other parts of

---

[39] The Majority Report to The Papal Commission on Population, the Family and Natality, can be found in *The Birth Control Debate*, Robert Hoyt ed., 'The Question is not Closed', The National Catholic Reporter, Kansas, 1969.

the world, this view has now been abandoned."⁴⁰

The failure to understand that natural law is based on reason and not on physical rhythms and laws has had lasting, adverse consequences, because the criticism surfaced above all at the time of the controversy over birth control and the encyclical *Humanae Vitae*. The critics who argued for a change to the Church's constant teaching maintained that it was based on a natural law theory that was 'physicalistic' and biologistic' and hence unable to claim immutability and universal validity. In other words, their attack was not only on the doctrine of birth control, but also on the natural law itself, as they had understood it. The claim of many was not that contraception was good, but that it was not wrong on each and every occasion within a good marriage and should be judged according to the merits of the marriage as a whole. They saw that their claim that it was not an intrinsically evil action contradicted the teaching of natural law and so they looked for an alternative theory, which they found in proportionalism. The latter has many flaws in it and much that is irreconcilable with Christian doctrine, which will be dealt with in a later chapter, but suffice it to say at present that their concept of the 'good' failed to overcome the 'naturalism' and 'physicalism' they criticized in their erroneous understanding of natural law, because they failed to grasp the moral identity, and hence the moral object, of an action.

The Theory of the Revisionists contradicts the Unity and Dignity of the Person

Here natural law is being understood according to a dualistic notion of man and his sexual acts and therefore being misconstrued, because according to this view sex is biology and the person is consciousness, hence laws about sexuality are biological. Of course, we can separate off biological facts, such as those about conception, the implanting of the embryo in the endometrium and so on, conceptually for the purposes of discussion. But to say that biology is separable from the person is not the same as to say it is separate; it is only conceptually separate. When exercised

---

[40] *The Tablet*, London, Aug. 27th 1994.

consciously, sexuality and biological action are always personal, in the sense that the whole person, mind and will is involved.

Veritatis Splendor explicitly rejects this revisionist view:

> This moral theory does not correspond to the truth about man and his freedom. It contradicts the *Church's teachings on the unity of the human person,* whose rational soul is *per se et essentialiter* the form of the body. The spiritual and immortal soul is the principle of the unity of the human being, whereby it exists as a whole – *corpore et anima unus* – as a person. These definitions not only point out that the body, which has been promised the resurrection, will also share in glory. They also remind us that reason and free will are linked with all the bodily and sense faculties. *The person, including the body, is completely entrusted to himself, and it is in the unity of body and soul that the person is the subject of his own moral acts.*[41]

Although some of the fundamental inclinations of the person, such as self-preservation and procreation, are also to be found in animals, in man they are not physical or biological but rational in virtue of the unity of the human person. The moral norms which are derived from them, via the goods and values which are the object of these inclinations, get their force from the dignity of the person.[42] Moral revisionists have tended to conceive of the natural law in a 'physicalistic' or 'biologistic' way because they have lacked an adequate understanding of personal unity and the power of human reason which gives it its rational nature.

The encyclical *Veritatis Splendor* emphasizes that man's biology is an integral part of his unity as a rational creature and hence all his conscious actions are rational and not just biological:

> The natural moral law expresses and lays down the purposes, rights and duties which are based upon the bodily and spiritual nature of the human person. Therefore, this law cannot be thought of as simply a set of norms on the biological level; rather it must be defined as the rational order whereby man is called by the Creator to direct and regulate his life and actions and in particular to make use of his own body. To give an example, the origin and the foundation of the duty of absolute respect for human life are to be found in the dignity proper to

---

[41] *Veritatis Splendor,* n. 48.
[42] Cf. *Veritatis Splendor,* n. 50.

the person and not simply in the natural inclination to preserve one's own physical life.⁴³

That is to say, the human person is of intrinsic worth and so his life is always inviolable, and indeed, so are the basic goods attached to it.

St Thomas did not, however, 'derive' natural law from an abstract idea of human nature, much less physical or biological human nature, but it is known by reason in the light of a correct anthropology. The Pope chooses his words very carefully:

> It is in the light of the dignity of the human person – a dignity which must be affirmed for its own sake – that reason grasps the specific moral value of certain goods towards which the person is naturally inclined. And since the human person cannot be reduced to a freedom which is self-designing, but entails a particular spiritual and bodily structure, the primordial moral requirement of loving and respecting the person as an end and never as a mere means implies, by its very nature, respect for certain fundamental goods, without which one would fall into relativism and arbitrariness.⁴⁴

We thus see from these last two paragraphs that the absolute nature of the common and fundamental principles of the natural law is discovered (*'invenitur'*) by reason and based on the intrinsic worth of the person and the absolute respect due to his fundamental goods, such as his life, the purpose of his sexuality, his property, his good name etc. And this is because the person exists for his own sake and must always be treated as an end and never as a means: this is the personalist principle. The natural law, properly speaking, corresponds to a true notion of the human person, and not a reductionist or dualist view, i.e. an inadequate one. So when *Veritatis Splendor* enumerates the basic principles of the natural law it is talking about rational ones and not ones based on mere biological inclinations.⁴⁵ The resulting goods get their force from the inviolable nature of the person. If we take the case of the good of life it is more appropriate to call it inviolable rather than absolute, since it is not the case that suffering human life must be kept alive on every occasion. Where treatment would

---

⁴³ Ibid.
⁴⁴ Ibid., n. 48.
⁴⁵ Ibid., n. 51.

require extraordinary or disproportionate means it is perfectly acceptable to let the dying die the death they are undergoing, as long as ordinary everyday nursing care, including food and hydration, is given.

Those who criticize natural law as 'physicalistic' also singularly fail to understand practical reason, insofar as its principles are based on reason and personal experience and apply to action. Even though there was probably some truth in their criticism as it related to the neo-scholastic interpretation of natural law which they had inherited, they failed to see that this was not the understanding of natural law of Aquinas himself. Nor did 'physicalism' or 'naturalism' feature in any way in the Aristotelian approach to ethics, which was rather through the activity of the practical reason of the acting subject, as is becoming more fully recognized once more. The failure to appreciate this came about, most probably, through an insufficient understanding of Aristotle's *Ethics* and the extent of its influence on Aquinas.

Freedom, Nature and Natural Law

The natural law is an unwritten law grasped by reason in virtue of its participation in the eternal reason and so does not come to us from without and conflict with our freedom. It is true that divinely revealed law comes from without, but (with the exception of the placing of the Sabbath on a fixed day of the week) it is essentially another form of the natural law given to confirm and deepen our understanding of it, in view of the weakness which affects our intellect. It fully respects our dignity and freedom and indeed enhances it.

By the same token, reason (and freedom) have their own autonomy as secondary causes, because God treats all creatures according to their condition, and the sense of right and wrong is 'in man', but this autonomy is not total independence, due to the participative character of reason. The same is true of freedom. There is a true autonomy and a false autonomy depending upon whether man's dependent character under God is acknowledged or not. This is the point made in Gen 2:16, that Adam and Eve may not eat of the tree of the knowledge of good and evil, since there is a threshold not determined by them that they may not cross. Man's self-determination and autonomy are limited, but nevertheless genuine. The human person is master of him or herself, within the confines of the truth of the human condition. Moreover, there is no conflict between freedom and law, if law is a 'rule of reason', and reason's purpose is truth to which genuine freedom is itself directed and in which it is fulfilled.

There are two types of obstacle to the understanding of natural law. One is to create a conflict between person and nature, (a variation of which is to see a corresponding difficulty between freedom and nature). The other is to see a similar impasse between the person and law, and hence, equally, as before, between freedom and law. Much of the alleged conflict, in both cases, is illusory but it is important to examine the problem briefly, and see what the basis for it is.

A conflict comes about with 'nature' if it is understood in the modern sense, as 'what simply happens' independently of consideration of a subject, or with the non-rational world of biological nature. When one says in modern speech, 'it happens by nature' one is emphasizing that an event takes place rather than that someone or some subject is the author of it. And this is the way 'nature' is understood in phenomenology and phenomenalism. In classical metaphysics, 'nature' is the principle of activity of a being and is integrated into the subject, or the person, as the well known definition of Boethius says, "an individual substance, or subject, of rational nature." In this sense, nature and person intersect continually and it is always the whole person that acts (*'actiones sunt suppositorum'*), and it does so in virtue of the 'nature'.

Karol Wojtyla writes, "the conflict between person and nature appears only when we understand nature in the sense in which the phenomenologists understand it, namely, as the subject of instinctive actualisation, as the subject of what merely happens... nature (understood) as the source of such actualisation excludes the person. The person, in turn, ... as the source of actions and deeds, stands above nature and is, in a certain sense, opposed to nature."[46] The underlying problem here is again the philosophy

---

[46] Karol Wojtyla, 'The Human Person and the Natural Law' in *Person and Community*,

of dualism, which identifies the human person with spirit, or consciousness, and the body with the material world. According to this mindset, the person is identified with freedom and 'nature' with determinism such that not only does the human being not act as a unity, but person and nature are actually at variance with one another. Furthermore, physical and biological laws are not seen as being on the same level as the laws of the spirit, and belong to a lower mechanistic order not compatible with freedom, so the latter must impose itself on the body. But this conflict only arises as a result of a certain type of philosophy, and not according to the classical and original meaning of the terms. To this extent we may say the conflict is illusory and besides it is, properly speaking, a problem of anthropology, not of natural law.

We have here a classic expression of the modern idea of freedom, of a voluntarist and Kantian hue, absolute and antecedent, not subordinate to reason and truth. It is a freedom, which 'dictates norms to itself' and does not accept being ruled by another. This gives rise to a notion of autonomy, itself the source of a number of spurious rights claims, which is opposed to a true notion of freedom and law. According to this a law that was above or outside of one would be an imposition (a 'dogma') incompatible with human dignity. This so-called 'heteronomy' would obliterate human freedom. However, as we have seen, this conclusion is derived from false premises, because although the law is, in one sense, outside of us, since we are not the origin of it, we do participate in it. This knowing participation in the order of the universe is called participated theonomy, which yields a valid and genuine form of moral autonomy, since while the law is not of us it is *in* us, which allows us to have a genuine self-determination and the creativity proper to a free secondary cause.

At various points in its exposition of natural law the encyclical makes use of the truth of the person to explain it more adequately and address misunderstandings. In particular, the full truth about the human being as a unity of body and soul, is essential in order to counter accusations that natural law is based on biological and physical laws rather than rational and personal ones. With good

---

op. cit., p. 182.

reason the encyclical says, "Faced with this theory (proportionalism), one has to consider carefully the correct relationship existing between freedom and human nature, and in particular *the place of the human body in questions of natural law.*"[47] If freedom is opposed to human nature and bodily life, this leads one to treat the latter as of a lower order and its laws as physical and biological. The writers of the so-called Majority Report on the contraceptive pill were guilty of this mistake. If, however, the person is a unified totality all his or her actions are rational and so are the laws of human nature.

So there is no conflict between the person, or freedom, and nature, as long as we have a certain understanding of the human being. Real conflict only occurs if we understand the person as "pure consciousness" or as "absolute freedom", that is as a being of unlimited freedom. In these cases, the human being is not subordinate to God, and so there is certainly a conflict with natural law since the latter is a participation of the human reason in the eternal law of God.

Universality and Immutability in a changing environment

Aquinas argues that the natural law is common to all men and all nations, but in explaining this he draws our attention to the difference between speculative and practical reason. The former is concerned with necessary matters which cannot be otherwise than they are, whereas the latter deals with contingent things, and although its general principles are necessary the more we descend to matters of detail, the more exceptions we find. The example given by Aquinas to illustrate this is that of returning goods and deposits held in trust to their rightful owner, which is true for the 'majority of cases' but in a particular case would be wrong if, for example, it was a weapon such as a knife, or a gun, that was going to be used to harm somebody. The right is forfeited as a result of a higher right of third parties to security of life and protection from harm.

What makes the fundamental precepts of the natural law always and for ever true (*semper et pro semper*) is not the fact that they are based on natural inclinations, but rather the dignity of

---

[47] *Veritatis Splendor*, n. 48.

the human person whose goods they protect:

> Human life, even though it is a fundamental good of man, thus acquires a moral significance in reference to the good of the person, who must always be affirmed for his own sake ... Only in reference to the human person in his 'unified totality', that is, as 'a soul which expresses itself in a body and a body informed by an immortal spirit,' can the specifically human meaning of the body be grasped. Indeed, natural inclinations take on moral relevance only insofar as they refer to the human person and his authentic fulfilment, a fulfilment which for that matter can take place always and only in human nature.[48]

A further objection to natural law frequently expressed is that it is static and does not take account of the evolutionary nature of man, historical progress, known as historicism, etc. Human beings do progress in the sense that they constantly develop new capabilities but these do not change human nature. Man's cultural condition does not exhaust his definition. The very fact that cultures progress, change and are different shows that there is something in man over and above culture and common to man as such, namely, his dignity and rationality. For example, the fact that life must be preserved is not simply because it is a human instinct to do this, but because of the intrinsic dignity and worth of a human rational life. We do not just have these values because we have been taught them, but we have been taught them because they are true and known by reason. We cannot say that the basic values are different for different cultures and historical periods, because the constant feature of the nature of the person, namely reason from which these values come, persists, even though the historical environment and circumstances change.

In this context it is often urged that moral norms, once taught as true, have changed, typically the prohibition on charging interest for lending money, and the acceptance of slavery which is now universally outlawed. It is of interest here to recall our distinction between personal goods and norms. The norms are derived from goods, as stated above and not the other way round and so in this case the norm has *apparently* changed but the goods and values on which it is based have not. What has

---

[48] John Paul II, *Veritatis Splendor*, n. 50.

changed is rather the culture and circumstances in which we are living, that is to say the matter to which the norm applied. Usury was prohibited at a time when money was simply a means of exchange and before it took on the role of capital under modern economic conditions. Since, from that time onwards, the use of capital enabled you to make further wealth it became reasonable for the borrower to pay the creditor for the economic resource made available to him, just as if he had lent him a plough, or a fishing boat. Aside from this, usury which means exorbitant and unreasonable rates of interest continues to be prohibited by the moral law.

Equally with slavery, while the law *apparently* allowed it up to recent centuries, under Christianity the moral values with regard to ownership of a person always obtained albeit a little less rigorously than today. What existed during the Christian centuries was servility, or serfdom, rather than slavery as such. The former gave the lord ownership of the serf's employment and activity in exchange for looking after his livelihood, which according to St Paul's letter to Philemon was supposed to be carried out according to human dignity, treating him as an equal brother in Christ. He was a tenant of his lord within the feudal system. It is true that in practice the serf would scarcely have been able to withdraw his service, but in the reality existing at that time, this would have left him without a livelihood, given that the range of choice was much more restricted than it is today. On the other hand, slavery meant ownership of the slave's very life, which contradicts the norm that he must be treated for his own sake and never as an instrument of another. It might be argued that servility comes very close to infringing the same value, but the progress made in this respect has required a process of social evolution. The Church never taught that slavery or serfdom was right, it simply regarded it as permissible in the circumstances. Hence, to reprimand 'serfdom' as *Gaudium et Spes* does, is not a reversal of its original position, but a development of understanding of human dignity.[49]

Revisionists argue that even those negative moral norms

---

[49] *Gaudium et Spes*, n. 71.

that have been traditionally considered universally valid and immutable admit of exceptions. They point out that the norm prohibiting killing allows for exceptions in cases of self-defence, war and capital punishment. The prohibition of killing a foetus is, they say, set aside under the terms of the principle of double effect, if the mother's life is threatened by cancer of the uterus, or an ectopic pregnancy. The norm against self-mutilation is, they say, waived in the case of organ donation. The revisionists, however, fail to take into account the four conditions for the principle of double effect. These conditions ensure that a basic value is not transgressed directly, except when another equally basic value is threatened. For this reason the principle of double effect is also called the indirectly-voluntary principle. In such cases the first value may be protected even though the second value, the foetus, or the ectopic pregnancy is lost, but this happens indirectly and is not directly desired or sought.[50] The relevant ethical principle regarding bodily mutilation is the principle of totality. This may occur, and all surgical operations are conducted in virtue of this principle, if it is in the interests of the whole person and does not harm or seriously threaten the life and well-being of the patient.[51] The prohibition on self-mutilation has been subsumed by the higher norm of saving a life by an act of heroic charity provided the conditions are met.

The result is that these so-called exceptions do not really fall under the moral norm in question, because they have a different moral object from actions classed as the direct killing of the innocent. A further instance of the same type is that of self-defence. So if an aggressor dies when a victim acts in self-defence, provided there is proportion and the other conditions of the double-effect principle are adhered to, we would say that the action was primarily aimed at saving a life rather than taking another. And wartime killing has as its object the defending of one's country, and perhaps one's freedom and livelihood, against an act of unprovoked aggression and tyranny. This is only

---

[50] For more on the principle of double effect including the conditions of its use and ectopic pregnancy see my book *The Moral Dignity of Man*, pp. 51-2, and 137-8. See also ch. 7 in the present work.

[51] See *The Moral Dignity of Man*, pp. 52-3.

superficially similar to the self-defence argument at the collective level, because waging a war is never an individual decision. A just war can only be declared by the legitimate authority of the state and must fulfil a series of conditions to be deemed just.[1] Another way of putting the point is to say that in all of these cases the moral object is different from that which is prohibited by the universally valid moral norm. This is a point which will be treated more fully in the critique of proportionalism.

---

[1] See the *Compendium of the Social Doctrine of the Church*, ch. 11, n. III for the conditions.

VI.

FREEDOM, AUTONOMY AND TRUTH

The history of modern times can be seen from one point of view as an account of the acquisition of human freedoms, individual, social and political, in accordance with the dignity and right to self-determination of persons and nations. This goes hand in hand with modernity's idea of progress understood as the gradual domination of nature, or the natural environment, by science and reason. The growth of freedom is part of this process and would signify liberation from ignorance and sub-human conditions of life leading to one's own self-fulfilment and that of society. But can one have freedom and self-fulfilment without a goal to aim at and guide one? We have already noted that genuine human advancement and progress only come about by means of moral truth and values. This enables us to make a useful distinction between freedom *for* a worthy objective, such as virtue, excellence in one or more fields, and holiness, and freedom *from* the potential slaveries of an inhuman existence. In the Enlightenment idea of freedom we see the origins of today's notion of it as unrestricted personal autonomy by putting freedom first, even before the right to life, as the cry of 'liberty, equality, fraternity' leads us to do. Modernity's concept of liberty no doubt has its usefulness, but the dangers of it are exemplified by the way the French Revolution, which attempted to put into practice Enlightenment ideas of liberty, led to the 'Terror' of Robespierre and subsequently the destruction brought about by the Marxist and Nazi dictatorships of the twentieth century.

A further truth that freedom must acknowledge, and allow itself to be limited by, is the freedom of others, although this cannot be the only condition, or the first. The principles of justice, and more specifically equality, dictate that everybody must equally enjoy freedom as long as it does not threaten the peace and stability of the common good or a nation. The link between freedom and truth does not mean that one can deny freedom of expression to those who believe in other truths, or differ from us, which, of course, is the nature of our pluralistic society. Nor does this entail that error has rights anymore than criminality does, but simply that human persons enjoy basic rights which include freedom of conscience and freedom of speech. Naturally, there are limits to this, since the common good demands that the authorities step in to restrict those who would overthrow democracy and the fundamental rights of citizens. As the United Nations *Declaration of Human Rights* tells us, "all members of the human family" have the "right to life, liberty and security of person".[2] Logically, however, life precedes liberty since without the right to life there would be no other. We, therefore, notice various conditions on the exercise of liberty which are going to mean that the principle of autonomy cannot be employed unconditionally.

Bearing in mind modernity's conception of freedom as personal autonomy it is becoming apparent why there is so much misunderstanding of the Church's teaching by secularism connected with this issue. Not only is there opposition on matters like contraception, abortion, euthanasia and embryonic stem-cell research in the name of freedom, but these things are considered 'rights' of the human person. People must be allowed to do as they see fit as long as their behaviour apparently does not do harm, or inhibit the freedom of others; often called in technical language, autonomy and non-maleficence. It is claimed ambiguously that each person enjoys his/her own moral autonomy, frequently by way of slogans such as, "it's my body to do with as I like", or "abortion is a woman's right", or "I am pro-choice", and increasingly "the right to die." One sees in these attitudes a freedom which is above all identified with individual choice and personal preference. In this

---

[2] See *The Universal Declaration of Human Rights*, article 3, 1948.

situation, which characterizes much of present European culture, ethical decisions are decided by consensus, personal preference or power. Interestingly, nobody, and no society, is a relativist when it comes to traffic laws, or the effects of obesity etc.

In the light of what we have said thus far it is not difficult to see where these ideas come from. We are able to trace back a voluntaristic conception of freedom (one in which will precedes reason) in European philosophy to the late middle ages. Such voluntarism goes together with legalism because it makes ethics depend on the will of the lawgiver, in the case of Ockham, God, and in more secular times, if God is removed from the equation, human persons themselves. Once the dependence of freedom on reason and truth is removed then freedom becomes its own lawgiver and the arbiter of moral choice. The Church's constant teaching goes in the other direction, namely that freedom can only be genuine if it is directed towards and informed by the true good of the person. If the delicate balance between freedom and truth is lost with the passage of time an individualistic and autonomous freedom emerges which does not liberate and can even destroy the freedom it cherishes both at the individual and social level. If freedom is not determined and guided by reason, it is literally irrational and not genuine liberty, but rather licence. Such a freedom has all the potential for ending up as slavery, to power, wealth, alcohol, drugs, sex, etc., when in fact it is only fully realised by ultimate truth and love in accordance with human dignity.

If we recall what we have already said about the free act it is clear that it encompasses a good deal more than free choice. By freedom, man is the principal agent of his activity, aware of acting through himself and thus master of his acts and responsible for them. We make ourselves with our free acts and to that extent freedom is concerned not just with individual actions, but also with their totality over a lifetime and so with personal fulfilment. Man is an autonomous subject, but this does not entail unlimited freedom. To will is always to will something and so freedom is not indifferent to goods and values and the inclinations to them since they are part of rational human nature. We must not confuse self-determination with indetermination, or licence to do as one wants. To ignore the natural inclinations and the goods they lead to would be to ignore reason, which, though possible for the human being, is the point at which his behaviour becomes an abuse of freedom. The moral value of man's actions depends on him judging, deciding and acting in accordance with the true good of the person. In this way freedom is always linked to the truth as Christ memorably taught, 'the truth will make you free.'[3] Only thus will the person grow in freedom and gain dominion over him or herself. If, on the contrary, he acts against conscience and truth knowingly, he will easily become enslaved to his passions and fall into behaviour below human dignity, as St Paul says to the Galatians.[4] Thus, if man pursues his freedom irresponsibly he exposes himself to losing it.

In *Veritatis Splendor,* the Pope explained that since the crisis of truth affects natural law and ethical principles it also affects conscience. He wrote, "once the idea of a universal truth about the good, knowable by human reason, is lost, inevitably the notion of conscience also changes. Conscience is no longer considered in its prime reality as an act of a person's intelligence, the function of which is to apply the universal knowledge of the good in a specific situation and thus to express a judgement about the right conduct to be chosen here and now. Instead there is a tendency to grant to the individual conscience the prerogative of independently determining the criteria of good and evil and then acting accordingly. Such an outlook is quite congenial to an individualist ethic, wherein each individual is faced with his own truth different from the truth of others."[5]

Scripture and Magisterium

For fallen human nature there are dangers in freedom as well as opportunities. Man's freedom is obscured by his inability to see the truth fully due to original sin. So true liberty is opposed by error and ignorance, by the passions and moral weakness of human nature. St Paul warns, "Do not be conformed to this world",[6] and

---

[3] Jn 8:32.
[4] Gal 5:13.
[5] John Paul II, *Veritatis Splendor*, n. 32.
[6] Rom 12:2.

"Do not use your freedom as an opportunity for the flesh."[7] If it is not used according to the truth it becomes licence and slavery. For this reason Christ has 'set us free for freedom.'[8] Freedom itself has had to be redeemed. Only when freedom is lived 'according to the spirit', that is, directed to its true end and good, is one truly free, otherwise one is enslaved in one way or another.

It is because of this equivocal character of liberty that Vatican II speaks of 'genuine freedom': "Genuine freedom is an outstanding manifestation of the divine image in man. For God willed to leave man 'in the power of his own counsel' (cf. Sir 15:14) so that man would seek his Creator of his own accord and would freely arrive at full and blessed perfection by cleaving to God."[9] These words indicate the depth of sharing in God's creation to which man has been called. God has entrusted not only the world, but man himself to his own care and responsibility so that he may attain his perfection by seeking his Creator. Freedom consists not simply in doing what one likes, but in doing what one ought. It can, of course, be used to sin (though Our Lord who was free could not sin), though this is an abuse of freedom which does not lead to liberation, but to slavery.

True freedom for this reason looks to the world like anti-freedom. It requires self-giving instead of self-will and selfishness, and domination and moderation of the passions, instead of self-indulgence. It comes through the acceptance of suffering and pain, (in the elderly, the disabled, an extra or difficult child in the family), which the world recoils from. Christians affirm that Christ has won our freedom for us on the Cross and for each of us this means being a follower of Christ crucified in the painful situations of life. Hence freedom does not consist in doing as one likes, but rather in the sincere gift of oneself to the service of God and others, or as the Gospel says, losing one's life in order to gain it.

Those who see morality rooted in individual choice consider the natural law or a moral code to be an imposition on one, limiting individual choice and therefore freedom. Such thinkers see obedience to a law of God as a *heteronomy*, an imposition

---

[7] Gal 5:13.
[8] Cf. Gal 5:1.
[9] *Gaudium et Spes*, n. 17.

from outside restricting freedom. They fail to see that God respects and treats us according to our freedom and that by reason man actually participates in the eternal law enabling him to act according to his own lights. His autonomy consists in this participation and he is able to make his own choices in virtue of the light it accords to him. In other words, natural lawyers, religious people, and, one suspects, the majority, see law not as inhibiting freedom, but as facilitating it and leading you to your true well-being and fulfilment. Truth and law, and indeed nature properly understood, are not opposed to freedom but actually enable it. The Church does not oppress but liberates, the Commandments do not restrict but vivify.

The truth of this teaching is spelt out in the Book of Genesis. Man has abundant freedom in Paradise. He is told, "you may eat of any tree in the garden", but there was a limit: "of the tree of the knowledge of good and evil you shall not eat. On the day you do eat you shall die."[10] When the devil encourages them with the words, "you shall be like God knowing good and evil", he is tempting them to cross the threshold between Creator and creature, between truth and falsehood, and be arbiters of good and evil and dictate moral norms to themselves.[11] Their freedom and clarity of vision are diminished by doing this, and by the resulting separation from God, they lose the fullness of freedom and self-dominion. Man is not the author of the moral order, he is not the arbiter of good and evil. Our very rationality and freedom are a participation in that of God Himself. We are free and autonomous, but under the universal autonomy of God.

In opposition, then, to those who see a higher law as an imposition and *heteronomy,* John Paul II writes:

> Others speak, and rightly so of *theonomy,* or *participated theonomy,* since man's free obedience to God's law effectively implies that human reason and human will participate in God's wisdom and providence. By forbidding man to 'eat of the tree of the knowledge of good and evil', God makes it clear that man does not originally possess such 'knowledge' as something properly his own, but only participates in it by the light of

---

[10] Gen 2:16-17.
[11] Gen 3:5.

natural reason and Divine Revelation ... by submitting to the law, freedom submits to the truth of creation.[12]

That freedom is not absolute and independent of our natural limitations, is obvious to common sense. One may like to drive Jaguar cars, or eat in expensive restaurants, and go on exotic foreign holidays, but the children's education has to come first. Equally, one is restricted by the rights of one's neighbours, as well as by one's own qualifications, skills and attainments when it comes to education and employment. Freedom is limited, therefore, by one's relations with others and the duty to respect their freedom. The dignity of each person implies the equality of each individual. The freedom to grow the garden hedge higher is limited by the right of the neighbours to enjoy sunlight, views etc. One would not normally consider that these things took away autonomy or independence even though they restrict choice. We think it natural that freedom is limited because it is human freedom, but it is none the less freedom; indeed limited freedom is the only one we have.

'Modern Freedom': Freedom of Indifference

Modern culture leads many of our contemporaries to see freedom in another way and the recent work of Servais Pinckaers has thrown instructive light on the origins of this.[13] For William of Ockham, following St Bonaventure and Scotus, who emphasized the superiority of will over intellect, in contrast to Aquinas, freedom actually *precedes* reason and will, since it is necessary to put them into action. The importance of this is that it has influenced the modern notion of freedom, and particularly the contemporary concept of moral autonomy. Ockham explained that we can choose whether to know or not to know, to will or not to will. This changed Peter Lombard's classic definition adopted by Aquinas: "Free will is that faculty of reason and will whereby one chooses the good with the help of grace and evil without that help."[14] Aquinas explained that freedom was an act of practical

---

[12] John Paul II, *Veritatis Splendor*, n. 41.
[13] Servais Pinckaers, *The Sources of Christian Ethics*, T & T Clark, Edinburgh, 1995, pp. 242ff, 330ff.
[14] "Liberum vero arbitrium est facultas rationis et voluntatis, qua bonum eligitur gratia

judgement *proceeding from* the prior deliberation of reason and will and leading to an act of choice. On the other hand, Ockham believed that freedom, or free will, *preceded* reason and will in order to move them to act.

Ockham tended to identify freedom with the will which is characterized by its ability to choose contraries or opposites, that is to decide to will or not, to act or not, to act according to reason, or according to the law or not. The will is indifferent to all of these choices and can be used as such, hence this view is given the name freedom of indifference. It is also free and indifferent to its ultimate end. His view therefore plays down finality in ethics. Freedom, according to this opinion, does not consist in attraction to the good and the true, exercised through love and desire, as in Aquinas. The core of freedom is precisely in radical indifference to inclinations and desires. We thus have a freedom which is in disharmony with human nature and the natural inclinations and fundamental goods, and tends to break up the different elements of the human personality and indeed, in some cases, oppose them to one another.[15]

This had the effect, whether intended or not, of separating freedom from its guiding principle of right reason and gradually loosening its connection to the truth. It describes human behaviour as a series of atomic acts, each one having no connection with those that go before, or afterwards. In doing this, it excludes and virtually denies that morality consists in the continuous and gradual growth of good habits and virtues and the ongoing tendency to a final goal. In place of the virtues, it emphasizes law and obligation. At the same time, paradoxically, it sets up a confrontation between freedom and law, because freedom is complete autonomy and law limits that. Your freedom begins where the law ends.

The voluntarist position of Ockham emphasizes the separation between freedom and the basic natural inclinations to life, knowledge, friendship, and even to the good itself, and from one's ultimate end and happiness. By making freedom antecedent to

---

assistente, vel malum eadem desistente" (Lombard, *Sent.* II, dist. 24, c. 3), quoted in Pinckaers, op. cit., p. 331.

[15] I am dependent in this section on the work of Pinckaers, op. cit., p. 243.

these tendencies it implicitly denies that it works in harmony with them. Later on, when Descartes makes man a dualism of spirit and matter, biological nature will be opposed not only to spirit but also to freedom since this is located in the sphere of spirit.

Thus in modern times freedom becomes the foremost right after life itself and the liberal tradition is born. We need look no further than the Lockean-inspired first line of the American Constitution, which guarantees the right to "life, liberty and the pursuit of happiness." No mention of truth or reason here. The primacy of liberty in Locke's philosophy is manifested by the emphasis he put on private property which guarantees it.

The Inadequacy of Freedom of Indifference

Man cannot claim freedom before, and to the exclusion of, all other goods that perfect the person. I don't have freedom in the first place, I have an intellect and a will. I cannot do anything I want with my freedom if I am not to risk losing it. Or rather, I am free to do all things but not all things are convenient. Genuine freedom, then, does not consist in pure indetermination, or autonomy, but rather it provides the potential for moral growth, personal fulfilment and excellence. It is not opposed to the natural inclinations, to law or to truth or grace, but is designed to work for and along with them.

Of course, it can work against them, but this is a defect of freedom rather than the essence of it, the freedom to sin which eventually is destructive. But you might say, freedom means independence and autonomy if it means anything. It means self-determination. Yes indeed, but self-determination to one's true end and goodness. Revelation explains this to us. Man could eat of any tree in the garden with the exception of the 'tree of the knowledge of good and evil'. There were limits to man's freedom. Truth and freedom are given to him; it is not in his power to determine them for himself. The mistake is to put will before reason, and therefore freedom before truth, which is what we mean by voluntarism.

The separation of freedom from truth entails ethical relativism, because it means that moral values depend on the subjective opinion of individuals or groups. Many rejoice at this, thinking it means more autonomy for the individual, but in fact it ends up leaving the individual more vulnerable. If ethical values are in the gift of individual choice then so are human rights and what is to stop a tyrannous regime taking power and making laws which put the rights, and even the lives, of the majority of human beings in jeopardy? If there are no moral absolutes this scenario is always a possibility. An alliance between permissive morality and democracy, where indeed it exists, as it surely does, finishes up threatening the very basis of the democracy.

Consequently, authentic freedom is founded on a rationally based and knowable moral order. And, therefore, freedom cannot precede basic, self-evident ethical principles, rationally known, but is dependent on, and subject to, them. How can there be freedom unless there are goods and values to make choices about? And this implies an ethical order. Man can, of course, use his freedom to ignore it and turn his back on it, but then he is pursuing false goods and following an illusory freedom. He is putting freedom before truth and the ethical order and must face the consequences.

For many of our contemporaries freedom is simply the response to instinctive forces, and will to power and enjoyment. It is independent of reason and truth and objective universal moral norms. It has ceased to be based on rational deliberation. As a consequence, all sorts of desires and claims are dressed up as 'human rights', such as the 'right' to an abortion or conversely to have a child, 'gay rights', or the claim that cohabitation has the same legal status as marriage. For Hume, for example, morals and therefore freedom were founded not on reason but on emotion, but a freedom which is not rational cannot be *human* freedom. What characterizes man is rationality which should guide him, and not emotion or instinct. Man is capable of acting against what is objectively good and truthful but he has a prior obligation to seek it. And that search is a rational one.

Those who hold such views see law as restricting freedom, and moral norms, or commandments, as a burden. They are unable to see that the law and the truth actually fulfil you and lead you to your goal. In the process they liberate you from your own limitations, fallen passions and the disorders of human nature. Most people would agree that the exercise of freedom must be responsible. It must not harm others, and insofar as possible, it must not harm oneself. So we take the steps we can as a society to stop people committing suicide, or harming themselves through drugs etc. When we say freedom should be responsible we mean it should be accountable and reasonable, that is, it should be exercised within the limits of right reason. But the object of reason is the truth. Reason judges and decides and concludes and learns in each case with the intention of acquiring true knowledge. This is what is meant by linking freedom and truth.

Freedom for Excellence

In contrast, the Thomistic and Catholic account of freedom may be called, with Pinckaers, freedom for excellence, because the human inclinations and appetites lead you, when guided by reason and law, harmoniously to your overall fulfilment. The moral subject goes through stages of growth, from beginner, through the progress and development of the virtues, to moral maturity and genuine freedom. This freedom consists in self-mastery and dominion and requires moral education. Hence, morals involve a training in the use of freedom throughout the whole of one's life. Freedom is not just freedom *from* oppression, ignorance, poverty etc., but freedom *for* moral, personal and social growth.

We saw above that man is the principal agent of his own activity, and that this self-determination implies self-consciousness and self-possession. But if this is the case, he must be accountable for it. He cannot transfer this responsibility to anybody else, since no one else has been a cause of his actions. He is aware of his actions as the subject of them, and the goods and values to which his actions are directed. This awareness of moral actions and values is conscience.

Furthermore, these actions also change and determine him as a person, as a subject. His actions and choices are not only free and accountable but also self-determining, that is to say, he makes himself to be the person he is and becomes and is responsible for the way he turns out. John Paul II finds a basis for this idea in St Gregory of Nyssa: "Now human life is always subject to change; it needs to be born ever anew ... but here birth does not come about by a foreign intervention, as is the case with bodily beings ...; it is the result of free choice. Thus we *are* in a certain way our own parents, creating ourselves as we will, by our decisions."[16]

Freedom, then, is not just the power to say 'yes' and 'no', or to choose this or that, but rather the ability to choose the good, and hence to attain personal fulfilment and happiness. Our freedom is given to us so that we may grow morally. Each act leads towards or away from that growth. We are destined to be whole and fulfilled human beings. As the well-known expression of St Irenaeus says, "The glory of God is man fully alive and the life of man is the vision of God".[17] The painter, journalist, poet, statesman and sportsman, or woman, who attain stature in their field have made good use of their freedom in that area of endeavour. The person who does this with regard to the meaning of life as a whole is a fully free and fulfilled human being. Freedom, then, is to attain excellence in the art and purpose of life.

That is why the Catechism in describing freedom speaks not only of individual choice, but of a power to shape one's whole life. It can only do this when it is aimed at the basic and true goods of the human person. It explains: "Freedom is the power rooted in reason and will, to act or not to act, to do this or that, and so to perform deliberate actions on one's own responsibility. By free will one shapes one's own life. Human freedom is a force for growth and maturity in truth and goodness; it attains its perfection when directed towards God our beatitude."[18] It, therefore, has the double purpose of enabling us to make individual choices and more globally and importantly to fulfil ourselves as persons.

Freedom dependent on the Ultimate Good and the Natural Inclinations

Freedom includes choice but the final end of man is not a matter of choice, because of freedom's dependence on the will and its appetite for universal goodness. In order to identify the ultimate

---

[16] John Paul II, *Veritatis Splendor*, n. 71.
[17] St Irenaeus, *Adv. Haer.* IV, 20, 7 : PG 7, 1037.
[18] CCC, 1731.

good we must ask ourselves with Aristotle which good is willed for its own sake. This will be the ultimate one. In practice, we will more immediate particular goods like the well-being of the family, employment, professional success, health or friendship, but these can also be treated as means to further ends. Nevertheless, the line comes to an end in happiness which is willed by all of us and cannot be a means to any further end. Though one cannot choose a different last end, one is still free to act in favour, or against it. While desiring their ultimate happiness, automatically men conceive it in different ways. If man were presented directly with the fullness of good there would be no option, but no created good exhausts goodness and in this life God can only be known imperfectly by man.

Only a good which is spiritual and universal can be adequate to satisfy the human will given the nature of the human person. The universal good is the foundation of freedom. The ultimate goal of the will transcends any limited material good, such as wealth, power, fame etc., and indeed all individual goods, and seeks happiness without end. This is testified to in the phenomenon of addiction. If one seeks happiness in drink or drugs etc., one constantly pursues more of the same in search of the elusive felicity. The will is never satisfied and in this very dissatisfaction we can see the universal nature of the will and its unlimited desire for fulfilment. It follows from this that the person is fully free when he, or she, makes the right choices, or takes the requisite steps to their ultimate end or good, i.e. to the truth.

The choice of the ultimate goal of our life may be said to be a 'fundamental option'. There are indeed in life small choices like how to decorate the bedroom, large choices, like the choice to contracept, and fundamental choices like those that determine the course of one's life, such as the choice to marry, the choice of career, or to be a priest etc. However, John Paul II identifies the fundamental option with a specific act of choice and rejects the sharp distinction between this and everyday choices that the revisionists and proportionalists make. All our free choices lead us to the person we become and thus to our ultimate end, even though some are bigger and more fundamental decisions than others.[19]

---

[19] Cf. John Paul II, *Veritatis Splendor*, n. 65.

Freedom, then, is not indifferent to the truth and other 'reasons', such as the basic goods of the person, inclining it to judge in one way or another. Nor is it opposed to man's nature or the other natural inclinations such as those to life and friendship, but rather acts in harmony with them, because it is not anterior to them, but part and parcel of them. Nor is it opposed to law, because law is a rule of reason, which is discerned in accordance with the very natural inclinations, and goods of the human person. For the same reason freedom is not opposed to grace, because God respects man's freedom and nature, and grace builds on the natural inclinations, and goods of man, in order to turn them into virtues and perfect them. Since true freedom consists in love of the supreme good and of those goods of the person which are basic participations in it, we can say that freedom is fulfilled in love and charity. Given that this is the purpose of the Commandments they are not an obstacle to freedom but the path to its fulfilment.

We caught a glimpse in the last chapter of the opposition which elements of our culture see between person and nature. From the same root comes an alleged opposition between freedom and nature, due once again to a dualistic anthropology and shifts in the meaning of nature, or denial of its existence. The latter is taken to mean anything below man, or to signify the material creation. The person and freedom are identified with spirit, and nature with matter, and it is the task of rationality to dominate and shape brute nature, including the human body, to its designs. One can see that from these presuppositions proceed many of today's bio-medical activities, be they IVF, embryo experimentation, embryonic stem-cell research, cloning, and trans-gender operations which do not respect the truth and dignity of the human person. In these cases the human body is used as raw material for alleged scientific and humanitarian purposes and benefits, as part of man's dominion over nature in the name of progress.

At the root of this is a lack of respect for the dignity of the human body which is lost sight of, and which in turn proceeds from treating the person as a dualism of spirit and matter rather than as an integral whole. The person is separated from their nature and, therefore, from their body. Freedom which is identified with the person is thus in confrontation with nature, which is more or less to say freedom is self-defining and creates its own values: "Indeed, when all is said and done man would not even have a nature; he would be his own personal life-project. Man would be nothing more than his own freedom." [20]

If, however, the truth of the human being is discerned in the unity of his/her spiritual and biological inclinations, then freedom will be understood not to be opposed to any part of the nature of the human person, but to be part of it. Freedom will respect this truth of the composite unity of the human person and work in harmony with it. Man's freedom is part of his creaturely condition as 'image of God' and, therefore, limited. It is subject above all to the truth about man, as *Veritatis Splendor* confirms. "This moral theory", it says, speaking about proportionalism, "does not correspond to the truth about man and his freedom. It contradicts the *Church's teachings on the unity of the human person,* whose rational soul is *per se et essentialiter* the form of the body."[21]

Freedom is only genuine and truly beneficial to mankind if it is guided by the truth of the person in the integrity of his rational and sensible faculties and inclinations which all work together according to the unity of the person. The Church's definitions on the unity of the person, says *Veritatis Splendor,* "remind us that reason and free will are linked with all the bodily and sense faculties";[22] in other words, all man's activities, even those done mainly with the body, are also rational and spiritual in virtue of the unity. This entails that freedom may not unconditionally shape the body and bodily life according to its designs, but must recognize that it is limited by it and more specifically by the moral value that human dignity gives to the body.

Freedom and Moral Absolutes

It will also be asked whether the dogmatic truths of faith and the absolute nature of some moral principles are not opposed to the freedom of the individual. They may well be opposed to some of the 'freedoms' we have discussed above, but not to a

---

[20] *Veritatis Splendor*, n. 46.
[21] Ibid., n. 48; and Council of Vienne, DS, 902.
[22] *Veritatis Splendor*, n. 48.

genuine freedom because both dogma and morals have truth as their foundation. This question should also be considered in its personal and collective dimensions.

Our autonomy is really a share in the autonomy of God. That is why it is not opposed to it. The very fact that we participate by reason in the eternal law and wisdom of God and know them as reflected in ourselves, is part of that freedom; freedom, that is, to share and live in the truth. It is proof that we are fundamentally spiritual beings who transcend the purely material level. There is no real morality without God, which does not mean that it cannot be known independently of Revelation. Indeed without God man himself is threatened. Man is indeed autonomous and self-determining, but under the universal autonomy of God.

Vatican II warns against a false concept of autonomy, i.e. one which would maintain, "that created things are not dependent on God and that man can use them without reference to the Creator."[23] On the other hand, the Council emphasizes the role of human reason in discovering and applying the moral law. But reason draws its own truth and authority from the eternal law not from itself. The rightful autonomy of man is that he possesses in himself his own law, received from the Creator. Autonomy cannot mean that reason itself creates values and moral norms.[24]

There are those who express a legitimate concern, more especially given the history of the last century, that a universal, or what they call a utopian, truth, valid for all on fundamentals, leads to dogmatism and is to the detriment of individual liberty. Two things may be noted here. Firstly, this tends to overlook the fact that it is *false* dogmatism that destroys freedom and, secondly, there is a need to distinguish between eternal realities to which dogma pertains and temporal ones where different opinions can be equally valid, or where they may need to be revised with the passage of time. Newman pointed out in *The Development of Christian Doctrine*, that truth needed to change and develop in order to stay the same since it faced different challenges and

---

[23] *Gaudium et Spes*, n. 36.
[24] Cf. *Veritatis Splendor*, n. 40.

controversies at different times and in this sense he concluded in some famous words, "In a higher world it is otherwise, but here below to live is to change, and to be perfect is to have changed often."[25]

In a word, truth itself is changeable or unchangeable according to whether it deals with temporal or eternal reality. It is a mistake, by no means unknown to human nature, to relativize dogmatic matters and dogmatize in opinable areas. Saint Josemaria Escriva constantly alluded to this point. "There are no dogmas in temporal affairs" he wrote. "To try to set up absolute truths in matters where the individual sees things from his own point of view, in terms of his own interest, his cultural preference and his own experience: this insults the dignity of man." He continued, "I am of the opinion that a Christian has to be passionately interested in civil and social progress while realizing the limitations of his own opinions thus respecting the opinions of others and showing love for legitimate pluralism."[26] Only a handful of moral norms are absolutes. Questions like the suitability of wind farms rightly admit of different opinions.

Equally, those who want to make all moral norms relative and reduce all law to positive law, made by man, are always subject to the danger that a regime will come along and impose its own system of justice on people who would have no recourse if all law and rights are dependent on the representative will of the people, the Assembly, etc. For this reason there must be a universal system of human rights and law independently of promulgation by any human authority and to which all such authorities must be made to answer.

Then questions are asked about whether a universal moral law incorporating absolutes is compatible with the freedom and individuality of the person. We have already said that in granting liberty God respects the freedom of secondary causes and by extension, therefore, their individuality. A universal truth about the good is not in any way opposed to the freedom of the individual, because it depends upon the very nature of the human

---

[25] J.H. Newman, *An Essay on the Development of Christian Doctrine*, Sheed and Ward, London & New York, 1960, p. 30.
[26] St Josemaria Escriva, *The Riches of Faith*, article in *ABC*, Madrid, 2-XI-1969.

person of which freedom is a part. Only if freedom is considered an absolute is there a conflict, but then the conflict is with truth itself and the nature of reason, not simply with the good.

Freedom and the Magisterium

In the years following the Second Vatican Council it was not infrequent to hear a theologian here and there claiming that while the Magisterium taught authoritatively on matters of faith this was not the case in morals and indeed the Church had not defined definitively any moral truths. This claim, of course, ignored what was said in *Lumen Gentium* (25), that the Magisterium speaks either through the solemn judgement of the Pope or ecumenical Council, or by the universal and ordinary day to day teaching of the Pope or of the bishops together in Council in communion with the Pope. In the first place, Catholics must believe with divine faith everything contained in the Word of God either written or handed down and proposed by the Church as divinely revealed, either in solemn, or ordinary, Magisterium. One can think here of the Church's teaching on the indissolubility of marriage, or the killing of the innocent.

In the second place, there are matters which, though not explicitly referred to in divine revelation, have an inseparable link with those that are. Pope John Paul said in *Ad Tuendam Fidem*, that "everything set forth definitively by the Magisterium of the Church regarding teaching on faith and morals must be firmly accepted and held; namely those things required for the holy keeping and faithful exposition of the faith; and therefore anyone who rejects propositions which are to be held definitively sets himself against the teaching of the Catholic Church."[27] The reference here is to doctrines which, though not proposed as divinely revealed, have an intrinsic connection with teachings of faith and morals and must be held with Catholic faith. Into this category fits, for example, the doctrine on euthanasia which, though not explicitly referred to in Scripture, has a logical connection with the prohibition on the taking of innocent human life. The Pope made this clear in

---

[27] Pope John Paul II, Apostolic Letter Motu Proprio, *Ad Tuendam Fidem*, (To Protect the Faith), 1998.

Evangelium Vitae, recalling that euthanasia is "a grave violation of the law of God" and declaring that "this doctrine is based on the natural law and upon the written Word of God, is transmitted by the Church's Tradition and taught by the ordinary and universal Magisterium."[28]

The third paragraph of the Profession of Faith states: "Moreover, I adhere with submission of will and intellect to the teachings which either the Roman Pontiff or the College of Bishops enunciate when they exercise their authentic Magisterium, even if they do not intend to proclaim these teachings by definitive act."[29] These teachings are an 'authentic expression of the ordinary Magisterium' and require religious submission of mind and will. The purpose of them is "to arrive at a deeper understanding of revelation, or to recall the conformity of a teaching with the truths of faith, or lastly to warn against ideas incompatible with these truths, or against dangerous opinions that can lead to error."[30] How do we recognise them? The non-definitive teachings set forth require different degrees of adherence according to the mind and will of the Magisterium which is shown "by the nature of the documents, by the frequent repetition of the same doctrine, or by the tenor of the verbal expression."[31]

In *Veritatis Splendor,* the Pope notes that rational reflection and daily experience remind us of the fragility of human freedom and its judgements.[32] The teaching of the Church in helping us to form our consciences is only giving us the criteria which we can find out for ourselves. In this sense it not imposing it on us, because the teaching of Christ authentically passed on by the Church is not a sort of force extrinsic to us, but simply presenting us with those elements which a well formed conscience will already have. The doctrine of faith includes a behaviour which the followers of Christ must strive to grow in constantly and be converted to, and therefore the teachings of the Magisterium should be accepted with the obedience of faith, also in moral matters where these

---

[28] Pope John Paul II, *Evangelium Vitae,* n. 65.
[29] *Ad Tuendam Fidem,* n. 2.
[30] Ibid., Explanatory note, n. 10.
[31] Ibid., Explanatory note, n. 11.
[32] *Veritatis Splendor,* n. 86.

have been definitively defined. These are no more than the truth and good of the human person which we are enabled to see more clearly in the light and truth which is Christ. The universality and immutability of the moral norm, far from being an imposition, serves and protects the personal dignity and inviolability of man and his basic goods and rights.[33]

Freedom to be Wrong as well as Right: Tolerance

This conclusion leads to a further question, but this time in reference to society at large: does freedom only consist in the freedom to be right, virtuous and so on? Or must we also allow a freedom to be wrong, evil, wicked etc? Speaking of Edmund Burke, Isaiah Berlin, a highly acclaimed writer on modern liberty, says,

> his doctrine of freedom, like Montesquieu's, tells us that man is only free to do what is right – there is not freedom of choice to act according to one's, perhaps deeply mistaken, convictions. If these beliefs are believed as anti-social or disgusting in some other way, then they infringe freedom. But liberty is surely what we normally mean by the word: freedom to be wrong as well as right, wicked as well as virtuous except that in the case of too much wrong or wickedness it is right to restrain such conduct. But restraint is not freedom ...[34]

In the present world, clearly, the rights of those whose views and actions are opposed to Christian, or accepted, moral standards, may have to be tolerated in some cases, provided that they do not cause major harm to the individual and the common good and public order. This was part of the purpose of Vatican II's teaching that religious liberty and freedom of conscience were fundamental human rights. But this does not mean error or wickedness is of the essence of liberty, since as the *Catechism* puts it, "the choice to disobey and do evil is an abuse of freedom".[35] Christ Himself, after all, was incapable of sin and yet perfectly free. Our response to Berlin is to reiterate that the fulfilment of freedom is in the attainment of the good and, therefore

---

[33] Ibid., n. 90.
[34] Conor Cruise O'Brien, *The Great Melody*, Sinclair-Stevenson, London, 1992, pp. 612-13.
[35] See CCC 1733.

in love and charity, as already outlined. The question, however, can be addressed both on the personal, or individual level, and also on the collective level of the public good, and therefore concerns the extent to which the civil law should uphold morals.

The Council was perfectly clear in drawing out the conclusions that had always been latent in general moral theology. Man has a right and a duty to follow a true conscience and also an invincibly ignorant one. In other words, those who are in good faith and ignorant of true moral norms through no fault of their own, must be respected in what their conscience tells them. This does not mean that error has rights, but simply that human beings and their consciences do. If they are in good faith they will, however, be seeking to inform their conscience and attain a fuller grasp of the truth. Such a person, though, is in a different position from the one who errs as a result of negligence and laziness, or indeed cultivates ignorance so as not to have to change his behaviour and be converted. This position is blameworthy and does not fulfil the Council's teaching about the obligation to seek the truth more fully all the time. What must be followed is not simply a certain conscience but a true one.

Since freedom and truth are in harmony and not opposition then man's freedom has nothing to fear from the truth, indeed it can only grow by acquaintance with it. Nor has the Church anything to fear from respecting those who err provided she insists on the obligation to seek the truth and proclaims it herself. Evil and error may sometimes be tolerated in the interests of a greater good, although we "may never do evil that good may come of it."[36] It may sometimes be necessary for the law not to prohibit, or penalize, certain forms of action (e.g. private homosexual ones), for the common good, but this is wholly different from approving it. Toleration never amounts to condoning the error, or the evil, that is perpetrated.

Morality, Civil Law and the Common Good

Isaiah Berlin raises the question of the right to be wrong, or 'wicked', and the common good, or public order. It is true that morality and law are not co-extensive in the sense that the law does not have an

---

[36] Cf. Rom 3:8.

obligation to enforce private morality in all respects. It must do so in matters which concern human life, since the State must ensure protection to everybody of what is the most basic right on which all others depend. However, it has long been recognized in the case of adultery and more recently in that of homosexuality that to penalize these actions among consenting adults can do more harm to the common good and to family life than de-penalizing them. They are thus 'tolerated' by law, rather than being mandated or encouraged by it. It is not the duty of the State to make people morally good, but rather to maintain public order and create the conditions for its citizens to live morally and virtuously.

What this tells us is that some choices are communal and social, though made by individuals, or a representative assembly or parliament on behalf of the citizens. If these choices are wrong, or wicked to use Berlin's phrase, and are tolerated and then accepted by society, they become embedded in the culture of that society. In this way, for example, the pro-choice position on abortion, or a "woman's right to choose" as the slogan has it, becomes an accepted principle of the time. This is the reality of social sin. A Christian who believes and reasons that a foetus is a living human being and the abortion of it an act that is intrinsically evil and always wrong to do on account of its object which is incompatible with the good of life of a human person, cannot at the same time vote to allow it for others. The basic good of life, the prohibition of doing harm to others, and the fundamental right to life do not allow of toleration of abortion by the civil law; though this is not true of adultery or homosexual acts. Why is this?

A milestone in matters of morality and law was the Wolfenden Report in England in 1957, which recommended that homosexuality between consenting adults in private not be prohibited and punished by law. This recommendation was later put on the statute book and Cardinal Heenan is reported as saying at the time: "It may be, however, that the civil law cannot effectively control such acts (private acts which affect the common good) without doing more harm to the common good than the acts themselves would do. In that case it would be necessary in the interests of the common good to tolerate without approving such acts."[37] The same doctrine applies to adultery since the imprisonment of a spouse would do great harm to family life. Notice that we are saying here the law may *permit* but not *condone*, we are not saying that the law makes these actions morally acceptable. They, too, are ethically intrinsically evil acts, but law and morality are not entirely co-extensive, and it is not the former's task to outlaw all sin, but to uphold human rights, public order and the common good and it operates within this remit.

There are, then, limits to this principle. For example, the State has the duty to protect the right to human life at all times by prohibiting and penalizing adequately its transgression, given the fundamental nature of this right, and the fact that it also affects the lives of third parties and that all other human rights depend on it. This is also true of the procreation of life and the right of children to be born of the personal love and marriage of their parents and not in a laboratory.[38] Christians are not trying to impose their views, but simply standing up for the rights of the unborn embryo and endeavouring to persuade mankind to approximate more to the truth. If not, and morality is consensus, where we all give a little, the right to life of the unborn and the elderly is compromised. We have recent historical experience (e.g. Nazi Germany) of the dangers of a State that can arbitrarily take the lives of its citizens. Furthermore, citizens are all but expected to uphold a law in public (doctors and pharmacists and even clergy), which goes against their conscience and religious belief. In this case, it is the State 'imposing' its ideology. If morality is in the gift of the individual and groups, one day it could be in the hands of a powerful clique that would use it to tyrannize over the majority and abuse human rights.

It should also be noted that Isaiah Berlin writes in the tradition of liberty which traces its roots back to 'freedom of indifference', spoken of above, that stresses the primacy of will and its separation from reason and truth. In departing from Peter Lombard's and Aquinas' definition as 'the power to reason and will', it sets in train a series of subtle nuances leading to contemporary relativism

---

[37] Quoted in Denis O'Callaghan, 'Theology 6: Law and Morality', *The Furrow* 22, pp. 358-9.
[38] Cf. *Instruction on Respect for Human Life in its Origin and on The Dignity of Procreation*, (*Donum Vitae*), CDF, Rome, 1987.

which is opposed to Christian freedom. As regards the State's toleration of badness or wickedness, the limit is reached by the State's duty to protect human life which is an integral part of the common good. So, the fact that a person is in pain, or imagines future suffering, and invokes the principle of autonomy to end their life, is not a sufficient condition. We all have duties to others, to society and to the common good, as well as to ourselves, which make up the principle of solidarity. This, together with the principles of equality, and non-maleficence, referred to above, mean that we do not have power over human life, our own, or others, making it wrong, not only to take life, but also to assist, or encourage, others to do so.

The common good, it should be noted, is not just the sum total of all individual goods, it is an integral part of the individual good of each one, that is, the personal good of everyone includes a concern for the good of others, not just our own. This translates into a duty to promote justice, fairness and equality as well as the charity which consists in wanting the good of the other person. The Church's statements of social morality have this concern as their motivation. Freedom both of the Church as a whole and the individual is directed not only to truth but ultimately to love because the will is orientated to the supreme good and the good of others. In contrast to all doctrines of self-interest, the disinterested and generous welfare of others is an essential part of one's own good and freedom.

PART II

CONTROVERSY AND RENEWAL

VII.

MORAL REVISIONISM: PROPORTIONALISM AND THE FUNDAMENTAL OPTION

Moral revisionists tend to underplay the importance of individual actions and insist on the overall moral character of the person, of his actions taken together and the consideration of the totality of circumstances involved. They would agree that a moral act is one done willingly and knowingly by a human subject, but would draw the line at saying that each of these acts can be classified as good or evil on all occasions independently of the facts of the case. They ask whether you can judge morality by one action without taking into account the overall moral worth of the person. It is argued that morality is not just about conformity of human actions to the moral law, but about virtues and vices and these take time to develop. Hence, to judge the moral character of a person you have to take into account the totality of his actions.

The 'situation ethics' of the 1940s and 50s which had already made these points, became the moral revisionism of the 60s and 70s onwards, above all as a result of the efforts of revisionists to justify some contraceptive acts after the invention of the birth control pill. Some said that contraception was justifiable and was only prohibited previously because of an overly biological, or physicalistic, view of the natural law, a position considered above. Others, however, agreed that contraception is not licit as a general rule, but disagreed with *Humanae Vitae's* teaching that it was wrong *on each and every occasion.*

They maintained that it can be justified in certain circumstances. In doing so they take issue with the assertion that it is absolutely wrong, or an intrinsically evil act, that is, an action that is always wrong independently of circumstances and intentions, simply as a result of the nature of the act and its object. But many of them soon came to see that the logic of this position means that if actions, hitherto considered intrinsically evil, can sometimes be judged as permissible, then this also applies to other actions such as homosexual acts, abortion and euthanasia under certain well defined circumstances as well. It also means that you have to take issue with the whole system which makes them moral absolutes, and the way moral absolutes are described.

Moral revisionism, or proportionalism, is offered as such a system which rationalizes this position and incorporates a number of observations made by well known theologians of the 1960s. According to Rahner, the natural law is objective and formal and can never cover all the circumstances of a particular act, or the peculiarities of a subjective dilemma. This is due to his historicist understanding of human nature which is never fixed and immutable, according to this view, but conditioned by the culture of the time which always determines one's self-understanding. He thus sees an opposition between subject and object, at least in some circumstances. For similar historicist reasons, Fuchs will go on to say that it is the concrete situation which each person finds themselves in, that is truly objective, since moral norms are produced by the mind and so are always, to some extent, conditioned by the limitations of the cultural situation obtaining at the time at which they are formulated.[1] And Häring will conclude that the Commandments and the moral norms of the Gospel represent an ideal to tend towards. Hence, conscience has to be 'creative' in its task of applying the law and makes its decision on the merits of each case. This means that it should apply the law in its fundamental orientation but not necessarily in its concrete normative directives.[2] This puts conscience above the law rather than being a faithful interpreter of it. According to

---

[1] See Livio Melina, *Moral: entre la crisis y la renovacion*, Ediciones Internacionales Universitarias, Madrid, 1998, 2nd edition, pp. 52-3, 111-12, 114.
[2] Ibid., p. 113.

the revisionists the Gospel and the Church do not give concrete directives, but offer prophetic ideals and propose values.

The revisionists make a distinction between the *ethical order* which is of human origin and relevant for this world only, and the *order of salvation* which makes reference to interior intentions and attitudes regarding God and neighbour, according to the way *Veritatis Splendor* summarizes the revisionists' different uses of terminology. In other words, they propose a two-tier system of morality according to which Divine Revelation does not give any specific moral norms which are universally valid. The Word of God limits itself to proposing and exhorting moral behaviour, known as 'paraenesis', leaving autonomous reason to work out moral norms which would be 'objective' for the concrete situation in hand. By extension the Church's Magisterium would not be able to teach specific moral obligations which have to do with the so-called human good. These norms would not be relevant for salvation. Such a double morality is at odds with the whole Tradition of the Church, and the notion that the Commandments do not express specific moral duties was explicitly rejected by the Council of Trent which we shall see more fully.[3] But first let us look more at the detail and background of this moral revisionism.

The Question of Moral Absolutes; Transcendental and Categorical Norms

If challenged as to whether their system admits of moral absolutes, revisionists reply affirmatively with the important proviso that their absolutes are different from those traditionally so called. A distinction is made between transcendental and categorical norms, called by some formal and material norms, and absolutes occur only on the first level. These transcendental norms tell us the inner attitudes and intentions we should have and they apply to the behaviour of the person as a whole, while the categorical refer to the concrete external act. The first apply on each and every occasion, while the second do not. The transcendental norms, however, are very general formulations inculcating us always to act in accordance with the love of God and neighbour, to follow

---

[3] Council of Trent, Session VI, Decree on Justification, Canons 19-21, Dz. 829-831.

right reason, and respect the dignity of the person and to be open to life, freedom, truth and justice, etc. The transcendental level engages the whole person, especially their relations with God, Christ and their neighbour. It comprises virtuous behaviour like the exercise of faith and love, consent to the Redemption, the imitation of Christ etc. This is what *Veritatis Splendor* refers to as the *order of salvation*.

Categorical norms refer to concrete individual situations. These are norms of the form that we are familiar with in the Commandments and throughout the ages, namely 'do not kill', 'do not steal, or lie, or commit adultery', etc. Revisionist thinkers find a problem with this type of moral law because, in their view, it can never cover all the predicaments and circumstances people can find themselves in. It does not have the flexibility necessary for everyday life. As far as they are concerned a norm like this, such as 'do not kill', means 'do not take life unjustly', and so is tautologically true, but there may sometimes be a 'just reason for doing so'. Or norms like, 'do not have sexual relations with a woman who is not your wife' may be 'virtually exceptionless' in that there is unlikely to be a 'proportionate reason' among the circumstances of an action to overturn it, though in principle it is always possible. Such actions are neutral and abstract, or, in their terminology, 'pre-moral' until a calculation of consequences has taken place.

First of all, this reveals the legalistic and casuistic nature of revisionism, by its very approach of trying to find exceptions and proportions to get round the law, but this in itself betrays a misunderstanding of what a moral absolute is. It throws some light on the subject to see how this term, or its equivalent, arose and hence what it means. The term 'moral absolute' is the one most commonly used in secular literature and throughout the English-speaking world. In the Church's moral tradition, up to and including *Veritatis Splendor*, the self same notion is expressed by the term 'intrinsically evil action'. It was coined in opposition to those who said that certain actions were wrong (e.g. masturbation), not in themselves, but only because they infringed the law. But the term 'intrinsically evil' is telling us that such actions are *of their nature* wrong, that is to say, in their *object*, and it is for that reason there is a law against them, not the other way round. The moral law is not arbitrary, since its purpose is to encompass, protect and uphold values and goods with its positive precepts, and equally by the rejection of their opposites. A system of proportionate reason only tells you whether things are better or worse. For example, proportionalism might say a dignified exit is better than living with a painful and terminal illness. But it cannot on its own premises state that such a conclusion is absolutely wrong.

More fundamentally, however, the revisionists' supposition of transcendental and categorical norms is only possible on the basis of a dualistic anthropology. The person is considered as consciousness and this leads them to locate morality principally on the level of interior attitudes and intentions while at the same time separating it from concrete bodily acts. There thus result two levels of morality for revisionists, namely an interior attitude and intention which may make the action right, even though the bodily action transgresses one of the commandments. However, *Veritatis Splendor* warns against just such a step:

> *A doctrine which dissociates the moral act from the bodily dimensions of its exercise is contrary to the teaching of Scripture and Tradition.* Such a doctrine revives in new forms, certain ancient errors which have always been opposed by the Church, inasmuch as they reduce the human person to a 'spiritual' and purely formal freedom. ... In fact *body and soul are inseparable*: in the person, in the willing agent and in the deliberate act *they stand or fall together*."[4]

The revisionist position is, therefore, unsustainable if the person is a unified totality, because in each concrete act the whole person acts and the individual action is the bodily expression of the decision of mind and will, as has already been noted. Let us look for a moment at where the distinction between transcendental and categorical comes from and its implications.

The distinction traces its origin from Kant, and so has impeccable rationalist credentials, though he did not exactly use categorical to refer to the particular level as these writers do. It therefore rests, as one would expect, on a dualistic concept of the human person inherited from Descartes. It is also tied up with the presuppositions of the Kantian philosophy and particularly its

---

[4] *Veritatis Splendor*, n. 49.

notion of the *a priori* conditions of knowledge. 'Transcendental' refers to the universal element in knowledge which is contributed by the mind. Knowledge of everyday matters and singular things, for Kant, is a synthesis of the categories of the mind with objects in the world, but few, if any, would accept this today. Since in Kantian thought the apprehensions and judgements of everyday experience (i.e. on the individual level) only reach the *phenomena* or appearances of things, and not the things in themselves, any universality, for example in the laws of physics, comes from the mind not from the empirical, or what these authors call, the categorical level. Once they had adopted this Kantian terminology, then, the revisionists had pre-determined the issue such that only transcendental norms, of the form 'one must always act in conformity with human dignity', would have absolute value in the sense that only they would be universally applicable. The error in theology is based on an error in philosophy. The Church has consistently pointed out the inadequacy of the Kantian epistemology for expressing true knowledge since it does not allow that reason can reach the being or essence of things. For the same reason it is not apt for use as a basis for theology.

The categorical level of right and wrong is arrived at by a calculation of the proportion of benefits over harm which arise from carrying out a certain action. Revisionists claim that no morality can be applied to an action before a calculation of consequences has been made by the acting subject of the 'pre-moral' goods involved. And in effect all goods have good and bad effects; eating, though nourishing and pleasurable, can produce health risks, promotion brings more work, and so on. So, on this criterion, there might be a higher degree of benefits over harm resulting from ending the life of an old person with a terminal illness and a low quality of life. As we have seen, such a procedure yields the useful good but not the moral good. The revisionists endeavour to retrieve the situation by arguing that the action would not go against the absolute value of life, because on the criteria of their transcendental level it would be in agreement with right reason and the dignity of the human person.

The Council of Trent had already condemned the separation of faith from morality as the proper object of the teaching of the

Gospel and the Church, as well as the notion that Scripture does not include specific moral precepts to be followed. A canon of the decree on justification rejected the proposition that "nothing is commanded in the Gospel except faith, and that everything else is indifferent, neither prescribed nor prohibited but free; or that the Ten Commandments in no way concern Christians." Others emphasized that the Decalogue is not only to be believed but also observed, and that God as well as Redeemer is also a law-giver.[5] The new revisionist theories fail to understand the unity between faith and morality and between divine law and natural law. In espousing aspects of the Kantian philosophy and the dualism of modern philosophy the revisionists failed to acknowledge the need of a philosophy of 'genuinely metaphysical range' as a foundation for Christian ethics and the unity of the human person as an essential element of it.

What is meant by Proportionalism?

In the process of constructing the ethical order by autonomous reason the revisionists invented a whole new moral theory, known as proportionalism, overturning natural law and objective morality, because a system of moral absolutes does not mix with one which allows exceptions and relativizes basic values. In reality, they tried to effect a compromise with the secular morality of utilitarianism, borrowing its consequentialist criteria, and for that reason it is sometimes called 'mixed consequentialism'. As we have seen, they have already taken a radical step by claiming that they are not opposed to moral absolutes, but at the same time denying that these are upheld by norms which refer to particular acts, but consist rather in living in conformity with certain interior attitudes and values.

Proportionalism is a moral theory constructed to deal with 'hard cases' and then widened to serve as a general moral system. It is designed to cater for situations like that of an under-age girl living in poverty who becomes pregnant. Human dignity, it is argued, may be served better by aborting the baby than by bringing it into the world to face a miserable and impoverished existence. Equally, with a terminally-ill aged patient whose quality of life has

---

[5] Council of Trent, Session VI, Canons 19-21, Dz. 829-831.

fallen below a reasonable level of decency expected for human dignity and who suffers great pain, it may be a greater 'good' to terminate the life immediately.

They maintain that actions such as these, which are generally wrong, may be right if there is a 'proportionate reason'. And to find out if there is such a reason it is necessary to take into account all the circumstances of the case, and weigh up the consequences, that is, the benefits versus the harm of the different possible positions taken. They point out that even traditional moral theology allows exceptions, e.g. taking life in self-defence, a just war and capital punishment. We might also add stealing if you are starving, or performing a hysterectomy on a cancerous womb.

The new theory arose by a widening of the conditions of the principle of double effect which is used to establish the right way of acting when it is known beforehand that any action taken will result in some evil consequences. Of the four conditions needed, namely a) that it be a good action, b) the first effect be good, c) there be a right intention, and d) a proportionate reason, the revisionists say that only the last one is necessary, namely that there be a proportionate reason for doing the action and that a significant degree of benefit over harm will ensue as a result. The revisionists' criterion of judgement is based on the relation of act to consequences, rather than act to object as Catholic Tradition teaches, and the right action will be judged by the balance of 'good', or beneficial, consequences.

Naturally enough, these decisions are not to be arrived at lightly. There are fairly stringent conditions on what constitutes a 'proportionate reason': 1) the value one is upholding must be equal to the value sacrificed, 2) all other ways of protecting the value have been exhausted and this is the least harmful, 3) the method used to protect the value will not harm it in the long run (for example, bartering life by killing one person to save another will eventually undermine the value of life, which would certainly rule this out, even on proportionalist grounds). How do we fulfil the criteria? Richard McCormick provides us with a number of tests. They include consulting widely to avoid self-interest, consideration of past experience, one's own and others, universalization of the case (what would happen if everybody did it?), consideration of the social implications and prejudices of society.[6]

By rejecting three of the four conditions given by the principle of double effect the proportionalists have endeavoured to use it as a thin edge of the wedge to justify exceptions to moral absolutes. However, they have changed the principle to the point of invalidating it. They use 'hard cases' as a licence to change the moral system. If there is a 'proportionate reason', they say, one may shorten the life of a suffering terminally ill patient, allow an abortion to an under-age girl unable to look after the baby adequately, and justify living together to a man and woman who are in love, but unable to get married for financial reasons etc. It is more in conformity with human dignity to allow these situations than to deny them, the argument goes.

The fact is that the proportionalists have radically changed the moral analysis of a human act. Instead of the moral object, a good or evil of the rational order sought by a free act of intellect and will, being the determining factor, it is now the 'proportionate reason'. The extent of the change here from moral tradition can hardly be exaggerated and it is a change rather than a development, as one of the Church's foremost moralists has pointed out.[7] The only type of change which is legitimate within Catholic tradition in faith and morals is one which is in homogeneous development with what went before, in other words, one which deepens the tradition, but does not substitute it, or depart from it.

The moral judgement, then, is made at the so-called 'pre-moral' level by considering the relation and order of the act to its circumstances and end, and calculating the ensuing benefits and

---

[6] Richard McCormick, *Notes on Moral Theology*, 1981, pp. 74-90.

[7] One of the Church's foremost moralists has summarized the situation as follows: "... a profound change has been introduced, a change of axis: a shift from a morality centered on the relation of act to object, this relationship giving to the act a moral quality that is intrinsic and independent of the intention of the agent, to a morality centered on the intention of the agent, and intention which constructs the object itself by means of the proportionate reason. The theory of the cause with the double effect, which in traditional casuistry had only a limited application in the solution of certain difficult cases, becomes a universal moral category; its application no longer begins with its first condition, the principle that one may not do what is evil in itself to attain some good, but begins instead with its last condition, the proportionate reason which subsequently determines what is good and what is evil. We are witnessing a kind of revolution within post-tridentine Catholic moral theology." S. Pinckaers, 'La question des actes intrinsèquement mauvais et le proportionalisme', *Revue Thomiste*, 1982, pp. 181-212.

'goods'. The interesting thing is that at this point the will has still not entered into the equation. It enters after the calculation and its role is limited to opting for, or against, what has already been declared good or bad. Consequently, morality, for the revisionists, rests on whether the acting subject has a good or bad intention and neglects altogether the moral object.

The proportionate reason is very closely connected with the intention of the person acting. If the doer of the deed can find a value apparently equal, or greater than the value sacrificed, then they proceed with the action. This has a subjective ring about it, recalling the adage, 'the wish is father to the thought'. If human dignity is salvaged in the early death of a terminal patient with a low quality of life, or an abortion saves a child from a miserable existence due to the inability of its mother to cope, then here is the value: a dignified life for a life.

Returning to their claim that traditional moral theology allows exceptions, this, indeed, is true. But in all of these cases the 'exceptions' actually change the moral object. Concerning life, the absolute moral prohibition is against taking *innocent* human life. None of the cases mentioned, namely self-defence, just war, or capital punishment, constitutes an exception to that. The moral object of these actions is different from the taking of *innocent* human life, so, for example, the moral object of self-defence is to save a life, that is, your own. Escaping prisoners of war in occupied France, or street children in South America, are entitled to take food because in situations of dire need the world's goods belong to everybody before they belong to anybody and so, in these circumstances, it is a good moral object and action. Hence, a starving person is not stealing in taking food as long as they do not put anybody else in the same position. But this is not an exception, rather the changed moral object has made it a different type of action.

Pre-Moral Good and Evil

A further implication of this way of thinking is that, until the weighing up of particular goods, evils and values has been done, moral good and evil do not exist in a particular case. Instead, at this stage, we only have so-called 'pre-moral' good and evil. Pre-moral, or ontic, goods are things like life, health, private property, knowledge of truth and so on. In other words, pre-moral (or ontic) good and evil cannot be given a moral evaluation until the whole process of proportionalist evaluation of consequences has been carried out.

We will argue in the next chapter that the category of a pre-moral good or evil cannot be a valid one in the sense intended here.[8] Once something becomes the object of the rational will, it is already good or evil, such as conspiracy to murder. Hence, something intended, or chosen, as the beginning of an action, though it is still in the mind, and even though it may never be carried out, is already good or evil. In another sense, of course there are physical goods and evils, but these are events or states of affairs, like a good property, or an earthquake, for example. They are not human actions or intended human activity.

The intention of the subject takes on a preponderant role in the proportionalist analysis and the object of the action is played down. Instead of considering the moral object and the intention and, in a supplementary way, the circumstances, separately, they lump all these together under circumstances. The aim here, presumably, is to consider the action as a whole, rather than the separate acts and elements that go to make it up. However, this leads them to pass over evil actions in the interests of the whole. They do not say this exactly, but rather that until the moral analysis has been made the goods and evils involved are 'pre-moral', or ontic, or physical goods and evils. Kiely makes a telling judgement in this regard:

> The object of moral judgement becomes the totality of the process under consideration. If this totality can be judged as positive, in terms of a prevalence of ontic goods over ontic evils, then any action bringing about such a positive totality will be justified. Rather than saying that the end can justify the means, it seems more accurate to say that the whole can justify any of its parts, if in the final outcome there is the desired prevalence of ontic goods over ontic evils.[9]

---

[8] See ch. 8.
[9] Benedict Kiely, SJ, 'The Impracticality of Proportionalism', *Gregorianum* 66, 1985, pp. 656-666.

The Sources of Morality: the Moral Object

The objection to proportionalism above all concerns its treatment of the traditional understanding of the morality of an action contained in the sources of morality and further its mistreatment of the principle of double effect. The mistake seems to lie partly in a misunderstanding of these two principles and partly in a misconceived and illegitimate development of them. A change has taken place from a morality which is based on the relation of act to object, to one which depends on the intention of the agent to the exclusion of the moral object.

The moral object is the good desired by the will, which therefore determines the will to be good or bad. The will chooses rightly, or wrongly, according to whether reason determines the action in conformity with the true good of the person, or not. Some actions such as murder, fornication, and theft are always wrong to choose. It will help us to understand the moral object if we distinguish it from the physical object. For instance, there are cases where the same physical action can have different moral objects. It is not the same to take an item from a shop with the permission of the owner as it is without that permission. Sexual intercourse is not the same, morally speaking, when done in marriage as it is done out of wedlock. It is not the same to have one's kidney out because it is diseased, or to donate it, as it is to have it out to sell it. Neither is it the same to become a bit annoyed with the children to correct them as to lose one's temper because one's pride has been upset. Nor is homicide the same as taking life in war, or in capital punishment.

The proportionalists pay attention to the intention and circumstances of the moral act, but seriously underestimate the importance of the moral object. It is the latter which anchors morality to the objectivity of the natural law and the truth of the human person. A moral object which is not in conformity with man's last end, or with any of the goods which are basic participations in the last end, such as life, truth, friendship, worship of God, justice etc., can never be good; or, by the same token, any action which is in opposition to any of the Commandments. These actions are called 'intrinsically evil' because they are wrong on all occasions and independently of circumstances (*semper et pro semper,* always and for always). We will look more thoroughly at the moral object in the next chapter.

Further Objections to Proportionalism

Let us turn now to consequentialism. Insuperable difficulties are encountered in trying to weigh the different types of human good against one another, because they are qualitatively different and not quantitatively only. One can weigh in the scales different amounts but not different types, or kinds. One cannot compare life (or health) and beauty, truth and friendship, or even human goods such as food and sleep. This becomes clear when you endeavour to exchange them with one another. It is no good having beauty without health, or friendship without truth, since they won't last very long. Nor can one substitute sleep for food, or vice versa: they are different types of need. Hence, human goods are not commensurable and so cannot be compared and weighed against one another.

A further well-known difficulty of a system that depends on a calculation of foreseeable consequences is that these can never be exhausted, or fully known. The future may always bring results we cannot envisage, and usually does. This rules out, at a stroke, the possibility of moral absolutes, since theoretically conditions may always arise leading us to change our moral rule, or criterion. The consequences of actions can be unpredictable and surprising even in the short and immediate term. Good actions can produce immediate bad effects and vice versa, as Benedict Kiely has shown with a couple of biblical examples. So the effect of Abel's acceptable sacrifice to God was to occasion his brother's jealousy and Abel's consequent death. In contrast, the selling of Joseph into the slavery of Egypt resulted in his rising to an influential position in Pharaoh's court to the benefit of his people.[10]

Perhaps the most devastating effect of a morality of consequences is that, at times, it can be used to justify the commission of manifestly evil acts, such as taking or endangering innocent human life. The principle of double effect and its four conditions is

---

[10] Ibid.

designed to cater for all *good* acts which have a foreseen evil effect, but not to do evil. Proportionalists have widened it by suspending all the conditions except the proportionate reason. This constitutes an unjustified departure from the general principles of moral theology because it means that the whole can justify the part to the extent that one can actually justify the doing of an evil act, which contradicts Romans 3:8. Of course, proportionalists would say, whether the act is evil, or not, is the point at issue, so we must consider the following dangerous scenarios of their position.

Judging the goodness of an act by its consequences does not allow you to extend protection to a human person's sovereign and unconditional right to life at all times. So, for example, during the Second World War cases arose where Nazi commandants bargained with peoples' lives, demanding to kill more people unless some were murdered. Spaemann[11] gives the example of a German policeman who was ordered to kill a twelve-year-old Jewish girl, otherwise his superior would order the execution of twelve innocent persons. The policeman went ahead and shot the young girl, knowing it to be wrong but with the excuse that he was saving the lives of twelve other innocents. Examples like this could be multiplied. The proportionalist argument could be used, for example, to risk the lives, or health, of some human guinea pigs now by experimenting with new drugs, albeit with their consent, in order to save the lives of hundred and thousands later on. Such are some of the dangers of any theory which refuses to allow that some actions are always and everywhere wrong, as does proportionalism.

The Fundamental Option

Together with proportionalism, the theory that has contributed most to the loss of the awareness of sin and descent in the practice of confession in recent decades is the 'fundamental option'. It maintains that for a mortal sin to be committed an action must be accompanied by an option against God, or one's ultimate Good. Failing this, even actions which are knowingly and willingly

---

[11] R. Spaemann, *Etica teleologica o etica deontologica?*, Quaderni CRIS, Rome, 1983, nn. 49-50.

committed in grave matter, such as taking life, adultery, stealing, or missing Sunday Mass, may not be mortal sins in the sense of cutting the person off from the life of God and communion with Him. There, thus result, it is alleged, not only two types of sin, mortal and venial, but also a third called 'grave' occupying a broad middle ground.

The theory is put forward to show why (allegedly) we cannot be constantly falling in and out of mortal sin and hence of the grace of God and participation in the divine life. External behaviour, according to this, is only a partial indicator of interior orientation and attitudes. Only some actions contribute to this basic commitment. Even serious or 'grave' sins, therefore, if they are not accompanied by an 'option' against God, and one's final end, do not separate you from it. The reference is to so-called 'grave' sins as opposed to mortal ones. Hitherto, that is to say, before Vatican II, it was always possible to find an exceptional commentator who would express the view that it must be exceedingly difficult to fall into mortal sin given the effects of this and the consequences if you die in this state. If he was a priest giving a retreat to schoolboys he would attain a certain notoriety for his view. It is this position which has been rationalized and has acquired a far greater clientele under the title of the 'fundamental option'.

This is tied up with the idea of fundamental freedom. According to this view there are some decisions in our lives which are of a more radical and life-determining nature. These are different from our everyday choices and operate on the transcendental level. A distinction is therefore introduced between freedom of choice, which covers most daily actions, and which is not self-determining, that is, our ordinary acts don't affect the sort of persons we are or become, and fundamental freedom which does. The latter is not comprised of particular acts but is comprised rather of deep attitudes (sometimes unconscious) underlying our behaviour, leading us towards our supreme Good, or away from it. Mortal sin is only possible when you act against fundamental freedom, or in other words, when you change your fundamental option away from love of God and neighbour etc. Though this is not done by particular acts, the latter can, and do, lead to such a change gradually.

The revisionists maintain, then, that only certain actions pertain to the last end, namely those in which fundamental freedom is engaged. This would necessitate a deliberate option, perhaps arrived at gradually, to separate oneself from the ultimate end because the action itself would not do it of its own accord. Particular actions are incomplete attempts to give expression to the fundamental option. The reason for this seems to be, according to its proponents, that the person, in his or her totality, is not engaged in everyday acts and, therefore, nor is the full use of freedom involved. The immediate object of such acts is not the ultimate good which belongs to the transcendental level, but particular goods pertaining to the categorical level. But the 'fundamental option' as it is called does not operate on the level of particular acts but on the transcendental level. By it, a person makes an overall self-determination, though not in a specific and conscious way, but in a 'transcendental' and 'athematic' way.

Particular actions, then can give rise to venial and 'grave' sins when the matter is serious. They do not admit that the latter, however, are mortal in the sense of separating one from love and union with God. They may lead to it, and this is why 'grave' sins must in no way be underestimated, but they do not necessarily cause it. It is in this way that they develop the tri-partite division of sins, mortal, 'grave' and venial, in contravention of the Tradition and teaching of the Church. The practical effect of this is to lead many to think of mortal sin as something which is very hard to fall into, given the rare and unspecific nature of it, and consequently they do not hesitate to approach communion when conscious of 'grave' sins.

A Severely Restricted Freedom

It is true that there are certain exercises of freedom in life which incorporate fundamental options and are life-determining. The Bible refers to many, such as when Our Lord invites the rich young man to "come follow me." Clearly, some of my free acts are much more important than others. Where should I go on holiday? when shall I get the house painted? or, sell my shares? are of very little consequence compared with, 'what must I do to attain eternal life?'

'what is the meaning of life?' or 'how can I fulfil myself?' etc. *Veritatis Splendor* confirms that, "It has been rightly pointed out that freedom is not only the choice for one or another particular action; it is also within that choice a decision about oneself and a setting of one's own life for or against the Good, for or against the Truth, and ultimately for or against God."[12] Emphasis has been correctly placed on choices which shape a person's entire life, as the decisions about marriage, a job or profession, a vocation obviously do.

However, two peculiarities about the fundamental option theory stand out. It claims that only some of our actions have a relation to the last end and it is stranger still to maintain that those that do are not necessarily particular actions, but simply attitudes prepared for by choices. As we have seen, although some of our choices have a fundamental character they are not different from all of our acts of free choice which in their own way contribute to our last end and the person we become. *Veritatis Splendor* teaches, "this capacity (of fundamental choice) is actually exercised in the particular choices of specific actions, through which man deliberately conforms himself to God's will, wisdom and law."[13]

Contrary to appearances, the theory does not do justice to freedom, maintaining as it does that we only make fundamental decisions affecting our whole life very rarely. Our freedom is not able to reach what is true and good most of the time, and when it does, it is only in a semi-conscious and athematic way. Thus freedom is severely curtailed, as is responsibility. We scarcely have our destiny in our own hands and are at the mercy of many uncontrollable forces and pressures. It begins to sound somewhat deterministic. Thus, although the fundamental option appears to offer the reassurance of distancing us from mortal sin it does so only at the price of severely and incorrectly limiting our power of self-determination.

Free Choice and Truth: Orthodox Moralists compared to Revisionists

In the tradition of orthodox morality, however, genuine free choice presupposes that there are a number of alternative goods from

---

[12] *Veritatis Splendor*, n. 65.
[13] Ibid., n. 67.

which to choose which are diverse and incommensurable, some of which may be wrong and some right. The subject's decision settles the question as to which action to take and, indeed, he or she is conscious of making the choice, able to reflect back on it, and aware that nothing makes him, or her, make it. One is aware of being free. Finally, and no less importantly, free choice also has a self-determining effect on the person even in ordinary everyday decisions. It not only produces an effect in the external world but also affects the person as well. By the action I become a philanthropist, a thief, a liar, depending on what the action has been. We become little by little what we do.

For the proportionalists, on the other hand, prior to choice we are not able to know which alternative line of action will produce the most benefit, or the least harm. Since for them this determines the right action to choose, they are claiming, not only that we can choose the moral good, but also that with our decision we make an action to be morally good. To be the arbiters of good and evil goes too far, recalling the temptation to Adam and Eve. We all have experience of choosing something morally bad as well as good. This implies we know good and evil prior to choice and hence we know truth. This is the basis of the link between freedom and truth. Hence there is no opposition between freedom and law or truth, because true law guides our freedom.

The rationale of the primacy of individual autonomy view, argues that the goodness of actions depends only on the good intention of the acting subject. But this leaves out the truth of the moral act which depends above all on the object chosen and not only determines the morality of the action but also determines the moral subject. There are moral objects which are always wrong to choose because they violate one of the basic goods of the person, made in God's image, such as bodily life, marital communion, private property etc. Actions such as murder, theft and adultery are always wrong to choose because they are incapable of being ordered to God, or the integral fulfilment of the person and his/her happiness.[14]

The revisionists (proportionalists) deny this and maintain that

---

[14] Cf. 1 Cor 6:9.

a person may choose an evil for a greater good, or lesser evil. So they would hold that a pregnant sixteen year old who is unable to give her baby a worthwhile life in accord with human dignity acts in line with this principle if she has an abortion. However, as *Veritatis Splendor* says, it is impossible to know what the greater good or lesser evil is prior to choice. Furthermore, as William May has shown, if we could know it before choosing a course of action, then that would be the only course of action to take thus ruling out the other alternatives.[15] But as we noted, free choice entails that a range of options be available. In this way, revisionism, which appears to favour personal freedom, actually restricts it

A False Anthropology

As we saw earlier, the affirmation of a double level of morality would seem to rest on a dualistic notion of the human person, but it is necessary to recall this point in order to comprehend more fully what is meant by 'fundamental freedom' and the deficiency of it. Man is conceived above all as a spirit imprisoned in the body. The spirit gives rise to freedom on the transcendental level which is able to direct its options to God or the supreme Good. It is thus not hampered by the limitations of the body and physical actions. Individual choices resulting from bodily passions and appetites do not have fundamental moral value. The person does not express, or commit, him or herself completely through such choices. If this is the case, then it rests on a mistaken anthropology, namely dualism, whereas the natural law requires the conception of man as a psycho-somatic unity as a pre-condition.

The mind/body dualism of much contemporary philosophy which underlies the thinking of the revisionists leads to an incorrect analysis of the human act. In every genuine human action the mind and body work together not separately, because the intellect works through the organs of the body in one action. The body forms part of the integrity and dignity of the person, as we have consistently underlined. If this is the case, then the whole

---

[15] William May, 'Scelta Libera' (Free Choice), in *Lexicon: Termini ambigui e discussi su famiglia, vita e questioni etiche*, Pontifical Council for the Family, Edizioni Dehoniane, Bologna, 2003. English version can be found online at www.christendom-awake.org.

human being, and its destiny and freedom, is fully committed in each act which can be properly called a human act. That is why *Veritatis Splendor* says that to dissociate the moral act from its bodily association is erroneous, as we saw.[16]

The root of the theory goes back to a distinction which Rahner derived from Kant, via Max Scheler, between the transcendental and categorical character of the human act. It is a distinction not between two kinds of act but between two aspects of a single act: "The categorical aspect is the choice of some particular concrete good, but the transcendental aspect is the fundamental attitude which the act embodies, an attitude which must be either open to God, or closed to him."[17] The transcendental element is the universal aspect and in the Kantian philosophy this is contributed by the mind, with the result that the categories and concepts of the mind make a synthesis with the empirical data given and produce knowledge not of the real objects themselves, but *phenomena* or appearances of things. The Kantian epistemology, therefore, does not allow of a realist theory of knowledge, which can actually reach the truth of things in themselves, demanded by Christian ethics.

The Meaning of Mortal and Venial Sin

The revisionists who are responsible for the fundamental option also propose a revised division of sins which conforms to their premises. Since only a few actions affect our last end, or eternal salvation, this is going to have the effect of cutting down drastically the actions which tradition has considered as mortal sins. The way they do this is to propose a revised presentation of sins, as follows: venial, grave and mortal. Hence, according to this classification, there would be grave sins which are not mortal and, therefore, do not take away sanctifying grace from the soul by which it is in communion with God. This corresponds to their premise that only acts of fundamental freedom affect salvation and therefore union with their last end. This theory, which has been widely repeated

---

[16] *Veritatis Splendor*, n. 49.
[17] B. Ashley, *Moral Truth and Moral Tradition*, Four Courts Press, Dublin, 1994, pp. 68-97.

at the level of everyday catechesis, has contributed considerably to the loss of the sense and meaning of mortal sin in the life of souls and been a major factor in the reduced number of penitents attending frequent confession. It has been explicitly rejected by the Magisterium in *Reconciliatio et Paenitentia* as has the wider theory, into which it fits, in *Veritatis Splendor*.[18] The loss of the sense of sin requires us to look in more detail at the Church's tradition on mortal and venial sin.

The Holy Scripture speaks of a sin which leads to death (1 Jn 5:16-21). St John seems to be speaking here of apostasy or idolatry, rejecting revealed truth and adopting idols and false gods, but he underlines that the essence of sin lies in rejection of God leading to the death of the soul. Likewise St James speaks of the sin which "when it is full grown brings forth death"(Jas 1:15). In this passage he traces its origin to temptation and sinful desire, but only when this has been succumbed to in grave matter with full consent and knowledge, the Church teaches, will it become mortal. Then again, Scripture's reference to the sin against the Holy Spirit as being the only sin that cannot be forgiven would appear to refer to a voluntary rejection of pardon, of the offer of the grace of salvation, and so *ipso facto* being impenetrable to forgiveness. It includes actions such as resisting the known truth, final impenitence and despair of one's salvation. Nevertheless, the Pope uses it to illustrate the existence of sins which bring the punishment of 'eternal death' to the sinner.

In the light of these and other passages the Fathers and Doctors of the Church, and subsequently the Magisterium, have divided sins into mortal and venial. St Augustine speaks of *letalia* or *mortifera crimina* as opposed to *venialia, levia (light), or quotidiana (daily)*. The latter are, therefore, light or everyday offences which are called venial because they are easily pardoned.[19] St Thomas Aquinas defines mortal sin in the following way: "those acts are of their kind mortal sins through which the covenant of friendship between man and God and between man and man is violated; for they are contrary to the two precepts of charity which is the life

---

[18] John Paul II, Post-Synodal Exhortation, *Reconciliatio et Paenitentia*, 1984, n. 17; *Veritatis Splendor*, n. 70.
[19] *Reconciliatio et Paenitentia*, n. 17.

of the soul."²⁰ Hence, it is called 'mortal' because by the loss of infused charity, the soul forfeits supernatural life, its life-blood, so to speak, and cuts itself off from its final destiny of union with God.

Venial sin, on the other hand, does not cause this separation from the final end and loss of charity and life of the soul, though it does harm to it. St Thomas taught that venial faults were sins in an analogous sense, since by them one does not act against the law (*contra legem*), but outside or beyond the law (*praeter legem*). If life is considered as a journey or a way or road, then by mortal sin one loses one's way and sense of direction entirely. By venial sin, however, one simply deviates from the way, going on secondary roads etc. and arriving more slowly.

The meaning and distinction of the two sins may be summarized by this quotation from *Reconciliatio et Paenitentia*, again using some more words of Aquinas:

> According to St Thomas, in order to live spiritually man must remain in communion with the supreme principle of life, which is God, since God is the ultimate end of man's being and acting. Now sin is a disorder perpetrated by man against this life-principle. And when 'through sin the soul commits a disorder that reaches the point of turning away from its ultimate end – God – to which it is bound by charity, then the sin is mortal; on the other hand, whenever, the disorder does not reach the point of a turning away from God the sin is venial.' (ST, I-II, q. 72, a. 5) For this reason venial sin does not deprive the sinner of sanctifying grace, friendship with God, charity, and therefore eternal happiness, whereas just such a deprivation is precisely the consequence of mortal sin.²¹

Hence, from the point of view of its consequences mortal sin leads to eternal punishment, if unforgiven, while venial sin merits temporal punishment which can be expiated on earth or in purgatory.

St Thomas himself compares sin to a disease of the body which if it is mortal, or lethal, the body's own defences cannot overcome. If however, it is not, the anti-bodies, or one's own defences, can conquer it. So with the soul, if charity remains, then the soul retains

---

[20] Aquinas, ST, III, Supplementum, q. 65, a. 4c.
[21] *Reconciliatio et Paenitentia*, n. 17.

an ability within itself to heal its sin through God's grace, but if not, the cure must come from outside, from God's forgiveness. Therefore, it remains true, teaches John Paul II, "that the essential and decisive distinction is between sin which destroys charity and sin which does not kill the supernatural life: there is no middle way between life and death."[22]

The Temptation of Ethical Relativism

One cannot help seeing a dangerous and counterfeit character in proportionalism, because it parodies the orthodox moral theology of the Church and ends up coming to opposite conclusions. It claims to be based on a teleological end, and to maintain moral absolutes like the traditional morality, albeit different ones. In effect, the revisionist theories are called 'teleological' by *Veritatis Splendor* "because they make the basic moral criterion the end of the action."[23] The 'end' in question, however, is a pragmatic, a technical, and a utilitarian one. It is the end which gives the greatest benefit over harm, of pleasure over pain etc., which has the best consequences. Hence, it is not a moral end, because none of the above is an end in itself but a means to something else like happiness, or quality of life etc.

This is a typical temptation for the industrial, consumer society and the scientific mentality. It is so used to calculating its benefits and its profits and level of well-being that it seems natural to transpose the same system to its moral reasoning. But this is a considerable and fundamental error. Of course, in deciding our behaviour we all consider the circumstances and consequences of our actions, but these are secondary factors, not primary ones, in deciding what is moral. The moral object and the intention are the deciding factors, as seen above, and circumstances can increase or decrease the goodness or badness of an action. If they are particularly significant they will change the moral object and this may affect the morality, but they will never do it on their own.

A true ethics is indeed teleological in that goodness depends on the supreme good, or ultimate end, of human activity. But

---

[22] Ibid.
[23] *Veritatis Splendor*, n. 71ff.

ever since Aristotle it has been abundantly clear that this end must be truly final and not a means to a further end, which a utilitarian end always is. Consequently, the revisionists in seeking for a teleological ethics have found an end and good, but it is the useful good and not the moral good. In other words, it is not a good that is sought for its own sake as it should be, but as a means to something else. One of the consequences of this is that it precludes the role of the virtues, since these must indeed be sought for themselves and for the perfections they contribute to the human person, but not for any lesser benefit, or advantage, that might accrue from them.

Sadly, therefore, what the revisionists have done is to turn the whole of morality into casuistry, something they would never have intended consciously. From the moment they took their cue for a 'new morality' from the principle of double effect it had to be on the cards. The latter was for the resolution of hard cases, but in basing their system on it they have tended to turn the whole of morality into a casuistry of hard cases. It is a form of legalism and the trouble with legalism is that it makes you ask the question, 'what can I get away with? what is the least acceptable level I can reach and still fulfil the law?' It turns you into a minimalist. Nevertheless, this is what they are trying to do from the beginning; they are trying to see how they can accommodate objective moral norms with the exceptions that life in a secular society and difficult personal circumstances, in their opinion, necessitate. They take this approach rather than that of striving to love God and goodness or Truth above all things and to be ready to sacrifice oneself and even one's life, if necessary. In this sense, the martyrs are the supreme witnesses of the love of God and moral absolutes.

In trying to compromise on basic principles the proportionalists finish up constructing a rationalist ethics at odds with the Gospel, in other words just the opposite of what Vatican II called for in asking for greater liaison between Scripture and morality. As Pinckaers puts it, they have appealed to the magisterium of reason rather than to the Magisterium of the Church.[24] It is to the

---

[24] S. Pinckaers, *Para Leer la Veritatis Splendor*, Rialp, Madrid, 1996, p. 82.

latter and to a genuinely evangelical morality, that is, to a closer connection between the Gospel and morality, that we must look for a solution to the problems they raise.

The Pastoral Problem

For the most part, the motivation of the revisionists may be pastoral and well-meaning, because the authors are trying to address the difficulties of Christians endeavouring to fulfil the moral law in a secular society, and particularly the so-called hard cases. However, this should be dealt with not by changing the law, or making exceptions to absolutes, but by shepherding the people in the way of following Christ's morality, step by step and by an encounter with the Person of Christ Himself through the means he has left us for the purpose. For this reason, we will finish the chapter by considering the pastoral approach to the problem.

The Gospel and the Church do not give concrete directives, but offer prophetic ideals and propose values, say the revisionists. Much of their concern comes from the obvious pastoral fact that people often find certain Christian moral teachings difficult and indeed agonizing to fulfil, because of their formation, circumstances, or personal weaknesses. And, of course, Christ himself addressed this problem in multiple ways, some of which are referred to in other parts of this work. There is one dimension which is worth treating of here, however.

This is the problem of the application of the universal law to particular cases which is the task of conscience. In solving this, the Magisterium teaches that it is perfectly proper to proceed according to the law of gradualness, as long as we avoid the gradualness of the law. This latter would be to adapt it to each situation and circumstance so that we end up with different laws for different people and different groups, which is the revisionist position. Where this principle has been followed in practice the conclusion has been drawn that one thing is true in the Gospel, in Church teaching, and natural law, and another in pastoral practice. Such an approach, however, yields a sort of double truth which is unacceptable since its contradictory character does not fit with the Church's teaching of unambiguous truth and its consistency and coherence.

The law of gradualness means that pastoral work has to be done with souls to achieve step by step progress to fulfil the demands of moral norms and increase the virtues that the Law nourishes and safeguards. Growth in virtue precisely requires this gradual advance and conquest. But we cannot 'graduate' the law. It is perfectly compatible with good pastoral practice, indeed it is the time honoured method, to lead people gradually up the inclined slope, by means of conversion and repentance, growth in the virtues and transformation in Christ, at the same time as upholding the moral law. This is the correct understanding of the 'law of gradualness'.

All of this is the task of the virtue of prudence, or practical wisdom, within which the judgement of conscience falls. Ethics is an activity of practical reason which proceeds from an apprehension of what is good and right to its application and ends with an action. Since ethical reasoning is about practical activity it is wrong to consider it as mere theory, and so, incorrect to suppose that there is an object-subject type opposition between moral norms and the concrete application of them. Rather, we should regard them as two aspects of the one activity of moral conduct. Discerning moral norms and applying them correctly is itself a virtuous activity, which is carried out well by the person according to the degree of goodness and holiness they have already achieved. The best judge of the right action is the good man, Aristotle would say. The equivalent for a Christian would be the person who is most identified with Christ and in communion with the Church.

VIII.

HUMAN ACTION AND THE SOURCES OF MORALITY

Intention and Moral Object

Some of the objections raised by revisionists, such as those to do with natural law and freedom, have been addressed, but their analysis of the morality of the human act remains to be looked at. For Thomists the human act is an act of the whole person, but principally shaped by intellect and will. The definition Aquinas gives of a human action considered from the moral point of view is "that which proceeds from a deliberative will."[1] It is the intention of the will and the object of the act together with the circumstances, the so-called 'sources of morality', which determine the morality of an act. Which, however, are the most determining factors? The Church teaches that the morality of the action turns on the moral object, that is the proximate end of the action and the intention of the person doing it.[2] The circumstances do not change the morality but they can increase or diminish its moral responsibility.

The proportionalists, on the other hand, say that the intention of the acting subject together with the circumstances and consequences are the most decisive. Their notion of pre-moral good and evil enables them to say this. As we have seen, for them, until

---

[1] Aquinas, ST, I-II, q. 1, a. 1.
[2] *Veritatis Splendor*, n. 78.

the weighing up of the effects of an action we only have physical or ontic goods, such as life, death, physical integrity, material goods etc. However, these moralists do not want to be considered simply utilitarians, or pragmatists, who derive the morality solely from a calculation of the effects, and so the action must be in accord with a higher series of values, like charity, the dignity of the person, mercy etc., and this depends on the intention of the agent.

And so, for revisionists, and consequentialists, *the intention* one has for doing an action, after carrying out a projected calculation of the effects, has more moral significance than the objective moral content of the act which for them remains neutral. In order to obtain 'good' results one may have to perform an action, which in other circumstances would be wrong, but here is classified as pre-moral. It may be necessary to lie to save a thousand lives, or kill seven people to save ninety three, as Paul Touvier, the Mayor of Lyon, did in order to placate the Nazis commander of the city, Walter Knab, who had threatened to kill a hundred in reprisal for an action of the French Resistance.[3] Or, they continue, the use of contraception may be needed to save the marriage and keep the family balanced. In a world which is always a mixture of good and evil, this, they claim, is the most sensible approach.

So, from the time of *Humanae Vitae* onwards the proportionalists invent their new system which, in effect, exchanges the moral object as a criterion of ethical judgement for the consequences of the act. This turns out to be a very loose and negligent account of moral action, for reasons which we shall see, which vastly underestimates and misunderstands the importance of the object of the act. *Veritatis Splendor* refers us back to what it calls the 'insightful' analysis of Aquinas, but we will find, when we go back to the original source, that it has not always been transparently and coherently explained by his neo-scholastic commentators.

The Moral Identity and the Natural Identity of an Act

In answer to these arguments of the revisionists two things need to be said. The first is that the proportionalists confuse the natural

---

[3] According to a press report of the case in March 1994, quoted in M. Rhonheimer, *La Perspectiva de la Moral*, Rialp, Madrid, 1994 & 1999.

and physical account of a human act with a moral account of it, which enables them to hypothesize the concept of pre-moral good and evil and fall into what is sometimes called 'naturalism'. However, if the distinction between the natural and moral identity of an act is maintained, there is no longer room for pre-moral good or evil but rather an action with a natural identity. As soon as an action is considered from the point of view of the will of the acting person under the aspect of good or evil, it becomes a moral act. Secondly, we will go on to explain why every action has two parts which are relevant for morality, namely the intention to do it and the object rationally chosen.

First of all, we need to describe and eliminate the natural or proper end of an action, or of a power or faculty. The will is a rational appetite and can only desire what is presented to it on the rational level. The sensitive appetites have sensible things as their object. But the passions and emotions to which these give rise can come under the control of the will when the contents of sensitive life are presented to it via the reason. The act of will is said to be either elicited, or commanded. The first is its decision to will or not to will, and the second is where it acts through the powers and organs of the soul and the body, by putting them into operation, which is what happens on the vast majority of occasions.

In the latter, namely commanded acts, the will acts through bodily organs and actions, so that the whole person acts in a unified manner. Human acts begin in the mind and will and work through the powers and organs of the body. So we say the person walks or eats, through the locomotive and digestive power by means of bodily organs, legs and mouth. We do not, however, say that the legs walk, or the mouth eats. However, the person walks with their legs, sees with their eyes, hears with their ears and procreates with the generative organs etc. Hence, the bodily act embodies the intention of the will, it puts it into practice such that the carrying out of the action is part and parcel of the original intention, but we are still at the level of the physical description of the act. Here we are speaking of the natural identity (*genus naturae*) of an action and the natural end (*finis proprius*) of a power or faculty.

In a moral action, or an action analysed from the point of view of good and evil, the will, therefore, does not simply choose the 'natural' or 'physical goods' of the bodily organs. We have left this level behind. Thus the moral object or end is not the same as the physical object. The latter is simply the description of walking, seeing, hearing or shouting, swimming etc., from the physiological viewpoint. Once any of these actions becomes concrete one can ask what exactly the person is doing and why. What is the rational good, or good of reason, they are seeking and their purpose in doing it. This yields the moral identity (*genus moris*) of the action and when we analyse it further it furnishes us with the moral object, that is, the objective moral content of the act, and the intention of the person. The moral content is the end or goal sought by the will, as presented by reason, because good and evil are the object of the will. However, at this point we have done no more than distinguish the moral identity and object of an action from the physical end and purpose of a human faculty and action and its physical description.

The moral object, therefore, is neither the object of a productive activity, nor the object of knowledge, nor the object of a physical or biological power. The latter is particularly crucial. In every human activity there is a natural, or proper end (*finis proprius*), as well as a moral end or object. The act may be described on the purely natural or physical level and on the moral level. The proper or natural physical end of an action can more easily be likened to an event, because it just describes the external action. Two actions may be exactly the same on the first level, but opposite from the moral point of view, as are an act of conjugal union and an act of fornication, or shooting an innocent person and shooting a soldier on the battlefield, or in self-defence, or in an authorized execution. Critics of natural law doctrine on birth control confuse the natural action and end of conjugal union with the moral end and object of it.

Instead of seeing moral action in terms of act to object, revisionists and many secular moralists see it in terms of act to consequences and this leads them to 'transfer' the moral content beyond the act to the effects and so overlook the content of the act, that is to say, what is actually being done. The moral act, for them, can more properly be described as an event than a human action, because they fail to notice, or stress, that it is the result of the deliberative will rather than something which just happens. They, thus, see it as a physical or external action whose morality depends on the effects it brings about, that is, its ability to produce more good than evil. We should choose the action, they say, which brings about the greater good, or the lesser evil. To do the opposite would be absurd and unthinkable in rational terms.

This ignores the fact that the object, or proximate end of the action, gives the end and form to the act, and conditions the will. And if the action is bad in itself it makes the will, and therefore the person, bad. It is always wrong to choose what is evil, no matter what the consequences, because that makes the will evil. Proportionalists overlook the fact that a moral act is intransitive and above all affects the person doing it and does not just have external effects, so a bad action cannot but affect the person correspondingly. As the popular saying goes, "the end cannot justify the means", a doctrine emphasized by St Paul who actually said that we cannot do evil that good may come of it (cf. Rom 3:8). It is necessary to look more carefully at the human act.

It must be admitted that the terminology used by the neo-scholastics, to distinguish the intention and moral object, namely the end of the agent (*finis operantis*) and the end of the action (*finis operis*), though correct, plays into the hands of the consequentialists and proportionalists in that it gives the impression the action is split between a personal intention and an impersonal action which can make it seem like an external event. It is thus liable to obscure the fact that both intention and moral object come from the will of the acting subject, and so are objects as well as ends, a fact which is particularly true of the latter. They are both part of one action and cannot be considered as subjective and objective dimensions of it, which are set over against each other.[4] To understand the one, and the other, one has to put oneself in the position of the acting person, because it is the person who makes the judgement. The only time Aquinas

---

[4] See Martin Rhonheimer, *Natural Law and Practical Reason*, Fordham, New York, 2000.

separates them is when the intention is distinct from the object, as when a doctor practices medicine simply to make money or achieve fame, rather than treat the sick.

A moral act (*qua* moral), then, is a human act, whose good, or evil, quality stays in the individual, and must be distinguished from all acts having a purely useful, or productive purpose, such as those of an architect, or craftsman, and work in general. The contemporary world has shown itself particularly tempted to identify the moral good with technological progress. There is, however, a difference between doing, or acting, and making. A moral virtue such as courage is different from the skills of an architect or craftsman which can be exercised by bad men, as well as good. So a human act has its own proper end and purpose, and also its moral object and classification. The specifically ethical act is also different from the natural act described biologically, anatomically, or psychosomatically, as we saw. The moral act is an action of the whole person, which proceeds from human freedom.

The Interior and Exterior Action: Intention and Moral Object

Certain ancient and modern theories from Abelard to the contemporary consequentialists have endeavoured to evaluate an action exclusively by the intention of the subject doing it. If the intention is good, no matter what the action is it will be good as well. This goes against the Thomist tradition according to which any defect in the intention, or the moral object, makes the act bad, or according to the well known phrase, *bonum ex integra causa, malum ex quoque defectu.*[5] It will be evident from our analysis so far that the intention is bound up with the object since they are two aspects of the one action. We will continue this analysis after a brief reference to the emphasis *Veritatis Splendor* puts on this point.

The encyclical teaches that the "morality of the human act depends primarily and fundamentally on the 'object' rationally chosen by the deliberative will." It goes on,

> The reason why a good intention is not itself sufficient, but a correct choice of actions is also needed, is that the human act

---
[5] Aquinas, *De Malo*, q. 2, a. 1, ad 3.

> depends on its object, whether that object is *capable or not of being ordered* to God, to the One who 'alone is good', and thus brings about the perfection of the person. An act is therefore good if its object is in conformity with the good of the person with respect for the goods morally relevant for him.[6]

That is to say, the object or proximate end of the act must be in conformity with the true good of the person and that is made up of all the personal goods which reason grasps in the light of the dignity and intrinsic worth of the human being. If the action goes against one of the fundamental goods of the person that action cannot be right because it is not capable of causing goodness in the will. The document stresses that by the object of an action one doesn't mean an event of the physical order which brings about a state of affairs in the world, but rather the end of a deliberate decision which determines the act of willing on the part of the acting person. It therefore causes good or evil *in* the person.

Any projected and willed human action always includes two elements, namely the original intention, or plan to do something like euthanasia for a terminally ill and suffering patient, and the gathering together of the means to do the actual deed of administering a lethal injection; or, the decision to give some of one's salary to charity and the action of writing and dispatching the cheque. The second step furnishes us with the moral content of the action: "Objects, according as they are compared with exterior acts, have the nature of *matter concerning which*; according as they are compared with the interior act of the will they have the nature of *ends*." (I-II, q. 72, a. 3, ad 2). These two elements both involve the will (in fact they both involve an interplay between reason and will), and are called the action of the intending will (*intentio*) and that of the elective, or choosing will (*electio*). It is the latter which sets off the action and so is the proximate end of it and this is called the moral object. It will be recognized that this is different from the originating decision to carry out an act of euthanasia or charitable donation. First one must conceive the plan (*intentio*) and then gather the means to achieving the end and these are the two elements which St Thomas calls the interior and the exterior action.

---

[6] *Veritatis Splendor*, n. 78.

Aquinas makes a distinction between the interior and exterior aspects of a single action in order to clarify the matter more exactly. The interior action is the goal, or end, of the intending will, namely, that for the sake of which something is done, while the exterior action is the product of intellect, will and the organic faculties, and therefore gives us the matter, or object of the action, but is predominantly the work of the reason. The object is the *materia circa quam*, the content of the action as it is proposed to the will by the reason. The object of the action is always a good of reason, and so it cannot be said, at this stage, that this good is pre-moral because it is only a natural good and so cannot specify the will. If this were the case, the moral quality would be determined by the inner act of the will alone. Though he was not privy to the modern problems in this area, St Thomas deals with this question.[7] A good presented to the will already has the character of a *genus moris*, precisely because it is a 'good of reason' and not simply a natural good.

The difference between the interior and exterior action is best explained by St Thomas in the *Commentary on the Sentences* where he is commenting on the difference between the intending and the elective act.[8] The object, as the immediate goal of the action, is the subject matter of the elective will, and the goal of the intention is the subject matter of the intending will, but we are speaking of one act of willing with two aspects. For the will to be good, therefore, the elective act must be good because this is what sets off the action and because what is intended is intentionally present in it. So, if the exterior act, that is the chosen object, is bad then the whole action will be bad because the will is involved in this action as well as the reason. It will be asked how we know an action is bad at this stage because after all the proportionalists will claim it depends on the circumstances and consequences. For them, at this point, the object is at least indifferent.

Considered in the abstract, there are acts, which are morally indifferent, like going for a walk, picking up a stick, raising one's arm etc. This ceases to be the case in a concrete particular action, because we have to ask, in each case, what the person is doing

---

[7] Aquinas, ST, I-II, q. 19, a. 1, obj. 3.
[8] Aquinas, *In II Sent.*, dist. 38, q. 1; dist. 40. For this analysis we are dependent on Rhonheimer, *Natural Law and Practical Reason*, pp. 430-1.

and why. If he is going for a walk as part of his daily exercise for health reasons, this is one type of moral object, if however, he is checking up to see if some local residents are away on holiday with a view to breaking into their houses this is wholly different. There are some actions which may be good, or bad, depending on the orientation given to them, and there are other kinds of action that are always wrong to choose, such as stealing another's property, giving a lethal dose of morphine to a patient, adultery or lying. The reason is that they go against the good of reason. And this is true even if the personal motivation is good, namely if one steals to help the poor, or one considers one is doing an act of mercy by giving a lethal overdose to a patient with terminal illness.

There are some objects that are always wrong to choose, as we saw, because they are unsuitable (*indebita*), no matter how good the intention apparently is. Such is the case of someone who steals to give money to charity, or commits fornication because they are "in love", or takes the life of a terminally ill patient to save them from more suffering. To such a person you have to say you may intend good, but the action chosen nullifies the good intention whether it is done in good faith, or not. This is surely what the age-old phrase, "the road to Hell is paved with good intentions", refers to. Such a situation is referred to by St Thomas in a passage quoted in *Veritatis Splendor*. He writes,

> 'it often happens that man acts with a good intention, but without spiritual gain, because he lacks a good will. Let us say that someone robs in order to feed the poor: in this case, even though the intention is good, the uprightness of the will is lacking. Consequently, no evil done with a good intention can be excused. 'There are those who say: and why not do evil that good may come? Their condemnation is just' (Rom 3:8)'.[9]

How, then, is the reason able to discern the *debitum*, the right and due action in each case? The *debitum* ensures that the moral object chosen is a right and fitting one and hence is part of the object and presupposed to it. It is part of the *materia circa quam* of which the moral content is made up and is the work of reason, the ordering of reason done by the mind. Fitting and due matter making for a right moral action would be, Aquinas says,

---

[9] Aquinas, *In Duo Praecepta Caritatis*, quoted in *Veritatis Splendor*, n. 78.

"giving a hungry person something to eat", whereas wrong matter (*indebita*) would be "taking something that belongs to someone else."[10] Again Aquinas writes, "good and evil in human actions is considered with regard for how the act accords with reason as informed by divine law, by nature, or by instruction."[11] The due, or fitting, matter is not derived from the will but rather from the reason. By 'nature' here Aquinas means natural law, which as we saw, yields those goods and evils which are discerned by reason according as they are or are not in conformity with the true goods of the dignity of the human person.

Certain moralists, such as Anscombe, and sometimes Finnis, use the word 'intention' for both aspects of the free act. The former applies it to the issue of birth control in order to explain to many who assume that in choosing to forego a child there is just one intention which may be followed up for good reasons. So Anscombe explains that a couple may formulate an intention not to have children for a period of time, but points out that in realizing that decision in practice there is a further intention, namely the use of the means to the end.[12] It is this second intention, which is what we have called the moral object, that may or may not be in line with the moral law, depending on whether the means used are natural methods of infertility, or contraceptive devices.

It is also important to stress that the type of action done has its origin in an intention of the will, and therefore, this intention must also be good for the action to be good. Usually, however, the two intentions coincide, even though the matter of the action has now been specified. In some cases, nevertheless, they do not, though for diverse reasons. It may be that a doctor who though healing children is actually motivated by fame, or making money. Or as mentioned above, a benefactor may steal to give to the poor. These examples certainly show there is a difference between the intention and object of the act. They also, however, show the connection, because while a bad object may invalidate a supposed

---

[10] Aquinas, *De Malo*, q. 2, a. 4.
[11] Ibid.
[12] G.E.M. Anscombe, *Contraception and Chastity*, CTS, London. Also in Janet Smith ed., *Why Humanae Vitae Was Right: A Reader*, Ignatius Press, San Francisco, 1993, pp. 119-146.

good intention, equally the original intention may throw more light on what a person, or persons, are doing and so invalidate the moral object of the action as in the case of Second World War bombing of cities because the action and its object embody the original intention.

In the analysis of any act we have to go back and ask what the acting subject is doing, we said. This is prior to and goes beyond, giving a description of what is carried out, which is the exterior action and completes the formation of the moral object. So, for example, in regard to the wartime bombing of cities it is not enough to know whether cities were bombed and civilians killed, one must ask what the intention of those who commanded the action was. Was it to bomb military and strategic targets knowing that this would cause collateral damage resulting in civilian loss of life? Or, was the intention directly to kill civilians and undermine enemy morale? These two intentions give us a different moral object and hence a different action. The carrying out of the exterior action is the assembly of the means to the end and the execution of them, namely the *electio*. This will, in good measure, confirm or deny the intention, but not necessarily entirely which is why we need to know the original *intentio*. These two aspects of intention, and execution of means, are two aspects of one act, not two acts, and *together* give us the moral quality of the action.

The 'Debitum'

Once the moral object is correctly formulated and chosen, it will be clear that there are actions which are always wrong to choose. We have already observed Aristotle's point that it does not make sense to ask whether one committed adultery with the right woman, at the right time, in the right place etc. All other things being equal, (that is, you are not starving, in which case the moral object changes), if you decide to take money that does not belong to you, or a magazine from a shop without paying for it, it does not make sense to ask whether the man is rich, or the shop is doing a good trade. The reason, in each of these cases, is that the action is incompatible with the goodness of the will.

The good and evil nature of an action can only be established on the level of reason and will, because it is these faculties that give the action its moral quality, its *genus moris*. So *Humanae Vitae*, in the core content of its teaching, is not referring simply to the biological separation between the unitive and procreative aspects of the conjugal act, which often happens on this level, but *to the rational and free decision of the protagonists to separate them*. Hence, there is a distinction between the natural end of an action, the *finis proprius*, and the right or due end of it, the so-called, *debitum*. This point was missed by many critics. And while they criticized the natural law for being 'physicalistic', understanding it wrongly, they went on to commit the same mistake of naturalism by not distinguishing the physical end and object of an action from the specifically moral end and object.

So, by way of example, it is not sufficient to say that the moral object of the conjugal act is the procreative good, but rather the responsible transmission of human life.[13] The full meaning of a human life is not contained in the expression 'procreative good' which refers merely to the generation of life on the natural, biological-physiological level. The only description of an object which is fitting morally and keeps due proportion to the nature of the procreative act is one which realizes it accounts for the body and soul, even though the spiritual soul is created by God, and hence it is a collaborative act with Him. The full understanding of the moral object of procreation also includes its unique connection with married love, and the responsibility of educating and bringing up the children.

There are a number of actions, which are externally the same, but which are, in fact, different actions. So an act of sexual union will depend for its classification on whether the partners are married and are of the opposite sex. Causing the death of an innocent person is murder, but with causing the death of another in self-defence, or in a just war, or the action of a hangman, each have a different moral object. For example, the objective moral content of the action of self-defence is to save a life (your own) not to take one, and the purpose of military action should be to defend one's country, or the just and fundamental rights of

---

[13] See Martin Rhonheimer, *Natural Law and Practical Reason,* op. cit.

citizens, against tyranny, etc.

It emerges from the foregoing that there certainly are goods, which are non-moral rather than pre-moral, and are natural, physical, or ontic, or however one wishes to denominate them. To identify the moral good with any of these would be to fall into 'naturalism,' that is to identify the good with the natural purpose of a faculty or action, the so-called *finis proprius*. Yet, for this very reason, the moral aspect cannot come from a calculation of consequences, which would only give us another 'naturalistic good'. Rather the good is to be found in a proper analysis of the human act, namely in the action of the deliberative will and its end which is the object of the action. The problems of the revisionists come from failing to identify the objective moral content of the action, that is, the moral object, and its relationship to the goal, or intention, of the will. This failure led to an alternative theory based on the 'proportionate good' and on a calculus of consequences, and therefore yields a 'useful' and certainly non-moral good.

Consequences of the Dualist Analysis

Unfortunately, revisionists have overlooked all this in their analysis of acts, but it is probable that their dualist and 'spiritualist' presuppositions about the person impede them from understanding it. It is not clear what a dualist analysis of a human act would be, but it is quite evident that it cannot be described as a single process from rational will through organs to accomplishment. Consequently, it is less easy to speak of an object of the act and more easy to speak of consequences, because the act itself is already a causal event from mind to body to action. In the process the action becomes less of a human act and more of an event – often even a physical event.

Given a correct anthropology, nor can there be such a thing as a pre-moral act. Each act, if it is truly so, and done with a rational will, necessarily has a moral value to it as soon as it is formulated. Another matter is that from the external description alone we may not know the moral evaluation, but this is simply due to a lack of the requisite information. So a man out walking is carrying out a neutral act until we enquire why he is walking. If it is to keep fit, then it will be a good act, but if, to return to our earlier example, it is to reconnoitre houses in order to size up which would be the best one to burgle, it would be bad. We simply have to find the motive and intention to give a full moral description.

Unless you describe the moral act correctly with its objective moral content, it will not be possible to affirm the existence of moral absolutes. If morality depends only on consequences and intention, there can always be a motive and some consequences which are good, even from bad acts. Furthermore, the consequences of an act can never be exhaustively described. An evil action is already wrong in its formation and cause, not simply in its effects, but understanding this depends on having a proper anthropology and act analysis. If the terminus of the act is an object of the rational will there are some acts, such as adultery, theft, lying, fraud, the abuse of children etc., which are always wrong to choose.

Those who say that a good intention can be separated from the physical doing of an action and, if necessary justify it, are guilty of a dualist understanding of man and his actions. In fact, the performance of an action gives bodily form to the original intention to do the action. In a correct anthropological understanding there is no reason for separating the interior act of rational willing from the exterior act performed.

To separate the external act from the interior act of the will, is to turn the human act into an event. The next step it to weigh the consequences of the event according to their good and evil effects. This, however, ignores the fact that moral actions are human, that is free acts of rational deliberation. Again we come upon the consequence that the revisionist and consequentialist analysis does not yield the moral good, but a sort of useful and naturalistic ethic. To consider an external action, such as procreation, as an event is to treat it as inferior to reason, which is to misunderstand that sexual actions like all human actions are acts of the whole person, not just of the body, due to the unity of the human being.

PART III

BIBLICAL ETHICS

IX.

THE BIBLICAL FOUNDATIONS:

LAW AND EVANGELICAL GRACE

Christian ethics is based on Revelation and its counterparts of grace and faith while natural ethics is founded on human reason. The two run parallel except that Christian morality deepens and confirms its rational counterpart which is subject to the weakness, scepticism and confusion which afflict human nature. Both are based on the fundamental goods of man and his ultimate Good, all of which are guaranteed by the natural law and the divine positive law, summarized in the Decalogue. Christian morality is about the good for man and about the meaning of life and this meaning is found in Christ. One cannot reach the plenitude of love or goodness by reason or human morality alone, because of sin and because we are called beyond our earthly condition.

Revelation shows how moral life consists in a transformation from one state to another, from what man is to what he ought to be, from fallen nature to 'new creature.' It is a vocation to live up to, and reach the dignity in which we all were originally created in Adam, which is holiness of life and communion with God. Christian morality demands fulfilment in the heart and the conversion of the person via a process of interior struggle and renewal. It includes certain virtues of its own like faith, hope and charity, namely the theological virtues, and humility, not common in rational ethics, which acknowledges one's creaturely condition and weakness and hence need of Redemption. It also makes use of concepts such as 'life according to the spirit' and 'life according to the flesh', 'old man' and 'new man' etc.

In other words, Christian morality is set within the parameters of creation and redemption. Scripture enables us to see three levels of man's existence. His pre-history prior to the Fall, his historical existence and his eschatological end, or eternal life. The full truth about man can only be known by examining all three stages. John Paul II wrote in *Redemptor Hominis*, "through the Incarnation God gave human life the dimension he intended man to have from the beginning."[1] Christian morality as a whole answers the question how man can again aspire to the perfection and holiness Adam enjoyed in the original creation.

To begin to answer this question and discern the truth about man we have to go back to the 'beginning'. In the original state of innocence man lived in happiness and liberty and was able to fulfil the law since he possessed the divine life of a child of God and integrity of nature. His freedom was not absolute, but conditioned by the limits of the Creator and the creation. Genesis confirms this when it relays God's command to Adam, establishing the first Covenant with man: "You may freely eat of every tree in the garden, but of the tree of the knowledge of good and evil you shall not eat."[2] The symbolism of the 'tree' tells us the source and content of the moral law and true freedom was not man but God. Man shares in knowledge of right and wrong and has to discern and apply it by himself, but he is not the origin of it. He has a very high degree of freedom, but is limited by the truth about himself and his freedom depends on that.

Sin is the result of Adam and Eve's refusal of God's love by transgressing his command. The consequence is that man becomes enslaved to a weakened nature and will, and a tendency to evil and malice, ignorance, pain, suffering and death and, as a result, further curtailment of liberty. Furthermore, he is inherently unable to fulfil God's Law and Will and so unable to reach the fulfilment of his vocation to happiness and communion with God. When the gifts were lost he passed from being a spiritual to being

---

[1] John Paul II, *Redemptor Hominis*, I, n. 1.
[2] Gen 2:16-17.

a carnal man, in St Paul's terminology, wounded in his nature by ignorance, malice, weakness and concupiscence, and therefore inclined to evil and unable to attain the goodness in its fullness which he could still glimpse. This situation drew from God an immediate promise of redemption. He says to the devil, "I will put enmity between you and the woman, and between your seed and her seed. He shall bruise your head and you shall bruise his heel."[3]

God did this by establishing a series of Covenants with the Chosen People which are centred on the Covenant of Sinai and the Ten Commandments. It is, indeed, an external law whose purpose is to point to Christ through whom it becomes internal by the work of the Holy Spirit. When the law is seen as something imposed on you from without, requiring external fulfilment, then it is understood as restrictive of freedom and burdensome. But law is a "rule of reason" for our own good, whether it has God for its legislator, as divine law does, or our own reason. Hence, (eternal) law is the wisdom according to which God created us, and which is also reflected in us. For a Christian, law is wrongly understood when it seen as something coming from outside to be fulfilled externally only. *Veritatis Splendor* traces a morality which is not just about prohibitions and obligations, but is rather about 'the meaning of life'. At the same time, it leads to a deeper understanding and fulfilment of the Commandments and the Covenant so as to aim at the perfection required by the Gospel which applies to everyone.

St Thomas defined law as a rule of reason, whether for one's own good, or that of the community: "The end of every law is to make men just and virtuous."[4] He divided law into five kinds: eternal law and natural law which is human reason's participation in the former; human law which is promulgated for the good of the community and is based on natural law. Revelation added the Old Law, or Decalogue (which is like a revelation of natural law), and the evangelical law of the New Testament, hereafter frequently referred to as the New Law. All laws are directed to,

---

[3] Gen 3:15.
[4] Aquinas, ST, I-II, q. 92, a. 1.

and fulfilled in, the Evangelical Law. To understand the New Law we have to grasp its relationship to the Old Testament under various aspects.

The story of how the law is to be fulfilled in the inner man, as well as outwardly, and thereby lead to growth in virtue and goodness, is the lesson of the Old and New Testaments. It is the lesson of the morality of the Bible. The law should, therefore, be fulfilled not simply for its own sake, but because we seek the good values that it inculcates. It is also the lesson of how the moral law, including moral absolutes, can be compatible with our nature as free, autonomous and sovereign individuals. While the law, both divine and natural, is in us, it does not take its origin from us. We have freedom and autonomy with regard to it, but can only be fulfilled and truly free according to the truth of the divine and natural law. Why we cannot fulfil either with our own strength alone, but only through faith in Christ, is a special lesson of Scriptural morality.

The Old Covenant and the Law

The Law was given as part of, and indeed as the expression of, the Covenant of God with his People. By the Covenant He entered into communion with them, He possessed them and they possessed Him, according to the well-known expression, "I will be your God and you will be my People." They will have Him alone as their God and no other. In turn, He will love them and always be faithful, in spite of their infidelity. The Covenant will later on be likened to spousal love in the prophetical literature of Hosea, Jeremiah and Ezekiel, as well as in the Song of Songs. Far from being simply a set of rules and regulations the law was an expression of friendship, love and communion between God and his people.

In the event of Sinai we see that laws are also set down regulating worship, indicating that only when God is seen as the source of law and morality and given due adoration are these firmly based and possible of fulfilment. While some writers speak truly of the natural law being known by reason without God, it is also the case that in its fullness it includes one's duties to God. Without God morality easily decays into relativism. Law is necessary for Israel to live as a People, respecting one another's goods, for without law there is no freedom and no security, only anarchy. The Law is necessary to give form and content to the Covenant, to point the way ahead, a way of life, but it is not simply an external code. It safeguards personal goods and so is based on ethics. Its purpose is not just to regulate external behaviour, but to lead to inner growth and happiness. And so on Sinai we have an early indication of the inner unity that exists between worship, law and morality.

The Law, which was given to Moses was linked to a promise of long life in the promised land. The New Law similarly was accompanied by a promise, though this time of eternal life. The Old Testament often refers to the law as 'holy' and 'spiritual' and exhorts man to follow it, as in the first psalm, 'Blessed is the man who walks not in the counsel of the wicked ... but his delight is in the law of the Lord'.[5] "Moral existence is a *response* to the Lord's loving initiative."[6]

The Catechism points out that, "the Law is holy, spiritual and good," and it adds, "yet still imperfect."[7] The Old Law consisted not only in moral precepts but also in juridical and ceremonial ones. These latter were circumstantial and destined to pass away. They were signs and shadows of the reality to come in Christ. Ritual laws like circumcision and the Passover were directed to the worship of God and the prefiguring of Christ. Once they had completed this latter task their purpose had been served and they were superseded. It was the moral law, or Commandments, which were to last and be perfected and deepened in the New Law which would be an internal law and possess other perfecting characteristics.

The Old Law is like a tutor that shows what must be done, but does not of itself give the strength, the grace of the Spirit, to fulfil it. A pedagogue in ancient times was a slave who led the pupil to school and looked after his physical and moral well-being, but was not himself an educator. The history of the Old Covenant is a perfect example of the way God leads His chosen People to the full understanding of the moral law by the law of gradualness, or step

---

[5] Psalm 1:1-2.
[6] CCC 2062.
[7] Ibid., 1963.

by step progress. It teaches us also that the law demands internal, not just external, fulfilment, perfecting the whole person, because every human act has both an interior and exterior aspect to it.

By the Law man is called to love God above all things, and be holy in spite of his sins: "You shall be holy; for I the Lord your God am holy."[8] Man's Redemption consists in recuperating the holiness in which he was constituted at the creation. But if God alone is good no human effort, not even the most rigorous observance of the Commandments, succeeds in fulfilling the Law, i.e. acknowledging the Lord as God and rendering him the worship which is his due. This fulfilment can only come as a gift from God, the offer of a share in divine goodness revealed and communicated in Jesus: "The gift of the Decalogue was a promise and sign of the New Covenant in which the law would be written in a new and definitive way in the human heart (cf. Jer 31:31-34), replacing the law of sin which had disfigured that heart (cf. Jer 17:1)."[9]

The Law and Sin: the Letter kills but the Spirit gives Life

The Law is the revelation of God's will and reason and since in the Old Covenant it was given externally to man and was beyond his capacity, it terrorized him. To the old man the Law was a painful reminder of his insufficiency before God, a sort of upbraiding conscience which drove him to fear. It became, as St Paul says, a 'law of condemnation', not because it was bad in itself (quite the opposite), but rather because it was an occasion of sin to men. In the words of St Paul, "sin indeed was in the world before the law was given, but sin is not counted where there is no law."[10] Once the knowledge was given sin abounded and led to death.

Because of sin which it cannot remove, it remains a law of bondage. According to St Paul, its special function is to denounce and disclose sin, which constitutes a 'law of concupiscence' in the human heart. If goodness consists in conformity to the law then sin will be a transgression of it, a refusal to answer God's call to

---

[8] Lev 19:2.
[9] *Veritatis Splendor*, n. 12.
[10] Rom 5:13.

us,[11] and a turning away from Him. Furthermore, for the natural man without grace such a transgression will be inevitable since he is carnal and God's standard is spiritual. Thus with the Fall, "the very commandment which promised life proved to be death to me. For sin finding opportunity in the commandment, deceived me and by it killed me. So the law is holy and the commandment is holy and just and good."[12]

The words of St Paul to the Corinthians, 'the letter kills but the spirit gives life,'[13] are equivalent to what he says elsewhere, namely, that the law is the occasion of knowing sin: "I should not have known what it is to covet if the law had not said, 'You shall not covet'". "In some strange way the very object that we covet becomes all the more pleasant when it is forbidden," says St Augustine.[14] The letter of the law which teaches us not to sin, kills if the life-giving spirit is absent, inasmuch as it caused sin to be known rather than avoided and therefore to be increased rather than diminished, because it adds to an evil concupiscence, the transgression of the law.

Through the law sin has abounded, but grace abounded more.[15] St Paul sees that perverse men may use this in the wrong way and so he asks, "What shall we say, then? Are we to continue in sin that grace may abound? God forbid. How can we who died to sin still live in it?"[16] In other words, if grace has led us to be free of sin, we would show ourselves ungrateful to grace if we continued to sin. The man who recognizes the virtues of medicine and drugs does not maintain that his diseases and sicknesses are of advantage to him. The law did not help man to fulfil it in order that he would see he needed a helper to observe it. The medicine is Christ's Passion and Resurrection. "Do you not know that all of us who have been baptized into Christ Jesus were baptized into his death? ... so that as Christ was raised from the dead by the glory of the Father, we too might walk in newness of life ... We know that our old self was crucified with him so that the sinful body might be destroyed, and

---

[11] Rom 7:8-10.
[12] Ibid., 7-12.
[13] 2 Cor 3:6.
[14] St Augustine, *De Spiritu et Littera*, 6, referring to Rom 7:7.
[15] Cf. Rom 5:20.
[16] Rom 6:1-2.

we might no longer be enslaved by sin. But if we have died with Christ we believe that we shall also live with him."[17]

We now see that no human being can be justified by the works of the law, or we might say by the 'law of works', which in turn emphasises that justification is by a *free gift* of God's grace, i.e. the law of grace. This, however, is not because of any defect in the law itself, but because of our fallen nature. St Paul says, "the righteousness of God has been manifested apart from the law, *although the law and the prophets bear witness to it*, the righteousness of God through faith in Jesus Christ for all who believe."[18] The law shows forth God's righteousness, that is, the righteousness by which he makes us justified. We are justified, not because we have merited it by good works, but so that we may be able to do them, in other words not because we have fulfilled the law, but so that we may be able to fulfil it.

If it emphasized man's infirmity then the purpose of the Old Law was to show both its limitations and man's insufficiency to fulfil it. The epistle to Timothy says, "Now we know that the law is good, if anyone uses it lawfully, understanding this, that the law is not laid down for the just, but for the lawless and disobedient ..."[19] The unrighteous man lawfully uses the law, because it leads him as a pedagogue, or schoolmaster,[20] so that he might become righteous. Once he is, he must not so use it, because it is not made for the righteous, because they are not justified by the law, but by grace: "For we hold that a man is justified by faith apart from works of the law."[21] Those who know the law by their own knowledge of it are not justified either, because the natural law known by reason does not give the strength to fulfil it to the fallen creature.

To call the Old Testament, the 'law of works', and the evangelical law, the law of grace, while true, hides a possible fallacy, because even the latter might kill if observed legalistically since it is the *letter* of all law that kills, not because there is anything wrong

---

[17] Rom 6:3-8.
[18] Rom 3:21-2.
[19] 1 Tim 1:8-9.
[20] See St Augustine, *De Spiritu et Littera*, 16; cf. Gal 3:24.
[21] Rom 3:28.

with it, but because it does not bring with it the capacity to fulfil, if not lived according to the Spirit. Furthermore, because the law of grace excludes Old Testament works it does not mean it excludes all works after grace, like sacraments, virtues and so forth; on the contrary it demands them. This can only be the result of God's gift and so the Christian must pray, like St Augustine, 'Lord, give what you command and command what you will.'[22] This is an example of the exercise of the virtue of humility which, by facilitating total reliance on God, and faith in Christ, must precede all good works.

No human being can be justified by his own deeds alone. The Book of Wisdom points the way: "But I perceived that I would not possess wisdom unless God gave her to me – and it was a mark of insight to know whose gift she was – so I appealed to the Lord, and besought Him."[23] St Paul: "Now we have received not the spirit of the world, but the Spirit which is from God, that we might understand the gifts bestowed on us by God."[24] What is the spirit of the world if not the spirit of pride, of those whose mind is darkened, and, not recognizing the righteousness of God, attribute whatever goodness they have to themselves, and like the Pharisee fail to thank God and ask for the further gifts they need, as St Augustine puts it. He writes, "a man is not justified by the precepts of a holy life, but by faith in Jesus Christ – in a word, not by the law of works, but by the law of faith; not by the letter; but by the Spirit; not by the merits of deeds but by free grace."[25]

"However, the Law remains the first stage on the way to the Kingdom. It prepares and disposes the chosen people and each Christian for conversion and faith in the Saviour God. It provides a teaching which endures for ever like the Word of God."[26] It guides man's freedom to maturity through training in virtue. As well as leading to virtue it also brings home to man his sinfulness and weakness and leads him humbly to seek the grace and power of God to fulfil them. In the well-known saying of St Augustine,

---

[22] St Augustine, *Confessions*, X, 29, 40.
[23] Wis 8:22.
[24] 1 Cor 2:12.
[25] St Augustine, *De Spiritu et Littera*, 22.
[26] CCC 1963.

"The Law was given that grace might be sought and grace was given that the Law might be fulfilled."[27]

The New Law is Internal

The Old Law was to act as the figure and sign of the New Law and New Covenant. The old was fulfilled in the new and the new was hidden in the old, as St Augustine famously taught. The meaning of the Law and its fulfilment in the inner man is best brought out by means of a well-known quotation from Jeremiah:

> Behold the days are coming, says the Lord, when I will make a new covenant with the house of Israel and the house of Judah ... this is the covenant which I will make with the house of Israel after those days, says the Lord: I will put my law within them, and I will write it upon their hearts; and I will be their God, and they shall be my people.[28]

As St Augustine observes, this is one of the few times the New Testament is spoken of in as many words in the Old and so it is of special value in teaching what God Himself has to say about the New Law. First, He attributes the breaking of the Promise to his peoples' infidelity and not to the law which Jesus Christ came to fulfil rather than abolish. Despite this, justification comes not through the law but rather through the vivifying Spirit, for if the law was life-giving then righteousness and goodness would proceed from it, and not from Jesus Christ. Nevertheless, considering that in both Testaments the same law is binding, in what precise sense is the one called Old and the other New? In the sense, says the great Father of the Church, that the letter of the Old Law did not cure man's wounds while the renewal of the Spirit does heal the infirmities of the old man.[29]

"By the law of works, then, the Lord says, 'Thou shalt not covet' (Ex 20:17): but by the law of faith He says, 'Without me you can do nothing' (Jn 15:5)" we read in *De Spiritu et Littera*. And St Augustine continues:

> It is, therefore, apparent what difference there is between the old covenant and the new – that in the former the law is written

---

[27] *De Spiritu et Littera*, n. 19; *Veritatis Splendor*, n. 23.
[28] Jer 31:31-33; cf. Ez 36:36.
[29] Cf. *De Spiritu et Littera*, n. 35.

on tables, while in the latter on hearts; so that what in the one alarms from without, in the other delights from within; and in the former man becomes a transgressor through the letter that kills, in the other a lover through the life-giving Spirit. We must, therefore, avoid saying, that the way in which God assists us to work righteousness, and 'works in us both to will and to do of His good pleasure,' (Phil 2:13) is by externally addressing to our faculties precepts of holiness; for He gives His increase internally (1 Cor 3:7), by shedding love abroad in our hearts by the Holy Spirit, which is given to us. (Rom 5:5)[30]

It is not possible to fulfil the Divine law with the resources of rational human nature alone, because it surpasses our natural end. This does not mean that God's law is against reason, because He works in conformity with it, but it goes beyond it. The purpose of all law is to lead man to growth in virtue, or as St Thomas puts it, the precepts of the Law are about acts of virtue.[31] The New Law raises man to a participation in the divine nature enabling him to fulfil theological and supernatural virtues. It identifies and protects the goods and values of man, and thereby leads him to moral growth. In doing so it guides man to fulfilment and happiness. This occurs when it is seen as addressed to the whole man and fulfilled internally as well as externally, that is, not just in a legalistic, or routine way. Only thus can it conduce to virtue, because the latter is a 'good operative habit', or 'quality of the soul', that is, it pertains to man's internal life.

Morality and the Law are fulfilled in Christ

Christ Himself is the purpose and fulfilment of the Scriptures and of the Commandments. He Himself testifies to this: "Do not think that I have come to abolish the Law and the Prophets; I have come not to abolish them but to fulfil them."[32] "You search the Scriptures …; and it is they that bear witness to me."[33] Christ has fulfilled the Law perfectly and his merits are superabundant so as to earn the redemption of the whole human race by the price of his blood. Christ brings the Commandments to fulfilment by interiorizing

---

[30] Ibid., n. 42.
[31] Aquinas, ST, I-II, q. 62, a. 1.
[32] Mt 5:17.
[33] Jn 5:39.

their demands and bringing out their fullest meaning. He shows they must not be understood as a minimum, but rather as the path of a moral and spiritual journey to perfection, to be understood as love. The call to "follow me" issued to the rich young man and all Christ's disciples means to fulfil the Commandments, not legalistically, but in the spirit of the Beatitudes and the Sermon on the Mount.[34]

In the parable the rich young man answers that he does indeed fulfil the Commandments, meaning that he lives in accordance with them as a sort of external guide, but he realises there is more to do because he asks, "What do I still lack?"[35] He is aware that he has not fulfilled them in the sense that Jesus is to explain in the Sermon on the Mount, that is internally, in the heart. Jesus indicates this by well-known phrases such as, "everyone who looks at a woman lustfully has already committed adultery with her in his heart"; or, "unless your justice exceeds that of the scribes and the Pharisees, you will not enter the Kingdom of Heaven."[36] In other words, He refers to acts which may not be external ones, or may not be fully completed etc., but they still transgress the Law.

The fulfilment of the Law, in this sense, has only been achieved by Christ Himself. So what more does he require of the rich young man? "If you would be perfect, go and sell what you possess and give to the poor … and come follow me",[37] that is to say, he is inviting him to surrender himself to God, make a gift of himself and practise detachment from external and material things in such a way that he makes union with Christ his overriding concern. But how does one follow Christ today, twenty centuries after he lived? *Veritatis Splendor* explains,

> *Following Christ* is not an outward imitation, since it touches man at the very depths of his being. Being a follower of Christ means *becoming conformed to him* who became a servant even to giving himself on the Cross (cf. Phil 2:5-8). Christ dwells by faith in the heart of the believer (cf. Eph 3:17), and thus the disciple is conformed to the Lord.[38] Following Christ is thus the

---

[34] Cf. Mt 19:21.
[35] Mt 19:20.
[36] Mt 5:28, 5:20.
[37] Mt 19:21.
[38] *Veritatis Splendor*, n. 21.

essential and primordial foundation of Christian morality. [39]

Currently, under the influence of the prejudice against law and exceptionless norms, it is sometimes thought that the Gospel has superseded the law, or that it does not apply in its entirety. What the Gospel does is to deepen the law to include the internal thoughts of the heart and, therefore, embraces not only an action, but the very roots of action. The grace of the Holy Spirit goes to the heart and reforms it, or in other words, it puts the law within us and enables us to fulfil it. The Gospel perfects the Old Law and brings it to fulfilment. And the encyclical makes abundantly clear that this call to perfection, or sanctity, addressed to the rich young man applies, not just to some of Christ's followers, which has been widely thought until now, but to all Christ's followers without exception, as the Fathers had taught.

We would be wrong to think that Christ has fulfilled the Law in our place and we do not have to observe all of it. It is not for us to make an exception for ourselves, or cut it down to size. Some years ago a cartoon was hung on a university notice-board showing the Ten Commandments written out in the form of an examination paper with the instruction at the bottom saying, 'only five should be attempted.' This is all too representative of the view that today they are not possible of fulfilment, although certainly they are not if we don't struggle to live in the grace of God. They are a law of love, and who can say he cannot love?, as St Augustine puts it.

The Evangelical Law of love and life cannot be thought of as a precept because no one can merit it or live up to it.[40] It is a gift that heals and transforms the human heart. However, it does not excuse us from fulfilling the Law or Commandments but rather increases the responsibility to do so, because Christ came to complete and fulfil them. "The New Law is the grace of the Holy Spirit given through faith in Christ."[41] The external precepts mentioned in the Gospel dispose one for this grace, or produce its effects in one's life. The New Law does not merely say what must be done, but gives the power to do it. This answers the question

---

[39] Ibid., n. 19.
[40] Cf. *Veritatis Splendor*, n. 23.
[41] Aquinas, ST, I-II, q. 106, a. 1.

of how the standard of the 'beginning', with regard to marriage and divorce, for example, can be aimed at and lived up to; not, of course, without effort and self-denial, or setbacks. This is due to the fact that in the present life we are in a lapsed and redeemed state at the same time (*lapsae simul ac redemptae*).

The New Law is a law of love in that it opens up the possibility of, and enables us to observe, the double precept of charity, love of God and neighbour in which the fulfilment of the commandments consists. The Decalogue is a gift of God, which should be received and observed with love, and, although to live up to it is beyond man's strength, he aspires to it by a further gift of His Spirit, the fruit of love: "As the Father has loved me, so have I loved you; abide in my love."[42] We might ask with St Augustine, "Does love bring about the keeping of the Commandments, or does the keeping of the Commandments bring about love?" And he answers: "But who can doubt that love comes first? For the one who does not love has no reason for keeping the Commandments."[43] In Christian morality, therefore, pride of place is held by charity, infused and lived out. Christ's gift is his Spirit whose first fruit is charity. Only by receiving the gift of love and grace from God can one fulfil the commandment of love and perfection.

The Role of the Holy Spirit

The Doctor of Grace brings out the contrasting roles of the Old and New Law by considering the manner of the giving of the Law under both Covenants. In the ceremony of Sinai fearful threats were given to the people to prevent them approaching the place where the Law was given. In the New Testament, on the other hand, the Holy Spirit descended on those who had congregated and awaited his promised arrival. The fact that Moses, following his vision, could not show his face to the multitude and had to speak to them through a veil signifies the externality of God and the law to man. In other words, it demonstrates that the letter

---

[42] Jn 15:9.
[43] St Augustine, *In Iohannis Evangelium Tractatus*, 82, 3, quoted in *Veritatis Splendor*, n. 22.

of the law justifies no one. A veil covered the Old Law until the coming of Jesus, and the arrival with Him of the law of grace, by which we are enabled to do what is asked of us.

St Paul writes to the Corinthians, "and you show that you are a letter from Christ delivered by us written not with ink but with the Spirit of the living God, not on tablets of stone, but on tablets of human hearts."[44] The letter of the law is the external law of olden times while the Spirit is the promise realized in the New Covenant, the grace of God enabling us to reach the standards set by the law and to be obedient to it. This distant relationship between God and man in the Old Testament, which is superseded in the New, is bought out by the above quoted verses of St Paul. Whereas on Sinai the Law was written on tablets of stone, at Pentecost it was written on the very hearts of those who received the Holy Spirit. Not until the law of the Spirit entered man's heart, until it formed part of him, could he be justified and fulfil it. The external Law, then, was given as a figure of the internal law which was to follow. This is referred to in some later words of the same chapter of Corinthians, "For if there was splendour in the dispensation of condemnation, the dispensation of righteousness must far exceed it in splendour."[45]

We saw that the Prophets, Jeremiah and Ezekiel, spoke of the writing of an interior law in the hearts of men and from these verses the Apostle took words to the same effect. The fulfilment of this prophecy comes about in the New Testament by the presence of the Holy Spirit in the hearts of men through whom the virtue of charity is infused into us.[46] By comparison with this the promises made in the Old Testament were all earthly, with the exception of the ordinances which were types of the future, such as circumcision; earthly, or carnal, that is, in the sense that they were promises of temporal goods which belong to corruptible flesh. In contrast, in the Gospel we are promised the fruits of the Spirit, in the heart and in the understanding.

---

[44] 2 Cor 3:3-6.
[45] 2 Cor 3:9-10.
[46] Cf. St Augustine, *De Spiritu et Littera*, n. 36.

The New Law brings about our Justification and Transformation

Transformed by the grace of the Gospel, the Christian becomes a 'new creature' capable of living, in St Paul's terminology, the 'life of the Spirit'. St Thomas explains that this expression can mean two things. Firstly, it refers to the Holy Spirit Himself dwelling in the soul who not only teaches and enlightens the mind, but also moves the will to action. Secondly, it may mean the effect of the Holy Spirit, namely faith working through love which instructs and urges to action.[47] The New Law contains other elements which are part of the action of the Holy Spirit, namely the Word of God and the sacraments. Consequently, the New Law is primarily an interior law, *lex indita*, and secondarily a written law.

The justification and sanctification which is brought to man in the Gospel consists in a change of state. It is a transformation from the state of nature and death, from a carnal state to a state of salvation and life, or a spiritual state: "He has delivered us from the dominion of darkness and transferred us to the kingdom of his beloved Son, in whom we have redemption, the forgiveness of sins."[48] To those who receive Him through faith He gives them the instrument of baptism to become children of God.[49] This transformation consists in justification being implanted within us. This is the work of the Holy Spirit, Person-Love and Person-Gift, who brings to our soul the supernatural virtues, gifts and fruits.

The theological virtues of faith, hope and charity are infused into the soul and transform the natural, cardinal virtues. In this way, the Holy Spirit makes the person capable of supernatural action and propels him to it. The gifts dispose him to receive spiritual graces and inspirations and so perfect the moral virtues. That is why St Thomas placed a gift beside each virtue to perfect it; counsel to prudence, piety beside justice, fortitude to courage, and fear of the Lord and hope beside temperance.[50]

---

[47] Servais Pinckaers, op. cit., p. 175.
[48] Col 1:13-14.
[49] Cf. Jn 1:12.
[50] Servais Pinckaers, op. cit., pp. 175 ff.

A Law of Grace and Charity

As the Catechism says, the Gospel is a law of charity because it makes us act out of charity and not fear, a law of grace because it confers the strength of grace to act by means of faith and the sacraments, and a law of freedom because it frees us from ritual observances of the Old Law and enables us to pass from slave to friend of Christ.[51] We should note, however, that as St Thomas teaches, grace is not the same as charity (or virtue), but rather is the nature, or principle, from which acts of charity proceed. Only when we become new creatures can we exercise the supernatural virtues including charity.

We have thus regained our spiritual dimension and hence there does not exist that unbridgeable gap between our carnality and the spirituality of the law. The gap has been bridged by what St Paul calls the 'dispensation of the Spirit' and the 'dispensation of righteousness'.[52] This righteousness enables man to fulfil the law which is why the New Testament insists so much on obedience. Only the Christian is able to respond to St Paul's exhortation to fulfil the 'righteousness of the law'. Our Lord himself is no less stringent, as we have seen, urging that our righteousness exceed that of the scribes and the Pharisees, if we want to enter the Kingdom of Heaven.[53]

This is precisely what was foretold by the prophets, namely that the righteousness of the law really would be fulfilled in us under the Gospel by the Holy Spirit. The law then for a Christian becomes the effect of the indwelling of the Holy Trinity in his soul. It is illegitimate to say, however, that the Law of God has been fulfilled once and for all by Jesus Christ and thereby abolished. The Gospel destroyed the Jewish law (ritual and juridical) but not the moral law of God contained in it. Christ Himself became the Christian's law, but this does not excuse him from the fulfilment of it, rather it enables him to achieve it, not perhaps perfectly and wholly but with a continual approximation to perfect obedience. The Christian enjoys freedom not from the law but in it.[54]

---

[51] CCC 1972.
[52] 2 Cor 3:9.
[53] Cf. Mt 5:20.
[54] Cf. J.H. Newman, 'The State of Grace', in *Parochial and Plain Sermons*, vol. IV, p. 143.

THE BIBLICAL FOUNDATIONS

The Evangelical Law is an internal law in the sense that grace inheres in the soul, raising it to share in the divine life and so be capable of supernatural acts. External acts have a twofold connection with grace: a) as leading to it, in the way that the sacraments, such as Baptism and the Holy Eucharist do, and b) as proceeding from it, as do the profession of faith, acts of charity and the other virtues. However, grace is antecedent to, and distinct from, the virtues and works which issue from it. It thus prescribes certain works like faith or chastity and forbids others, such as unbelief and adultery, but it leaves other matters at the discretion of the individual, or a spiritual director.[55]

When Christ summed up the Commandments saying that they consisted in the love of God and neighbour he was referring to the two tablets given to Moses, the first three relating to God and the other seven to our neighbour. So one cannot love God and neighbour without fulfilling all Ten Commandments. That is why each one is a moral absolute not admitting of any exceptions. The Catechism explains, "the Ten Commandments reveal grave obligations. They are fundamentally immutable, and they oblige always and everywhere."[56] Moreover, 'to transgress one commandment is to infringe all the others.' [57]

The second tablet lists the duties which make up the love of neighbour. It, therefore, affirms the dignity of the person, protects his goods and indirectly his rights. The Ten Commandments "teach us man's true humanity. They shed light on the essential duties, and so indirectly on the fundamental rights inherent in the nature of the human person."[58] They tell us the same as the natural law tells us by unaided reason, although this can become obscured and confused by the influence of evil, and hence the Decalogue is essential so that man may know these precepts with certainty and some ease. One cannot, however, fulfil the second commandment without fulfilling the first, or vice versa. The moral law consists in the fulfilment of the double precept of charity, which is the summary and completion of all the virtues.

---

[55] Aquinas, ST, I-II, q. 108, a. 1.
[56] CCC 2027.
[57] Ibid., 2069; cf. Jas 2:10-11.
[58] CCC 2070.

The Commandments can be seen as a law of charity in the sense that they protect the essential goods of the human person and where they are widely neglected, as in today's society, it is not surprising to witness serious harm done to the individual and society despite the overwhelming emphasis on human rights and dignity. The Decalogue upholds the right to life, the goods of marriage and family life, private property and one's good name; and yet State-sponsored abortion tramples on new life before birth, sex education takes away the innocence of children depriving them of the chance of gaining proper control of their instincts, crime on an unprecedented scale puts property continually at risk, while people's good name is continually compromised by scandal and gossip in the media. Looked at like this the Commandments, far from being an imposition, or a burden, are in the interests of every upright and law-abiding citizen and the common good of society as a whole.

Today people are very anti-law, or antinomian, and tend to see law only in the restrictive sense. What this view overlooks is that the law encapsulates goods and values which are essential to the person and society in general. Consequently, one obeys it not simply out of cold duty, but with the freedom and love of someone who is conscious of doing something for their own good and that of others. The Commandments are not fulfilled, in a Kantian sense, for duty's sake alone, but for love. One fulfils them willingly, recognizing that they are the path leading to fulfilment and truth. The negative precepts point to the minimum level beyond which we must not fall, but they are complemented in the Gospel later on by the beatitudes which signal the ideals at which we must aim, and the attitudes and dispositions we must cultivate. In this way, the Commandments put us on the road to the virtues and should not be considered apart from them.

The fulfilment of the law and the central role of charity are spelt out especially in the Sermon on the Mount after the beatitudes. There we are told to 'turn the other cheek' when harmed, or in other words, not to repay evil with evil, and to go two miles with the person who forces us to go a mile, namely to overcome selfishness with generosity, and to be compassionate with others, taking care not to judge or condemn anyone. Only God knows sufficiently well to be able to judge and if we were all-seeing like Him we could well find it easier to forgive. All this is the content of the 'Golden Rule': 'treat others as you yourself would be treated.'[59]

A Law of Liberty

Those who live by the 'flesh', or according to worldly standards and fashions, see God's Law as a burden and as a denial or restriction of their liberty, often because they put freedom of choice before all else. Those who walk 'in the spirit' know that as creatures their freedom is limited, and must not supplant truth and love but be subject to them. They see no opposition between freedom and God's Law, but, on the contrary, recognize the latter as the guide and pathway to genuine liberty. Man has autonomy under God's universal sovereignty, but his freedom is that of a secondary cause subject to the universal causality of the supreme Good. The Law, then, should not be seen as a heteronomy by which God imposes on man a series of duties by compulsion, but as a theonomy whereby man freely pursues goods and virtues, the knowledge of which he participates in through his reason, leading to his fulfilment.

The Law becomes a pathway to liberty because it teaches and guides us to live the virtues spontaneously. The Commandments encapsulate the goods of the person which the virtues incarnate in him and, in this sense, the virtues and beatitudes complete the Law. This, says Pinckaers, is why the New Law is called a 'law of freedom' because "the action of the Spirit through the virtues creates within us a spontaneous personal movement towards good acts ... But we need to understand very clearly that inspired by charity this spontaneity, far from acting against the precepts, tends to bring to perfection the moral qualities they would safeguard."[60] For the Christian who has matured in the interior law of the beatitudes and virtues under the influence of the Holy Spirit, the well-known phrase of St Paul is applicable: "where the Spirit of the Lord is, there is freedom."[61]

Our liberty is recovered in the Incarnate Son of God who

---

[59] See Mt ch. 5; Lk ch. 6.
[60] Servais Pinckaers, op. cit., p. 185.
[61] 2 Cor 3:17.

enters into solidarity with the human race. It is the same freedom and grace of Christ which Adam enjoyed in the original creation though without the preternatural gifts and with the inclination to sin. The Redemption of Christ carried out through his Death is a re-creation. This freedom is, however, the fruit of the Cross and it is matured and developed in the Christian by a prolonged participation in his Passion, which is carried on throughout history in his members and, therefore, throughout the life of each one of us. Albacete writes, "this liberty is exercised as loving obedience of the one who belongs to Jesus Christ. It is a liberty which in the fallen world appears as non-liberty, a liberty expressed as suffering, as the suffering of expiatory love. It is expressed as sacrifice." [62] The same writer quotes *Veritatis Splendor* n. 25: "The identification of Christ with the men and women of each age is brought about in the living Body of the Church" (my translation); and comments on it in the following way:

> Through the Eucharist, the sacrifice of Jesus on the Cross as a vicarious suffering creates the personal possibility for a share in his salvific mission made possible by the Holy Spirit. It thus sets liberty free. It makes possible the moral life according to the good of the person. It is the Eucharist of the Church (the Body of Christ) that thus makes it possible for everyone to have an encounter with Christ like that of the young man remembered in *Veritatis Splendor*."[63]

The Eucharist builds up the Church because, "as often as the sacrifice of the Cross … is celebrated on the altar the work of our redemption is carried out."[64] The act of the redemption is made eternally present in the Eucharist. It makes us into one Body because wherever the Mass is celebrated the whole Church is present. The Church is a Body of which Christ is the Head. Body in the biblical sense means the whole person looked at from the bodily point of view just as, on other occasions, spirit means the whole person. The analogy with the body shows just how closely we are drawn into the divine life of Christ won for us so as to be in communion (*koinonia*) with Him without losing our individuality.

---

[62] L. Albacete, 'The Relevance of Christ or the *Sequela Christi?*', *Communio*, Summer, 1994, p. 262.
[63] Ibid.
[64] *Lumen Gentium*, n. 3.

Like the bridegroom and bride we have a similar identity of life and love while remaining two subjects, such that we truly live one life, the life of Christ. It is this share in the divine life which is increased by our participation in the Eucharist.

The Mystical Body and the Communion of the Church

Union and oneness with Christ is made possible by the Incarnation, and by his 'vicarious satisfaction' for us on the Cross thus enabling him to pay the punishment for sins on our behalf. A new relationship with Christ, his Life, mysteries and merits is established. A new liberty is obtained for created nature, the liberty and sonship man had enjoyed at the beginning of creation. Indeed, the basis for the new relationship is the creation of human nature in Christ from the beginning.[65]

The only way to follow Christ so as to fulfil the moral and spiritual demands he makes on us is by becoming one Person with him. In the Incarnation he joins himself to the human race by the assumption of our human nature given to him by his mother Mary. We are thus enabled subsequently to become one moral, or mystical, Person with him while remaining two individual subjects. In other words, we become part of the Body of which Christ is the Head, and of which we are members by belonging to the Church. This is precisely what he has made us by means of the Holy Spirit at baptism, which is incorporation into Christ. It enables us not only to live 'in Christ' and 'put on Christ', but to be 'other Christs' and 'Christ Himself'.

What exactly does this grace of incorporation into Christ, and therefore his Body, the Church, consist in? It is the grace by which we receive again the 'glory and freedom of the children of God.' It is a gift of the Holy Spirit that is sent to us as a fruit of the Passion and Death of Christ which brings about our Redemption. It is the fruit of the Cross. We are children of God again, enjoying a share in the divine life as our first parents did because by it we become 'sons in the Son.' Our filiation is a participation in the subsistent filiation of the second Person of the Blessed Trinity. There is only one Sonship of God and we are made part of it as

---

[65] Cf. John Paul II, *The Mystery of Original Innocence*, General Audience 30-1-80.

adoptive children of God.

This explains how the two facts that Christ dwells in us as in a Temple and that we are all members of Christ are both parts of the one reality. In effect we are one Body and one Person with him and so come to share his merits and his triumph over sin. "Let us rejoice", says St Augustine, "that we have become not only Christians but Christ."[66] "Christ enables us to live in him all that he himself lived, and he lives in us."[67]

Our understanding of the Mystical Body is further enlightened today by the use of the notion of communion (*koinonia*) to describe the Church. By it we are united with the Trinity through Christ from baptism and with the other members of the Church. The early Christians, we read, persevered in "the teaching of the apostles, fellowship (*koinonia*), the breaking of bread and the prayers."[68] This communion is increased and fostered by the Holy Eucharist: "Because there is one bread, we who are many are one body, for we all partake of the one bread."[69] When eating ordinary food, which is inferior to human beings, it is assimilated into us, but when eating Christ's Body, (superior to us), we are assimilated to it. We thus share more fully in Christ's life and his Body the Church is built up. This union of the human (ourselves) and Christ's life is made possible by, and is similar to, the union of the two natures in the Incarnation. The divine nature neither absorbs the human, nor are they two completely different spheres of activity, rather the former completes and enhances the latter. In the case of the will, for example, the human will identifies itself with the divine will, it is not supplanted by it. In the same way Christ builds up the Church with the infusion of the divine life into the human members, raising up and transforming the latter.[70]

It can be seen from this how closely the triad of worship, law and ethics, which we noted is present at the outset of the Old Covenant on Sinai, is mirrored at the end of the New Testament. The worship of God in the Church, the new People of God,

---

[66] St Augustine, *In ev. Jo.* 21, 8: PL 35, 1568. See CCC 795.
[67] CCC 521.
[68] Acts 2:42.
[69] 1 Cor 10:17.
[70] Cf. Cardinal J. Ratzinger, 'Communion: Eucharist-Fellowship-Mission' in *Pilgrim Fellowship of Faith*, Ignatius Press, San Francisco, 2005.

and consequent participation in the divine life makes possible, especially through the sacraments, the living of the Christian moral life. It now remains for us to spell out the details and content of the evangelical law in the virtues, beatitudes and gifts of the Holy Spirit. Before doing this we will first consider virtue on the human level, so as to have a complete picture and be able to grasp more readily the theological and supernatural virtues.

X.

THE PURSUIT OF VIRTUE AND THE SERMON ON THE MOUNT

The law is the beginning of morality and not its fulfilment; its purpose is to lead to virtue. To make man free it must be fulfilled inside him. The virtues perfect man internally as well as externally. Here is the way Aquinas puts it: "the proper effect of law is to lead its subjects to their proper virtue; and since virtue is 'that which makes its subject good' it follows that the proper effect of the law is to make those to whom it is given good, either absolutely, or in some particular respect."[1] A virtue denotes a certain perfection of power, and is also a habit and by means of these two characteristics guides the actions and behaviour of the person so as to perfect him/her.

Not to recognize the pre-eminent role of the virtues is to run the risk of falling into legalism, with its tendency to external fulfilment and to seek to do the minimum necessary to comply with the law. It leads people to reduce morality to a discussion of ethical issues such as for example, the morality of cloning or minority rights, rather than as a means to grow as a person and in freedom. Legalism tends to see the law as a necessary, yet somewhat hostile, agent, in the battle to be good. It fails to understand that the law is written into us and that its acceptance and guidance enable us to live with interior freedom.

---

[1] Aquinas, ST, I-II, q. 92, a. 1.

A true and renewed morality in putting the emphasis on virtue ethics in no way downgrades the law, which always remains the standard of objectivity and truth to which freedom is subject, if we are not to fall into autonomous morality. The law is a means and not an end, which for some it had become. The end is virtue lived in goodness according to truth. The balance between the objectivity of law and its interior root and fulfilment frees us from the twin perils of legalism and autonomous morality. And the interiority of the law ties in with the increased interest today in the subjectivity of the person to which we have also devoted attention.

The basic inclinations establish the fundamental goods of the human being whose purpose is to fulfil and perfect the person. The ordering of the passions and the sensible goods also contribute to this purpose. This yields the moral virtues which moderate the concupiscible appetite, namely all the virtues falling under temperance, and the irascible appetite, that is all those that fall under fortitude. The virtues are the goals to which the rational and sensible appetites, that is the will and the passions, feelings and dispositions, are directed by reason. Virtues are habits formed out of good dispositions which interiorize and personalize the norm or law.

Human Virtues

Ethics, then, is not only about moral reasoning, or even simply about human behaviour, but rather about the virtues and vices which issue from that behaviour and perfect, or corrupt, the person. Healthy morality is about growth in the virtues. Aristotle distinguishes between intellectual and moral virtues, pointing out that the former (or knowledge) can be taught in stages and through experience, while the latter can only be fully acquired by practice. The very name 'ethics' comes from 'ethos' meaning habit (as we saw), and thus a virtue is a good habit or disposition developed by means of repeated acts.

A moral virtue, then, is different from an intellectual habit or a skill in that it can only be acquired in action. Because one has a mind or sight one can carry out acts of thinking or seeing, but where a virtue is concerned many actions must first be practised before one can be said to be just, or temperate etc. Nobody is born virtuous; the most that can be said is that one has a facility to perform acts of virtue. However, to be quick-witted, or well-sighted or physically strong, is an endowment of nature. "The moral virtues, then," writes Aristotle, "are produced in us neither by nature nor against nature. Nature, indeed, prepares the ground for their reception, but their complete formation is the product of habit."[2] To be just, or have self-control, is a trait of character that has been acquired.

Passions and Feelings

Aristotle distinguishes virtues from passions and feelings, though it is the job of the former to moderate them. We looked at emotions when considering anthropology, suffice it to recall then that by passion, we mean the feelings of love or hatred, sorrow, joy, anger, fear, daring, jealousy, pity etc. By dispositions are meant "states of mind in virtue of which we are well or ill disposed in respect of the feelings concerned."[3] We have a good disposition in regard to fear if we do not become excessively afraid, or insufficiently so, when faced with danger, or challenging circumstances.

Now virtues and vices are not to be identified with feelings. We do not receive praise or blame because we feel angry, sorrowful, joyful or frightened etc. Virtues and vices have to do with the will and the character. They have to do with dominating your feelings so as to strike a balance between excess and deficiency in the control of them. This is what we mean by virtue being a mean between two extremes, expressed in the well known saying *in medio virtus*. Health is ruined by eating and drinking too much, or too little, and physical strength by doing too much, or too little, exercise. A man who is afraid of every challenge and danger is a coward and one who feels no fear is foolhardy. A person who indulges in all the pleasures he fancies becomes incontinent and intemperate, but he who enjoys no pleasures and has no affections is hard-hearted and reclusive and becomes a bore. So temperance

---

[2] Aristotle, *Nicomachean Ethics*, Bk 2, ch. 1, p. 55.
[3] Ibid., Bk 2, ch. 5, pp. 62-3.

consists in enjoying the good things of the world in just measure.

This does not mean that virtue consists in mediocrity. In fact, when someone reaches the mid-point in which virtue consists, he must carry it to perfection. The virtue must take firm root in him and be maintained by the continual exercise of it. Therefore, the state of mind in which we are well disposed in respect of a particular passion according to the golden mean, in a firm and stable way, is what we call a virtue: "Human virtues are firm attitudes, stable dispositions, habitual perfections of intellect and will that govern our actions, order our passions and guide our conduct according to reason and faith. They make possible ease, self-mastery and joy in leading a good life." [4]

A virtue is also different from what today are called values. A value refers to something considered to be worth pursuing, a quality which enriches us or the experience of a good. But here we are still at the level of the *knowledge* and *experience* of what is worthwhile, or the *desire* and *appetite* for it. The value only becomes a virtue at the level of personal and concrete action. The virtue is the finished product. Value is more of a subjective term; virtues and goods are objective.

Socrates considered virtue to be knowledge of the good implying by this that you only had to identify what is valuable and worthwhile and be sufficiently convinced about it, and you will do it, not an uncommon view, even today. However, it does not take into account human weakness, especially of the will, and the tendency to backsliding. Nor does it take account of the passions and feelings of human nature. To know that it is virtuous to give some of your salary to charity does not mean you will do it. Nor will the requisite moral knowledge mean you will be faithful in marriage, loving and peaceful at home, just and fair in your dealings with your neighbour, and self-controlled when you are wronged, or enjoying yourself. This is because of man's passions or feelings and thus the passions are the testing ground of human virtue. This point raises the question of the role of prudence, or practical wisdom (*phronesis*), which due to its pivotal role in the mosaic of the virtues demands our immediate attention.

---

[4] CCC 1804.

Prudence

At all times, and especially in a climate of ethical pluralism, it is clear that to choose what is right is itself a virtuous act and requires moral goodness in the subject. That is to say, it is not possible consistently to make correct ethical choices without being a good person. The virtue which enables one to judge rightly, and so be of sound judgement, is prudence, a good habit which perfects both the intellect and the will. Morality, unlike other types of knowledge, such as mathematics or history, is affected by one's behaviour. We see here a key answer to why there are so many different views about well-known moral problems.

Prudence has a decisive role among the virtues because it has a part to play in the acquisition and development of all of them, and for this reason, is traditionally known as *auriga virtutum,* or the charioteer of the virtues. As already noted, it is both an intellectual and moral virtue because it consists, not only in knowledge, but also in the habit of deciding 'the right way of acting' and putting it into practice. It is practical wisdom. You can speak of the prudence of an architect who draws up the plans of a house, or even that of a thief who works with cunning and sagacity, which is what St Paul is referring to when he talks about the 'prudence of the flesh'. But prudence is a true moral virtue only when it orders human acts to their true end and chooses the right means to that end.

The task of prudence is to apprehend the moral law and apply it to individual circumstances. It is related to the general principles of moral theology and to conscience, and by study and reflection gains an ever deeper grasp of the former so as to apply them to a greater and greater number of individual cases. Moral theology is the norm and rule according to which prudence should be formed. Conscience, whose job is to judge and decide on the evidence given to it, is an act of prudence. Prudence, however, as we have already noted, requires not only truthfulness and knowledge in the intellect but goodness and rectitude in the will and in the subject's consequent behaviour. One can easily imagine that an unchaste person will find it difficult to understand the Church's teaching (indeed the natural law teaching) on sexual ethics for this reason.

It is significant that moral revisionists and proportionalists speak little about the virtues in general and prudence in particular. In fact, practical wisdom is the virtue which fills many of the gaps they point to in moral decision making, and solves many of their dilemmas. It is the mediating capacity a person has, to a greater or lesser degree, between the universality of the moral law and its application to particular cases. Rahner, as we saw, sees a conflict between the objective and abstract law and the subjectivity of the person's moral choice and action. But prudence fills the gap. When we understand this we will not see a conflict, or opposition, between subject and object in moral decision making, but a process which harmoniously combines both.

In *Veritatis Splendor*, John Paul II goes out of his way to underline that the universality and immutability of the moral law does not contradict the individuality and freedom of the human person. He writes, "*this universality does not ignore the individuality of human beings*, nor is it opposed to the absolute uniqueness of each person. On the contrary, it embraces at its root each of the person's free acts, which are meant to bear witness to the universality of the true good."[5] God's law is not an alien imposition on man, but rather something in which man participates in virtue of his rationality and which he freely accepts for his own benefit, because of its truth, or rejects for his own destruction. That is why "man's *genuine moral autonomy* in no way means the rejection but rather the acceptance of the moral law."[6]

Hence, prudence and conscience should be formed by higher principles which include the doctrine of the Church and hence, normally, should not find itself opposed to it. For the acts of prudence to be carried out properly they need to be accompanied by the supplementary parts of the virtue.[7] There are three

---

[5] *Veritatis Splendor*, n. 51.
[6] Ibid., n. 41.
[7] A summary of these given by Prummer is enlightening. 1. Memory. This means knowledge both of one's personal past experience and of history, because there is truth in the expression 'there's nothing new under the sun.' 2. Intellect. Knowing present circumstances and their relation to the end and particular moral principles. 3. Docility. Actions and events have so many sides to them we cannot know them all and should be willing to learn and take counsel. 4. Shrewdness. Perspicacity and sagacity, or ability

subordinate parts which are virtues concerned with secondary acts and secondary matters:

a) *Eubulia*. The habit of seeking right counsel, because, as is said above, prudence does not come immediately, but as a consequence of study and consultation.

b) *Synesis*. The virtue of judging rightly according to the rules of natural and positive law.

c) *Gnome*. The virtue of judging rightly from higher principles. It may be a judgement which departs from the letter of the law but not from the mind of the legislator. Hence, *'epikeia'* in the interpretation of the law proceeds from this virtue. It involves judging with sympathy and mercy.

This brings us to the contrary vice of precipitousness which is caused by lack of thought and neglect of the factors listed above. It involves leaping into action before due consideration is given. St Thomas likens it metaphorically to bodily precipitousness. If someone jumps from a higher to a lower level without proceeding according to the right order, going the right way etc., he exposes himself to grave danger and possibly bodily death. Morally, too, one must take account of present circumstances and future events. When precipitousness proceeds from contempt for the rules it is called temerity.

Much of prudence is common sense, but it is also moral and supernatural sense as well. The need to have the right ethical first principles, the right presuppositions, and the right notion of man and his dignity in its totality, as well as a knowledge of Scripture and doctrine, to come to the right moral conclusions, is emphasized by the virtue of prudence. One may know what to do and still not do it and prudence is, as has been repeatedly said, knowledge and virtue rolled into one, and these points are echoed in *Veritatis Splendor*.

---

to be able to make a quick decision about the means to be used to an end. 5. Reason. Readiness to infer one thing from another, because often one has to deliberate for some time before coming to a practical judgement. 6. Providence. Consideration of future events which is taken here in a double sense. Either ordering of the means to the end, or the consideration of future events which can follow from the act. St Thomas says that providence is the principal part of prudence to which two other parts are ordained, namely memory of the past and knowledge of the present. 7. Circumspection. Careful consideration of the circumstances to see if they are good and adequate for attaining the end in question, or bad and useless for the purpose. 8. Caution. Care in avoiding evils and obstacles which can go against the good work and the virtue and impede it.

It is the 'heart' converted to the Lord and to the love of what is good which is really the source of *true* judgements of conscience. Indeed in order to 'prove what is the will of God, what is good and acceptable and perfect' (Rom 12:2), knowledge of God's law in general is certainly necessary, but it is not sufficient: what is essential is a sort of *'connaturality' between man and the true good*. Such a connaturality is rooted in and develops through the virtuous attitude of the individual himself: prudence and the other cardinal virtues and even before these the theological virtues of faith, hope and charity and the beatitudes, gifts and fruits of the Holy Spirit. This is the meaning of Jesus' saying: 'He who does what is true comes to the light (Jn 3:21)'[8]

Virtue as a Habit, a Power and Excellence in Actions

St Thomas defines a virtue as a 'good operative habit' and a habit is sometimes understood as a custom or pattern of behaviour developed by repetition of acts. If you repeat good actions a sufficient number of times, such as tidiness, gratitude or generosity, they become deeply rooted habits which form the basis of virtues. In ordinary life, however, a custom is understood as an inclination to act in a certain way, with ease and without effort. On the other hand, a custom of this sort often leads to a certain routine and mechanical way of doing things. Custom sometimes means an attitude of indifference by which one does things automatically. If you define virtue in terms of custom understood in this sense, then virtue diminishes in the measure in which custom grows and we are faced with a paradox.

If virtue and goodness only consisted in the repetition of acts, then they would just be mechanical. There would be no need, or room, for freedom. Hence, it is necessary to deepen our understanding of virtue. The specific characteristic of a virtue is its goodness, though the latter is not simply what is in conformity with the moral law, but something much richer than this, according to Aquinas. He adopts Aristotle's definition of virtue: *virtus cuiuslibet rei determinatur ad ultimum in id quod res potest*: "the virtue of a thing is fixed by the highest degree of its power."[9]

---

[8] *Veritatis Splendor*, n. 64.
[9] Aquinas, ST, I-II, q. 55, a. 3.

Virtue, then, is a capacity in a person to respond to the highest degree he is capable of in a particular area. A virtue gives us the power to perform more perfect and excellent actions and thus distance ourselves from a mechanical way of acting. Furthermore, there are as many virtues as there are distinct aspects of goodness. St Thomas points out: "For every act in which there is found a special aspect of goodness, man must be disposed by a special virtue."[10]

Not surprisingly, there are degrees of virtuous activity and we find Aquinas distinguishing between perfect and imperfect virtue.[11] For example, a good quality in a person, such as self-discipline which leads him to do good work in a particular area, but not in all departments of his life, would be called secondary or imperfect virtue because it lacks the conditions for true virtue. Perfect moral virtue requires that an individual's knowledge of a good and his dispositions result in specific actions. It is not enough for an individual's actions to be in conformity with moral norms, but goodness must also inform his will, and his passions and appetites. Virtue requires not just that the agent does the right thing according to an objective standard, but that a particular aspect of goodness, such as courage, inform his will, his passions and appetites in an habitual way. The will and the passions can only be formed by education, practice and right judgement.

It is enlightening to see what Aristotle made of Socrates' doctrine that virtue consists in knowledge of the good, implying that by knowing good you will do it and become virtuous, because all virtues are forms of prudence or practical wisdom. Aristotle's view is more complete: "True virtue cannot exist without prudence any more than prudence without virtue," he says.[12] Of Socrates he comments: "He was wrong in thinking that the virtues are forms of sagacity, right in saying that they cannot exist without sagacity."[13] This is because, "Virtue is a disposition in accordance with the

---

[10] ST, II-II, q. 109, a. 2.
[11] ST, I-II, q. 65, a. 1.
[12] *Nicomachean Ethics*, Bk 6, ch. 13, pp. 190-1.
[13] Ibid., p. 191.

right principle",[14] and the right principle is discerned by sagacity. Every virtue is brought into being by prudence or sagacity. But we must go a little further. Virtue is not merely a disposition in accordance with the right principle, but in *collaboration* with the principle which in human conduct is prudence. Here the emphasis clearly points to the difference between speculative theory and action. Socrates thought virtues are principles; Aristotle says they work along with a principle and require habit-forming actions which are brought about by practice and training.

A proper understanding of the virtuous, or moral life, can be gained from likening it to golf or chess, for example. The best player is not the one who knows the rules perfectly, but the one who is able to think out new moves and methods of play, practice and train in them, and execute them with precision. Virtue, then, is a quality which enables one to create acts of a high calibre in the moral order. And it does this in such a way that it goes beyond the law – though not against it – as charity does when it inspires all our actions. Hence, the proper exercise of virtue is a far cry from routine behaviour which is the sepulchre of true virtue.

This by no means implies going against the traditional doctrine that virtue is built on the repetition of acts, because it includes it, but nor does the development of habit-forming activity exhaust the meaning of virtue. It all depends on a correct understanding of the human act. The interior act proceeds from the will and reason, whereas the external act is the product of other faculties. So, for example, in the case of fortitude, the interior act of reason consists in discovering the mean, or mid-point, between recklessness and fear. The external act is an act of the physical prowess, emotions and senses directed by reason and commanded by the will. Thus the virtue which principally brings about fortitude is in the interior of the action and so is not acquired by the mere repetition of acts.

A virtue, as we have seen, is a disposition to do the right thing with a certain promptness. On the other hand, the simple repetition of external actions is done without the dominion of

---

[14] Ibid., p. 191.

intellect and will. Custom can produce facility but not joy. The practice of virtue is the means by which man grows in fulfilment, and in the case of the supernatural virtues, greater spiritualization. For example, in the prayer, the Mass and the Communion of a saint there is no routine or boredom, but only fascination and novelty, even though they are done everyday, and even though at times it might be against the grain.

External actions help, but you cannot achieve virtue with external acts alone. It may, therefore, be more satisfactory to say that virtue is achieved not just by repetition of acts, but by education. You teach children to be grateful by reminding them to practise external actions, but gratitude becomes a virtue when it becomes internal. Repetition of acts does, therefore, contribute to the acquiring of virtue, but what must be avoided is a purely material repetition which leads to the loss of the personal and moral character of human action.

Growth in virtue is a lifelong task which includes the linking and development of all the virtues. Moral maturity is not achieved by a lopsided progress in virtue. The continual need for ongoing moral formation can be illustrated by considering the following instances of persons who possess moral education, but nevertheless require ongoing formation: a) Pre-virtue morality. The person who has had a good upbringing and possesses the ability to practise good actions and customs, but who can easily be changed by temptation and provocation, by peer pressure, the desire to be accepted by others, role models etc. b) The continent person. He carries out the right actions resisting strong passions to the contrary, but lacks the right order to the end, and is not necessarily practising his actions on account of the moral good and ultimate end. He is not entirely free. c) The docile person. He does the right actions simply because they are right, but is unable to decide for himself which are the right actions and why they are.

Types of Virtue

Traditionally, since the Greeks, the moral virtues have hinged around four principal ones, known for this reason as cardinal (from *cardo*, hinge). They are prudence, justice, fortitude and temperance. Every virtue requires the exercise of one or other of these, and they refer to special activities that require the control of virtue, like the exercise of the irascible and concupiscible appetites, and the relations between the part and the whole, i.e. between individuals and society. Each one of the cardinal virtues includes under it a number of supporting and supplementary virtues. So, for example, the virtue of religion falls under justice, chastity under temperance, and magnanimity and patience under fortitude. This does not mean that the cardinal virtues are superior to those that fall below them, in fact religion is superior to justice since its object is more noble.

To these human virtues a Christian must add the supernatural ones starting with the theological virtues of faith, hope and charity which are so called because their immediate object is God Himself. The moral virtues may be supernatural as well as human. The difference is that a supernatural virtue is infused by God through grace as opposed to being acquired by repeated acts. The end and purpose of a supernatural virtue is also different, so, for example, the reason for human temperance and moderation is bodily health, while supernatural temperance is concerned with the dominion over the body so that it serves the spiritual well-being of the person. Human virtues facilitate the doing of an action while supernatural ones make it possible but not easier. The dual supernatural and human aspect of moral virtue shows how for a Christian the human virtues are the basis on which the supernatural are built.

For the Christian, temperance includes the virtues of self-denial, mortification, fasting and abstinence. This should never be done in a way which is prejudicial to health, but to the point that it is necessary to strengthen our fallen nature so as to avoid sin. Evil can only be overcome in the measure in which we bring our unruly nature and passions under control. In general, today we are more familiar with temperance or self-control when it is broken down into its smaller virtues, of sobriety, chastity, modesty, continence etc. But virtue, of course, is not all about negation and discipline. On the contrary, man's purpose, indeed his moral responsibility, consists in striving to cultivate all the virtues. He is called to seek excellence and perfection by pursuing them.

But that excellence is achieved not simply by seeking his own well-being, but, above all, that of others. We are inter-dependent beings. As the well-known text of Vatican II has it, "he (man) only fulfils himself by making a sincere gift of himself",[15] in other words, by openness to others, by his concern and service of them, and by the equal recognition of their rights. This is covered by the virtues of justice and charity which save us from falling into the trap of creating the stoical individualist, selfishly obsessed simply with his own well-being and perfection. Concern for the common good is an integral part of one's own self-fulfilment. The virtues are inter-connected and just as man is one being (soul and body), so human life, if it is to be virtuous, requires their cultivation in a balanced way avoiding an exclusive emphasis on some aspect of human activity to the detriment of another area.

The Supernatural Life

Here, we pass, however, from the human to the supernatural virtues. Just as the former derive from dispositions and repeated acts so the latter take their origin from the gift of God who infuses them directly into the soul. Aquinas, and the rest of Christian tradition, hold that we have a supernatural end which consists not simply in union with an impersonal first and last Cause, but rather in the love and friendship of a personal God, which exceeds our natural powers and capacities to attain it. It can only be achieved when these capacities are raised up by God, "entirely from without."[16] Once God has done this, He must also give us the wherewithal to live and operate at the supernatural level, since no purely human power could sustain it on its own. The purpose of the infused virtues is to raise the faculties of the soul to the level of grace and make them capable of supernatural acts. These together with the gifts and fruits of the Holy Spirit and the acts of the beatitudes make up the pattern of supernatural life.

The theological virtues (faith, hope and charity) are distinguished from the moral (prudence, justice, fortitude and temperance) in that the former refer directly to the end, that

---

[15] *Gaudium et Spes*, n. 24.
[16] ST, I-II, q. 63, a. 1.

is, God and eternal life, and the moral ones cover the means to the end, that is the cardinal and other virtues which enable us to reach the end. The existence of the theological virtues is revealed by some well known texts of St Paul, such as, "the love of God has been poured into our hearts by the Holy Spirit".[17] Faith enables us to know God as the first Truth; hope, to desire and trust Him as the supreme Good; and charity unites us to Him by a love of communion and friendship, insofar as He is infinite Goodness.

Sacred Scripture explicitly teaches the existence of the infused cardinal and moral virtues, both in the Old and New Testament. We read in the Book of Wisdom: "If one loves justice, the fruits of her works are virtues; for she teaches moderation and prudence, justice and fortitude, and nothing in life is more useful for men than these."[18] St Peter, after speaking about the promises made to us in virtue of God's divine power to overcome the corruption of this world, encourages Christians to live up to the call to share in the divine nature by cultivating the virtues: "For this very reason make every effort to supplement your faith with virtue, and virtue with knowledge, and knowledge with self-control, and self-control with steadfastness, and steadfastness with godliness, and godliness with brotherly affection, and brotherly affection with love."[19]

The supernatural virtues follow the command, or dictates, not only of reason, but also of reason enlightened by faith. Their purpose is to elevate the faculties to the divine level and enable them to carry out actions of the supernatural life, which would be impossible without them. However, there are differences between the supernatural and human virtues, because the repeated actions of the human virtues confer a facility in acting which the infused virtues do not have. The latter confer an intrinsic inclination to do good, but not an external facility to overcome impediments to the practice of virtue. So, we notice that converts, or beginners in the faith, carried away by religious fervour, or repentant sinners, do not always have the ability to sustain their enthusiasm in daily

---

[17] Rom 5:5; see also 1 Cor 13:13.
[18] Wis 8:7.
[19] 1 Pet 1:5, 6; cf. also Phil 4:8.

life, or successfully remove the obstacles to virtuous living arising from bad habits and vices acquired in their former life.

The infused virtues also have different ends and are lived and experienced differently from their analogues, the acquired virtues.[20] They are directed not just to attain human ends, such as the health of body reached by temperance, but the self-control and detachment necessary for the salvation of the soul and the living of divine life and love, such as the self-denial to take up the Cross and avoid sin and the occasions of it. Equally, they give the fortitude not just to have the drive and stamina to succeed in business, but the strength to persevere in prayer. The infused virtues are able to raise the capacity of the soul to respond to the demands of the Gospel, to a life of evangelical love and self-giving, and to the Commandments and the beatitudes.

The Sermon on the Mount

The Evangelical Law gives the Christian the ability to fulfil its precepts and gradually be transformed into a 'new creature' able to live according to his dignity and divine calling. This occurs in virtue of the riches and merits of Christ's Redemption, but these are transferred into the human subject, specifically into the faculties of the soul, through the grace of the Holy Spirit by the infusion of His virtues, gifts and fruits. The life and workings of grace complement and are built on nature, and work by analogy with it.

The most complete expression of the Evangelical Law is to be found in the Sermon on the Mount. In its postulation of true happiness as the end and meaning of a human life and in its analysis of human actions and the acts of virtue associated with them and its directions for the avoidance of the occasions of sin, it not only lays the foundations for moral theology, but points to its fulfilment. It demonstrates St Thomas' teaching that the precepts of the law, when adhered to, lead to acts of virtue. The living of the virtues makes us blessed, or happy, although, strictly speaking, the beatitudes are acts, while the virtues are habits, either formed by repeated acts, or infused into the soul

---

[20] ST, I-II, q. 63, a. 4.

by the Holy Spirit. More specifically, they are acts which flow from habits. The Sermon requires that the law be fulfilled in the inner man, transferring it from tablets of stone to the heart of human beings.

The key reason why the New Law, and its most emblematic expression, the Sermon on the Mount, is the fulfilment of the Old, and of the Commandments, is because it is a portrait of Christ and a portrait of charity. Far from opposing the Commandments, the Sermon shows us how we are called to the perfection of love of God and neighbour. It urges us to an interior, as well as exterior, love of Christ and his virtues and therefore to a greater fulfilment of the Commandments which must be practised, not simply out of obligation and as a minimum, but out of love and opening up to a greater perfection which is given by the virtues of the Sermon. In the latter we are able to see the characteristics of the spiritual face of Christ offered to us as a model and companion on the journey to the Kingdom which is marked out by the Commandments.[21] For this reason the Sermon has been called the great charter or 'magna carta' of evangelical morality. It is the fundamental constitution of the People of God. The New Law is either the Holy Spirit who lives in the soul or the effect of the Holy Spirit, namely faith working through charity.[22]

Our Lord makes clear in the Sermon that the negative precepts of the Commandments prohibit not only the external act of murder or adultery, for example, as the Pharisees thought, but also the internal thoughts and desires, and also the occasions of evil deeds: "I say to you that everyone who looks at a woman lustfully has already committed adultery with her in his heart."[23] He goes on to speak very graphically about the need to put aside occasions of sin in a determined fashion: "If your right eye causes you to sin, pluck it out and throw it away."[24] Something similar is said of the hand if it becomes an occasion of sin. He also makes reference to the occasions of sin when speaking about perjury or telling lies under oath. Our Lord enjoins his followers to avoid performing

---

[21] Cf. Servais Pinckaers, *Para Leer la Veritatis Splendor*, Rialp, Madrid, 1996, p. 38.
[22] Ibid., p. 39; *Veritatis Splendor*, n. 16.
[23] Mt 5:28.
[24] Mt 5:29.

oaths, or swearing, so as not to risk falling into perjury. [25]

In addition, there is the personal intention for doing the action, namely that for the sake of which something is done. Christ expresses this by warning against doing good actions like praying, giving alms or fasting to gain the praise of men, thereby indicating that the intention is not only different from the end or object of the action as such, but that, if evil, it can vitiate the whole action. "Beware of practising your acts of piety before men in order to be seen by them." So, "when you give alms do not left your left hand know what your right hand is doing."[26] Nor should one do actions in order to attain riches as if they were an end in themselves: "Do not lay up for yourselves treasures on earth, where moth and rust consume ..."[27] Sometimes it surprises us to see how many of the principles of moral theology are already contained in the Gospel and especially in the Sermon. The detail into which Our Lord enters at times in this passage reminds us of a modern treatise on the subject.

Then, Our Lord goes on to forbid certain interior and exterior actions concerning one's neighbour, such as judging rashly, unjustly or presumptuously. He further forbids approaching the altar, that is to say, what is sacred, while in an unworthy state, and urges us to be reconciled to those who have something against us. These warnings are, so to speak, the backdrop for the standard set by the new law of the Gospel, to love our enemies, which involves not only forgiveness, but the generosity, if someone does us harm, of 'turning the other cheek' and, if they ask us a favour, to 'go the extra mile'.

The Evangelical law makes abundantly clear the new standard which the era of Christ and his Redemption ushers in and which is required of his followers. But it is equally manifest that this standard can only be achieved by communion with Christ in prayer and action. "Which of you", He asks, "by being anxious can add one cubit to his span of life?";[28] your Father knows all your needs both spiritual and material. He advises us

---

[25] Cf. Mt 5:33.
[26] Mt 6:1, 3
[27] Cf. Mt 6:19.
[28] Mt 6:27.

that we will be able to fulfil the Gospel by imploring God's help, entering by the narrow gate of virtue and being vigilant and alive to the danger of evil influences such as false prophets who appear in sheep's clothing but inwardly are ravenous wolves.[29] To reach Heaven it is necessary to fulfil the Commandments and it is not enough simply to listen to His words, or make a profession of faith. In the light of these passages we can be in no doubt about the close connection between moral theology and the spiritual life.

The Sermon on the Mount of the Beatitudes fulfils the Law and perfects it and internalizes it without taking anything away from it. The list of acts of virtue which are there contained brings out the values which are inherent in the Law. Those who criticise law on the grounds of legalism fail to recognise the way in which it is a plan of wisdom leading to beatitude and happiness. "The beatitude we are promised confronts us with decisive moral choices," the Catechism tells us. "It teaches us that true happiness is not found in riches or well-being, in human fame or power, or in any human achievement – however beneficial it may be – such as science, technology and art, or indeed, any creature, but in God alone, the source of every good and of all love."[30]

The Beatitudes

The beatitudes are more about basic attitudes and dispositions than about particular rules of behaviour, *Veritatis Splendor* tells us. However there is no separation between them and the Commandments since they both orient us to eternal life, it goes on. The beatitudes are above all promises from which 'normative indications' flow.[31] They show us how we attain happiness by the fulfilment of our duties to ourselves, our neighbour and God, according to St Thomas Aquinas. Happiness is thought by some to consist in material well-being, honours, power and fame etc., while for others it is achieved by active life and still others by contemplation. But material happiness is false and contrary to

---

[29] Cf. Mt 7:15.
[30] CCC 1723.
[31] Cf. *Veritatis Splendor*, n. 16.

right reason, given a true anthropology, while the active life in the service of others disposes one to virtue and therefore, future happiness, and contemplative life, if perfect, is the very essence of future happiness and, if imperfect, is the beginning of it.[32]

Consequently, in the list given by St Matthew, the first three beatitudes are dedicated to removing the obstacles which purely material goods can present to genuine happiness. Hence, *Blessed are the poor in spirit*, refers to the need for detachment either from riches or honours, which results from humility. The next two beatitudes restrain and moderate the irascible and concupiscible appetites respectively. Thus, *Blessed are the meek*, protects man's irascible nature from falling into excessive anger and keeps it within the bounds of reason. And *Blessed are those that mourn*, moderates man's desire for pleasure by keeping it in proportion, which is the effect on us when we suffer trials, tribulations and the death of loved ones.

The active life should be devoted principally to one's duty and spontaneous inclination to serve one's neighbour. One's duty to one's neighbour is a matter of justice which inclines one to give everyone what is due to them, and the corresponding gift enables one to do it, not as one who is pressed into service but ardently and willingly, just as one eats and drinks eagerly when one has a good appetite. Hence, it is written, *Blessed are those who hunger and thirst after righteousness*. But spontaneous inclination also leads us to go beyond what is strictly due to others and show them generosity, understanding and forgiveness, and indeed gratuitously without expecting anything in return.[33] This is what we mean by mercy and, hence, the next beatitude is, *Blessed are the merciful*.

Those things that concern the contemplative life are either final happiness itself, or the beginning of it, and so they are listed in the beatitudes not as merits but as rewards, although the effects of the active life which lead to contemplation and which perfect man himself are included as merits. Hence, we say of men who triumph over the passions, *Blessed are the pure of heart*. The virtues and

---

[32] Cf. ST, II-I, q. 69, a. 3 for this and what follows on the beatitudes.
[33] Cf. Lk 14:12-13.

gifts which perfect man in his relations with his neighbour have peace as their effect, as we read in Isaiah: "The work of justice shall be peace" (32:17). Hence the seventh beatitude tells us, *Blessed are the peacemakers.*

The Gifts of the Holy Spirit

The gifts differ from the virtues in their origin, but they both perfect man in relation to doing good, the gifts in disposing him to follow well the promptings of the Holy Spirit and the moral virtues dispose the appetitive powers to be guided by the reason, or reason illumined by faith.[34] Both infused virtues and the gifts can be considered as habits, which come about not by repeated acts, but by infusion of the grace of the Holy Spirit according to his sevenfold gift in the latter case (see Isaiah 11:2-3.) The difference, however, is that the infused virtues function under the guidance of reason and are limited to a human mode of action, the mode of reason, whereas the gifts are directly activated by the Holy Spirit, and therefore operate in a supernatural way. Hence, presupposing an actual grace, the virtues can be activated at will, whereas the gifts only function when the Holy Spirit chooses.

There are gifts, such as fear, which we do not consider to be virtues, underlining the difference between the two, namely that the gifts dispose us to be responsive to the inspirations of the Holy Spirit. When St Thomas considers whether the gifts, or the virtues, are more excellent he answers that that is higher which is moved by a superior cause, and since the Holy Spirit is higher than reason that puts the gifts ahead of the virtues.

The infusion of the Holy Spirit is the infusion of charity because He Himself is love, Person-Love as He is called nowadays. Just as prudence perfects reason and through the moral virtues directs the appetites towards good on the natural level, so charity is the guiding light of the gifts of the Holy Spirit disposing man to his supernatural end.[35] The gifts are good habits which perfect the speculative reason, the practical reason, relations with others, and the irascible and

---

[34] Cf. ST, I-II, q. 68 a. 3.
[35] ST, I-II, q. 68, aa. 3, 5.

concupiscible appetites. Wisdom and understanding perfect the speculative reason, and knowledge and counsel the practical reason. For the apprehension of truth, understanding perfects the speculative reason and counsel perfects the practical. In order to judge rightly, the speculative reason is perfected by wisdom, the practical reason by knowledge. Piety governs and perfects our relations with others, and fortitude and fear the irascible and concupiscible appetites respectively. Fortitude protects man against the fear of dangers, and fear against an inordinate lust for pleasures.[36]

We can see that in their different ways the gifts and the virtues are going to dispose and enable us to practise the beatitudes, which brings us to the question of the relation between the gifts and the beatitudes. With one exception, St Augustine had assigned a gift to each beatitude in order to facilitate it. Aquinas does not go that far but he underlines that the beatitudes have as their purpose to conduce us to happiness, for which we need works of virtue and above all the works of the gifts, if we are referring to eternal happiness. Some of the beatitudes, such as mourning and peace, are neither virtues, nor gifts. Consequently, the beatitudes are deeds or works and so are related to the gifts, not as habit to habit, but as act to habit.[37]

The Fruits of the Holy Spirit

The fruits of the Holy Spirit enumerated by St Paul,[38] are different from the virtues or gifts in not being habits, and from the beatitudes in not being so all-embracing and comprehensive, not so perfect as Aquinas would say, although like them they are acts. The word 'fruit' is being used here as a metaphor, taken from a tree of which it is the final product. Applied to man, then, it refers to what he produces as, so to speak, the end product, and also what he gathers. Fruit does not refer to any and every end product, but rather that which gives enjoyment and delight. To the objection that some fruits, namely charity, meekness, faith and chastity, are

---

[36] ST, I-II, q. 68, a. 4.
[37] Cf. ST, I-II, q. 69, a. 1.
[38] Gal 5:22-23.

virtues, St Thomas points out that sometimes the word virtue is used to apply to its actions, as faith is 'to believe what is unseen' and charity is the action of loving God and neighbour. There is a finality about the fruits: they have the nature of an end in which one delights.[39]

Since a fruit is something that proceeds from a source, like a seed or a root, the different fruits come in different ways from their source in the Holy Spirit. The work of the Holy Spirit orders man's mind with respect to itself, to things around it, and to things below it. The mind is well disposed to itself when it has a good disposition both to what is good and what is evil. The first disposition of the mind is love towards what is good, and so charity is the first fruit of the Holy Spirit which mirrors Him Himself because He is love. And the result of charity is joy since everyone in love rejoices at being united to the beloved. The perfection of joy is peace because somebody at ease with himself is at peace. One cannot rejoice fully in something if one is not at peace and secondly peace calms restless desire, because one cannot perfectly enjoy something if one is not fully satisfied with it. Peace, then, implies two things, namely that one is not disturbed by external things and that our desires are centred on one object.[40]

Man is well disposed to his neighbour when he wills to do good to him, and when he executes those desires in a kind and generous way, which is benignity. At times he has to put up with the sufferings and annoyances his neighbour causes him and this is meekness, which as we have seen, controls anger. He must also avoid treating his neighbour deceitfully or fraudulently, and this is faith in the sense that he is faithful and sincere with others.

Finally, the human being is well disposed to what is beneath him by modesty according to which he observes the mean in external actions whether of word or deed. As regards internal desires, continence separates one from lawful desires and controls them, and chastity does the same for unlawful desires.

---

[39] Cf. ST, I-II, q. 70, aa. 1-2.
[40] Cf. ST, I-II, q. 70, a. 3.

These works of the Spirit are opposed to the works of the flesh as St Paul has just said in the passage of Galatians before he enumerates them. Thus chastity and charity are opposed to fornication which is the satisfaction of lust outside marriage, patience is opposed to quarrels and enmities, and kindness helps to cure them, and goodness to forgive them, and continence is opposed to drunkenness and revelry. In general, we can say the works of the flesh move the person to sensible goods which are beneath him, and the fruits and works of the Spirit move the mind to what is in accord with reason and above it.[41]

---

[41] ST, I-II, q. 70, aa. 3-4.

PART IV

SPECIAL QUESTIONS: GENDER, CONTRACEPTION AND THE RENEWAL OF MARRIAGE

XI.

THE THEOLOGY OF THE BODY DISCOURSES ON THE HUMAN PERSON IN GENESIS

John Paul II uses his personalism to achieve a markedly deeper understanding of the account of man's creation in Genesis. The immediate purpose of his analysis of these texts is to follow Our Lord's directives to go back to the 'beginning' (cf. Mt 19:8; Mk 10:6) when they ask Him about divorce. Hence, the Pope is concerned to understand the original and fundamental meaning of human sexuality, marriage and conjugal love and thereby throw more light on today's problems of divorce, cohabitation, contraception and so on. Their overall consequence is to establish more adequately 'the full truth about man' which is done here by means of Revelation through the prism of creation and redemption. The author is mindful of the well known saying of Vatican II: "The mystery of man becomes clear only in the mystery of the Incarnate Word."[42] He thus overcomes any reductionism about the human person, that is, to a materialist or behaviourist vision and underlines particularly the unity of the human person, and the dignity and sanctity of human life.

In addition, these writings of John Paul II, which show striking originality and gather together ideas flowing from certain currents of philosophy in the last century, are then used to gain greater insight into the sacred text. Specifically, it can be said that by means of the phenomenological method Wojtyla is able to supersede the dualistic

---

[42] *Gaudium et Spes*, n. 22.

concept of man (as mind and body) which has dominated the post-Cartesian world, and today influences many of the secular and revisionist theories of sexual morality and bio-ethics. We say Wojtyla's phenomenological approach 'supersedes' Cartesian dualism because this philosophy understands the body as 'revealing' or 'expressing' the person. The body, then is an integral part of the person, not something attached or juxtaposed to personal consciousness.

Hebrew thought did not divide man into body and soul as later Greek Platonic thought was to do. For the former, the whole man is sometimes referred to as 'body' and sometimes as 'soul' or 'spirit'. Flesh, or 'basar', means the concrete person and refers to his bodily and non-bodily aspects. This has great relevance as applied to the Genesis statement that man and wife become 'one flesh', namely one moral person, because it shows how the unity is both spiritual and bodily at the same time. 'Nephesh', (soul or spirit), expresses the fact that man is a spiritual and rational being of bodily existence. In effect, for Genesis, man is 'a living being' (2,7) that is, an animated being, an ensouled body. John Paul II takes his starting point from the biblical view of person which underlines his unity, not from personalism which is used as a tool to further understand the scriptural text.

Scripture and Christian Tradition acknowledge the special dignity of man and his unity. The first sees the person as God's 'image and likeness' set apart from the rest of the world. The solitude that man experiences in the Genesis account, together with his ability to name the animals and his joy at finding a common and equal partner in Eve, all serve to distinguish him from the material creation. What seems indisputable is that the writings of Edith Stein, which fascinated Karol Wojtyla, set him on course to develop an anthropology which would serve as a unique preparation for his pontificate which came at a time when bio-ethics and the feminist question would be major issues for the Church to deal with. Edith Stein wrote extensively, both on women and the man-woman relationship, from a theological and philosophical, as well as social point of view. Indeed, she had begun in a limited way to study anthropology in Genesis and other parts of the Bible.[43]

---

[43] See Edith Stein, *Essays on Woman*, ICS Publications, Washington, D.C., 1996, espe-

The Person as a Human Subject

In fact, these writings can be better understood if we call them the theology of the body-person or the body-subject. The author often refers to, "the body in the structure of the personal subject." Hence, to understand them, first of all, we have to put ourselves in the correct perspective. This enables us to comprehend in what way man/woman is conscious of him/her self where the 'self' includes the body and is part of it. There are four perspectives from which we can analyse the body: i) from the scientific and empirical point of view studying the biology and anatomy etc. This can never be the basic analysis because it presupposes a subject; ii) from the point of view of a third person observer in its ontological/metaphysical composition according to the ultimate definition of rational animal, as "an individual substance of rational nature"; iii) from the viewpoint of one's own awareness of oneself, that is, one's own subjective consciousness; iv) from the cultural point of view as it is depicted in art and photography, for example.[44] Wojtyla goes on to explain how the first and second accounts of creation in Genesis look at the person in the second and third way respectively.

Christ's words in Mt 19:4 make reference to the first account of creation ("Have you not read the Creator from the beginning made them male and female ...") as well as the second. In these words, Our Lord makes clear that the 'one flesh' means an indissoluble union between man and wife from the time of the beginning of creation. The first account, or Elohist, as it is called on account of the name given to God, is considered to be of later composition than the second one and has a different character. It gives a more theological account in the sense that the human person is defined on the basis of his relationship to God, indeed we can say man is a person precisely because he is similar to God ('image and likeness') in whom we find the model and perfection of personhood, and this essential truth applies equally to men and women. This indicates to us the absolute impossibility of

---

cially, the essay on 'The Vocation of Man and Woman'.
[44] See Jorge Arregui, 'The Nuptial Meaning of the Body and Sexual Ethics', in *Issues for a Catholic BioEthic*, ed. L. Gormally, Linacre Centre, London, 1999, pp. 122-24.

reducing man to the world, although notwithstanding this, man is also a bodily being through which we get the distinction between masculinity and femininity. Indeed, the Holy Father tells us the image of God comes out fully in the dual nature of mankind as male and female. We can also see here a reference to the communion of persons in which marriage consists and the blessing of fertility which is its purpose though not its sole meaning.

The Elohist account also contains a powerful metaphysical and ethical content as well as anthropological. The mystery of creation is linked with the perspective of procreation, the *fieri* or 'coming to be' of future, contingent beings. Equally, there is the aspect of the good, or value, which is emphasized throughout the chapter, especially of the creation of man and woman. The first chapter of Genesis, then, contains material for metaphysics and ethics as well as anthropology according to the principle that being and goodness are convertible ("ens et bonum convertuntur"), as the medieval philosophers taught.[45] Nevertheless, John Paul II saves the bulk of his analysis for the Yahvistic account of creation in the second chapter.

The Body expresses the Person

Very central to an understanding of the theology of the body is a principle already referred to various times, namely that the body is the visible expression of the person. In these discourses the Pope goes beyond saying that the body is part of the dignity of the person to saying that the body reveals the divine plan of God with respect to mankind. Using more theological language he says that the human person through the body becomes a sacrament, that is, a visible sign of the economy of truth and love. And, in turn, the person is the highest expression of the sacrament of creation. When we look at the body correctly, as an integral part of the person we see that it reveals the human person as someone chosen by God to participate in the divine life. And if the body is part of this calling it is going to determine the ways we should treat it and therefore have important ethical consequences, both for human love and marriage and for bio-ethics.

---

[45] General Audience 12-IX-79.

The union in 'one flesh' took place in the state of original innocence, in virtue of the grace of Christ. Our first parents were chosen *in Christ* before the beginning of the world, and so in the original state they shared in the divine life. This innocence, then, signifies divine life, grace and holiness. When they lose it they harm and wound their human nature, including their intellect, so that mankind in his present state is not what he ought to be which is one reason why "only in Christ does man understand his true self."[46] Nevertheless, as Leo XIII had already taught, the 'one flesh' foreshadows the Incarnation which was the divine plan of truth and love hidden in God since time immemorial and revealed in Christ.

Pope John Paul II writes: "It can be said that the visible sign of marriage in the beginning inasmuch as it is linked to the visible sign of Christ and the Church ... transfers the eternal plan of love into the 'historical' dimension and makes it the foundation of the whole sacramental order."[47] "Christ's union with the Church is the summit of the salvific economy of God," the Pope adds. The Redemptive Incarnation has raised up our human nature once again to share in the divine nature and life. Christ has died and risen for every single individual since all are equal before God. Christ's gifts come to us through the visible realities. This is what we mean by the sacramentality of creation and redemption. They come to us through the 'sacramentality' of our lives, family, work, suffering etc.

Theology's recent retrieval of a wider patristic meaning of 'mystery' and 'sacrament' is adopted by Pope John Paul and applied to the 'signs' Genesis gives us about God's eternal plan. It is much broader than the way we have become accustomed to using the word to refer to the seven Sacraments. *'Mysterion'* in Greek tends to emphasize what is hidden, and *'sacramentum'* in Latin what is revealed. Creation is a sacrament in the sense that it reveals signs of God's plan for mankind, and the person is the highpoint of it and marriage is the primordial sacrament. The Church is described in the same vein in *Lumen Gentium* as being

---

[46] *Gaudium et Spes*, n. 22.
[47] General Audience 29-IX-82.

in the 'nature of a sacrament' and we can see that this is what the Pope means by the sacrament of redemption. Reading backwards from the New Testament it can be seen that in Ephesians (5:25) 'one flesh' is explicitly linked with Christ and the Church and through these signs the 'sacraments' of creation and redemption are referred to. Hence, the image of the 'one flesh' can be understood as a sign that refers to the mystery of the plan of salvation hidden in God until the coming of Christ (cf. Ephesians 3:9) which is completed in the union of Christ and the Church of which marriage is an analogy.

Wojtyla's personalism develops from the subject's direct awareness of himself and this includes the experience of his body. He knows the body from its actions, those which happen in it, and those he causes. This, then, is carried over to theology. The two expressions, 'this is bone of my bones' and 'the two became one flesh',[48] have special meanings, the first signifying that the body reveals the person, as it did to Adam, and the second, the personal union in marriage through the body. The body, therefore, we can say, according to Wojtyla, has theological value in that it is a sign of the person who is the 'image of God'.

Hence, the union of man and woman becomes a sign of the mystery of man's eternal salvation in Christ by means of the Church. The two signs, i.e. the 'one flesh' of the beginning and the union between Christ and the Church, form one great sign of the mystery of salvation and sanctification. The grace of original innocence lost through sin is recovered in redemption. However, while there is continuity between the state of innocence and historical redeemed man there is also difference because the threefold concupiscence is still present in the latter. The continuity between the two orders cannot be achieved without the Cross. Spouses who collaborate in the 'redemption of the body', progressively rediscover and live according to their original dignity and in this way are enabled to aspire to that to which they are called. The Pope writes:

> Man appears in the visible world as the highest expression of the divine gift, because he bears within him the interior

---
[48] Gen 2:24.

> dimension of the gift ... Thus in this dimension there is constituted a primordial sacrament, understood as a sign that transmits effectively in the visible world the invisible mystery hidden in God from time immemorial. And this is the mystery of truth and love, the mystery of divine life in which man really participates ... The body, in fact, and it alone, is capable of making visible what is invisible: the spiritual and the divine. It was created to transfer into the visible reality of the world the mystery hidden since time immemorial in God, and thus be a sign of it.[49]

He goes on to say that, therefore, the sacramentality of creation, of the world is revealed in man. Creation, then, as theology tells us, is the gift of God, the fruit of his self-giving and superabundance, and therefore of his love. Man carries the divine gift of God's love and life within him. He is the supreme expression of it, he is the image of God. In God, then, creation, that is the giving of life or calling into existence, and love are united. This union of love and life in God is prolonged in man.

We are thus witnessing here the incarnational theology of John Paul II. It is, of course, based on his adoption of the patristic meaning of 'sacrament', through which what is visible, namely the body, the 'one flesh', the Church, reveal what is invisible, namely the eternal plan of God. But the highpoint of this revelation, the Incarnation itself, by which God reveals Himself to us, follows the same principle. John Paul shows how these other realities referred to are linked intimately to the Incarnation.

The body transfers into the world the mystery hidden in God for generations (cf. Eph 3:9), the mystery of truth and love. It is the mystery of the love of God for man, and of man for woman, according to Genesis 2:24, and the mystery of the prolongation of the creation through the procreative power proper to marriage (Gen 1:28). The model for married life must come from the 'beginning' where God's plans are clearly seen, before sin, in the perfect state, the state of original innocence. The reason why this is a model is because it is the gift of divine life, or election in Christ, given in the beginning, but now rehabilitated in man, by the life and redemption of Christ, but without man losing his fallen nature.

---

[49] General Audience 20-II-80.

Image of God

John Paul II goes beyond his predecessors in affirming that the 'image of God' is not simply in the reason, will and memory, but also in the body. In what aspect of the body do we find this 'image'? The answer given is that it is in its sexuality, in the duality of masculinity and femininity, and their complementarity and reciprocity, which enable them to become a communion of persons. God Himself is a communion of persons in the Trinity and duality in human nature reflects that communion. This does not mean that sexuality applies to God who is above it, but only that it mirrors the communion of persons in Him. In this sense, the image of God also extends to the body, although naturally this does not imply bodiliness to God, but is based on the *relationship* of persons which in humans is through the body. Human existence is a gift and the person fulfils him, or herself, by continuing that self-giving throughout life, by being a person-gift for others.

The expression 'image of God', therefore, does not only refer to the rationality and freedom by which man is similar to God but also to his capacity for communion both with God and with other human beings. To be a person is to exist in a relationship to others, that is, in an I-thou relationship.[50] Such a relationship includes the I-Thou relationship with God which is the basis of the Covenant God establishes with man, and Revelation itself. It is because of this that man can enter into personal communion and friendship with God. The first narration of Genesis (Elohist) seems more theological and seems to bring this out.

The expression "flesh of my flesh and bone of my bones" (Gen 2:23) means precisely 'the body reveals man':

> This concise formula already contains everything that human science could ever say about the structure of the human body as organism, about its vitality and its particular physiology etc. In this first expression of the male-man ... there is also contained a reference to what makes that body truly human, and therefore to what determines man as a person, that is as a being who, even in all his corporality, is 'similar' to God.[51]

---

[50] Pope John Paul II, *Mulieris Dignitatem*, n. 7.
[51] General Audience 14-XI-79.

It is at this point that we understand what is meant by the phrase 'theology of the body' because at the core of the person, and therefore of the body since man is a unity, is a theological dimension since what makes man a person is that he is created 'in the image of God'. Thus, the theology of the body becomes, in a way, the theology of sex and of masculinity and femininity, and of medical ethics, all of which has its beginning in Genesis.

A little reflection on the contemporary mentality also shows us the urgency and necessity of a theology of the body. Descartes bequeathed to the modern mind a mechanistic model of the human body. If, however, it is just a machine, separate from the soul, then like a torch or a television set, it has no proper nature of its own, but only an extrinsic one given it by man, and so has no goal or purpose to fulfil, other than its usefulness to man. So if human life has no inherent value, when its quality of life falls below the desired standard it becomes dispensable. But if the body is an integral part of the dignity of the person, then it also has an inherent meaning given it by the sanctity of human life.

The theology of the body, then, seems to bring out the sacred nature of the body. The human body, we are reminded, has a sacramental and ethical dimension which no other living body has. This is because it is part of a person and a person is the 'image of God'. God is the the source of personhood 'par excellence' and man is his image and so also a person, and his/her body forms part of the dignity of the person. This has implications not only for sexual morality but also for bio-ethics. In the first place, we will draw the consequences for sexual morality, and subsequently it will be necessary to examine further the way in which the communion of persons of man and woman completes the 'image of God'.

We have already seen from the purely rational point of view the dignity and inviolability of the human person including the body. Now from a theological viewpoint we can talk about the sanctity of human life and the human body. St Paul indicates this other source for the dignity of the body when he reminds the Corinthians, "Do you not know that your body is a temple of the Holy Spirit within you, which you have from God? You are not your own, you were bought at a great price",[52] that is to say by the redemptive Incarnation. He explains in the first letter to the Thessalonians that "this is the will of God your sanctification: that you abstain from unchastity, that each one of you know how to control his own body in holiness and honour, not in the passion of lust like heathens who do not know God."[53] Therefore, for the believing Christian, purity becomes a new capacity in virtue of the gift of the Spirit as long as he collaborates with grace by 'living according to the same Spirit'. Therefore St Paul urges the Corinthians, "Shun immorality. Every other sin which a man commits is outside the body; but the immoral man sins against his own body."[54] In shunning immorality he keeps the body 'in holiness and honour.' John Paul II summarizes the Pauline doctrine in the following way:

> It is difficult to express more concisely what the mystery of the Incarnation brings with it for every believer. The fact that the human body becomes in Jesus Christ the body of the God-Man obtains for this reason, in every man, a new supernatural elevation, which every Christian must take into account in his behaviour with regard to his 'own' body and of course with regard to the other's body ... The redemption of the body involves the institution in and through Christ, of a new measure of holiness of the body."[55]

The Meaning of Original Solitude and Original Unity

But man may also be studied from the angle of his own subjectivity and consciousness. By his cognition, self-knowledge and self-determination, man is a personal subject. He may, of course, analyse himself, as he does others, as an external observer, as an object of knowledge. But even prior to this he knows himself through his own personal experience, in the first instance in a pre-reflective way. It must be stressed that we are not talking here of introspection but of man's knowledge of himself through his actions, his use of language and his work, for example.

---

[52] 1 Cor 6:19-20.
[53] 1 Thes 4:3-5.
[54] 1 Cor 6:18.
[55] General Audience 11-II-81.

This self-knowledge, according to John Paul II, is implied in the concept of original solitude referred to in Genesis 2:18 and shown in man's subjective reaction to the creation of woman in verse 2:23. As we have seen, this second account of the creation of man, which is considered to be the older version, is told predominantly from the point of view of man as a personal subject. Man is aware of being 'alone', that is, different from the surrounding creation. Such awareness presupposes subjectivity, self-consciousness and self-determination. It presupposes he is a thinking subject experiencing his own activities and able to interpret and communicate them. In Genesis, two activities are highlighted, that of naming the animals and hence use of language and rationality, and work and dominion over creation; he was placed in the Garden of Eden 'to till the earth and keep it' which demonstrates his superiority and dominion over it.[56]

Man's solitude has a twofold significance. First of all, it marks him out from the material and brute creation because of the above-mentioned activities which he has experience of carrying out. His experience of his own body which places him in the world does not lead him to identify himself with the world, but rather to detach and distinguish himself from it. In realising he is distinct from, and superior to, material creation, he becomes aware of his dignity and that of the body. Genesis makes it clear that man's experience of original solitude is not just a theoretical reflection, but is the result of experiencing the action of his body at work and naming the animals. Through them man realises that he can act in a rational and organised way and fulfil himself in the process. In a word, he is aware of his spirituality, knowledge and will.

The original solitude of man, which is not spoken of in the first, or Elohist, account of creation, is part of the meaning of original unity. By 'unity' the Pope has in mind the union in 'one flesh' which Christ spoke about in Mt 19:5. The Yahvistic account of solitude makes us think only of the man in the first instance and then pass on to the double solitude by which the two recognise each other as help-mates and soul-mates, able to live in harmony, equality and reciprocity with one another. The first solitude leads him to

---

[56] Gen 2:15.

think of the fact that by the body he belongs to the visible world, differing from the other animals, but goes beyond this first stage to think of man according to the dualism of the sexes. Logically and really speaking, corporality and sexuality are not completely identical, because the former is more basic. The fact that man is a body, belongs more to the structure of the personal subject than that he is also male and female. The latter is based on two ways of being a body. For the same reason original solitude precedes original unity. We can deduce that man is the 'image of God', not only through his rational and free humanity, but also through the communion of persons which man and woman form from the beginning.

The common realization of their difference from the world of other living beings, that is their double solitude, gives the couple the possibility of being and existing in a special reciprocity and companionship and enables them to form a communion of persons. The concept of 'help' (Gen 2:20) also expresses this reciprocity in existence which no other living being could have provided. The couple are united by sharing two different forms of a common human body. The word 'rib' is also used to express the reality that they possess the same humanity. The true interpretation of 'helper fit for him' is the direct opposite of its use by some radical feminists' groups who understand it to mean she is a kind of servant or 'lackey' of the man. But the reciprocity in existence could not have been given by any other living being, or by one who was not equal in humanity. Here, we have the first society of persons, of which the rest of society is made up. "Indispensable for this reciprocity was all that constituted the foundation of the solitude of each of them, i.e. self-knowledge and self-determination, that is, subjectivity and consciousness of the meaning of one's body."[57]

"'This at last is bone of my bones and flesh of my flesh; she shall be called Woman, because she was taken out of Man'. Therefore a man leaves his father and his mother and cleaves to his wife and they become one flesh."[58] When the first man says the words at the beginning of this passage, he seems to say 'here is a body

---

[57] General Audience 14-XI-79.
[58] Gen 2:23-4.

that expresses the person!'[59] It is not good that he be alone and he is created not only *with* someone but also *for* them, otherwise he would not completely realize his essence. 'Alone' and 'helper' indicate that the relationship and communion of persons is constitutive for both of them: "Communion of persons means existing as a mutual 'for' in a relationship of mutual gift. And this relationship is precisely the fulfilment of man's original solitude."[60] The unity of man and woman is through the body ('the two will become one flesh') and possesses a multiform dimension – an ethical dimension as Christ's answer to the Pharisees shows, and also a sacramental dimension as seen in St Paul's words to the Ephesians (5:29-32).

The Nuptial Meaning of the Body: the Person as Gift

When Adam utters the words at the beginning of the last paragraph (Gen 2:23), he makes it clear that he realizes that the woman is a gift for him and we may take it that this is mutual. The body expresses the person and the person is a gift for the other. They are a product of God's love, and the body expresses that gift or love. In this way the body is a sign of the love of God and should always, and only, be used to express love. This is the nuptial meaning of the body. The spousal element is "the capacity of expressing love: that love precisely by which the man-person becomes a gift – and by means of this gift – fulfils the very meaning of his being and existence."[61] As the Council taught, persons can only fulfil themselves by 'a sincere gift of themselves', that is to say, in the majority of cases by giving of oneself in marriage, and in the remainder by some service to mankind and especially to God.

The nuptial meaning of the body is really the awareness man had in the state of original innocence, of the fact that he was a gift and the other a gift for him. This can be deduced from the way they see nakedness in this state. They see the body as expressing the whole person, and not the body as an object of use, pleasure, or manipulation, which is the way it is seen by historical man. It

---

[59] General Audience 9-I-80.
[60] Ibid.
[61] General Audience 16-I-80.

was impossible to conceive the human body as an object in the original state, but this truth (of the body as part of the gift of the person) has become blurred in our present condition and is now experienced as a 'distant echo'. Hence, the Bible teaches quite clearly that the body is for married self-giving love, and indeed that this is the purpose of our gendered nature, man and woman (cf. Gen 2:24). Scripture here clearly comes out against alternative sexual lifestyles, as being contrary to the truth of the person and the body. Sexual love is for marriage, and the use of it outside of this goes against the truth of our nature.

The whole creation is above all a gift and man is a visible sign, through the body, as image of God, of God's self-giving. We are told in the General Audience Discourses that "man appears in the world as the highest expression of the divine gift."[62] Through the body man becomes a visible sign of God's love which was the source of creation. Sexuality, then, is a visible sign and expression of the gift of creation and of the love by which the world was created. Each marriage is, in a sense, a renewal of the mystery of creation and an expression of love to which sex should always be linked and subject.[63] Sex, then, makes its appearance in the world as an expression of the love and self-giving of God of which it is always a manifestation. This has the obvious ethical implication that if it is to be true to the nuptial meaning of the body (that is, to express the love of God), sex must always and only be used to form 'one flesh' with one's wife, to express love to her, to which is added the blessing of fertility. Any other use of it opposes God's plan, the nuptial meaning of the body, and the truth of person and their true love.

Precisely because the body is an integral part of the person and not an instrument of it, it has a nuptial meaning in that it can express the love of a person. It can be the vehicle by which he/she makes a gift of themselves. Just as the body expresses the person, so the sexual act expresses, and is a sign of, the two-in-oneness, or unity of the two of marriage. The biblical term for this personal marital union is 'one flesh' which means the stable moral union of

---

[62] General Audience 20-II-80.
[63] General Audience 14-II-79, n. 5.

two persons without prejudice to their separate individuality and identity. Indeed, the latter is enriched by their union. If the sexual act did not express a union of persons given to each other by a union of wills and therefore of love, it would be a lie.

The nuptial meaning of the body in the original state leads on to what the Pope calls *the freedom of the gift*.[64] This quality was enjoyed by man in his primordial, and prototype, condition, in the state of original innocence before the Fall. By freedom we mean here especially self-mastery which is essential in order that man be able to give himself. In this state he/she is able to affirm his/her love for the other for his/her own sake without any self-interest, concupiscence etc. This condition of man at the beatifying beginning is shown in the nakedness of the body. They were able to stand before each other selflessly, but simply desiring the good of the other in which love consists. Hence, we may say the state of innocence is brought out in the state of the body in which man and woman were able to look at each other and recognize the unity of a common humanity, seeing their own humanity in each other. They thus penetrated beyond the purely physical dimension of sexuality to the person and looked at each other with the 'peace of the interior gaze'.

Christ also revealed the vocation to celibacy and virginity over and above the vocation to marriage, and far from opposing this truth about the relational value of the person it confirms and illustrates it. By celibacy man and woman make a gift of themselves for the Kingdom of Heaven, which proves, the Pope says, that the freedom of the gift is in the human body. It shows this body to have a full nuptial meaning.[65] Through this state man and woman are called to a spousal relationship of service to the Kingdom of Heaven and therefore to the Church and their fellow men and women with their whole life and being. In this way they are also especially conformed to the celibate Christ and to the eschatological Kingdom, where there will be no giving and taking in marriage and, thus, they are a sign of it in this world.

Here, then, is Pope John Paul's biblical foundation for sexual

---

[64] General Audience 16-I-80.
[65] Ibid.

ethics. Much of it may be summed up by some well-known words from *Familiaris Consortio*. He writes:

> Sexuality by means of which man and woman give themselves to one another through the acts which are proper and exclusive to spouses, is by no means something purely biological, but concerns the innermost being of the human person as such. It is realized in a truly human way only if it is an integral part of the love by which a man and a woman commit themselves totally to one another until death. The total physical self-giving would be a lie if it were not the sign and fruit of a total personal self-giving, in which the whole person, including the temporal dimension, is present: if the person were to withhold something or reserve the possibility of deciding otherwise in the future, by this very fact he or she would not be giving totally."[66]

Original Nakedness, Shame and Sin

The original state of innocence represents a great contrast with the state of man and woman after the Fall. The shame the person experiences at nakedness after sin reveals that the very meaning of nakedness and, in turn, the meaning of the body has changed. What has gone is the acceptance in the state of original innocence of the body as a sign, or expression of the person. Sin has caused a greater separation between the person and the body such that the body represents the person to a lesser degree. The important thing, however, about these original experiences (i.e. also original solitude and unity), is not simply that they belong to man's theological prehistory, but that there is still an echo of them in our present state and so they are at the root of all that we experience and especially of all that we are called to become, that is the holiness that is our goal by overcoming sin through redemption.

Together with shame they experienced fear, as we learn from the dialogue between God and Adam. The "Lord God called to the man, and said to him, 'Where are you?' And he said, 'I heard the sound of you in the garden, and I was afraid, because I was naked; and I hid myself.'"[67] This fear expressed something deeper than the physical shame bound up with nakedness. It is caused

---

[66] John Paul II, Apostolic Exhortation, *Familiaris Consortio*, n. 11.
[67] Gen 3:9-10.

by the breach in the original covenant with God, as is indicated by the words of God which follow: "Who told you that you were naked? Have you eaten of the tree of which I commanded you not to eat?"[68] The Pope writes: "Actually through 'nakedness', there is manifested man deprived of participation in the Gift, man alienated from that Love which had been the source of that original gift, the source of the original good intended for the creature."[69]

The results of this state are according to the traditional teaching of the Church, the loss of the supernatural (faith, hope and charity) and preternatural gifts (immortality, impassibility etc) with which man had been originally endowed though they were not due to his nature. "Furthermore, he suffered a loss in what belongs to his nature itself, to humanity in the original fullness 'of the image of God'. The three forms of lust do not correspond to the fullness of that image, but precisely to the loss, the deficiencies, the limitations that appeared with sin."[70] The reduction of the image of God in man means, for example, that he ceases to participate in the divine perception of the world and its goodness, he ceases to see his transcendence over the world of material things *(animalia)* so clearly.[71]

The experience of sin seems also to have affected the inner unity of man between spirit and body. Maybe, this also makes it more difficult for man to perceive himself as a spirit/body unity which could explain why thinkers so often assume a mind/body dualism. John Paul II writes:

> "The body, which is not subordinated to the spirit as in the state of original innocence, bears within it a constant source of resistance to the spirit, and threatens, in a way, the unity of the man-person, that is, of the moral nature, which is firmly rooted in the very constitution of the person. Lust, and in particular the lust of the body, is a specific threat to the structure of self-control and self-mastery, through which the human person is formed. And it also constitutes a specific challenge for it. In any case the man of lust does not control his own body in the

---

[68] Gen 3:11.
[69] General Audience 14-V-80.
[70] Ibid.
[71] Cf. ibid.

same way ... as the man of original innocence did."[72]

Sin, and the threefold concupiscence that accompanies it, has caused a separation from the state of original innocence, ushering in lust which inclines a person to look upon a member of the opposite sex as an object of pleasure and use. Man is called to overcome this concupiscence by true personal love of another. He must do this by keeping before his mind the three originating experiences, original solitude, original unity, original nakedness, which antedate original sin and pursue the goods they represent. This process enabled by grace is called the 'redemption of the body.'

The Redemption of the Body

The union in 'one flesh' took place in the state of original innocence in virtue of the grace of Christ. Our first parents were chosen in Christ before the foundation of the world and thus at creation they shared in divine life. The original union is called by John Paul the 'primordial sacrament', in the wider sense of sacrament meaning a visible sign which reveals a deeper reality. As we saw, *'mysterion'* in Greek translates into *'sacramentum'* in Latin, giving us 'mystery' and 'sacrament' in the vernacular, where the first emphasizes what is hidden and the second what is revealed. The state of innocence signifies divine life, grace and holiness. When our first parents lose this state by original sin the result for mankind is the historical state of 'fallen human nature' which involves the loss of the grace of divine life, the wounds of sin and the threefold concupiscence.

The Redemptive Incarnation has raised up human nature once again to share in the divine nature and life. Christ's gifts come to us through visible realities, which is what we mean by the sacramentality of creation and redemption. In Ephesians 3:9, St Paul speaks of the mystery hidden for ages in God, which is the mystery of truth and love for man and now realized in Christ. Pope John Paul goes on to declare that this mystery hidden from ages past is definitively revealed in the union of Christ and the Church referred to later on in Ephesians 5:21-33. The Church

---

[72] General Audience 28-V-80.

is the sacrament of redemption and the union of Christ and the Church is foreshadowed in the 'one flesh' of Genesis with which St Paul explicitly links it. The Pope writes: "It can be said that the visible sign of marriage in the beginning inasmuch as it is linked to the visible sign of Christ and the Church ... transfers the eternal plan of love into the historical dimension and makes it the foundation of the whole sacramental order."[73]

The sacramental sign not only proclaims the mystery, but also accomplishes what it signifies. The two signs referred to above, that is the 'one flesh' and the union of Christ and the Church, form one great sign of the mystery of salvation and sanctification. The spousal significance of the body is completed with its redemptive significance and with its sanctifying value. The grace of original innocence lost through sin is recovered in redemption. Spouses who collaborate in the 'redemption of the body', progressively rediscover and live according to their original dignity. Only by sanctifying their married life, by living according to the grace of redemption, can spouses achieve that to which they are called. In this way marriage is a vocation to sanctity. Christ's union with the Church has both a unitive and life-giving dimension. It is unitive when the Church responds to the gift of the Bridegroom, and life-giving through the grace of the Church's spiritual motherhood.

The theology of the body is an incarnational theology, rather than a simply sacramental one in the sense that the latter, i.e. sacramental theology, falls within the incarnational principle. Working on the access opened up to the Fathers by Vatican II when it characterized the Church as being "in the nature of a sacrament"[74] and as "the universal sacrament of salvation", John Paul II developed this theology beyond the confines of marriage and bio-ethics to cover ecclesiology and give a deeper treatment to the Church as Body and Bride of Christ. He shows how within the sacrament of Redemption, not only marriage, but also other human realities such as work and suffering, are taken up by Jesus and united through the humanity to the divine life. Work,

---

[73] General Audience 29-IX-82.
[74] Cf. *Lumen Gentium*, nn. 1, 48.

in the words of St Josemaria Escriva becomes a "redeemed and redemptive reality".[75] We will deal more fully with the 'sacrament of Redemption' and its consequences when we come to the chapter on marriage.

The Purpose of the Theology of the Body

The theology of the body discourses successfully achieve what they set out to show, namely that the nature of marriage and masculinity and femininity 'in the beginning' reveal that sex is part of, and subject to, an indissoluble union of love between man and woman. However, they also do two other things. The analysis of original innocence sets the scene for a deeper presentation of the Incarnation and the Redemption which is, after all, a re-creation of the original model intended by God and described in the first three chapters of Genesis.

They also, however, provide invaluable criteria for the many issues and dilemmas of bio-ethics with which contemporary man is faced. The features which are underlined are the complete difference of the human body from other material bodies and organisms, and the dignity and, indeed, the sanctity of human life and the human body because they share integrally in these characteristics of the human person himself. Such activities as IVF, embryonic stem-cell research and cloning, especially the creation of animal/human hybrids, which involve damaging and destroying many embryos, go against the dignity and sanctity due to the human body and marriage, as does the obtaining of human foetal tissue and stem cells to be used for medical purposes from abortions. We can thus understand the root of the Church's condemnation of them, but this 'sanctity of human life' needs more precise explanation.

Man and woman share the title 'person' with God because they have a similarity and likeness to God which is brought out by the biblical phrase 'image of God'. This sets human beings apart from other 'living beings' in the world and also the human body from the matter of the earth. It shows us the reason for the sanctity of human life and also of the body, because it is an integral part of

---

[75] St Josemaria Escriva, *Christ is Passing by*, Scepter, London, n. 47.

the person. Of course God does not have a body, but mankind through the body is capable of forming a communion of persons which reflects the communion of the Trinity. The human body, the Pope says, in the most general way enters into the definition of a sacrament in that it is the visible expression of the invisible side of the person. It also has the potential to be the 'temple of the Holy Spirit' and a means of grace. This points to the inviolability of the person and has implications for how we must protect human life from the beginning and must treat the body in an ethical way in sexual matters.

John Paul II spells out the sanctity of human procreation by explaining how God is present in it. He writes:

> When a new person is born of the conjugal union of the two, he brings with him into the world a particular image and likeness of God himself: *the genealogy of the person is inscribed in the very biology of generation.* In affirming that the spouses, as parents, cooperate with God the Creator in conceiving and giving birth to a new human being, we are not speaking merely with reference to the laws of biology. Instead we wish to emphasize that *God himself is present in human fatherhood and motherhood* quite differently than he is present in all other instances of begetting 'on earth'. Indeed God alone is the source of that 'image and likeness' which is proper to the human being, as it was received at Creation. Begetting is the continuation of creation.[76]

It reminds us again of what we have often noted, that there is a big difference between Christianity and secularism concerning anthropology and the nature of personhood. Secular thought tends to believe that a person is consciousness in a body and hence that the person is there when there is awareness. Christians, on the other hand, hold that a person is present from conception and since all the genetic information which will go to make up that person is there at the one cell stage, then that first cell is already a subject and a distinct individual. John Paul II, citing passages from the Old and New Testaments, speaks of "the indisputable recognition of the value of life from its very beginnings" and emphasizes that "life is always a good", even the life of a one or two week-old embryo,

---

[76] Pope John Paul II, *Evangelium Vitae*, 43, quoting his own *Letter to Families*, n. 9.

because mankind is different from all other living beings, has spiritual faculties and a particular likeness to God.[77]

A Summary of the Theology of the Body

In these discourses the Pope establishes i) the original unity of man and woman, whereby they lived in harmony and equality and possessed a complementarity and reciprocity which enabled them to become 'one flesh', and live in indissoluble union; ii) original solitude in which man realises his difference and superiority over the rest of creation and his need for communion with, and self-giving to, another person; iii) the human body is an expression of the person and an integral part of it and, therefore, has a sacramental value in the wide sense of the word of being the visible expression of an invisible spiritual reality. But this 'sacramental' value confers on the body and its actions a special dignity and sanctity. It is part of the 'image of God'; iv) persons are gifts for one another in virtue of their spiritual/bodily nature and thus can give themselves to one another through the body, which the Pope calls *the nuptial meaning of the body*. This is the root of personal and sexual love; v) Original nakedness. In the state of original innocence man and woman saw through the body to the person and loved and respected one another *for their own sake* with what the Pope calls 'the peace of the interior gaze', that is, without any intermingling of sensuality, or selfishness, and therefore also without shame. Sin has caused a separation from this state, ushering in lust which inclines a person to look upon a member of the opposite sex as an object of pleasure, manipulation and use. Man is called to overcome this concupiscence by true personal love of another. This process enabled by grace is called the 'redemption of the body'.

---

[77] Ibid. nn. 45 & 34 respectively.

XII.

SEXUALITY, GENDER AND FEMINISM

One of the many relevant consequences of the theology of the body is that it explains the nature of the sexual difference between man and woman and the purpose of it. Today, in some quarters, this is thrown into confusion by the 'ideology of gender', that is, the opinion that gender roles in society are socially generated, and should be a matter for the free choice of individuals. The reference is to the social gender role, whatever one's biological sexuality may be, but many go on to imply that the use of one's sexuality should also be a matter of personal choice. This has the effect of seeking to justify a series of alternative life-styles, cohabitation, gay 'marriage', or any other consensual union as equal to marriage, thus undermining the self-giving and commitment of the family as the basic cell of society and its unique contribution to the common good of mankind.

As we have already seen, sexuality, that is, being male or female, is through the body but affects the whole person, and the social aspect of sexuality (referred to by some as gender) is only a consequence of the personal biological truth and not a completely separate category of its own. Until the twentieth century philosophy had considered man as a human person in the abstract without trying to describe what it means to be a masculine or feminine person. Since sexuality is to be found in the *person* and not in the nature, it belongs to the existence or subsistence of the human being. A concrete human being, not only has a rational nature, but also a personal subsistence making them a unique unrepeatable individual and by which they are in the world as man or woman, which is what we mean by sexuality.

Masculinity and femininity are two irreducible ways of being a human person, as is testified by Genesis, "male and female he created them."[1] But man recognized his uniqueness (he was alone) until a 'helper' was made for him who was 'bone of my bones'. In this way man and woman recognized their common personhood and, by a second level of solitude, their superiority over the world of things in virtue of their spiritual nature deriving from being the 'image of God'. John Paul II writes that:

> when the Book of Genesis speaks of 'help', it is not referring merely to acting but also to being. Womanhood and manhood are complementary *not only from the physical and psychological points of view*, but also from the *ontological*. It is only through the duality of the 'masculine' and 'feminine' that the 'human' finds full realization.[2]

There is rightly an emphasis on equality of personhood between the sexes, but equality does not mean identity. Man and woman are equal and different in all aspects of their being. There is a unity of human nature, a unity in difference, a dual unity. Neither male nor female alone can represent the whole of human nature. This dual dimension not only distinguishes the sexes but also points to the communion, reciprocity and complementarity between them. Pope John Paul writes: "Being a person in the image and likeness of God thus involves existing in a relationship, in relation to the other 'I'."[3] And as we shall see more fully, by this dual dimension man is more properly the 'image of God' who is Himself a communion of persons.

Feminism and the Ideology of Gender

Some of the traditional assumptions concerning women have been superseded in our time, such as those that saw a hierarchy of superiority between men and women, or the tendency to see man as active and woman as passive, or man as the only breadwinner.

---

[1] Gen 1:27.
[2] Letter of Pope John Paul II to Women, CTS, London, 1995.
[3] John Paul II, *Mulieris Dignitatem*, n. 7.

Hitherto, many considered the caring professions to be the principal, and sometimes the only, ones for which women were fitted, yet women have shown themselves to be the equal of men in many activities previously regarded as a male preserve, such as business and finance, various types of management whether of the commercial or public sector, etc.

These developments, which simply do justice to the equality between men and women and ensure that it is reflected socially and economically, have undoubtedly been driven by the Feminist Movement since the late 1960s. Modern feminism, founded on writings such as Simone de Beauvoir's *Second Sex* and Betty Friedan's *The Feminine Mystique* passed from the emancipation sought on and off since the French Revolution to a more militant liberation, and hence it came to be known as 'Women's Lib'. The more radical side of feminism was never espoused by the majority of women though it had the capacity to influence mainstream views, even if by the end of the twentieth century it showed a marked tendency to be on the wane.

From the beginning of that century feminism had been, to a greater or lesser degree, associated with Marxism because the early feminists equated Socialism with social progress and saw in it an opportunity to bring about greater civil equality before the law, together with sexual liberation. Women were considered to be subject to male 'power structures' in the workplace and in social life, and this in turn was thought to be influenced by their so-called subjugation to child-bearing, household activities, marital laws making divorce difficult, etc. It is for this reason that radical feminism espoused sexual autonomy as part of its wider programme, claiming so-called 'reproductive rights' to easy or free contraception, abortion, child care facilities. These, together with claims to easier divorce, cohabitation, and sterilization, are considered by some to be 'rights' denied by a patriarchal society.

In the second half of the twentieth century the women's movement took on a more militant character. Whereas before it had been a battle for equality between the sexes, there was now talk also of 'gender war' among radicals. Previously, the predominant aim had been equivalence with the male model, although the suffragettes had rejected this approach, but now the emphasis was put on the difference, and even the superiority, of women. Among some of the more extreme exponents there was talk of a previous matriarchal society which worshipped the goddess Gaia, and was ruled by women, with inheritance through the female line. The later Hellenic and Christian civilizations displaced this and imposed a patriarchal society. It must be said the evidence for this hypothesis is meagre to say the least. Nevertheless, the view prospered among radicals that the sexual morality of patriarchal society, based on pre-marital virginity and marital fidelity, became a tool to oppress women. Hence, women's independence socially, economically and legally was linked to their sexual autonomy. One can also see here, in this so-called independence, one of the currents that fuels the growth of the practice of cohabitation from the female side.

Indeed, historically, it would be foolish to deny that women have often been denied equality of professional and social opportunities and progress to which they have a right. However, there has also been a tendency to over-emphasize the subordination of women in order to raise the stakes and create conflict and tension in order to empower women. But we must be careful to note that, according to the old saying, "the abuse of a thing does not invalidate the use of it." Unfortunately, what we witness in this scenario is an application of the warning given in Genesis to Eve, as a result of original sin, "(your) husband shall rule over you";[4] the unity and equality in the state of original innocence has been damaged but not lost.

There will always be tension between the social progress of women and their domestic life, but it will only be true progress if it is sought within moral truth. The link between women's emancipation and so-called sexual liberation has also been vastly exaggerated under the influence of false ideologies. One of the first perpetrators of it in modern times was Saint-Simon, the atheistic founder of sociology, and it was later taken up by Marxists. A recent female writer, Angela West, sounds a warning that to blame the patriarchal society for women's afflictions, and thereby proclaiming by implication their own innocence, can only

---

[4] Gen 3:16.

be harmful to women in the long run.[5]

Opinion polls are apt to reveal that a high percentage of women would rather stay at home and look after the children than have to go to work, but presumably they have become accustomed to the income, and doubtless there is a certain social pressure to conform. Some observers question whether the frustrations and tensions women often feel are not due to the need to juggle too many occupations at once.[6] What the few can manage cannot necessarily be a norm for the many. And what of research showing that teenage children of professional parents often under-perform in exams, due in part to the sparse time and attention afforded them by their parents?

Edith Stein's Description of Woman's Soul

Very pertinent in this regard are the thoughts of Edith Stein, herself a prominent proponent of the advancement of women during the early part of the twentieth century. Their particular interest lies in the fact that she looks at the question from the point of view of overall personal development and fulfilment, rather than just the socio-economic angle, which is surely the key to the dilemmas that arise. She emphasizes what she calls feminine singularity, namely that women, though equal, are different from men in that they have their own gifts and qualities which must be identified if their true well-being and development is to be served. The point had been hotly contested by the suffragettes a decade or two earlier, just as we have seen it was to be in the 60s and 70s. This position overlooks what Stein calls 'intrinsic feminine value' which most women (and indeed men) are able to identify with the majority of the time.

She points to two criteria distinguishing men from women, without wishing to be in any way exhaustive, in order to bring out this singularity. Males appear to be more objective in that they are in the habit of dedicating themselves at work to a discipline, be it business, technology, or academia, and so are subject to the

---

[5] Angela West, *Deadly Innocence, Feminism and the Mythology of Sin*, London 1995, quoted in Aidan Nichols, *Christendom Awake*, T & T Clark, Edinburgh, 1999.
[6] See Nichols, op. cit., p. 123.

laws of the discipline. "*Woman's attitude is personal*; and this has several meanings: in one instance she is happily involved with her total being in what she does; then she has particular interest for the living, concrete person, and indeed, as much for her own personal life and personal affairs as for those of other persons."[7] These are characteristics rather than values at this stage and we shall see that they can be the source of defects and failings as well as virtues if they are not responsibly cultivated.

The second criterion is that while the very specialization may lead to one-sided development in men, in women there is a natural drive towards totality and self-containment. By this she means there is an innate tendency to become a complete human being fully developed in every way, and by the same token she would like others to fulfil the same destiny. This call to become a whole person in whom the image of God is fully developed, and his gifts flourish under the influence of a rationally-led will, which in turn guides and contains the lower faculties, is the vocation of every person, man and woman.

However, Edith Stein finds this directedness to be particularly strong in woman in view of her task as companion and mother, since if she is indeed to be a support, she must herself be of firm character which can only be the case if inwardly there is order and equilibrium. Motherhood involves nourishing and protecting the true humanity of her children which can only happen in the measure that she possesses it herself. Nevertheless, nature does not by itself furnish us with virtue, but is only the breeding ground of virtue and indeed it can lead to vices or failings. Stein identifies a concern a woman may have for her own personal importance and an over-sensitivity to criticism and desire for recognition. Her husband must be acknowledged as the best and the children as clever, beautiful etc., to the point of loss of objectivity. Along with this, may go an excessive interest in others and a desire to enter into their lives. A perverted desire for totality can lead to an excessive desire to know everything and thus skim the surface, and go deeply into nothing. More men, comments Stein, have

---

[7] Edith Stein, *The Significance of Woman's Intrinsic Value in National Life* in Collected Works, vol. II, p. 255, ICS Publications, Washington, 1996.

an objective and perhaps deeper formation than women, though more women come closer to the full goal of humanity.[8]

She then considers how it is possible to purify the feminine character of these possible faults and weaknesses and finds the answer, interestingly, in 'thoroughly objective work' of whatever sort, whether it be housework, or professional paid employment of all kinds. The reason is that work subjects the whole person with their moods, thoughts, and dispositions to a discipline which, since it means submitting oneself to the laws of work, breeds self-control, inner depth and maturity. The development of full personal humanity and the overcoming of the faults of feminine singularity seems to be a very original, or at least rare, argument for equality of opportunity between men and women, but it also appears to go to the nub of the issue. It does not, however, stop there, because Edith Stein is keen that the virtues of feminine singularity be brought to bear for the good of society as a whole, for example by women's voice being fully heard in the enactment of parliamentary laws. She was also more than aware of the need to start at an early age and educate young girls according to feminine singularity so as to avoid the pitfalls and maximize their virtues and the potential.

The Sexuality/Gender Distinction

As we have indicated, there are those who argue for a distinction between sexuality and gender but this view is based on sociological criteria rather than anthropological or theological truth. Sexuality is founded on the biological reality, but gender is understood in terms of one's role in society, professionally and personally, and so subject to choice, as we have noted. We are here back to a 'freedom' which is separated from truth, in this case the truth of our sexual nature. As with all such freedom and autonomy it so easily becomes licence. The distinction features in major international conferences on women and population issues, as for example that of Cairo in 1994, and deserves closer scrutiny.

All talk of human nature, or the biological differences between

---

[8] See Edith Stein, Collected Works, vol. II, pp. 255-8, for the material of this and the following paragraph.

man and woman, is set aside by the present cult figures in studies of sexuality such as Michel Foucault who influence radical feminism. It is claimed that there is no reason why we should define ourselves in terms of the reproductive system. Why not understand ourselves in terms of talent and merit? Differences up to now have been determined by power structures, where men were prioritized above women according to the reproductive system. Differences between the sexes are a matter of social fabrication which benefit certain people who are in power. They are the result of what is called 'social constructivism'. This movement is an attempt to show that many of our assumptions are not based on truth, but on vested interests of the powerful and reactionary. Hence, sexuality is a matter of choice. One cannot fail to see the former Marxist interest in social science, and its preoccupation with the structures of class and power elites, behind this view. However, it also has the effect today of promoting cohabitation, homosexuality, bi-sexuality and choice in general, as a way of undermining the predominant 'power structure' represented by heterosexuality and marriage and the family. The insistence on inclusive language, the neutrality of children's toys, and certain forms of literature, can be contributions, wittingly or unwittingly, to this movement.

The proponents of the sexuality/gender distinction accept the biological differences between males and females based on chromosomes, hormones and genitalia, but maintain that these are of less significance than the fact that we are all persons. This is the position put forward by radical feminists and some homosexual groups. Because, allegedly, gender roles are largely socially generated it is within our power to change them. In other words, they are the result of nurture rather than nature. Individuals must be free to choose the gender they assume whatever their biological sexuality. To this end, education of children should be non-sexist, avoiding even gender-stereotype toys, such as giving trains to boys and dolls to girls, etc. If gender roles are largely the result of environment and social conditioning, therefore nurture, it is in our power to remould them and so those who are on this side of the argument deliberately underestimate a human nature which would establish a unity in difference between the sexes. This is an instance of endeavouring to separate freedom from nature, so that women are liberated from child-bearing and homosexuals from being expected to be heterosexual, if they so choose, and so on. We have already pointed to the fallacious distinction between freedom and nature, which are in harmony and not conflict. Freedom, we remember, is not unconditional or unlimited or indeterminate, but subject to the truth of man and therefore human nature.

There is in all of this a confused mixture of dubious sociological data forming the basis for ethical, or more correctly, amoral conclusions. One can merely emphasize that ethical conclusions can only be derived from the true good and freedom of the human person in its masculinity and femininity, according to the principles we have outlined throughout this study. It is not idle to note that radical feminism does not give an adequate rendering of the latter. So feminists reach the conclusion that women must have 'freedom' over their bodies and 'natures' to control their fertility with contraceptives or abortion. And the same argument is used to reach the opposite conclusion, that sterile women have the 'right' to recur to in-vitro-fertilization to conceive a child. Again, this is a use of freedom which exceeds the truth and nature of the person. What we are talking about here is technological control which does not accord with human dignity. A person grows as a human being by acting according to true moral values and not by merely utilitarian attitudes.

Sexuality: Unity in Difference

Whether one is a man or a woman affects every aspect of one's being, life and every cell in the body, the tone of voice, the way of walking, dressing etc., to say nothing of the predominant emotions, interests, ways of seeing things of the sexes. The most obvious difference is the female hormonal system which works on a more cyclical basis than a male's, and this together with the female potentiality for pregnancy and birth gives rise to significant psychological differences between men and women.

Masculinity and femininity go to the very core of the person and represent a sexual value for each other. In fact, man only knows who he is sexually by knowing woman and vice versa. Were either to exist alone in the world they would never understand themselves as man or woman respectively. Sexuality is a constituent part of the person and not just a quality. Pope John Paul has written, "Precisely the function of sex, which is, in a sense, a constituent part of the person (not just an attribute of the person), proves how deeply man, with all his spiritual solitude, with the uniqueness, never to be repeated, of his person, is constituted by the body as 'he' or 'she'."[9]

Sexuality belongs to the male or female body, but the body, in turn, is an integral part of the person, not an adjunct of it. If man is a unity then the body shares in the value of the person and enjoys the dignity and reverence due to the latter. It is for this reason that civilized systems of law, together with upholding the right to life have usually also defended the right to bodily integrity. Dualism makes it impossible to draw a proper distinction between male and female, and show their similarity and difference, because it separates body and spirit too radically, not allowing for their unity, and thus is unable to see how different biological make-up can affect the whole person.

It must be stressed that a correct account of sexuality entails the radical unity of the human person as body and soul, matter and spirit. John Locke argued long ago that personal identity is based on consciousness,[10] and many, wittingly or unwittingly, hold to the same view today. In other words, a human being who is unable to exercise intelligence, or other self-conscious abilities, is not a human person. If one accepts this, the notion that human life possesses a fundamental, intrinsic value is no longer tenable, because the 'consciousness view' makes personhood depend on what one does rather than what one is. Nor does it possess the spirit/body definition of a person necessary to describe human sexuality adequately.

From a theological point of view, the foundation for the difference between male and female is to be found in man's condition as the image of God. As we saw, the image of God, which was

---

[9] General Audience 21-XI-79.
[10] J. Locke, *Essay on Human Understanding*, Bk II, Ch. 27, § 26.

traditionally understood to reside in intellect, will and memory, also extends to the body. What aspect of the body? Precisely its sexuality by which man/woman can be a person-gift for one another and form a communion of persons. In this respect, mankind images the communion of Persons of the Trinity by which the Father and Son are eternally related to each other by the Person Gift of the Holy Spirit. In this way, the body reveals something of the mystery of God and so forms part of the sanctity of human life. No wonder St Paul says, "Your body is a temple of the Holy Spirit within you, which you have from God ... so glorify God in your body."[11]

Only in Christ and Christian Revelation can the creation of man as male and female be fully understood. Male and female were created to be 'one flesh', that is, to form a communion of persons in order to express love and thus together to be the image of God. The closeness of the union implies that the two are complementary and reciprocal, which can readily be seen on the biological and psychological level, but is also true ontologically. The fullness of human nature requires both sexes, because neither the one nor the other, on its own, exhausts what we mean by the human person. The difference between man and woman points to the 'great mystery' of conjugal union and its analogical portrayal of the relationship between Christ and the Church. Not only is this love a symbol, but it participates in the love that Christ shows towards the Church, as St Paul makes clear when he says, "Husbands, love your wives, as Christ loved the Church and gave himself up for her."[12]

The Pope points out that the mystery works both ways and the reality of male and female throws light on the relationship of Christ and the Church just as the latter does on the union of male and female. This indicates how damaging is the present tendency to blur the distinction between the two. It is a great 'mystery' and rationalism does not tolerate mystery. In words, which are truly profound and prophetic about our own time, the Holy Father says:

---

[11] 1 Cor 6:19.
[12] Eph 5:25.

It does not accept the mystery of man as male and female, nor is it willing to admit that the full truth about man has been revealed in Jesus Christ. In particular, it does not accept the 'great mystery' proclaimed in the Letter to the Ephesians, but radically opposes it. It may well acknowledge, in the context of a vague deism, the possibility and even the need for a supreme or divine Being, but it firmly rejects the idea of a God who became man in order to save man. For rationalism it is unthinkable that God should be the Redeemer, much less *that he should be 'Bridegroom',* the primordial and unique source of the human love between spouses.[13]

The reciprocity and communion between the sexes is shown by one's own experience of the ability of the body-person to make a gift of oneself to another person and, in turn, receive the gift of the other. Indeed, in the one action there is both giving and receiving. It clearly happens at the biological level, and the biological mechanism is able to reciprocate by reception of the gift. This is an expression of the mutuality and complementarity of the husband's and wife's love for each other in that they can both give to, and receive from, the others' affections. Analogically we can say, Mary received the gift of God in her heart and then consequently in her body, and this reception was the result of giving and entrusting herself to the gift of God received.

Human beings are a gift for one another. It is part of the essence of human persons that they are made for others, because they are relational beings. Since the whole of creation is a gift, and they reflect the Creator, they are able to make a gift of themselves and in that measure they fulfil themselves. For them to make a total sexual gift of themselves, however, they must respect the truth about the person, and the unity in difference of sexuality, which makes the complementarity and reciprocity of the gift possible. The understanding of the human person as a gift builds on the traditional metaphysical understanding of the person as 'an individual substance of rational nature' and is inclusive and not exclusive of it. It brings out more fully the subjectivity and consciousness of the human being, concepts which are largely ignored by the traditional objective definition. But subjectivity is

---

[13] *Letter to Families*, n. 19.

important for expressing love and friendship, the emotions and so on.

The fact that man and woman can enter into relationships with one another, and that this is part of their sexuality, shows that sexuality is not just biological, but personal and spiritual. Only spiritual persons can love and form relationships; animals are incapable of it which is why their sexuality is instinctual. This fact points to the radical difference between animal and human sexuality and is based on the human body's participation in the image of God, the unifying complementarity of male and female, and hence their ability to enter into personal communion.

Sexuality through the Body to the Person

Bodiliness distinguishes human beings into male and female, but this does not entail that sexuality is biological. On the contrary, precisely because the body is an integral part of the person, sexuality extends to the whole person and their actions. Masculinity and femininity are two ways of existing as a human person and so point to a unity in difference. It follows that between the sexes there is complementarity and reciprocity and the human person can only be fully described in terms of both of them. The masculinity and femininity of the body make it possible for human beings to make a spousal gift of themselves to one another.

At the same time as affirming the selfhood of the person, personalism goes on to confirm that the relational aspect, or dimension, of the person as a gift for others is a constitutive aspect of personhood. The deepest manifestation of this self-giving on the human level is spousal self-donation. This ability of male and female to give themselves to one another, on account of their complementarity and reciprocity, is called by John Paul II the 'nuptial meaning of the body.' This is an important concept in the Pope's treatment of marriage and contraception. The person experiences, and is aware of, self-donation such that spousal self-donation, or the lack of it, is something consciously lived through. In that sense, the Pope sees a subjective awareness by contracepting spouses of a holding back: "The act of contraception ... expresses an objective refusal to give all the good of femininity and masculinity."[14]

The person including the body is an acting subject to be distinguished from things and objects. When another person is not perceived as a gift, but as an object to be possessed and enjoyed, then their sexuality and dignity suffer. The body, and the sexuality of the other, are not seen as a sign or expression of their personal subjectivity. The person is then reduced from being a subject to an object. The other is not now loved in themselves, or for themselves, but is reduced to the level of an object to be used. Our Lord condemned adultery in the heart which occurs in thought or attitude before it occurs in an external act.

The exercise of sexuality, therefore, is a personal action in which the whole conscious and free person is involved and not just a biological action, as we shall see. Human sexual love is thus spiritual and bodily at the same time. Love proceeds from the senses, but the crucial point about genuine love is that bodily and sensual attraction be directed by reason and integrated into spiritual love. Only thus can it be fully personal and human. This is what we mean by chastity. This self-mastery must be achieved throughout a lifetime. Sexual activity which is merely instinctual and not subject to a love which consists in personal self-giving and concern for the good of the other is unworthy of human dignity and is selfish.

The fact that the body reveals the person, or is a sign of the person, is going to enable him to say that the body has a sacramental value in the sense that it is an integral part of something much deeper. This, in turn, will constitute a norm of behaviour with regard to the body and the good of the person, based on the truth of the person. Anyone with a dualist mentality, very widespread today, is going to find the Catholic Church's doctrine on sexuality, life and bio-ethical questions, very difficult to understand.

Sexuality is Personal as well as Biological: some psychological and social consequences

Hence, sexuality is spiritual and personal as well as bodily, or we might say, because it is bodily, if we understand the integrity of the person correctly. The body expresses and reveals the spiritual

---

[14] General Audience 17-IX-83; and *Familiaris Consortio*, n. 32.

person in virtue of the unity. Because sex is expressed bodily it does not mean it is biological; far from it. Sexuality may be described as the sharing of the gift of self in a life-giving and love-giving way in and through the body. The human body, then, clearly has a spiritual dimension in a way that the animal body does not. This is one of the lessons the Pope draws from the reference in Genesis to the original solitude of Adam in creation. First of all, he was aware through consciousness of his body that he was different from other bodily beings and the material creation. Secondly, the account of the creation of woman and appearance of the dual nature of man shows man was made for communion and to relate to another and to others.

It shows also that bodiliness and sexuality are not fully identifiable, bodiliness being the deeper notion, ontologically preceding sexuality. Adam said, "this at last is flesh of my flesh and bone of my bones," confirming that personal and bodily identity precedes sexuality. In other words, identity is not decided entirely by sexuality even though the latter affects every aspect of one's being. This takes on special importance in the case of homosexuals since it means that their personal and bodily identity, and their personal rights and duties flowing from this, take precedence over their sexual orientation.

In fact, through the bodily biology, sexuality affects the whole person and therefore it will have an impact on male and female psychology. We must be careful here because, in a sense, we can see the whole range of psychological types in both sexes. However, as we've said, every aspect of one's being is touched by whether one is male or female and one area is bound to be influential and that is the female capacity for childbirth. Woman's body is orientated towards the conception and harbouring of new life, and then the sustaining of it during the early months, which is bound to have social and psychological consequences. It turns woman more towards the person giving her a greater capacity of empathy and sympathy, an ability to enter inside the person, a greater attention to detail based on the necessities of life.

"In this perspective, one understands the irreplaceable role of women in all aspects of family and social life involving human relationships and caring for others."[15] The particular gifts of women stemming from their role as nurturers of life gives them a significant and active role in the family, since it is here that the character and virtues of new life are shaped. "They (the children) learn to love inasmuch as they are unconditionally loved, they learn respect for others inasmuch as they are respected, they learn to know the face of God inasmuch as they receive a first revelation of it from a father and mother …"[16] Where this is lacking, society suffers violence and becomes in turn the progenitor of more violence.[17]

All of this means also that women should take their place in the world of work and the organisation of society and hold positions of responsibility which enable them to inspire and affect the policies of nations. "However, in this respect it cannot be forgotten that the interrelationship between these two activities – family and work – has for women characteristics different from those of men."[18] The Congregation is thinking here of those characteristics of women more turned to the person, to the family and to love, and so when appropriate this is their primordial task, bearing in mind that the family is part of society anyway, and the most important and influential part at that. For this reason society should recognize financially the work of those women who dedicate themselves more fully to domestic life. It should also be born in mind that these values such as love, respect, teaching, caring for others which women have a particular talent for, are not simply feminine values, but human values necessary for all, men and women.

The Role of Biology and the Body

What part do biology and the body play in our nature? As has been indicated above, the body is an integral part of human nature since we are a unity of body and soul, or body and spirit, if one prefers. Matter and the body are important realities, not taboo

---

[15] Congregation for the Doctrine of the Faith, *Letter on the Collaboration of Men and Women in the Church and the World*, May 2004, n. 3.
[16] Ibid.
[17] Cf. ibid.
[18] Ibid.

topics for Christianity, exemplified by the Incarnation in which Christ took a material body to redeem us. It is an instance of the sacramental principle whereby visible material signs reveal to us deeper invisible realities. The body makes the person visible. The body is certainly not disposable or dispensable in the Christian economy. The human body is an important part of what the Pope calls the 'sacrament of creation', and the work of salvation will not be complete until we receive the 'redemption of our bodies'.[19] St Augustine reminded us that at the final resurrection we shall be like the angels only "in immortality and felicity, not in body ... He who establishes the two sexes will restore them both."[20]

Pope John Paul II takes this a step further when he tells us that the body enters into the definition of a sacrament. He writes:

> The 'body' also signifies that which is visible; it signifies the visibility of the world and of man. Therefore, in some way, even if in the most general way, the body enters the definition of sacrament, being 'a visible sign of an invisible reality', that is of the transcendent, divine reality. In this sign – and through this sign – God gives Himself to man in His transcendent truth and in His love. The sacrament is a sign of grace, and it is an efficacious sign. Not only does the sacrament indicate grace and express it in a visible way, but it also produces it and effectively contributes to having grace become part of man, and to realizing and fulfilling in him the work of salvation, the work begun by God from all eternity and fully revealed in Jesus Christ.[21]

John Paul II has already told us that the body is a sign which makes visible the mystery hidden in God from time immemorial; now he tells us that the body is in a general way like a sacrament, through which grace comes, the grace of love and redemption. He thus tells us that the body understood in this way reveals to us the mystery of man's creation as male and female, namely to form a loving communion of persons and participate in the creation, but, in addition, the 'great mystery' of male and female conjugal union is an analogy of, and participation in, God's love for His chosen people and for the Church.

---

[19] Rom 8:23.
[20] St Augustine, *The City of God*, 22, 17.
[21] General Audience 28-VII-84.

This stands in the most utter contrast to the modern dualistic view according to which the spirit/consciousness and body are opposed to each other and the person is identified with the former. The consequence is that the body is sub-human, something we possess and use, a tool which we may do with as we wish, employing it as a means to an end, even if it is for 'humanitarian' research, or for selfish pleasure or profit. According to this view, the body does not contain signs which point to the truth of human and sexual relationships, nor does it contain any meaning which may be called theological. Herein lies the difference between contemporary rationalism and the depth of truth contained in Christ's Incarnation and Revelation. We can see here why modern rationalism does not understand the difference between male and female and goes as far as it can to make the difference disappear. Here we see also the root of the confrontation between secular and Christian sexual morality and bio-ethics and the former's misunderstanding of the latter.

Saint Josemaria Escriva adverted to the Modern Age's misunderstanding of the consequences of the Incarnation by speaking of Christian materialism: "Authentic Christianity, which professes the resurrection of all flesh, has always quite logically opposed 'dis-incarnation', without fear of being judged materialistic. We can, therefore, rightfully speak of a *Christian materialism*, which is boldly opposed to those materialisms which are blind to the spirit."[22] This in the tradition of the Fathers, as is exemplified in the words of St John Damascene: "I will not cease to venerate matter, through which my salvation was brought to pass."[23]

While it is true that bodiliness and sexuality are not identical, as shown above, they are inextricably linked. Ontologically one is a person before one is male or female, but nor can one be a person without being masculine or feminine. Gender, therefore, is in turn linked to sexuality which comes through the body, but the body is an integral part of the identity of the person. So the distinction between person and sexuality is a distinction of reason, not a real one. Consequently, the alleged 'freedom' to choose one's gender

---

[22] *Conversations with Mgr Escriva de Balaguer*, Scepter, Dublin, 1968, p. 193.
[23] St John Damascene, *First Homily in Defence of the Holy Icons*, PG 94, 1245AB.

role is an exaggeration of freedom that transgresses the unity there is between freedom and nature. Freedom is neither unlimited, nor omnipotent, and is indeed conditioned by the nature and truth of the person. The latter, however, makes for true and not illusory freedom.

XIII.

MARRIAGE AND THE RENEWAL OF THE FAMILY

Marriage is a communion of persons of the opposite sex whose twin essential dimensions are lifelong personal love and self-giving and openness to the procreation and education of children. The current widespread practice of cohabitation owes much to the frequency of divorce and loss of confidence in lifelong commitment, as it does to contraception where couples routinely separate love-making from procreation. Consequently, the phenomenon of living together obliges us to examine personal love and the nature of procreation in marriage more deeply. The first will be dealt with in this chapter and the second in the following one. First, we must attend to the anthropology of sexuality and marriage. In addition, we shall initially consider it from the point of view of reason before bringing in Scripture, because the fundamental principles of marriage and family life are a matter of natural law applying to everybody, not only Christians.

Opposed to the divine-natural plan for the family based on a life-long union of man and woman is the contemporary secular notion of family diversity. This is the idea that the family has evolved and now comprehends co-habiting couples, one-parent families and civil unions. It is based on the presupposition that the family is a social construct, rather in the way that some people hold that gender itself is socially generated. The argument goes that we have socially constructed the family in the past according to the monogamous model and, therefore, we are at liberty to re-construct it according to changing attitudes and circumstances.

Such a position, challenges the Christian belief that marriage is ordained and revealed by God, and at the same time, responds to the nature and truth of man and woman who through their complementarity and reciprocity are both ideally equipped to form a loving communion of persons and have children by means of acts which are procreative in type, as well as to bring them up. Sociological surveys tend to support this conclusion, which in turn benefits the children who have the right to be conceived in the love of their parents and know their heritage; and benefits society through providing citizens with greater social responsibility, and delivering lower crime rates, drug and alcohol offences and so on.

While a silent majority may acknowledge this, many will not say so for fear of the accusation that they are being judgemental or discriminatory towards other lifestyles. However, the fear tends to evaporate decidedly when the question is turned round and looked at from the point of view of the well-being of the children. The Church has no intention or desire to offend or marginalize any group, but is aware of the obligation to testify to the anthropological truth of man and woman and their fittedness to form a stable communion of persons, and to her pastoral experience that it leads to the greater happiness and security of individuals and society. Moreover, her position, as articulated by John Paul II in the theology of the body, is not simply that the nuclear family is divinely ordained, but that this plan is also discernible by reason in an adequate anthropology whose signs can be read in the bodies of the different genders though applying to the whole male and female persons.

The Anthropology of Marriage

For that reason, two characteristics of the human person, already recognized, should be recalled in order to enable us to understand the truth and meaning of sexuality and marriage. One is that persons are body/spirit unities and the other is that the full truth of persons includes their subjectivity and consciousness. The first radically affects our understanding of the whole purpose of the body and its sexual identity and meaning and consequently the nature of human conjugal love. If the person is considered a dualism of spirit and body, then sex is identified with the body and once it is separated from procreation and genuine love it easily becomes thought of as an instrument to be used, rather than as an integral part of the subjectivity and dignity of the person. The result is that sex becomes a commodity, an object of use and enjoyment, to be indulged in at will for recreation as well as for love, which accurately describes the present situation, casting shadows over marriage and obscuring its true nature.

As we have seen, however, experience and subjective awareness testify that we act as a unity of body and soul, hence human love is bodily and spiritual at the same time. Consequently, the body and sexuality enter into the dignity of the person and the bodily actions and language must be in accordance with the truth of the person. This truth is known by the aforementioned nuptial significance of the body which consists in the subjective awareness one has of sexual identity and difference and its purpose, namely its spousal and procreative meaning. It also takes into account that sexuality is not just bodily but personal and is directed not just to a partnership of persons of the opposite sex, but to a real communion of persons, that is an exchange of love between all that each person has and is.

Subjective awareness enables us to understand why *Gaudium et Spes* and *Humanae Vitae* spoke about the 'meanings', rather than the 'ends', of marriage which had been used up to that time. The two 'meanings' of love and procreation, or the unitive and procreative significance, as *Humanae Vitae* puts it, are realities of which the spouses are consciously aware; they do not just know them theoretically or objectively, as happens with the 'ends'. Conjugal love and human dignity require self-mastery and dominion through the practice of chastity and continence. This means that for spousal love to be genuine the sexual inclination and drive need to be integrated into a love which is purified of selfishness through an overriding concern for the other rather than self, called by the Catechism the *integration of the person*.[1] The self-giving or donation of self which results, and is the core

---

[1] CCC 2338 ff.

of conjugal love, is referred to as the *integrality of the gift of self*.[2] The dignified practice of sexuality requires the integration of bodily passions and emotions into human action and love under the direction of the rational will. Without this it is not genuinely human activity.

Since the body is a sign and sacrament of the person, the visible body reveals the invisible reality and expresses the person and hence it has meaning, such that we can speak of the language of the body. The gestures, or actions, of the body express states of the soul, the inner core of the person. So crying, or shouting, reveal emotions of fear, sadness or anger, while cheering or applauding express satisfaction and happiness. Bowing or curtseying are a form of showing respect; shaking hands, friendship; and kissing or hugging, love. Like all language it can be true or false and so the language of the body must conform to the truth of the person and nuptial meaning of the body. The use of sexuality for cohabitation, free-love, divorce, and re-marriage, as well as for contraception and homosexuality, will be seen to be false language of the body because it does not correspond to its spousal meaning or dignity. Further reflection on conjugal love will deepen our appreciation of this.

A good deal of study has been done on the nature of conjugal love in the past half-century, because many believed it to have been overshadowed by the emphasis put on procreation until then. Efforts were made to upgrade its importance, culminating in *Gaudium et Spes* and *Humanae Vitae* teaching the unbreakable link between the two and showing how love was part, both of procreation and unity in marriage. Love takes many forms; it does not just mean one thing. It includes attraction, desire, friendship and sympathy between persons. But here we are talking about married love between a man and a woman, which, in addition to the foregoing, has its own characteristics. It includes the notion of mutual self-giving, a oneness of life giving rise to a shared and common existence, signified by the biblical expression, 'one flesh'. The communion of persons thus resulting is characterized by trust, loyalty, and fidelity, which is why this aspect of marriage was

---

[2] CCC 2346 ff.

referred to by the ancients as 'the good of faithfulness', (or *'bonum fidei'*). The uniqueness of marriage as compared to all other types of friendship is its *total and unconditional self-giving to the other person*. It will become clear that this is reflected in all aspects of married life and especially in the sexual act itself.

It is only persons who can form a stable communion of life. By a person we understand a unity of body and soul such that the sensible faculties are under the control of the intellect and will. A person, therefore, is a rational being who is able, as Adam was, to name the animals, capable of self-determination and self-reflection and hence of verbal communication. All man's actions bring both body and soul into operation in virtue of the unity of the person. That is to say, when man acts the whole person acts, not just the body. Hence, human love is both spiritual and bodily. And so it is crucial that the matrimonial act is a union of persons and not just of bodies. Two persons are united by means of the body, and thus it is a union of persons.

The body, therefore, has a language which makes the whole person visible. This is a consequence of the unity of the person. The person exists in the whole of their soul and body, but is made visible by the body. In his/her actions the whole person acts. There is, therefore, an appropriate behaviour for the body, that is, there is a correct and incorrect way to treat and use it. The body must never be used in ways that degrade the person, or pretend to separate it from the person, since it is an integral part of the latter. Hence, the person and, therefore, the body, must never be used or manipulated as an object of pleasure, profit or convenience. Sexuality must not be separated from its personal dimension by limiting it to the body only. All human actions are carried out by the whole person, but this applies in a special way to sexuality, because it is intimately connected to the relational aspect of the person, that is to say, his/her capacity for communion with others.

This communion of persons, of one's whole person, all that one is, and has, is therefore more than a communion of bodies only. Consequently, if there is to be personal union there must be a commitment of wills, minds and hearts. It must be unconditional in time and exclusive of all others, otherwise it is not a *total* commitment of the whole person in their spiritual and bodily nature by which the couple become 'one flesh'. The bodily sexual union, which is procreative in type is an expression and sign of total love, the love of whole persons for one another. Hence, the sexual act cannot simply be a union of bodies, but must express a union of *persons*; the body and the person are a unity. Consequently, if the sexual act is performed outside marriage it is false language of the body, because it does not express the commitment of the whole person.

It is for this reason that marriage enjoys the characteristics of unity and indissolubility, namely because its total and all embracing nature makes it unconditional. A spouse who shared his or her spouse with another partner, as in polygamy, would not fulfil this characteristic, nor would one who put a temporal condition on the union, or otherwise failed to make it definitive, as occurs in divorce and remarriage. The only adequate way to treat one's spouse is with an unconditional and exclusive love, otherwise it would not be conjugal love. As *Familiaris Consortio* puts it: "The total physical self-giving would be a lie if it were not the sign and fruit of a total personal self-giving, in which the whole person, including the temporal dimension, is present: if the person were to withhold something or reserve the possibility of deciding otherwise in the future, by this very fact he or she would not be giving totally."[3] Once this is established, we can see the convenience of it for parenthood. It is clearly in the interests of the children that their parents, who have a duty to educate them and bring them up, stay together indefinitely. Monogamous marriage, then, is true to the nature of sexual love, the institution of marriage and the interests of children.

A Deeper Analysis of Personal Love in Marriage

Like knowledge, love begins on the sense level and passes to the intellectual and spiritual level of reason and will, to become human. It then becomes personal love. It runs the risk, however, of staying on the sense level, which is characterized by the search for pleasure and self-interest egged on by the consumer pressures

---

[3] John Paul II, Apostolic Exhortation, *Familiaris Consortio*, n. 11.

of the present time and, as a consequence, not reaching the personal level. Man and woman in their fallen nature are subject to the triple concupiscence, namely the pride of life, lust of the flesh and the lust of the eyes. This lust is a separation from the order we have noted in the state of original innocence. Chastity in marriage, that is to say, the virtuous exercise of sexuality, demands the control by the higher faculties of the passions, emotions and sensual and carnal tendencies, and, thus, the integration of the latter into a behaviour that is truly personal. Further explanation of how this happens has been carried out by Karol Wojtyla in his work entitled, *Love and Responsibility*.[4]

Emotions, Passions and Concupiscence

Between his sense life and intellectual powers of mind and will man also has emotions, or passions. These are movements of the sensitive appetite which "incline us to act, or not act, in regard to something felt or imagined to be good or evil."[5] Knowledge is either sensible, or intellectual, and every act of knowledge is followed by an appetite, that is a tendency to, or away from, an object. The sensitive tendency which follows on a feeling, or instinct, about the goodness or evil of an object, is called an emotion. From the judgement of the intellect about the goodness or otherwise of the object, follows the intellectual tendency of the will. The most basic passion is love, which desires the absent good and the hope of attaining it, and which finds its completion in the pleasure and joy of the good possessed. The loss of it causes sadness. Animals also have sensitive appetites or emotions, but man in addition also has a will. It is this that either accepts, or opposes, the desires and attractions he feels at the sense level.

The emotions and concupiscences are in themselves morally neutral, but they become moral once they fall under the dominion of the will. They are humanly good or bad when they are directed by right reason, or against it, according to the dictates of the natural moral law. Consequently, the same criterion applies to love. It only becomes fully human and personal when it rises

---

[4] Karol Wojtyla, *Love and Responsibility*, Collins, London, 1981, pp. 166 ff.
[5] CCC 1763.

above the emotional level to the level of the will. If love stays at the sense, or emotional, level, that is, if it is only bodily, then it is not fully human and personal. It is not properly speaking married love. It is not yet the product of a rational and free commitment and so, at this stage, inclines more to the sensual and carnal in man rather than the properly personal. This is what is wrong with a man and woman simply living together; they have not made an unconditional commitment of wills which can only be done by marriage.

A man and a woman represent a sexual value for one another. The impression a man and a woman make on each other begins on the sense level, since each of them is a body exposed to the senses of the other. The impression is easily accompanied by an emotion because they represent a value for one another. All this is brought about by the sexual inclination which is a natural characteristic of human beings. So far, we are on the sense level and what is described here goes under the name of sensuality. Sensuality is directed towards the body and, furthermore, the body as an object of enjoyment. However, we are not yet at the moral level. Sexual desire may either be purely selfish, seeking pleasure and enjoyment, or it may be connected to the totality of the other person in their spiritual, psychological and sexual dimension, and seek their good and happiness.

Conjugal Love

Every human being is made not to live alone, but to be *with* and *for* others. In other words, the relational dimension is a constitutive part of personhood. This enables them to share interests, serve, support, and love one another. It enables them to make a gift of themselves and their lives to one another. This ability of the person to express communion and friendship with others, to give themselves and share their life, or part of it with others, in and through the body, is called by the Pope, the 'nuptial meaning of the body'. This phrase does not mean that everybody is called to be married, but refers to the fact that everybody is aware of the innate capacity to give themselves to one another in which marriage consists, that is, to be an expression of love for another person, in the last analysis an expression of the love of God Himself. This gift when used in its totality by two persons of the opposite sex is called marriage, but it may also be expressed by celibacy for the Kingdom of Heaven, or various types of service to mankind.

Making a gift of oneself to the other is to live for them and not for oneself. It is to pass over the fact that man exists for his own sake and to exist *for* another, and their well-being, in a disinterested way. And this we call love. But the other is also a gift for him. The spouse reciprocates. And insofar as she has made a commitment of the will, i.e. of love, she is a gift for him. The person is never a thing, object or a commodity and so is, therefore, a treasure, a gift, a value in themselves and must be treated as a priceless gift, someone of intrinsic worth. And to treat a person of the other sex like this, to whom one has committed one's life, is married love. They realise they are a gift for each other and say to one another, so to speak, 'you are the rest of my life.'

What effect, then, does the exchange of wills have on the interpersonal relationship? It means they each seek the good of the other person above all else. And this conditions their search for pleasure and tendency to selfishness, freeing them for true love. Only with the will can one make a gift of oneself to the other, can one desire the good of the person. In cohabitation this cannot be guaranteed and is, indeed, unlikely because it is based on convenience and maybe personal satisfaction and pleasure, rather than the unconditional good and happiness of the other person, at the expense of one's own. This self-giving and self-denial of one's own interests is, therefore, only fully catered for in the institution of marriage. The other is treated as another, and better, self. One learns to put oneself in their shoes, to understand their ways and forgive their weakness and so live together in mutual love and respect.

The attraction of a man and a woman initially on the sense level may be the occasion for the will with its natural aspiration to the infinite good to start wanting the good and happiness of another person too, the person who is for the senses and emotions an object of desire. The will, therefore, controls the sexual inclination, by practising self-mastery, and integrates it into conjugal love, or according to the nuptial meaning and truth of the body. In this way, because of the natural orientation of the will, true love gives the relationship between man and woman a thoroughly unselfish character, freeing it from utilitarian attitudes.[6]

This is the significance of what Wojtyla calls the struggle between love and the sexual instinct. The latter wants to take over, to make use of another person whereas love wants to give, to create a good, to bring happiness. Conjugal love needs to be permeated by friendship – the desire for the unlimited good of another 'I'. The integration of love into sexual desire and reactions ensures the unqualified affirmation of the value of a person and thus keeps the interpersonal relationship on the level of a true union of persons. There is nothing wrong with pleasure as such, as long as it always accompanies a worthy object, such as the good and value and happiness of another person, otherwise, on its own, it is opposed to happiness. There cannot be a unity of persons based on pleasure, but only on happiness.[7]

Chastity

The virtue that governs sexual desire and integrates it into love is chastity. In St Thomas the virtue of chastity is linked with temperance or moderation. It resides in the concupiscible appetite and has as its purpose to restrain the instinctive appetite for material and bodily goods. If man lacked it, the will might easily become subject to the senses and choose, as good, what is enjoyable to the senses. The virtue of moderation steers man away from this perversion of his true nature. But is the essence of chastity in moderation? No, the true nature of chastity must be seen in the light of love itself, properly understood. The purpose of chastity is to free love from utilitarian and hedonistic attitudes and to enable love to affirm the value of the person and seek their good.[8]

Chastity does not consist in inhibiting and pushing down the

---

[6] Cf. K. Wojtyla, *Love and Responsibility*, p. 137.
[7] K. Wojtyla, *Love and Responsibility*, p. 153.
[8] Cf. ibid., p. 169.

values of the 'body' and 'sex' to the subconscious where they await an opportunity to explode.[9] True chastity does not lead to a disdain for the body, or to the disparagement of marriage and the sexual life, because recognition of the true value of the body is conditional on raising these values to the level of the person. Thus only chaste men and women are capable of true love.[10] Chastity frees one from the tendency to use a person, which is incompatible with loving kindness.

The reason why man has a tendency to seek selfish, egoistical enjoyment at the sense level is because one of the effects of original sin is a lessening of the unity of the person. Instead of being the obedient servants of the will and intellect, the sensual and emotional appetites tend to rebel, or seek their own satisfaction and go their own way at times. This dominion of the higher powers over the lower has to be achieved by man's efforts to master himself over the course of a lifetime. This is why love must be *personal*, given and received by the whole person. The will must integrate sensual and carnal love into personal love.

There can very well be friendship between men and women, as there can be between any group of persons. But once that friendship begins to be expressed sexually then it takes on special characteristics. Why is that? Because we must safeguard here the truth that the body is the vehicle and sign of the whole person. An incipient love can be expressed by gestures, a kiss, a hug, etc., but the sexual act is a total bodily expression of love and therefore should be an expression of total personal love. This requires union of mind and will, in a word, commitment, as we shall see more fully.

Cohabitation

Today, with increasing numbers of couples cohabiting in Britain, and the West as a whole, the stigma which once attached to it socially has disappeared. Among the reasons for the phenomenon are: the widespread experience of divorce, either in themselves or their parents, and the nervousness connected with making a long-

---

[9] Ibid., p. 170.
[10] Cf. ibid., p. 171.

term commitment. It is seen as a way of enjoying the benefits of a close relationship and supposed sexual fulfilment without the responsibilities of marriage. Above all, it is an instance of the priority of freedom of choice over all else, where two people can combine independence and autonomy with the need for affection and companionship. Broadly speaking, they divide into those who regard it as a trial marriage, and those who reject the notion of marriage altogether.

Naturally enough, this supposed paradise turns out to be highly illusory. There are many dangers associated with cohabitation of a moral, physical and psychological nature. The illusion is created that you have the closeness of the relationship without the responsibility, and move on if it does not work out. However, the heartache and pain of separation, when it does come, is underestimated and can be traumatic. Furthermore, this is relatively common because these relationships do not have the stability of marriage, since research shows that such couples have a higher rate of unfaithfulness than spouses in marriage.

Cohabitation is often justified as 'trial marriage', namely a time of probation to test the waters and determine whether the couple are suited to one another. In fact, the evidence shows the opposite, that a greater number of marriages break down where the couple have lived together beforehand.[11] The engagement, traditionally, was, and is, a time for the man and woman to get to know each other. What is important is that they know one another, as well as possible, as *persons* and not simply sexually or bodily, a fact which will almost certainly distort the knowing process. Living together cannot be compared to marriage, because it lacks the element of commitment and permanence, and this lack introduces uncertainty and precariousness into the relationship.

There are also health risks. In cohabitation there is a higher incidence of sexually transmitted diseases. More women smoke,

---

[11] For women in their 40s, 39% of those who cohabited are now divorced, compared with 21% of those who did not. Taking all groups together, the divorce rate for those who premaritally cohabited, compared to those who did not, is 1.8 to 1, meaning that cohabitation is 80% more likely to lead to divorce. (Flanagan, Declan and Ted Williams, *Cohabitation or Marriage?* London: Belmont House, 1997, p. 15.)

perhaps reflecting a higher degree of tension among those living together, especially among women who know they may have to face a pregnancy without the support of the man. The stress may also be noted in higher levels of psychological and neurotic disease.¹²

The increased availability of contraception has played a big part in the rise of cohabitation. There is a perception that you can have a relationship with, or without, children, due to increased control of fertility. Or alternatively, changes in social attitudes mean you can have children with, or without, a husband, or a partner. All these taken together are dubbed the 'social liberation of women'. But what sort of liberation is it which ends up in so much pain and suffering? There is considerable anecdotal evidence that the new sexual permissiveness leads to increased domestic violence towards women and children.

What is Wrong with it?

Many cohabiting couples will maintain that their relationship is no different from that of married people. They will argue that the only difference is that they have not been through the wedding ceremony, and ask what difference a piece of paper makes. This rhetorical argument hides the truth, because rather than a 'piece of paper' it is the commitment of wills which creates the communion of persons. The union of bodies is an expression of the union of persons (i.e. union of wills), and never the other way round. It ratifies and seals the covenant, the act of commitment and self-giving. The Catechism underlines this point: "Carnal union is morally legitimate only when a definitive community of life between a man and a woman has been established. Human love ... demands a total and definitive gift of persons to one another."¹³

Cohabitation, on the other hand, is a union of bodies, but not a full union of persons, because there has been no union of wills. There has not been a sufficient act of commitment, no saying or affirming, 'I give you the rest of my life.' Sexual union without

---

[12] Ibid.
[13] CCC 2391.

it, is false language of the body, because the mind and heart are saying one thing ('I love you as long as it works') and the body is saying another ('this is an act of unconditional love'). The body is not acting appropriately or truly and, therefore, self-enriching love is not occurring and hence mutual growth is not taking place as it should be. Can we not see here the reason why a greater number of cohabitations fail in comparison with marriages, and also a greater number of marriages which have been preceded by a period of cohabitation?

One can perceive in all attempts to justify sexual relations outside marriage, such as cohabitation, an underlying dualistic notion of the person, whether it is realized or not; that is to say, an attitude that is prepared to separate the sexual giving of the body from the giving of the person and that implies a belief in the separation of the person from the body. If it is not a personal act it is simply a bodily act, and so not a fully human action. In these circumstances, instead of a giving it easily becomes a taking. If the other is not received as a person then they are more like an object.

The objection to cohabitation, and therefore, to fornication, and hence also adultery, which is the same but adds the sin of injustice, is that while doubtless, in some sense, loving each other, the partners are running the risk, to a greater degree than in marriage, of using each other. Conjugal love demands that one love one's spouse for their own sake, and desire their good and well-being often at the expense of personal sacrifice. This is sometimes difficult for fallen human nature, which is exposed to the temptation to use and manipulate others for its own ends. This may, of course, happen in marriage at times, but the conjugal commitment and the grace of the Christian sacrament can atone for human selfishness and weakness, and are a safeguard against them becoming the over-arching principle of the relationship. On the other hand, cohabiting couples leave themselves without such resources, and the *rationale* of living together is the bi-partisan self-fulfilment and independence of the parties together with a close sexual relationship. It may well be wondered whether such a combination is possible, but at any rate a degree of self-interest and 'use' is built into the very nature of the arrangement.

A further implication of cohabitation is that it will continue as long as it works, or is mutually acceptable, or a better arrangement with a third party does not intervene. Such a relationship 'ad tempus' inevitably entails that spouses treat each other for their own convenience and pleasure to some extent, and pleasure by itself is selfish. To love one's spouse for his or her own sake requires a totality of relationship, an unconditional self-giving, and so must be to the exclusion of all others during the spouse's lifetime. For a man to have more than one wife, or lover, would be to use them for his own purposes, and treat them as objects of pleasure, hence impeding his capacity to love them fully. Cohabitation is open to the same objection because, at least in principle, the door has been left open to somebody else coming along.

In a sense, the experience of cohabitation enables us to understand marriage and conjugal love better. The example of the 'beginning' (cf. Mt 19:4, 8; Mk 10:6-9) teaches us that true love between a man and a woman consists in their being a disinterested gift for one another, seeking only the good of the other. In this state, there is no room for treating the other as an object. In a very real sense, the self-interest and 'use' elements of cohabitation make it the very antithesis of the self-giving in which marriage consists. We have forgotten the notion of gift in our utilitarian atmosphere. Chastity is really the quest for dominion and mastery over oneself so as to be a disinterested gift for the other. It is chastity which genuinely upholds human dignity. The uniqueness of marriage cannot be set aside as culturally conditioned, because otherwise Our Lord's reference to the 'beginning' would be meaningless. His words obviously refer to the 'beginning' as a prototype model valid for all time expressing the eternal law and the truth of the human person.

Divine Institution in Scripture

The scriptural account of creation confirms that marriage is not a man-made reality, but is of divine institution and conforms to an eternal plan for mankind. In the second chapter of Genesis, which is said to be earlier than the first chapter and deals with the separate creation of man and woman, the unitive aspect of the sexes is uppermost. They were created for one another: "It is not good that man should be alone."[14] The woman is a companion and support for him, endowed with complementary qualities. The woman is his equal in humanity which becomes clear when Adam says: "this at last is flesh of my flesh and bone of my bones."[15] In using these words on seeing Eve, he is first of all recognizing another human person. Up to this point he had been alone, but now he recognizes a being to whom he is united by nature, a rational animal with a human will. This unity and equality of humanity is not, however, an identity, brought out when the text says, "male and female he created them."[16] Masculinity and femininity are two irreducible ways of being in the world, two ways of being the 'image of God' and therefore equal in dignity and rights but with different roles to play in certain important respects. Equality, here, does not mean sameness but rather implies complementarity.

The text goes on to say, "Therefore a man leaves his father and his mother and cleaves to his wife and they become one flesh."[17] We pass here from the genealogical and biological unity with one's parents to the *chosen* unity with one's spouse. Man's free will enters into this covenant. The expression, 'one flesh' was not understood by the Jews simply in a narrow physical sense, and thus does not refer to conjugal union only, but rather to a moral union of two *persons* who do not lose their individuality. It refers to a communion of persons and communion of life. It highlights the totality of the union, the way in which they give themselves to one another holding nothing back. It thus refers also to the legal bond, which is created when man and woman consent to give themselves to one another. This bond, though freely chosen, is not simply human but has a divine element in it, insofar as it responds to a plan of God, and is a divine institution. This plan can be seen in the body, and the ability which man and woman have to give themselves to one another which is 'the nuptial meaning

---

[14] Gen 2:18.
[15] Gen 2:23.
[16] Gen 1:27.
[17] Gen 2:24.

of the body.' This interpretation is confirmed by Our Lord's words later on: "What therefore God has joined together let no man put asunder."[18] The unity of the two, which results from this chosen union, thus gives rise to a lifelong commitment in virtue of the totality of the bond which is created.

And so the marriage covenant consists in a mutual self-giving of man and woman to each other totally and unconditionally. In the present state of mankind it is not possible to give oneself totally, due to selfishness, but in the original state of Adam and Eve it was. Adam loved his wife for her own sake, and vice versa, and respected her for her dignity and treated her as an equal. After the Fall, however, God said to Eve "your husband shall rule over you",[19] which indicates the proximate danger of disharmony between spouses and the tendency for one to want to possess the other and treat the other as an object of self-gratification. In the original state where man was not a slave to his passions he enjoyed what the Pope calls 'the freedom of the gift'.

Why does Christ demand indissolubility and sexual purity, i.e. abstinence, outside marriage? Because it corresponds to the truth of man and woman 'in the beginning'. It might be objected that Moses allowed the patriarchs to have more than one wife. Since then, however, Christ has brought the grace of Redemption, the renewal of the grace of original innocence, though not of that state, because we still carry with us our fallen nature and the threefold concupiscence. John Paul II calls marriage in Genesis, that is, the one-flesh union of our first parents, 'the primordial sacrament', because it is the centrepiece of the 'sacrament of creation'. It is the gift of God's love to man, an entrusting to man and woman with the continuation of the work of creation in collaboration with Him. It is completed in the 'sacrament of redemption'.

With Christ, the sacrament of marriage thus becomes one of the seven sacraments of the New Law and by its likeness to the union of Christ and the Church it actuates the graces of Redemption in the spousal union. This includes the so-called 'grace of state', to enable them to confront the challenges and difficulties, as well

---

[18] Mt 19:6.
[19] Gen 3:16.

as the ongoing graces from the other sacraments. The spousal analogy works in two directions. On the one hand, to a certain degree it illumines the mystery of Christ and the Church, at least to the extent that those who do not understand, or accept, the difference between male and female, will not understand the union of Christ and the Church either. At the same time, it unveils the essential truth about marriage which is shown to be intimately related to the Head-Body analogy. Spouses form one organism, one moral person, while remaining two individuals, and the unity in plurality which results, images Christ and the Church and the communion of persons in the Blessed Trinity.

The sacraments effect what they signify and their purpose is to sanctify. The fifth chapter of Ephesians shows us how, and in what way, marriage is a path of sanctification, a state which calls for holiness in the Christian. St Paul writes: "Husbands love your wives as Christ loved the Church and gave himself for her, that he might sanctify her, having cleansed her by the washing of water with the word, that he might present the Church to himself in splendour without spot or wrinkle or any such thing, that she might be holy and without blemish."[20]

The Great Mystery

In the light of the cautious approach to commitment and the claim to equivalence to marriage that the cohabitation mentality exhibits, the Pauline passage about marriage being a great mystery which relates to the union of Christ and the Church, is a strong reassertion of its sacramental character.[21] It completes the teaching of Genesis concerning the 'one flesh' to which it is explicitly linked. At the same time, it is a confirmation that marriage is an essential part of the eternal plan of God for man and woman, as well as responding to anthropological truth. This serves as a response to the secular claim that marriage in contemporary society is evolving and taking ever newer and different forms which are equally valid, in other words that it is simply a sociological reality.

---

[20] Eph 5:25.
[21] Eph 5:1-33.

Consequently, the 'one flesh' points to a 'unity of the two' in marriage which is so close that they become like one moral person. There is an identity between them, an identity of difference since they remain two individuals. So a personal and juridical unity is created. The use of marriage in Scripture as an analogy for the union of Christ and the Church, brings out both the closeness of this unity and the fact that marriage and family life are a central part of the redemptive work of Christ. This unity, though principally expressed in the conjugal act, is also manifested in many other ways on the psychological and personal and everyday level. The particular closeness of the unity of the two which is demanded by the nature of the person and conjugal love, as well as by the will of the Creator, demonstrates why the goods of indissolubility, exclusivity and fidelity pertain to marriage. If the union is total then it admits of no conditions whether of a temporal or personal nature. Were marriage to be *ad tempus,* or were there to be another person involved, then the self-giving would not be total; nor could it be compared to Christ and his Body, the Church, who are inseparably united.

In the most general way, the body enters into the definition of a sacrament as the visible sign of what is invisible. Thus, we may speak of the sacrament of the person with the body as its visible dimension and a sign of grace when it is used in a nuptial way. This is borne out in Ephesians (5:21-33) where the body and nuptial union are presented as a great mystery which refers to Christ and the Church. If it is a sign with sacramental value then it accomplishes what it signifies, and that is the sanctification of the spouses giving them grace to surmount the many obstacles to fruitful and fulfilling spousal love. There is a link with Christ's human nature and body which are the instrumental cause of the grace of salvation.

The linking of marriage with Christ and the Church, and therefore with the Redemption, brings with it the invitation to collaborate with the redemption of the body and the rehabilitation of marriage according to the dignity of original innocence. To do this, spouses must take up the redeeming Cross of Christ in order to progress towards the harmony, unity and love of the original state. This is necessary in order to overcome the tendency to self-gratification to which the concupiscence of the fallen creature inclines. It is done by striving towards purity of heart and the chaste use of marriage which is the characteristic of original innocence. To accomplish this, spouses are called to live, in St Paul's terminology, 'according to the spirit', and not 'according to the flesh'. Such a stance enables them to seek the good of one another before self, and to regard the other as a better self. Spouses are called to model their lives, not only on the 'one flesh' of the beginning, but, especially, on the union of Christ and the Church.

The linking of the spousal significance of the body with the redemptive significance means that marriage is a true sacrament, of which the body is a sign, and that man is called to love with the body, a love that is spiritual as well as bodily. It means marriage is a way of sanctification. Some associate the sacramental sign with the consent, i.e. marriage vows; others associate it with the consummation of the marriage. John Paul II brings the two together. The language of the body should correspond to the vows, and when this happens the language is being used according to truth. The communion of persons is brought about, not only by conjugal intercourse which expresses it, but by the whole marriage which therefore also constitutes the sign.

But sin impedes man and woman living marriage properly unless they are redeemed, or in the process of redemption, which is the purpose of the union of Christ and the Church. This process is called the redemption of the body.[22] Marriage serves as an analogy for the Covenant of God by which he demonstrates his love for his people, Israel, as well as his union with his Body the Church. Indeed, for this reason we must say that marriage is a covenant between two people, not just a partnership, but a real *union* of persons. For the same reason, Christ's Body is sometimes called his Bride to confirm the analogy and similarity with marriage. Thus from sacramental marriage comes 'the grace of state' to surmount the challenges and difficulties of married life.

Cardinal Ratzinger, now Pope Benedict XVI, summarizes what

---

[22] Cf. Rom 8:23.

we have been saying in this way:
> History is interpreted – again following the example of the Old Testament – as a love story involving God and man. God finds for himself a bride for the Son, the one bride who is the one Church. On the basis of the saying in Genesis, that man and wife shall 'become one flesh' (Gen 2:24) the image of the bride blends in with the idea of the Church, which is in turn anchored sacramentally in eucharistic piety.[23]

Pope John Paul II often referred to the nuptial character of the Eucharist, calling it the "Sacrament of our Redemption. It is the Sacrament of the Bridegroom and the Bride."[24] In addition, as the Catechism tells us, "the entire Christian life bears the mark of the spousal love of Christ and the Church. Already Baptism, the entry into the people of God, is a nuptial mystery; it is so to speak the nuptial bath which precedes the wedding feast, the Eucharist."[25] The fruitful practice of eucharistic life therefore nourishes and strengthens the indissoluble unity of the marriage bond.[26]

By the same token, marriage and the body are also a sign of the death and Resurrection of Christ through the self-giving, self-denying love of the spouses. Faithful spousal love, therefore, throws some light on the nature of Christ's compassionate, enduring and fruitful redemptive love of his people and is a constant reminder of it in the everyday world. All these meanings are inscribed in the body giving rise to the aptly named 'prophetism of the body' and also underlining its dignity and sacral nature.[27] Were the body not an integral part of the person, and if the person did not have a likeness to God, neither the one, nor the other, could form part of an analogy linking God and his people. It further emphasizes that the body cannot simply be used for utilitarian purposes, for pleasure or experiments etc. Each person including their body is inviolable and cannot be manipulated. For this reason St Paul reminds us: "Do you not know that you are God's temple and that

---

[23] Joseph Ratzinger, *Pilgrim Fellowship of Faith*, Ignatius Press, San Francisco, 2005, p. 134.
[24] John Paul II, Apostolic Letter, *Mulieris Dignitatem*, 1988, n. 26.
[25] CCC 1617.
[26] Cf. Benedict XVI, Apostolic Letter, *Sacramentum Caritatis*, n. 27.
[27] Cf. John Paul II, General Audience 26-I-83.

God's Spirit dwells in you? ... For God's temple is holy, and that temple you are."[28]

Clearly, at the heart of conjugal love is the self-giving of the spouses to one another, and the consent by which this is expressed. What, however, is the nature of this self-donation? St Paul refers to it in this way: "The wife does not rule over her own body, but the husband does; likewise the husband does not rule over his own body, but the wife does."[29] The context in which the author is speaking here is that of conjugal rights, but since the body is part of the whole person and sexual union is an expression of personal union, we can see here an indication that marital union consists in the spouses dispossessing themselves, surrendering themselves to one another and yielding themselves and their rights to one another. Love, then, consists in putting the good of the other first, a point that is confirmed by texts from Ephesians: "Be subject to one another out of reverence for Christ", and later on St Paul uses the language of self-surrender when he says, "Husbands love your wives as Christ loved the Church and *gave himself up for her.*"[30] There is obviously here a reference to the yielding of the will and the whole of one's person, that is, all that one is and has, or will be and have.

The phrase, "Wives, be subject to your husbands, as to the Lord," is to be understood in terms of the preceding one, "Be subject to one another out of reverence for Christ."[31] So in the first statement St Paul is using the customs of the time to show that there should be a mutual and reciprocal self-giving between the two spouses. This becomes clearer still when the passage urges husbands to love their wives as Christ loved the Church and gave Himself for her. In this way, as we have said, marriage is a sign of love between Christ and the Church and vice versa. The analogy works both ways and throws light on both realities, leaving no doubt about the sacramental character of marriage as an eternal plan of God and vehicle of grace. We were chosen in Christ before the foundation of the world, according to a plan of love of which

---

[28] 1 Cor 3:16-17.
[29] 1 Cor 7:4.
[30] Eph 5:21, 25.
[31] Ibid., 5:21-2.

marriage is both a part and a sign which accomplishes what it signifies. The sign has two parts, one the union in 'one flesh' of Genesis 2:24 and, secondly, the union of Christ and the Church of the letter to the Ephesians forming one great sign.

The virtuous use of sexuality by the gift of oneself and seeking the good of the other, dominating one's own selfish and egoistic tendencies, is made possible by sharing in the power given by Christ's salvation to the Church and received in the sacraments so as to bring about gradually the redemption of the body from concupiscence and the slavery of sin. Perhaps this enables us to understand that Christian teaching on marriage is not a utopian ideal impossible of accomplishment. And so St Paul does not hesitate to present Christ's gift of himself to the Church as the objective, but also the means, of love and self-donation required in marriage. When properly utilized it brings about the transformation of our nature.

The language of the body of spousal union actuates the mystery of Christ and the Church by renewing the grace of creation and redemption. When this language is read in truth it has sacramental value and becomes a means of grace for the couple and for the Church. In this sense, Pope John Paul is able to refer to it as 'liturgical' language. The Catechism tells us that liturgy "means the participation of the People of God in the work of God" and God's work refers to the Great Mystery of our redemption in Jesus Christ. The Fathers of the Church are known to have compared the marriage bed to an altar on which spiritual sacrifice is offered to God.[32] Marriage lived in fidelity sanctifies the world as a living sign of redemption: "It is this mystery of Christ that the Church proclaims and celebrates in her liturgy so that the faithful may live from it and bear witness to it in the world".[33]

---

[32] Cf. Rom 12:1.
[33] CCC 1068.

XIV.

HUMANAE VITAE:

A TEST-CASE FOR CHRISTIAN ETHICS

Hindsight enables us to see with more clarity both the circumstances that contributed to the furore over *Humanae Vitae* and how it fits coherently and consistently into the Church's overall teaching on married love and procreation. This is the case as long as we make an accurate study "of the biblical foundations, the ethical grounds and the personalistic reasons behind this doctrine (of the encyclical)", as John Paul II requested in *Familiaris Consortio*.[1] In urging theologians to illustrate these reasons ever more clearly he laid particular emphasis on the close connection between the Church's doctrine on marriage and her understanding of the human person, a task which is indispensable for upholding the rights both of the family and the human being, not to mention society at large. The biblical foundations of marriage, for their part, are expressed clearly and unambiguously in the first two chapters of Genesis which tell spouses to 'procreate and multiply and fill the earth' and to form a 'one flesh' communion of persons. This leads to St Augustine's doctrine of the three 'goods' of marriage, namely the good of the spouses, the good of children, and the good of faith ('fide') meaning the indissolubility of the bond and fidelity. If marriage is to be open to these dimensions and 'goods' then the problem of explaining the encyclical can be reduced to

---

[1] *Familiaris Consortio*, n. 31.

HUMANAE VITAE: A TEST-CASE FOR CHRISTIAN ETHICS

demonstrating that if there is to be a 'one flesh' communion of persons there must necessarily be openness to procreation in each marital act.[2]

Before doing that, however, a number of introductory remarks need to be made. If the doctrine was so intrinsic to Catholic teaching on marriage, why was there so much confusion and dissent following the encyclical? Two reasons suggest themselves within the Church and theological environment at the time, and a third one was the tremendous social pressure for birth control in Western society which had been building up for most of the twentieth century. We will detail these reasons a little more.

Up to 1968, the date of the publication of *Humanae Vitae*, insufficient attention had been paid to the nature of conjugal love within marriage, and faced with the barrage of criticism that ensued after the encyclical many found themselves poorly prepared to explain and defend spousal love adequately. The work of Dietrich von Hildebrand had begun to rectify this with his little book *Marriage: The Mystery of Faithful Love*. This is taken up by *Gaudium et Spes*, which devotes a section to the topic, and *Humanae Vitae* itself which did give an account of married love, but many who had already formed an opinion did not appreciate how crucial this was to the argument at the time. A fuller, more extensive and deeper treatment was needed and this was forthcoming in the 'theology of the body' at the beginning of John Paul II's pontificate, although this was difficult for the average reader to grasp initially.

A further difficulty was that many theologians and philosophers at the time had a deficient understanding of natural law. A voluntaristic explanation of it tends to lead to a rather legalistic concept of natural law since it is made to depend on the will of the lawgiver rather than on reason. Those who from a secularist viewpoint take God out of the equation, then replace the lawgiver with their own will, end up with the present phenomenon of

---

[2] At the time of *Humanae Vitae* the formulation of the teaching spoke of three 'ends' of marriage, namely 1) procreation and education of children, 2) mutual aid and support, and 3) remedy for concupiscence. The change from 'ends' to 'goods' and 'meanings' is a technical one and the whole matter is best dealt with by speaking of the 'goods' of the person and of marriage.

'moral autonomy'. Such a view obscures Aquinas' explanation of it as a 'participation of the eternal law in the rational creature' or 'human reason in eternal reason'. It is the rational basis of natural law which gives it its strength and opens it up to comprehension by those who do not have faith.

However, voluntarism, together with the influence of anthropological dualism, which sees the human being as consciousness in a body, led revisionist theologians to understand natural law as referring to the biological or physical rhythms of the body. If this were the case, then they would be biological laws and not have the universal and moral foundation which only reason can furnish. This is naturalism not ethics. These points were clarified in *Veritatis Splendor* which emphasized that natural law was based on reason's grasp of the 'goods of the person'. It showed that the revisionist rejection of natural law was founded on a mistaken idea of the Church's traditional understanding of it. The revisionists saw that to accept contraception they had to reject natural law thereby rejecting other doctrines of sexual ethics. For these reasons the crisis surrounding *Humanae Vitae* caused a crisis in moral theology as a whole and of dissent in the Church.

A host of other cultural reasons contributed to the furore which greeted the encyclical in 1968 and which has continued in the post-*Humanae Vitae* period until the present time and eventually also came to affect Catholics. These include the birth-control movement which has been gaining ground and social approval since the early 1900s; the rise of a more radical feminism, which sees contraception as a 'liberation' for women from the yoke of child-bearing; and a wider conventional view which would see it as giving women and families wider choice concerning whether, and when, to have children. It is part of an outlook which almost takes it for granted that advances in science and technology automatically contribute to a more civilized lifestyle for mankind and that it would be irrational not to make use of them, just as it would be not to make use of medical progress. It sees the advent of the oral contraceptive as part of man's advance in the process of the domination of the forces of nature. Furthermore, the conventional wisdom sees contraception playing a special role in the 'overpopulated' third world countries, and at the present time in the struggle against AIDS. As we saw, it denounces Catholic teaching for its 'harshness' in condemning the poor and unfortunate to further misery, as it sees it, by rejecting contraception.

Whatever the supposed short-term advantages of the revisionist positions, they will all go by the board in the long run, if contraception is not in accord with the truth of the human person, and therefore not in his, or her, long-term interests. In time, we will come back to all, or most, of these points, but initially and most fundamentally, it is the underlying notion of the human person and his or her goods and actions that is at issue. We have to ask what the true meaning of conjugal love and sexuality is in the life of couples. How should they be exercised according to their intrinsic meaning and truth?

The change of emphasis in *Humanae Vitae* to a more personalistic understanding of marriage takes into account the 'turn to the subject' of modern thought and, therefore, the spouses' own experience of marital love. Without considering the interior perspective we only reach "abstract considerations rather than man as a living subject".[3] The 'nuptial meaning of the body' is one's *awareness* of sexual identity and difference, of one's own body and the spousal significance of it, i.e. that it is meant for marital union and procreative life. In this sense, the theology of the body is very concrete and eschews the abstraction of a purely objective account. It talks about personal, subjective experiences, and herein lies the importance of the switch in *Humanae Vitae* from speaking of the 'ends' of marriage, to speaking of personal values and the 'meanings' of marriage. It is only by grasping this point more fully that we can understand the subtle change of presentation at the time of *Gaudium et Spes* and *Humanae Vitae*, which all the work of John Paul II on subjectivity has served to illuminate.

The doctrine of the encyclical is in continuity with the traditional formulation and, at the same time, is a homogeneous development of it. The objective teaching spoke of three 'ends' of marriage, namely 1) procreation and education of children,

---

[3] General Audience 26-XI-79.

2) mutual aid and support, and 3) remedy for concupiscence. Some commentators, in their concern to bring in love, have understood number two to be mutual *love* and support, thus separating it from procreation. Others go further, and thinking love to be primary, construct a theory to invert the supposed 'ends'. This hypothesis availed itself of a dualistic view of man, which concluded that 'love' was personal and sexuality biological, in which case the former precedes the latter. But this was not the case in the traditional formulation, since love was not a separate end, but was considered to cover all three ends of marriage and, thus, be present in all of them. This somewhat legalistic language was replaced from *Gaudium et Spes* onwards, by a concentration on the 'goods' of the person, marriage and society as more comprehensible to people of the present time, though they continue to express the same truth. The other development was the use of the word 'meaning' to refer to the psychological awareness of the two dimensions of marriage, unitive and procreative.

Central to the contraceptive mentality of the contemporary climate is the dualistic view of the human person and its consequences. For the dualist, a person is consciousness in a body, as we have seen, with personhood principally identified by the former, and the body considered as something the person owns and uses, rather than being an integral part of personal identity. This means that the body is simply biology and sub-personal and, since sexuality is identified with the body on this view, the same applies to that. Sexuality, then, instead of being seen as something personal and integral to you, that is part of the subjectivity of the person, is regarded as something you possess and use, and hence it may be used for pleasure, as well as for the more responsible activities of conjugal love and procreation. Since the person is co-terminus with consciousness, according to this view, then so are love and freedom, and hence these goods are superior to the body and sex. If the body is like the physical world then you tame it and subdue it according to your design just as you do the forces of nature. This allows the revisionists to invert the order of ends and say personal love is prior to the biology of sex and procreation, which must come under the control of man. Such a step can lead to a perception of conjugal love which is divorced from the objective goods and meanings of marriage. In this sense, the separation of loving communion and procreation is the result of the previous unwarranted separation of mind and body.

But if, on the other hand, the body is an integral part of you, then it must be guided to virtue according to its inner truth, which requires mastery of self and self-dominion. The body, rather than part of 'nature', or the 'natural world', is part of the subjectivity of the person and, therefore, pertains not to the domination of nature but to the mastery of oneself. Love requires discipline and control if it is not to degenerate into selfishness. Because the body belongs to personal subjectivity, one does not use or instrumentalize it, whether it be one's own or another's. Sex and sexuality, therefore, are personal and not just biological, which means that the procreative capacity cannot be demoted below personal love, or opposed to it, because it stands on the same level. Love, then, becomes, not an end, but the inner meaning and truth of conjugal life, uniting the two ends of marriage. Back in 1929 von Hildebrand had said that love was the primary meaning of marriage while procreation was the primary end and it was his insight that led to the development.[4] In the previous explanation, accurate as it was, the experience of the spouses was being left out and with it their awareness that mutual love and procreation together accounted for the meaning of married union. If *Humanae Vitae* said that procreation and communion of persons were the *meanings* of marriage, this personalistic language was used in order to emphasize how spouses are subjectively aware of them, and also that in marriage the *whole* person is given to the other and not just the body, and this is the reason for the change in terminology with regard to the traditional formulation.

John Paul II has written that, "The power of love – authentic in the theological and ethical sense – is expressed in this, that love *correctly unites 'the two meanings of the conjugal act'.*[5]" In his definition of love the Pope unites subjectivity with objective

---

[4] Dietrich von Hildebrand, *Marriage – the mystery of faithful love*, Sophia Institute Press, Manchester, New Hampshire, 1991.
[5] General Audience 10-X-84.

truth.⁶ He says, "*love* from the subjective viewpoint, is a *power* ... given to man in order to participate in that love with which God himself loves in the mystery of creation and redemption."⁷ The objective reference point of love is ultimate truth, or God himself. The further away from God one gets the more ambiguous, and the less authentic and objective, love becomes as a consequence of original and personal sins. Christopher West points perceptively to the need to avoid two erroneous extremes: that of subjective 'love' which is not guided by objective truth, or the sterile and loveless conformity to abstract and objective principles.⁸ In *Gaudium et Spes* and *Humanae Vitae* the language of the hierarchy of ends is dispensed with, but nevertheless the documents "deal with what the traditional expressions refer to." They clarify "the same moral order" but they do so "in reference to love".⁹ "In this renewed formulation the traditional teaching on the purposes of marriage (and their hierarchy) is reaffirmed and at the same time deepened from the viewpoint of the interior life of the spouses, that is, of conjugal and family spirituality."¹⁰ Love, then, becomes not an end but the inner meaning and truth of conjugal life.

The Truth of the Person and Conjugal Love

Familiaris Consortio noted that the cause of much of the misunderstanding of the encyclical *Humanae Vitae* is anthropological. Speaking of the difference between contraception and periodic continence, it says that it is "one which involves in the final analysis two irreconcilable concepts of the human person and human sexuality."¹¹ Those in favour of contraception see sexuality and procreation as biological and physical whereas Catholic tradition and natural law consider them to be personal, that is, actions of the whole person. Behind these two visions there is a different understanding of man himself and his actions. The question of contraception has to be decided in the context of

---

⁶ Cf. Christopher West, *Theology of the Body Explained*, p. 444, and for what follows in this paragraph.
⁷ General Audience 10-X-84.
⁸ West, op. cit..
⁹ General Audience 10-X-84, n. 3.
¹⁰ Ibid.
¹¹ John Paul II, Apostolic Exhortation *Familiaris Consortio*, n. 32.

conjugal love which has already been looked at.

Pope Paul explains that spousal love is human, that is to say, it is 'a compound of sense and spirit' like man himself.[12] It is also total, faithful and exclusive. To say that love is human, therefore, means that it is both bodily and spiritual at the same time. It is guided by reason like all human actions and is not just instinctual and emotional. If it were, it would be sub-human. Consequently, fully human love is spiritual in such a way that the emotional drives and biological processes are integrated into the personal unity of the subject by coming under the control of reason. In this way, human sexuality and parenthood are responsible, a fact which separates them completely from animal sexuality which is simply instinctual. The underlying reason for this is the substantial unity of the human being who is both spiritual and material at the same time and whose actions are also both. Human sexuality is, therefore, never simply biological and nor is procreation. Its bodily aspect is part and parcel of a personal/spiritual reality into which it has to be integrated and by which it has to be responsibly guided. This is not just true of sexuality but of all man's actions.

The encyclical emphasises that questions about the birth of children must be based on an integral or 'total vision of man'.[13] By this it means that we must have a complete understanding of man as a substantial unity of body and soul, sense and spirit; it is insufficient to look at him from a biological, psychological, demographical or sociological point of view. Equally, it is inadequate simply to look at him from the objective point of view but it is also necessary to consider the subjective dimension, that is, taking into account his inner life and his own awareness of himself. Man is a composite such that his actions have their origin in the soul and work through the organs of the body. These are known as the powers or faculties of the soul, i.e. the nutritive, growth, reproductive, cognitive, appetitive and locomotive faculties. Although some of these activities are shared with plants and animals, in man they are all human and personal. The reason for this is that man does not have separate rational, animal and vegetable souls, but a rational

---

[12] Paul VI, *Humanae Vitae*, n. 9.
[13] Ibid., n. 7.

soul, which directs the three types of activity.

There is an incorrect dualist personalism, which considers personalist goods as those which one is subjectively and consciously *aware of*, such as love, freedom, enjoyment, etc. These are goods *of* the person, while the so-called biological goods, such as sex and procreation, are goods *for* the person. But the distinction is a spurious consequence of dualism. If a person is defined solely in terms of consciousness, or awareness of self and others, it means that such bodily life that exists without consciousness is not personal life, nor are its goods, goods *of* the person. This is true of the early foetus and the embryo, and also of those in PVS, hence by this criterion bodily life is not personal life. And here we have a major issue of the day, the wrong estimation and underestimation of the body and physical life. An effect of dualism is to make this aspect of life sub-personal, and according to this biological sex has to be 'assumed' into the personal sphere. A true personalism based on the unity of the person would say, why does it have to be assumed into the personal sphere if it is already an integral part of the person?

The Personalist Argument against Contraception

When stating its doctrine of the non-separation of the unitive and procreative meanings of marriage the encyclical says that it is due to "the fundamental structure (i.e. nature) of the marriage act" and the "laws written into the nature of man and woman for the generation of new life."[14] By 'structure' here the encyclical does not just mean the physical nature of the act, but rather the more fully personal nature of it. And by 'laws' governing the procreative act, it does not just mean biological laws, but personal and rational laws, which govern human procreation and conjugal love. And by 'man and woman' here it means human beings in their subjective, as well as objective, dimensions, who are consciously aware of their fertility, which is much more than merely physical, and who, in turn, are also conscious of being a loving communion of persons. It is a question, first of truth in the ontological dimension (*fundamental structure*), and then in the subjective, psychological

---

[14] Paul VI, *Humanae Vitae*, n. 12.

dimension (*significance*). There is a primacy of the objective reality, but linked up with the subjective experience. *Humanae Vitae* tries to demonstrate that its moral norm is not imposed from outside, but wells up from within man and is in accord with the deepest truth and desires of man. So we now come to the point of explaining the teaching of *Humanae Vitae* with the help of the later writings of the Magisterium.

A fuller explanation of the structure of the marriage act and laws governing the generation of new life is given by aspects of the teaching of John Paul II's theology of the body. According to it, the sexual marriage act is a sign and expression of the marital bond which results from the consent of a man and woman to give themselves unreservedly to one another in mind and body with all that they have, and will have, in perpetuity. It is a love through the body, but of the whole person, in which they realise they are a gift for each other, and therefore their union requires total self-giving. It is personal love (i.e. love by the person-spouse), not just sensual love (i.e. lust for the body) it is what we have called spiritual and bodily love at the same time, and therefore chaste love.

Relationships with others are integral to human personality. There are different types and degrees of friendship with others, all of which involve you in giving yourself (time, talents, interests), within certain limits and specifications, to another, or others. But conjugal love requires *total* self-giving of the whole of one's life and self. It means, not only sharing one's possessions, one's time, etc., but one's whole self. Its purpose is to form a communion of persons according to the 'one flesh' model that was presented to mankind in the beginning. Spouses only have to think of the vows made on their wedding day when they gave themselves unreservedly to one another.

The exercise of sexuality, therefore, is a personal action in which the whole conscious and free person is involved and not just a biological action.[15] Love proceeds from the mutual attraction of two persons, but the characteristic of genuine conjugal love is that bodily and sensual attraction is directed by reason and integrated into spiritual love. Only thus can it be fully personal and human.

---

[15] Cf. *Familiaris Consortio*, n. 11.

The effort to achieve this is what is meant by chastity, which requires a self-mastery that must be sought throughout a lifetime. Sexual activity which is merely instinctual and not subject to a love which consists in personal self-giving and concern for the good of the other, is unworthy of human dignity and selfish.

The marriage act is, therefore, an expression of the *total* self-giving of the two spouses who become 'one flesh'. Hence, to deprive the act deliberately of one of its meanings and hold back the procreative capacity, is not to give oneself fully to the other, and so does not fulfil the conditions which are necessary for a full communion of persons. It is a bodily union, but not a fully personal one, in the sense that the whole person is not being given to the other. And since it does not do what it signifies, it is false language of the body. Thus, if it is not an act which is procreative in type, then nor is it an act of conjugal love and it is for this reason that the encyclical says that the unitive and procreative dimensions must not be separated. Hence, the contraceptive act, instead of fostering and building up spousal love between two people, has the potential to hinder it. As John Paul II was later to write in *Familiaris Consortio*: "The total physical self-giving would be a lie if it were not the sign and fruit of a total personal self-giving, in which the whole person ... is present. This totality which is required by conjugal love also corresponds to the demands of responsible fertility."[16]

The argument depends on the understanding that the human person is a unity of body and spirit, so that where the body acts the spirit is also present and vice versa. Let us recall that 'flesh' (or *basar*) for the Hebrews meant the person from the bodily point of view, whereas '*nephesh*' (soul or spirit) means that man is a spiritual and rational being of bodily existence. In the last paragraph we looked at man primarily as a rational/spiritual being, now let us look at the whole person again but from the bodily point of view. The total self-giving of a sexual nature, according to the explanation of David Crawford, means the communication of man's very self (his 'flesh'), genetically inscribed in his semen and sperm, to the woman whose body is uniquely made in its sexual organs to receive it. And by

---

[16] Ibid., n. 11.

receiving it she gives back her own 'flesh', i.e. her own identity, to her husband. Such an act, as can readily be seen, is *'per se* apt' for procreation. Because it is an act of love it is capable of fruitfulness in progeny, whether that fruitfulness occurs or not.[17] In other words, the total self-giving results in a one-flesh union and such a union is *ipso facto* procreative in type. Thus, if the generative dimension of the act is deliberately precluded it is not properly speaking a marital act either.

This is also true, as Crawford argues, when condoms are used within marriage to stop the spread of AIDS, because even though the intention is not directly to prevent procreation the action nevertheless ceases to be procreative in type and therefore not properly speaking a marital act. It is because the link between marital sex and procreation cannot be broken, that all forms of sexual activity outside marriage, which do sever the link, are wrong. If, however, it is claimed, as it is by the Church's critics, that contraception is valid, then sex can be used for its own sake, that is for reasons other than procreation, such as recreation, enjoyment etc., then it follows that other types of sexual activity such as homosexuality, cohabitation, masturbation etc., are also justified. And this, as predicted by *Humanae Vitae*, is very much what has happened. Notice, however, that what we have established is that every marital act, to be marital, must be *procreative in type*. Not procreative alone, because we know that most acts do not turn out like that, but Catholic doctrine requires that each act be *'per se* apt' for procreation whether it happens or not. This will help us later to explain why Natural Family Planning can be used for serious reasons.

The 'nuptial meaning of the body', as we said, consists in the awareness of the characteristics of sexual difference, communion in love with the other, and procreative ability. This language, which can be 'read' in the body, gives it its ethical significance. For there to be total self-giving, all three are necessary. The person experiences and is aware of self-donation, such that spousal self-donation or the lack of it is something consciously lived through. In

---

[17] Cf. David S. Crawford, 'Conjugal Love, Condoms, and HIV/AIDS', *Communio*, Fall 2006, pp. 509-10. I am indebted to this article for this expression of the matter.

that sense, the Pope sees a subjective awareness by contracepting spouses of a holding back: "The act of contraception ... expresses an objective refusal to give all the good of femininity and masculinity."[18] The description of contraception as false language of the body depends on the fact that the body 'mirrors' or reflects the person and, therefore, there is an inner truth for the body to follow. Just as a lie is to speak against what one is thinking, so to contracept is to act against the meanings of intercourse, which are mutual love and procreation, and persons as the acting subjects are capable of being aware of that in their inner consciousness, or conscience.

The contraceptive act is an act against spousal love and marital chastity, because there is no union of the two in 'one flesh' due to the deficiency in self-giving. Conjugal love is personal, that is love of the person, and not just sensual love, or lust for the body. It is spiritual and bodily love at the same time, which means it is personal and chaste love. The two spouses realize they are a gift for each other. If the other is not perceived as a gift, then he or she easily becomes de-personalized and treated as a body to be possessed, with prejudice to the dignity and love to which one's spouse has a right. The other is not now loved in themselves or for themselves; but, even though there may still be personal love, the other spouse is in danger of being treated as an object of pleasure.

The arguments against contraception are not primarily physical or biological, as the critics of *Humanae Vitae* often assumed them to be in the early stages of the debate, but personal and ethical. Once we look at it from a personal, or better still personalist, point of view we realise that the key to marital love is the virtuous pursuit of chastity. Sexuality is guided to personal love by chastity and away from it when sex is treated as a commodity to be used for pleasure, recreation or gain. Chastity enables spouses to show personal self-giving love to one another and not make use of one another selfishly. Love is opposed to use. Openness to procreation in marriage guides human passion and sensuality and, in a sense, 'atones' for it. On the other hand, separating sex from procreation

---

[18] General Audience 17-IX-83; cf. *Familiaris Consortio*, n. 32.

opens up the temptation to infidelity and promiscuity to a much greater degree, as *Humanae Vitae* predicted.

The Theological Argument

The evidence used so far is based mainly on reason and anthropology, but is confirmed too by the Word of God, thus providing us also with a theological argument. God's design for the world is a product of His free and gratuitous creative act of love and self-giving. In order to bring out the dimension of mystery in the account of the 'beginning', Pope John Paul II refers to the 'sacrament of creation', using 'sacrament' here in the wider meaning of a visible element which reveals a greater invisible reality. He, then, sees as the central point of the sacrament of creation, the union of male and female in marriage, with the purpose of continuing this mystery as partners of God. In this sense, marriage is said to be the 'primordial sacrament'. It is at the heart of God's plan and exhibits the central features of His design – self-giving love and creativity, or co-creation. Thus, marriage is capable of being an analogy of God's love and design in the Old Testament and of Christ and the Church in the New.

Taking this a step further, it can be seen that the body reveals the divine plan of truth, love and procreation. God is 'Creator' and 'Love' at the same time. And we are the 'image of God' so that these two characteristics are also shared in by us. In God they are not separated, and thus love or superabundance of goodness, is the reason for the creation. The same prerogative is participated in by human creatures, in whom they should not be separated either. But why is this the case? God has inscribed his own Word, his own language in the body, in order to reveal his mystery to the world. God's love all the way through the Scriptures is a self-giving gratuitous love. The epistle to the Ephesians makes it clear, "husbands love your wives as Christ loved the Church *and gave himself for it*." Reason also tells us that love in the first place desires the good of the beloved, not its own good.

Let us return to our question. Man *on his own initiative* must not separate the unitive and procreative dimensions of the sexual act, *Humanae Vitae* teaches; but why? The reason is because the sexual act may lead to a new life which requires the direct action of God, namely the infusion of the soul. Therefore, God is present in human sexuality and must not be excluded by man. When NFP is practised God is not left out since the action remains procreative in type. It respects the requirement that the act be open at all times to the twin purposes that God has written into human sexuality even if it does not result in new life. In other words, the sexual act as the expression of marital union must remain faithful to the purposes of marriage as a whole, namely communion in love and procreation and education of children. God, in whom love and life are not separated, has inscribed his own image and, with it, his own laws, in human beings. It is therefore his will that these twin purposes be respected at all times and in each case.

The contemporary mentality and pleasure ethic does not readily help people to understand self-giving. This notion, which goes to the heart of Christianity, is like a present day rendering of the Gospel's injunction to us to lose our lives if we want to gain them. To live we must die, to conquer we must overcome selfishness, to receive we must give, and so on. Present day thinking, however, finds a way round this, because if the body and biology are sub-personal, then so is sexuality and, if this is so, then it does not detract from the fullness of personal self-giving. Sex is an instrument, even a toy to be used, not something constitutive of personality to be integrated into human love-making and conjugal union. But this way of thinking runs contrary to the Church's tradition regarding human sexuality. So, it can readily be seen that there are two opposing concepts of sexuality, as there are of anthropology, which explain the modern age's difficulty in comprehending the Church's teaching on contraception.

Answering Dualist and Physicalist Objections

Let us recall that man has the power to procreate as he has the power to see, hear, walk, eat and sleep. These powers of the soul work through bodily organs, but the power is neither the organ, nor the use of the organ alone. We do not say that the reproductive organs give life but that the person does. The person becomes a father or mother, not the generative organs. You do not say 'My feet walk', or 'My mouth eats', but I walk or eat, just as we do not usually say our eyes see or our ears hear but that I see or hear. In other words it is the whole person who is the subject of his actions. The reason for this is rooted in the unity of man's being. There is a unity between the human powers and their exercise, which should not be broken. If it is, violence is done to the being of a person.

In contraception, a separation is made between the power of generation and the organic act of generation, in the same way as deliberate vomiting involves the separation of the power of nutrition and digestion from the act of eating. It has been said that if the encyclical were true we would not be able to eat or drink for pleasure, or for social reasons, since we would be denying the primary purpose of eating. But this, of course, is false, because both in procreation and eating (as in any human action) it is enough that you do not impede the primary purpose. Hence, for the eating analogy to be equal to contraception it would have to be a case of preventing digestion by deliberate vomiting and most people would still allow this to be wrong. But, it is *morally* wrong, not simply because of the physical impediment to digestion, but because it violates temperance and is an act of gluttony. Similarly, contraception is wrong because its moral identity violates the virtue of chastity.[19]

What, then, is the nature of contraception? It is not enough to say it is an anti-life type of act. This fits many other types of action such as euthanasia and abortion, from which contraception is morally *specifically* different.[20] Abortion and euthanasia are acts against life already conceived, whereas contraception is an act against marital chastity. It is the intentional impeding of the transmission of human life by deliberately altering the marriage act. It is generically anti-life, but the immediate object is clearly specifically different from acts which directly take life. However, abortion and contraception are linked like fruits from the same tree and the contraceptive mentality often leads to abortion,

---

[19] John Paul II, *Evangelium Vitae*, n. 13.
[20] Ibid.

either when the modern abortifacient pills are used, or when contraception fails.

It should be noted that it is not only because it goes against nature in a physicalist, 'natural' way that contraception is wrong. This has long been known as the 'perverted faculty argument', in other words, you distort the procreative power deliberately, just as you pervert the nourishing power in deliberate vomiting. Is it wrong to use one's teeth to chew gum which does not nourish, or cut one's hair? For one thing, this assumes the purpose of teeth is to nourish and of hair to grow which is clearly doubtful.[21] The physical side of the action of intercourse is separated from the generative power or faculty in contraception, but this alone is not what is ethically wrong with it. The physical side without the personal aspect is not enough to reach an ethical verdict, but this does not mean that the physical side is neutral, as Crawford's previously mentioned article shows, because the body is an expression of the person.

It is the separation of the two aspects of marriage, one-flesh union and procreation, and therefore, the impeding both of the transmission of human life and spousal love which is wrong. Now the signs of both these dimensions may be read in the body, but they are not simply bodily but personal. Spousal sexual intercourse is of a different order from the other actions referred to above, because sexual identity is so bound up with the identity of the person as such. John Paul II says it is constitutive of it. It is often pointed out that surgical operations, which imply physical change and disfigurement, are morally justifiable if they are for the good of the whole person by the principle of totality. However, the principle of totality is ruled out by the encyclical as irrelevant to the problem of contraception, because it (i.e. the principle of totality) only refers to the total physical good of the person and in contraception we are concerned with the personal and moral good.[22]

---

[21] Cf. Crawford, op. cit.
[22] See *Humanae Vitae*, nn. 3-6.

Is the Church's Doctrine Unrealistic?
The Role of Continence and Self-Mastery

However, spouses are not condemned to failure and frustration in their attempts to live up to the demands of Christian marriage. It is sometimes argued that the obligation indicated by *Humanae Vitae* to maintain the unitive and procreative aspects of marriage on all occasions, deprives them at times of expressing their love for one another. But a question arises as to what sort of love we are talking about? And whose love? That of man and woman redeemed by Christ and thus acting under the power of the Holy Spirit and grace, or that of the man of concupiscence? Thus love "is 'poured into (the) hearts' (Rom 5:5) of the spouses as the fundamental spiritual power of their conjugal pact."[23] And this conjugal love assists them in the fulfillment of the ends of marriage, that is the true communion of persons and responsible parenthood. In other words, those who live according to the Spirit, realize that there is no contradiction "between the divine laws pertaining to the transmission of life and those pertaining to the fostering of authentic conjugal love."[24] However, a number of means need to be employed so that we gradually overcome concupiscence, which should not be confused with genuine love.

When it is said that *Humanae Vitae* is unrealistic and out of touch, inattentive to the real needs of spouses and so on, what is really happening is that there is a confusion of concupiscence with real love. Concupiscence is "the movement of the sensitive appetite contrary to the operation of reason"[25] and though neutral in itself, if willingly followed it leads to sin. Concupiscence of the flesh would be an inclination of the sensitive appetite contrary to the nuptial meaning of the body. Concupiscence is not concerned with maintaining the truth of sexual union as an expression of God's life-giving love, it is concerned with its own satisfaction and shies away from authentic love. Love, however, "rejoices in the truth" (1 Cor 13:6) whatever the cost. Love is self-giving, thinking

---

[23] John Paul II, *Reflections on* Humanae Vitae, *The Power of Love is given to Man and Woman as a share in God's Love*, n. 4, p. 58, General Audience 10-X-84.
[24] *Gaudium et Spes*, n. 51.
[25] CCC 2515.

of the good of the other, rather than its own, and not self-taking, to which concupiscence pushes it. Ultimately, it can be said that contraception is used not simply to avoid pregnancy, but also to avoid the sacrifice and inconvenience required by self-control and continence, which is essential to authentic love.[26]

So true love requires, not the unleashing of one's emotional and sexual drives, but rather the discipline and control of them. In other words, true love and self-giving require restraint and this is what we call continence. This is so important that the Pope says that without it we cannot arrive "either at the heart of the moral truth, or at the heart of the anthropological truth of the problem" of understanding *Humanae Vitae*.[27] Hence, there is a struggle in fallen man between the inclination to the concupiscence of the flesh and authentic love, to the point where the latter can only be realized through the overcoming of concupiscence. This struggle with the waywardness of the flesh is one which is capable of a positive solution under the influence of grace and man's cooperation, along the path leading to the 'redemption of the body'. Sacrifice and restraint, therefore, far from being antithetical to love and married happiness, are an integral part of it. The story of Tobias and Sarah, in which they begin the first night of marriage in prayer in order not to be overcome by lust in their relations with one another, is a good example of this.[28] Lust tends to see the other person as a sensual body, or object, to be possessed and enjoyed for one's own gratification, rather than as a person to be loved for his or her own sake. A successful and happy marriage has to make this step.

Continence, temperance and chastity, nevertheless, tend to be understood by our society in a predominantly negative way. They are 'anti' something (concupiscence) rather than 'pro' something. The Pope answers this by saying that while this is true, it is not complete, because like other virtues continence does not act on its own, but always together with virtues such as prudence, justice, fortitude and especially charity. He therefore concludes that

---

[26] Cf. Christopher West, *The Theology of the Body Explained*, Gracewing, England, 2003, p. 447.
[27] General Audience 5-IX-84.
[28] Tob 7:8 – 8:21.

continence is "not only – and not even principally – the ability to 'abstain.'" This role would be regarded as 'negative': "But there is also another role (which we can call 'positive') of self-mastery: it is the ability to direct the respective reactions [of emotion and desire], both as to their content and their character."[29] Self-mastery is an integral part of love and has an upbuilding role to play, according to the law of gradualness, in the quest for authentic self-giving and the overcoming of the selfishness of concupiscence.

The argument is often put forward that human scientific and technological progress, such as medical drugs and surgical operations, contribute to a more civilized human life and, therefore, to the good of the person. Here, however, a distinction must be made between 'dominating the forces of nature' and 'mastery of self'. Mankind has a right and duty to impose his reason on the forces of nature, or the physical world. However, the human body cannot, as our anthropology has already shown, count simply as part of the physical world, since it is already an integral part of the person and of personal dignity and, therefore, part of the self. The body belongs to the subjectivity of the person. And, therefore, what is at stake, far from the domination of nature, is the mastery of self, a wholly different notion. It is mastery over one's personal emotions and drives, which is achieved by the cultivation of the virtues and good habits. What is at issue here, is the virtue of self-control or temperance and more specifically that part of it which we call chastity.

Why is Natural Family Planning permitted?

In contraceptive sex there is a separation between the self and the body and between freedom and nature. This does not happen with natural family planning, which makes use of the cycles of the body to identify the infertile period. By contrast, it involves avoiding intercourse during the fertile periods. However, to omit to seek a particular human good is not the same as transgressing it. Take, for example the value of truth. One is not obliged to tell the whole truth all the time, but only to avoid statements which are contrary to it. Similarly, with the procreative good, one does not have to

---

[29] General Audience 31-X-84.

will it consciously on each occasion, it is enough that one does not oppose it. This is the precise case of NFP where the action that one does is good because it is *'per se* apt' for procreation, and would be fruitful if God or nature chose it to be. Provided one's personal reason for doing it, one's further intention as Elizabeth Anscombe would say, is genuine then the action is in line with the moral and personal good and hence ethical.

This is what happens in natural family planning. A couple may decide for serious reasons that they cannot have a child for the immediate future, or even for an indeterminate period. These reasons may be of a psychological (ability of the wife to cope), economic, or social kind and it is for the spouses, not the priest for example, to decide if they are fulfilled. If this is the case, they are justified in using marriage in such a way as to avoid a pregnancy. In these circumstances, the intention of the will is correct, but they must also ensure that the action actually carried out is valid, which it will be if they do not interfere with the nature or structure of the act *on their own initiative.* As we have seen, continence and self-mastery give a positive orientation to the virtue of conjugal love in the battle with concupiscence, and so, for the right reasons, the use of periodic continence is an exercise of self-dominion and an integral part of love.

To understand how to use natural methods properly spouses need to have an integral vision of man and his vocation. Specifically, they must have a family and procreative attitude, namely they need to "acquire and possess solid convictions about the true values of life and the family."[30] Children can be looked upon as a burden rather than a joy and a blessing. Such a contraceptive mentality leads couples to think in terms of starting a family when they decide the time is right, that is to say, according to self-will and independent freedom. Even if the methods used in this case were natural methods, they could be contraceptive if the inner intention of the will were contraceptive, because this would invalidate the proximate object of the act, that is, using natural methods to avoid children. Natural methods are only valid, therefore, if there are reasonable grounds arising

---

[30] *Humanae Vitae*, n. 21.

from the physical or psychological condition of husband or wife, or external circumstances.[31]

Such an understanding of NFP answers those critics who regard the use of natural methods as just another form of contraception. Continence, then, is a virtue and, therefore, when abstinence is practised in the case of natural family planning, it is not simply a technique that is being applied, but the spouses are conducting themselves according to a virtuous way of living. Not to see it in this way could make it equivalent to contraception. As Christopher West puts it:

> In other words, not only does exercising one's freedom to abstain from intercourse when there is sufficient reason to avoid a pregnancy constitute an act of virtue ... but it also fosters the freedom necessary to ensure that when spouses do become 'one flesh' they act out of authentic love and do not merely indulge concupiscence. In this way we begin to see, as John Paul points out, that the role of continence lies not only in protecting the procreative meaning of intercourse, but also the unitive meaning.[32]

This is what we meant by saying, if it is not a procreative act neither is it, properly speaking, one of communion.

Marital Spirituality

Within marriage according to John Paul II, sexual intercourse has an exceptional significance because it is a sign and instrument of bringing about a communion of persons, according to the 'one flesh' of the beginning. Being open to this communion in each act and bringing it about constitutes "the internal problem of every marriage."[33] But this is only possible with the strength that comes from the Holy Spirit: "Those two who ... become one body cannot bring about this union on the proper level of persons *(communio personarum) except through the powers coming ... from the Holy Spirit* who purifies, enlivens, strengthens and perfects the powers of the human spirit."[34] Only

---

[31] Ibid., n. 16.
[32] See West, op. cit., p. 448.
[33] Karol Wojtyla, *Love & Responsibility*, p. 225.
[34] General Audience 14-XI-84.

then by 'life according to the Spirit',[35] that is, by the gifts the Holy Spirit brings, can spouses live marital chastity according to the truth of the 'one flesh'. In this way chastity is then perceived "not only as a moral virtue (formed by love), but likewise as a virtue connected with the gifts of the Holy Spirit – *above all the gift of respect for what comes from God.*"[36] The Pope is thinking here of the gift of piety which St Paul refers to when he says "defer to one another out of reverence for Christ."[37]

The excitement and emotion of spousal manifestations of affection are directed by chastity to this purpose of achieving a communion of persons. Marital spirituality then has the task of protecting the dignity of the sexual act. This enables them to love and cherish the other spouse for their own sake as a person and "gain a deep appreciation for the disinterested gift of the 'other'."[38] In the process they gradually overcome the concupiscence which treats the other as an object of gratification, which makes spouses feel used and manipulated rather than loved. Contraceptive intercourse is not properly speaking a marital act, that is, an act of conjugal love, because it is not so much a union of persons as a union of bodies. Consequently, the use of contraceptives does not contribute to the growth in married love and union between spouses in the way that the marital embrace should when it is carried out as a sign and fulfilment of the marriage vows, and indeed it presents an impediment to this growth.

The solution to the issue of human procreation demands that we have a concept of the human person as a spiritual and material whole, which takes us back to the principles of anthropology established in our early chapters. This leads us to acknowledge that in the generation of each new life God intervenes to create the spiritual soul. As we established earlier, the object of sexual union, in addition to the unitive love of the spouses, is not simply reproduction or even procreation, but the transmission of human life. It is required of free human beings that they show respect for the work of God in the generation of each human life, and

---

[35] Gal 5:25.
[36] General Audience 14-XI-84.
[37] Eph 5:21.
[38] General Audience 21-XI-84.

recognition of Him as the source of all life. Only thus do we do justice to the spiritual and fully personal aspect of human sexuality and procreation. Hence, St Paul's phrase, "defer to one another out of reverence for Christ",[39] can be seen as a plea not to leave God out of their thoughts and actions when it comes to the generation of new life.

The issue of contraception, for John Paul II, falls into the wider context of the dignity and vocation of man and woman, that is to say, of human love, in the divine plan. And the true response to this question and the living out of it are the foundation of ethics and society. Family life according to the truth of male and female is the basic building block of society and of the flourishing of the human being. The criterion of human progress must be what is good for man as man and not simply the most efficient way to solve problems, or the short-term solutions to problems of hunger and starvation: "The analysis of the *personalistic aspects* of the Church's doctrine contained in Paul VI's encyclical, emphasizes a determined appeal to measure man's progress on the basis of the 'person', that is of what is good for man as man – what corresponds to his essential dignity."[40]

In the last analysis, the confrontation between secular morality, which considers that contraception is the answer to many of the problems which hold up human progress, such as malnutrition, poverty and the spread of AIDS and sexually transmitted diseases, and natural law and Church teaching, is based on two different conceptions of the human person and progress, and therefore on two differing versions of what ethics consists in. Is it not rather the case that the latter affliction is aggravated by Western society's rejection of the truth and purpose of human sexuality and the genuine dignity and well-being of the human person as such, and by its promotion of condoms? Does the problem not arise, or at least reach its present grave proportions, from a non- acceptance of God's plan for human love and sexuality and the family based on the 'one flesh' of marriage? One side endorses an ethics which is based on

---

[39] Eph 5:25.
[40] General Audience 28-XI-84.

the usefulness of technology to bring about an efficient solution, or as the Pope puts it, in modern civilization there is an explicit tendency "to measure this progress on the basis of 'things', that is material goods."[41] The other argument is based on the true good and flourishing of the individual human person as a whole and the purpose of human sexuality.

Conclusion

The acceptance by society of contraception has been followed not only by 'alternatives' to marriage such as cohabitation and civil partnerships but also by the pioneering of IVF and the widespread use of technology not simply to assist childbirth but to replace it. The 1960s proved to be the curtain raiser to an overwhelmingly anti-life agenda. The lack of responsibility for human life and human procreation led to an undervaluing of life at its end as well as at its beginning, issuing in a euthanasia mentality. The separation of the marital act from procreation took place with the opposite effect in IVF. In the bio-medical and bio-scientific developments since then, we see a willingness to disregard ethical considerations in favour of 'moral autonomy' which is prepared to give the go-ahead to everything that can be achieved scientifically. But in all these issues the same principles are misunderstood and overlooked again and again, namely a correct anthropology, an accurate notion of natural law, and other ethical principles, such as an understanding of the moral act, a grasp of genuine freedom, and an awareness of the dangers of naturalism and physicalism in ethics as well as utilitarianism and consumerism.

This latter exposes us to the danger of treating humans as objects, and not as persons to whom the only adequate attitude is love. One cannot put technology before persons, or allow it to replace personal love in marriage, without exposing oneself to the danger of treating people, and especially children, in one way or another as a means to an end rather than for their own sake. Technology delivers many services to us, but man and human love are superior to things. Being is more important

---

[41] General Audience 28-XI-84.

than having. Every child is a gift and not a commodity, the Church reminds us. Hence the ultimate issue is not what works or what appears to be most efficient. Such a mentality has led to a Huxleyesque brave new world of artificial insemination, and ultimately cloning and embryonic stem-cell research, saviour siblings, etc. Many of these leave children not knowing who their father was, and their heritage, or whether they came into the world with the love of their parents. In this sense *Humanae Vitae* was prophetic, not only in its predictions about the growth of promiscuity, but also about the ethical limits of human biological research:

> Consequently, unless we are willing that the responsibility of procreating life should be left to the arbitrary decision of men, we must accept that there are certain limits, beyond which it is wrong to go, to the power of man over his own body and its natural functions – limits which, let it be said, no one, whether as a private individual, or as a public authority, can lawfully exceed. These limits are expressly imposed because of the reverence due to the whole human organism and its natural functions …[42]

---

[42] *Humanae Vitae*, n. 17.

CONCLUSION:

MORALITY AND EVANGELIZATION

Evangelization is as old as the Gospel, but contemporary experience teaches that it is in the countries of long Christian tradition, especially, and, therefore, among many of the baptized, where a new catechesis in the Faith and moral principles is required. This re-christianization, which the Polish Pontiff spoke of on many occasions, requires a deeper understanding and presentation of the mysteries of faith and moral principles to people who, across the board, have reached a higher degree of education than hitherto. It involves following much of the thinking we have been highlighting, such as the linking of objective truth with the subjective experience of it and making it more real and comprehensible to the people of our time. It means communicating the 'unsearchable riches of Christ' and what St Paul calls 'the mystery hidden for generations' (Eph. 3:9) and now revealed in the Incarnate Word. The theology of the body makes a great contribution to this process because it explains more fully the relationship of Christ and the Church, which is, in turn, an image of the union of man and woman in marriage.

While John Paul II clearly links the new evangelization to the proclamation of Faith he also applies it in a special way to morality. He speaks of peoples and communities once rich in faith and Christian life that have become de-christianized, through loss of faith, or its apparent irrelevance for them, and also of a decline and obscuring of the moral sense. This comes about through a

CONCLUSION: MORALITY AND EVANGELIZATION

loss of the awareness of the originality of Christian morality and an eclipse of fundamental principles and ethical values themselves. The new evangelization will show its authenticity by proclaiming the truth of faith, "and even more so in presenting the foundations and content of Christian morality", not only "by the word proclaimed but also by the word lived, through a life of holiness." This message, he says, must be "new in its ardour, methods and expression."[43]

The teaching of John Paul II shows a marked tendency to identify the radical nature of Christian revelation and bring to life its continual relevance. In going back to the 'beginning' he is able to divine the original truth of the human condition and its contemporary importance, which is what he means by the phrase, 'the originality of Christian morality'. He speaks not just of original sin but goes back further still, to the state of original innocence to which we have to tend, because it keeps the standard we are called to before our eyes. Although they belonged to a time when man lived in the perfect state of grace, the importance of the so-called original experiences, of solitude, unity of man and woman, and nakedness, is that they still have an echo in man's everyday life and represent the full truth about man found only in Christ (*Gaudium et Spes* 22), because the original state of grace was due to the gift of Christ. The Pope writes:

> The important thing, therefore, is not that these experiences belong to man's prehistory (to his 'theological pre-history'), but that they are always at the root of every human experience. That is true, even if, in the evolution of ordinary human existence, not much attention is paid to these essential experiences. They are, in fact, so intermingled with the ordinary things of life that we do not generally notice their extraordinary character.[44]

John Paul's insistence on the interiority of man, and that experience and consciousness is part of human action, enables him to explain more adequately another central tenet of revealed Christian ethics, namely that the Law of God and the virtues are fulfilled inside man, that is, in biblical language, his heart.

---

[43] *Veritatis Splendor*, n. 106, quoting speech to CELAM, 9-III-1983.
[44] John Paul II, *The Meaning of Original Human Experiences*, General Audience 12-XII-79.

This, therefore, corrects a deformed vision that sees moral life as conformity to an external law with the overtones that it is imposed on you and alienates you as an individual. This is overcome by the realization that it is within us, it wells up inside of us, in our own moral consciousness, and participates in a law that indeed is also without, in that it is common to all. We needed the study of interiority and the philosophy of consciousness in order to deepen and cement this crucial truth.

Nevertheless, evangelization must take into account both the culture of peoples and the culture of a particular time, as for example, the way in which relativism characterizes contemporary society. It also requires a true understanding of the fact that freedom and reason are directed to the truth and guided by it. These conditions, as we have seen, contrast with many aspects of today's culture and illustrate not only the challenge the Church faces according to the eternal plan, but also the necessity of faith and Christian ethics to enable man to live according to his dignity, to know the goods and rights of the human person, to understand the parallel path and harmony of faith and reason, and to be able to contribute to the peace and justice of society. By way of summary, we will expand now on these four aspects, of cultural relativism, freedom and rational truth, human rights, and the necessity of the Christian life given by the Church.

We have frequently reiterated throughout the narrative that if truth is neglected relativism results, because without truth, coherence and even the principle of contradiction go by the board. With relativism there are no moral absolutes, no truth which is applicable to all, because according to this position the power of human reason does not reach that far. But by the same token relativism itself is not capable of being defended rationally, because there is no truth by which the question can be decided. Each one's view is equally valid, but some of these views will contradict each other, as the Greeks, especially Socrates and Plato, found. If, therefore, relativism cannot be defended by rational truth, then it becomes 'dogmatic relativism' and is unreasonable dogma. Hence, there is a need for harmony between faith and reason, so that they can enable each other to fulfil their tasks. Benedict XVI writes:

CONCLUSION: MORALITY AND EVANGELIZATION

> Faith by its specific nature is an encounter with the living God – an encounter opening up new horizons extending beyond the sphere of reason. But it is also a purifying force for reason itself. From God's standpoint faith liberates reason from its blind spots and therefore helps it be ever more fully itself. Faith enables reason to do its work more effectively and to see its proper object more clearly.[45]

Faith is then an ally of reason, a transcendent ray of light raising the mind to the full extent of its powers which have been blinded by original sin. However, the best of classical Greek philosophy proves that great light can be given to reason alone, even independently of faith, when the powers of the human mind are at their highest, though it is never complete, but it is not the general condition of mankind throughout history and hence the need of faith.

If, therefore, attempts are made to undermine knowledge and introduce a radical scepticism, as has occurred at times throughout history, notably in Ancient Greece with the Sophists, or at the Enlightenment, or today with the movement of post-modernism and certain theories of meaning and language, then morals will suffer. According to such theories truth is limited to the perception of the observer and hence everyone is his own moral judge and relativism results. In Christian ethics, however, reason furnishes us with basic moral principles which are universally applicable and not simply personal preferences. But for this you need foundations for your knowledge which are very different from the contemporary presuppositions.

The grip that relativism holds over us makes it salutary to recall the lesson of the Sophists who had taken a correspondingly relativist position in ancient Greece and for similar reasons. The two diametrically opposed philosophies which preceded them, of Heraclitus ('all is change') and Parmenides ('all is one and there is no change') led to the belief that knowledge is unattainable. Thus our minds cannot get beyond the appearances to the core of reality. In these circumstances say the Sophists, the important thing is to get on in life and make the most of our situation to advance our position and well-being. Their teaching has come down to us through Protagoras whose well known assertion

---

[45] Benedict XVI, *Deus Caritas Est*, n. 28.

that 'man is the measure of all things' emphasizes the radical subjectivity of knowledge, even though its exact interpretation is disputed. But as Socrates was to point out, the problem with such statements is they cannot be universally true on their own premises. If someone disagrees with it, he is asserting the truth also. Relativism of this sort lands you in contradictions and a sort of double truth emerges, which seems to vindicate those who maintain reason's ability to know some universal truths.

This contradictory character of relativism entails that it cannot be rationally defended or argued for, otherwise it would be proposing the ability of reason to know the truth. If it tries to defend itself rationally it contradicts itself because it then has to admit the possibility of non-relative truth, or of relative and absolute truth coexisting and so cancelling each other out. In this sense, relativism shows itself to be a 'belief', or an assumption, in fact a dogma if this is understood as something that is accepted without evidence and so in a dogmatic manner. It was for this reason that the former Cardinal Ratzinger spoke of 'the dictatorship of relativism' shortly before being elected Pope. Furthermore, it cannot be demonstrated by mathematical-empirical reason because it is not a fact but a philosophy.

What Christian ethics and faith give to rational ethics, or rather to reason itself, is the confidence that there is an underlying truth that is permanent. Such universal truth or foundations cannot purely be the result of sense knowledge or empirical generalization, or pragmatism, as Plato saw, since that knowledge is constantly changing, or being revised in the interests of greater accuracy. It must therefore be the result of a more foundational or abstract knowledge, namely a philosophy of being, that is to say, metaphysics or ontology. Indeed, it is the Christian contention that God's nature is rational and his creation mirrors this rationality. The current relativism considers all religion as myth without foundation, a position which goes against the whole history of Christian thought. In fact, both Greek thought and the whole Judeo-Christian tradition conceive religion as knowledge and God as Logos, or Creative Reason.[46] Hence, the difference

---

[46] Joseph Ratzinger, *Introduction to Christianity*, Ignatius Press, 1990. See section 'The

between Christians and atheists implies more than the existence or otherwise of God and also includes the order of nature and the ability of reason to discern moral values from these truths.

It was predicted in *Humanae Vitae* that the acceptance of contraception would lead to an explosion of promiscuity due to the separating of sexual union from the responsibility for procreation. In fact, it has lead to a mindset which sees sexual activity as recreation, and as justified for pleasure alone once any responsibility is taken from it. The teaching and promotion of sexuality only in a biological way with no moral guidelines to young people and even to pre-teens, has obscured the moral conscience of youth leading to a considerable fall in religious practice. It also leads to the perception of all 'sexual orientations' as equal. This, however, ignores the personal and biological reality of sexual difference which gives rise to complementarity and reciprocity, and leads in principle to fruitfulness, which means that sexual union should be procreative in type. We see here another reason for the importance of the 'theology of the body' which uses human experience, philosophy and Scripture to give us deeper insights into gender difference, as well as how union in 'one flesh' and procreation are inseparable meanings of human sexuality and marriage.

Power often opposes truth, but accusations of power structures, as alleged by Foucault and radical feminism's attack on sexual difference and the consequent separation of sexuality and gender, are often used to put in place further power structures. In fact, what is happening is that sexuality is being re-described positivistically without reference to being and ontology, including biology, and therefore truth. The result is that sexual difference is replaced by the sexless person, such that sexuality does not enter into personal identity. Truth obliges us to show the utmost respect for the equality of women and the rights of homosexuals as persons, but if we neglect truth we can easily replace one injustice with another, and allow children to grow up without a father, or knowledge of their genealogy for example. These are instances of the ways in which the truth, identity, freedom and dignity of the

---

God of Faith and the God of the Philosophers', pp. 93-104.

person can be opposed by power and relativism when truth is dispensed with.

A look at the rights of the human person as expressed by the *Universal Declaration of Human Rights* will show how the basic human rights are founded on the goods of the person, including the child, and hence are self-evident and part of natural law. In article 3 the 1948 document states that "everyone has the right to life, liberty and security of person" and in the Preamble affirms that by 'everyone' it means 'every member of the human family'. It is founded on the notion that there are human values and that these values are inherent in the human person. It states in the Preamble that "the foundation of freedom, justice and peace in the world" is the "recognition of the inherent dignity and of the equal and inalienable rights of all members of the human family".[47] In practice, however, they tend to be fudged by the legislation of individual member states, particularly in regard to abortion and embryo experimentation and destruction. This question was raised (in regard to abortion) by a number of countries in a proposed amendment to the *International Covenant on Civil and Political Rights*, in 1966, but rejected on the grounds that it would be impossible to determine the moment of conception and hence to undertake to protect life by law from that moment.

The sentiments expressed in the 1948 Declaration are commendable but the question remains as to how much they are practised and lived up to. Human freedom is today frequently confused with a rather unlimited personal autonomy, yet it is necessary to affirm many ways in which personal freedom is limited by truth if it is not to be lost. For a start, the freedom of each one is necessarily curtailed by the freedom of everybody else. One cannot grow one's garden hedges irrespective of one's neighbour's rights to sunlight, views etc. Indeed, our freedom must be exercised in conformity with the justice and equality due to all human persons.

Historically, social freedom has been based on the power of property and wealth which puts it on a collision course with social

---

[47] On this question see the work of Fr John Fleming, 'What Rights, if any, do the unborn have under International Law?' in *Common Ground, Seeking an Australian Consensus on Abortion and sex Education?*, St Pauls Publications, 2007, p. 278.

equality. In order to maintain slavery, the Chief Justice of the United States in 1857 overturned Dred Scott's appeal, that his condition as a slave contradicted his rights as a person, on the grounds that he was a non-person.[48] Nevertheless, due to the human condition, the rights to freedom, justice and equality of the human being continue to be frequently abused, for example, by the use of power in the workplace and employment practice, by discrimination in the hiring of staff and in the treatment of them at work based on ageism, 'cronyism', ethnic discrimination etc.

The linking of freedom with justice and equality makes it clear that no individual has power over the life of another. If capital punishment, or the judicial taking of life, has been traditionally justified it is because it is done on the authority of the State – never by a private individual – which has responsibility for the common good, that is for the protection of its inhabitants. Of course, if this can be achieved by imprisonment it removes the main justification for it. The right to life is the most fundamental on which all others rest; we cannot give it or take it away. Since life is a gift held on trust no supposed principle of autonomy can override it. It is a gift and right not only to the individual, but also to one's family and society to whom one, therefore, assumes obligations in charity and justice, and naturally also to the Creator Himself. The Church, then, and particularly John Paul II, draw attention to the contradiction that exists in Western countries between laws on abortion, embryo experimentation, the freezing of embryos, therapeutic cloning, etc., which all involve the destruction of human persons, and the United Nations *Declaration of Human Rights*, to which they have all signed up, which requires that the equal and inalienable rights of 'all members of the human family' be protected.

Similar considerations apply to the rights to freedom, justice and equality of spouses and children in marriage. The dignity of marriage requires that the spouses have a right to become a father or mother through each other, and that children be born of the personal love of their parents, and therefore know who their parents are, without the predominating use of technology.

---

[48] Ibid.

Experience testifies to the justified anger of young people when they find out they were conceived by anonymous donor sperm. The Gospel of Life and the Gospel of the Family are an integral part of the new evangelization and consequently of the Church's whole mission. In stating its position on matters of marriage and bio-ethics the Church is not trying to impose its morality on society, but rather fulfilling the indispensable role of educating consciences.

Can we know such an unseen, hidden truth such as that which the Christian Gospel tradition has handed on to us? Yes, if language has representational meaning and the sign is able to relay the reality of the thing signified, which is surely the purpose of language. On the level of faith, Christian Revelation provides confirmation of this, since by the Incarnation of the Word the sensible signs make known to us the unseen God. The sacramental principle, much beloved of Newman, teaches us the same truth, because through the visible signs of the sacraments the invisible grace and strength of the Holy Spirit are made present to those who receive them worthily. For believers, at least, signs and symbols, such as the words of Scripture, are able to furnish us with a non-empirical truth such as the Incarnation. Hence, do we not assume also on the human level that reason is able to grasp a common and universal meaning through the words and symbols of language, notwithstanding the claims of post-modernism and radical subjectivism that we can never know the meaning of an original text, but only the way we understand it now?

Words are signs and symbols of a deeper reality which is different from the sign; the body is a sign of the person etc. Signs and images are used extensively in Scripture, so the shepherd is the sign of the pastor of souls and the sheep of the faithful; the banquet represents the kingdom of Heaven; the body is a sign of the Church and its members, and the head represents Christ the head of the body. The Church herself is a sign and sacrament as *Lumen Gentium* tells us in the following words: "The Church, in Christ, is in the nature of a sacrament – a sign and instrument, that is, of communion with God and of unity among all men."[49] In

---
[49] *Lumen Gentium*, n. 1.

another place, it spoke of the Church as the "universal sacrament of salvation",[50] similar but not the same as the seven sacraments, because it is being used in the wider meaning of 'sacrament', but nevertheless it shows how Christ reaches our lives in all their particularity through the sacraments by means of the Holy Spirit and the Church.

John Paul II also spoke of the 'sacrament of creation' and the 'sacrament of redemption'. The first is the way in which the world is a reflection of the Creator and leads us to know Him, as well as the fact that in the account of creation in Genesis in the state of original innocence we are able to glimpse the eternal plan of God and his grace for all mankind. The 'sacrament of redemption' is the work of Christ communicated to us through the Church in the word and Sacraments in its journey through the world leading mankind to its final destiny. We can also see other signs and symbols of the 'sacrament of redemption' in the world, such as work, family, suffering, human relationships, sorrows, joys, in other words, ordinary life which through the following of Christ and the life of the Church become sanctifiable. There is, however, an important difference between the seven sacraments instituted by Christ and lived in the Church and the use of 'sacrament' in the wider sense. The former confer the grace they signify *ex opere operato*, given the state of grace, whereas the 'sacrament of ordinary life', as it has been called, does so only if the person sanctifies it by his life of faith and moral behaviour.

However, the importance of the sacramental principle to religion and life is clear, both in order to know truths and the ultimate Truth and also to practise the truth. We have here another indication that the great ethical problems of mankind can only be ultimately surmounted with the worship of God, as we saw, and therefore working in harmony with the light and assistance which are given us by the sacrament of redemption brought to us by His Body, the Church on earth. An example is one of the major ethical issues of this, or any other time, namely marriage and family life. The union of man and wife is a sign, we saw, of the unity of Christ and the Church, and where it is lived as a sacrament it receives the

---

[50] Ibid., n. 48.

strength, light and assistance from Christ through the Church to live up to its characteristics of unity, indissolubility, faithfulness and fruitfulness. We see here the importance of unity between religion and ethics and between faith and moral living. There is, of course, a separation between rational and Christian ethics, as a way of knowing morality, but it is nevertheless a difference seeking unity and harmony, in the same way as faith and reason should harmonize, both for the individual good and the well-being and peace of mankind.

Select Bibliography

Anscombe, G.E.M., *Contraception and Chastity*, CTS, London, 1975 (also collected in Janet Smith, ed. See below pp. 119-146)

Aquinas, *Summa Theologiae*, (first Tr. of Fathers of English Dominican Province), Great Books of the Western World, Benton, Encyclopaedia Britannica Inc, Chicago, 1952

———, *Summa contra Gentiles*, in Basic Writings of Saint Thomas Aquinas, ed. Anton Pegis, Random House, New York, 1944

Arregui, Jorge, 'The Nuptial Meaning of the Body and Sexual Ethics', in *Issues for a Catholic Bio-Ethic*, ed. L. Gormally, Linacre Centre, London, 1999

Ashley, B., 'What is the End of the Human Person', in *Moral Truth and Moral Tradition*, ed. L. Gormally, Four Courts Press, Dublin, 1994

———, *Living the Truth in Love*, Alba House, New York, 1996

Augustine, *Confessions*, Library of the Fathers of the Christian Church, ed. Philip Schaff, vol. I, T & T Clark, Edinburgh & Eerdmans, Grand Rapids, Michigan, 1994

———, *De Spiritu et Littera, Anti-Pelagian Writings*, ibid., vol. V

———, *De Trinitate*, ibid., vol. III

———, *The City of God*, ibid., vol. II

Aristotle, *Nichomachean Ethics*, ed. J.A.K. Thompson, Penguin Classics, 1963

Beckwith, Francis J., *Defending Life*, Cambridge University Press, Cambridge, 2007

Braine, David, *The Human Person; Animal and Spirit*, Duckworth, London, 1993

Bristow, Peter, *The Moral Dignity of Man*, Four Courts Press, Dublin, 1997

Buttiglione, Rocco, *Karol Wojtyla, The Thought of the Man who became Pope John Paul II*, Eerdmans, Grand Rapids, Michigan, 1997

Cafarra, Carlo, *Living in Christ*, Ignatius, San Francisco, 1987

Cessario, Romanus, *Introduction to Moral Theology*, Catholic University of America Press, Washington D.C., 2001

Cicero, Marcus Tullius, *De Republica*, Loeb Library ed., Harvard University Press, Cambridge Mass. & London, 1928

Copleston, Frederick, SJ, *A History of Philosophy*, vols I-IX, Burns & Oates, London, 1946-67

———, *Contemporary Philosophy*, Search Press, London, 1973

Covey, Stephen, *The Seven Habits of Highly Effective People*, Simon & Shuster, London, 1992

Crosby, John F., *The Selfhood of the Human Person*, Catholic University of America Press, Washington D.C., 1996

Descartes, René, *Principles of Philosophy*, 1, 51 Descartes, *Key Philosophical Writings*, Wordsworth Editions, London, 1997

DiNoia, J.A. and Romanus Cessario, eds, *Veritatis Splendor and the Renewal of Moral Theology*, Midwest Theological Forum, Chicago, 1994

Escriva, St, Josemaria, *Christ is Passing by*, Scepter, London, 1974

———, *Conversations with Mgr Escriva de Balaguer*, Scepter, Dublin, 1968,

Finnis, John, *Natural Law and Natural Rights*, Clarendon Press, Oxford, 1980

———, *Aquinas*, Oxford University Press, Oxford, 1998

———, *Fundamentals of Ethics*, Clarendon Press, Oxford, 1983

———, *Moral Absolutes*, Catholic University of America Press, Washington D.C., 1991

Flannery, Kevin, *Acts amid Precepts*, T & T Clark, Edinburgh, 2001

Fleming, John, 'What Rights, if any, do the unborn have under International Law?', in *Common Ground, Seeking an Australian Consensus on Abortion and sex Education?*, St Pauls Publications, New South Wales, 2007

George, Robert, *In Defense of Natural Law*, OUP, Oxford, 1999

———, (with Christopher Tollefsen), *Embryo, A Defense of Human Life*, Doubleday, New York, 2008

―――, *The Clash of Orthodoxies*, ISI Books, Wilmington, Delaware, 2001

Grisez, Germain, *The Way Of the Lord Jesus*, (vol. 1), Franciscan Herald Press, Chicago, 1983

Hogan, *Confronting the Truth*, Darton, Longman & Todd, London, 2001

Hoyt, Robert, ed., 'Majority Report to The Papal Commission on Population, the Family and Natality', can be found in *The Birth Control Debate, The Question is not Closed*, The National Catholic Reporter, Kansas, 1969

Hume, David, *A Treatise of Human Nature*, 1, 4, 6, ed. Ernest C. Mossner, Penguin Books, London, 1985

John Paul II, *Crossing the Threshold of Hope*, Jonathan Cape, London, 1994

―――, *Memory and Identity*, Weidenfield and Nicholson, London, 2005

Kant, Immanuel, *Fundamental Principles of the Metaphysic of Ethics*, tr. T.K. Abbott, Longmans, London, 1962

Keown, John, *Euthanasia, Ethics and Public Policy*, Cambridge University Press, Cambridge and New York, 2004

Lawler, Ronald, Joseph Boyle and William May, *Catholic Sexual Ethics*, Our Sunday Visitor, Huntingdon, Indiana, 1985

Locke, John, *An Essay concerning Human Understanding*, II, 27, 9, ed. Peter H. Nidditch, Clarendon Press, Oxford, 1979

May, William, *An Introduction to Moral Theology*, Our Sunday Visitor, Huntingdon, Indiana, 1991

―――, *Human Existence, Medicine and Ethics*, Franciscan Herald Press, Chicago, 1977

―――, *Catholic Bioethics and the Gift of Human Life*, Our Sunday Visitor, Huntingdon, Indiana, 2000

MacIntyre, Alasdair, *After Virtue*, Duckworth & Co., London, 1990

―――, *Whose Justice? Which Rationality?* Duckworth & Co.,

London, 1988
———, *Three Rival Versions of Moral Enquiry*, Duckworth & Co., London, 1990
———, *Dependent Rational Animals*, Duckworth & Co., London, 1999
Martin, Francis, *The Feminist Question, Feminist Theology in the Light of Christian Tradition*, T& T Clark, Edinburgh, 1994
McCormick, Richard, *Notes on Moral Theology, 1981, 1965-1980*, University Press of America, Washington D.C., 1981
McInerny, Ralph, *Ethica Thomistica*, Catholic University of America Press, Washington D.C., 1997
Melina, Livio, *Sharing in Christ's Virtues*, Catholic University Press, Washington, 2001
Melina, Livio, *Moral: entre la crisis y la renovacion*, Ediciones Internacionales Universitarias, Madrid, 1998, 2nd edition

Newman, J.H., *An Essay on the Development of Christian Doctrine*, Sheed and Ward, London & New York, 1960
———, *Apologia pro Vita sua*, J.M. Dent & Son, Everyman's Library, London, 1955
———, 'The State of Grace', in *Parochial and Plain Sermons*, vol. IV, n. IX, Rivingtons, London, 1868
Nichols, Aidan, *Christendom Awake*, T & T Clark, Edinburgh, 1999

O'Brien, Conor Cruise, *The Great Melody: A Biography of Edmund Burke*, Sinclair-Stevenson, London, 1992
Ocariz, Fernando, 'Dignidad Persona, Trascendencia e Historicidad del Hombre', in *Naturaleza, Gracia y Gloria*, Eunsa, Pamplona, 1999

Pinckaers, Servais, *The Sources of Christian Ethics*, T & T Clark, Edinburgh, 1995
———, *The Pursuit of Happiness – God's Way*, Alba House, New York, 1998
———, *Para Leer La Veritatis Splendor*, Rialp, Madrid, 1996

Quay, Paul, *The Christian Meaning of Human Sexuality*, Credo

House, Evanston, 1985

Ratzinger, Joseph, *Introduction to Christianity*, Ignatius Press, San Francisco, 1990. See section 'The God of Faith and the God of the Philosophers'
———, *Pilgrim Fellowship of Faith*, Ignatius Press, San Francisco, 2005
———, *Called to Communion*, Ignatius Press, San Francisco, 1991
———, 'Communion: Eucharist-Fellowship-Mission', in *Pilgrim Fellowship of Faith*, Ignatius Press, San Francisco, 2005
———, *Truth and Tolerance*, Ignatius Press, San Francisco, 2004
Rhonheimer, M., *Natural Law and Practical Reason*, Fordham University Press, New York, 2000
———, *La Perspectiva de la Moral*, Rialp, Madrid, 1994 & 1999
Richard of St Victor, *De Trinitate*, IV, 23, *La Trinité*, Gaston Salet S.J., ed., coll. *Sources chrétiennes*, 63, Paris, 1959

Schmitz, Kenneth L., *At the Center of the Human Drama*, Catholic University of America Press, Washington, 1993
Shivanandan, Mary, *Crossing the Threshold of Love*, T & T Clark, Edinburgh, 1999
Singer, Peter and Helen Kuhse, 'On Letting Handicapped Infants Die', in *The Right Thing to do: Basic Readings in Moral Philosophy*, ed. James Rachels, Random House, New York, 1989
Smith, Janet, *Humanae Vitae; A Generation Later*, The Catholic University of America Press, Washington D.C. 1991
Smith, Janet, ed., *Why Humanae Vitae was Right: a Reader*, Ignatius Press, San Francisco, 1993
Sokolowski, Robert, *Introduction to Phenomenology*, Cambridge University Press, Cambridge, 2005
Spinello, Richard, *The Genius of John Paul II*, Sheed and Ward, Chicago, 2007
Stein, Edith, St, *Essays on Woman*, ICS Publications, Washington, D.C., 1996
Teichman, J., *Social Ethics*, Blackwell, Oxford, 1999

von Hildebrand, Dietrich, *Marriage – The Mystery of Faithful Love*, Sophia Institute Press, Manchester, New Hampshire, 1991

von Hildebrand, Dietrich (with Alice), *Morality and Situation Ethics*, Franciscan Herald Press, Chicago, 1966

Warnock, Mary, *A Question of Life*, Basil Blackwell, Oxford, 1985

West, Christopher, *The Theology of the Body Explained*, Gracewing, Leominster, 2003

Woodall, G. J., *Humanae Vitae, Forty Years On*, Family Publications, Oxford, 2008

Wojtyla, Karol, *Love and Responsibility*, Collins, London, 1981

———, *The Acting Person*, Reidel Publishing Company, London, 1979

———, *Person and Community, Selected Essays*, tr. by Theresa Sandok, OSM, Peter Lang, New York, 1993 (Most of these essays have been crucial to my work, especially, parts II and III.)

Yepes, Ricardo, *Fundamentos de Antropologia*, updated by Javier Aranguren, 4th ed., EUNSA, Pamplona, 1998

Documents of the Magisterium

Vatican II
Lumen Gentium
Dei Verbum
Gaudium et Spes
Dignitatis Humanae
Optatum Totius

Paul VI
Humanae Vitae, 1968

John Paul II
Theology of the Body Discourses (given between 5-IX-79 and 28-XI-84). Edition used, St Paul's Publications in four volumes:
Original Unity of Man and Woman, 1981

    Blessed are the Pure of Heart, 1983
    Reflections on Humanae Vitae, 1984
    The Theology of Marriage and Celibacy, 1986
  Encyclicals
    Redemptor Hominis, 1979
    Dives in Misericordia, 1980
    Centessimus Annus, 1991
    Veritatis Splendor, 1993
    Evangelium Vitae, 1995
    Fides et Ratio, 1998
  Post Synodal Apostolic Exhortations
    Familiaris Consortio, 1980
    Reconciliatio et Paenitentia, 1984
  Other
    Instruction on Respect for Human Life in its Origin and on The Dignity of Procreation, (Donum Vitae), CDF, 1987
    Mulieris Dignitatem, 1987
    Letter to Families, 1994,
    Letter to Women, 1995
    Ad Tuendam Fidem, (To Protect the Faith), 1998
    On the Collaboration of men and women in the Church and the world, CDF, May 2004

Catechism of the Catholic Church, Geoffrey Chapman, London, 1994

Benedict XVI
  Encyclicals
    Deus Caritas Est, 2005,
    Spe Salvi, 2007
    Caritas in Veritate, 2009
  Apostolic Exhortation
    Sacramentum Caritatis, 2006
  Instruction
    Instruction Dignitas Personae on Certain Bioethical Questions, CDF, 2008

Index

Abelard, Peter 213
abortion 25–27, 33, 37, 41, 72, 115, 157, 165, 177, 183, 190–191, 200, 242, 291, 296, 302, 351, 368–369
adultery 70–71, 92, 98, 141–142, 177–178, 185, 196, 199–200, 218, 221, 235, 241, 263, 307, 326
AIDS 26, 55, 94, 339, 347, 359
Anscombe, Elizabeth 69, 217, 356
Aquinas, St Thomas 5, 13, 29, 35, 37, 41, 44–45, 48–50, 55–64, 67, 71, 73, 75, 77–78, 80–81, 83, 98–99, 101, 105, 108, 119–120, 130, 134–139, 141, 143, 148, 151, 162–163, 166, 178, 202–203, 208–209, 212–217, 226, 234, 236, 241, 248, 255–256, 260, 265, 268, 338
Aristotle 5, 11, 29, 44–49, 51, 57, 60–63, 67, 70, 77, 96, 101–103, 108, 131, 133, 135, 137, 148, 168, 205, 207, 218, 249–250, 255–257
Augustine, St 23, 29, 64, 202, 230–233, 236–237, 246, 268, 310, 336
autonomy 5, 9, 24, 38, 54, 62, 68, 78, 93–95, 104, 112, 117, 130, 148–150, 156–157, 161–165, 171, 179, 199, 227, 243, 253, 296–297, 300, 324, 338, 360, 368–369

Beatitudes 8, 30, 45, 235, 242–243, 247, 255, 260, 262, 265–266, 268
de Beauvoir, Simone 296
Benedict XVI 6, 332, 364.
  See also Ratzinger, Joseph
Bentham, Jeremy 68
Berlin, Isaiah 175–178
biologism 13, 144–146.
  See also naturalism and physicalism
biology 117, 144–146, 274, 292, 308–309, 340, 350, 367
body 6, 10–12, 22–23, 32, 34, 37–38, 72, 75–77, 83, 85–89, 92–95, 97, 100, 104–108, 114–118, 123, 129, 132, 136, 138–140, 144, 146, 150–152, 157, 169–170, 177, 186, 200, 203, 210, 219–220, 230, 259–260, 262, 273–275, 277–294, 302–311, 314–318, 320, 322–323, 326, 328–335, 338–341, 343–350, 352, 354–355, 357, 361, 370
Bonaventure, St 63, 162

Buttiglione, Rocco 49, 106, 109, 116, 118, 120–122

cardinal virtues 239, 255, 259
categorical norms 28, 184–186
charity 61–63, 154, 169, 176, 179, 202–203, 209, 214, 216, 224, 237–243, 251, 255, 257, 259–261, 263, 267–270, 288, 354, 369
chastity 26, 37, 116, 241, 259, 268–270, 307, 315, 319, 322–323, 327, 346, 348, 351, 354–355, 358
cohabitation 5, 12, 33, 98, 165, 272, 294, 296–297, 301, 313, 316, 321, 323–327, 330, 347, 360
Commandments 27–31, 63, 137, 140–143, 161, 165, 169, 183–186, 188, 193, 226, 228–229, 234–237, 241–243, 262–263, 265
communion of persons 22, 36–37, 89, 97, 142, 279–280, 283–284, 292, 295, 304, 310, 313–317, 325, 328, 330, 332, 336–337, 341, 344–346, 353, 357–358
communion of the Church 245–246
concupiscence 55, 125, 226, 229–230, 277, 286, 289, 293, 319, 329, 332, 335, 337, 340, 353–358
conscience 5, 9, 21, 26, 28–29, 31, 39–40, 42, 48, 51–53, 82, 106, 110, 119–122, 127, 131, 133, 157, 159, 166, 174–176, 178, 183, 206–207, 229, 252–253, 255, 348, 367, 370
consequentialism 13–14, 16, 25, 28, 30, 41, 45, 61, 67–73, 188, 194, 209, 212–213, 221
continence 259, 269–270, 315, 342, 353–357
contraception 5, 11, 26–27, 29, 94, 98, 144–145, 157, 182, 209, 272, 296, 306, 313, 316, 325, 338–339, 342, 344–352, 354, 357, 359–360, 367–368
Covenant New 229, 233, 238
Covenant Old 227–229, 233, 246
'creative reason' 53–54, 366

Declaration of Human Rights 157, 368–369
Descartes, René 40, 74, 77, 83, 85, 88, 106, 132, 164, 186, 273, 280
Dominian, Jack 144
dualism 22, 28, 37–38, 42, 60, 72, 76–77, 83, 85, 87, 93–94, 101, 114, 117, 144–

145, 147, 150, 164, 169, 186, 188, 200, 220–221, 272–273, 273, 283, 288, 303, 307, 311, 315, 326, 338, 340, 344, 350
Duns Scotus 162

embryonic stem-cell research 23, 25–26, 33, 37, 88, 115, 157, 169, 291, 361
embryo research and experimentation 27, 33, 80, 93, 95, 169, 368–369
emotions 49, 58–60, 64, 97, 105–107, 109, 115, 117, 135, 210, 250, 306, 316, 319, 321, 355
Enlightenment 5, 24, 40, 156, 365
equality 37, 62, 141, 156–157, 162, 179, 282, 293, 295–297, 300, 328, 367–369
Escriva, St Josemaria 127, 172, 291, 311
essence 49, 50, 77–78, 107, 109, 131, 187, 284, 305
ethical order 49, 165, 184, 188
Eucharist 241, 244–246, 333
euthanasia 214
evangelical law 8, 28–31, 226–227, 231, 236, 241, 247, 262, 264
Evangelium Vitae 32, 34, 174, 292, 351
evangelization 8, 15, 31, 362–364, 370
experience 5, 10, 12, 15, 34–35, 45–47, 51, 56–59, 98–114, 116–119, 121, 123–124, 126, 128, 130, 133, 134, 137, 148, 172, 174, 187, 189, 199, 249, 251, 253, 277, 281–282, 285, 287, 305–306, 315, 339, 341, 345, 362, 363, 367

faith 5, 7, 12, 16, 23–24, 38–40, 43, 142, 170, 173–175, 185, 187–188, 190, 224, 227, 231–233, 235–236, 239–241, 251, 255, 259–261, 263, 265, 267–269, 288, 336, 338, 362–366, 370–372
feelings 58, 105, 107, 115, 249–251
feminism 13, 294–302, 338, 367
Fides et Ratio 16–17, 24, 38–40, 42–43, 119–120
finis operantis 212
finis operis 212
Finnis, John 69–70, 217
freedom 5, 9–10, 13–16, 19–20, 23, 25–30, 32, 35–36, 38, 40–42, 45, 48–57, 61–62, 65, 68, 71, 73, 75–76, 78, 80–82, 87, 89, 94–95, 100, 107, 109–110, 112, 115, 118–122, 125–126, 132–133, 136, 143–144, 146–151, 154, 156–176, 179, 185–186, 196–201, 213, 225–228, 232, 240, 242–245, 248–249, 253, 255, 279, 286, 300, 302, 311–312, 324, 329, 340, 344, 355–357, 360, 364, 367–369
freedom for excellence 62, 166
freedom of indifference 62, 162–164, 178
fruits of the Holy Spirit 31, 238–239, 255, 260, 262, 268–270
fundamental option 28, 168, 195–198, 201

gender 5, 9, 11, 13, 15, 37, 294–296, 300–301, 311, 313, 367
Genesis 11, 40, 161, 225, 272–293, 295, 297, 308, 327, 329–330, 333, 335–336, 371
gifts of the Holy Spirit 31, 239, 247, 255, 260, 262, 267, 358
goods of the person and good 5, 9, 10, 22, 26, 29, 32–33, 39, 44, 47, 48–52, 55, 58–59, 61–62, 64–73, 77, 79, 82, 84, 89–90, 94, 110, 119, 129–133, 136–144, 146–147, 151–152, 158–159, 163–169, 179, 187, 191–194, 199–200, 209–210, 211–212, 214, 217, 220, 224, 234, 242–243, 249, 338, 339, 340, 344, 364, 368
grace 12, 29, 31, 63–64, 127, 162, 164, 169, 196, 201–202, 224, 230–233, 236–241, 244–245, 259–260, 262, 267, 276–277, 281, 289–290, 292–293, 310, 326, 329–332, 334–335, 353–354, 363, 370–371
gradualness of the law 206
Gregory of Nyssa 166
Grisez, Germain 6

habit 30, 49, 59–61, 72, 124, 163, 234, 248–251, 254–256, 262–263, 267–268, 355
happiness 5, 21, 27, 29, 35, 44, 48–49, 61–70, 89, 122, 163–164, 167–168, 199, 203–204, 225, 228, 234, 262, 265–266, 268, 314, 316, 320–322, 354
Heraclitus 365
heteronomy 150, 160–161, 243
historicity 125–126
Holy Spirit 28, 30–31, 226, 234, 236–240, 243–245, 247, 255, 260–263, 267–269, 280, 292, 304, 353, 357–359
hope 59, 224, 239, 255, 259–261, 288, 319
human action 13, 15, 39, 41, 54, 57–58, 72–73, 77, 99, 182, 192, 200, 208, 212, 214, 217, 221, 258, 262, 316–317, 326, 343, 351, 363
Humanae Vitae 10, 12, 20, 145, 182, 209, 219, 315, 316, 336–361, 367

human right 5, 15, 22, 42, 73, 81, 91, 114, 129, 165, 172, 175, 178, 242, 364, 368
Hume, David 86, 121, 165

ideology of gender 294–298
in-vitro fertilization (IVF) 37, 88, 93–94, 94, 169, 291, 360
indissolubility 173, 318, 329, 331, 336, 372
intention 13–14, 30, 35, 55–56, 70, 73, 112, 120, 122, 166, 183, 184, 186, 189–193, 199, 204, 208–218, 220–221, 264, 314, 347, 351, 356
intrinsically evil acts 14, 28, 32, 82, 84, 145, 177–178, 183, 185, 193
intrinsic worth 21, 33, 77, 84–85, 88–89, 91–93, 96, 100, 140, 142, 147, 214, 321
Irenaeus, St 167

John Paul II 5, 8–11, 15–17, 19–20, 22–23, 31–42, 67, 69, 74–75, 82–83, 88–89, 93, 97, 100, 112, 114, 117, 119, 127, 133, 141, 161, 166, 168, 173, 204, 225, 253, 272–273, 275–276, 278–279, 281–282, 286, 288–290, 292, 295, 303, 306, 310, 314, 329, 332–333, 335–337, 339, 341, 345–346, 349, 352, 357, 359, 362–363, 369, 371. *See also* Wojtyla, Karol
justice 15, 17, 92, 129, 131, 138, 157, 172, 179, 185, 193, 235, 239, 258–261, 266–267, 354, 364, 368–369
justification 31, 188, 231, 233, 239

Kant, Immanuel 37, 45, 56–57, 67–68, 82–83, 111, 118, 150, 186–188, 201, 242
Kiely, Benedict 192, 194
killing the innocent 70, 130, 154, 173, 195, 209, 218
koinonia 244, 246

law of gradualness 206–207, 228, 355
Locke, John 74, 86, 164, 303
logos 23, 53, 54, 366
Lombard, Peter 13, 60, 162, 178
love 10–12, 15, 21–22, 29, 31, 33, 37, 47–48, 58, 61–63, 68–69, 83, 88–89, 95–98, 116, 123–125, 127, 133, 135–136, 140–143, 158, 163, 169, 172, 176, 178–179, 184–185, 190, 196–197, 205, 219, 224–225, 227, 229, 234–237, 239, 241–245, 250, 255, 260–267, 269, 272, 275–276, 278, 284–291, 293, 304–310, 313–323, 325–327, 329–337, 339–350, 352–361, 369
Love and Responsibility 12, 76, 82, 102, 319, 322

MacIntyre, Alasdair 6, 133
Magisterium 6, 8, 10, 14, 39, 53–54, 159, 173–175, 184, 202, 205, 345
Majority Report 144, 151
marriage 5, 9–12, 15, 22, 25–26, 33, 97–98, 123, 140–142, 145, 165, 173, 178, 193, 198, 209, 237, 242, 251, 270–272, 275–278, 284–286, 290–291, 294, 301, 306, 313–321, 323–324, 326–327, 329–337, 339–342, 344–354, 356–360, 362, 367, 369–371
May, William 142, 200
McCormick, Richard 189–190
metaphysics 17, 21, 29, 40, 51, 102–104, 107, 111, 125, 149, 275, 366
moral absolutes 5, 14, 19, 27, 32, 67, 71, 77, 82, 114, 138, 165, 170, 183–186, 188, 190, 194, 204–205, 221, 227, 241, 364
moral object 13, 14, 27, 30, 55–56, 61, 72, 112, 122, 143, 145, 154–155, 190–194, 199, 204, 208–220
moral revisionism 6, 12, 16, 27–28, 70, 182–184
mortal sin 28, 195–198, 201–203
Mystical Body 245–246, 290, 330–332, 371

Natural Family Planning (NFP) 347, 350, 355–357
naturalism 41, 63, 72, 122, 130, 143, 145, 148, 210, 219–221, 338, 360
natural law 10, 12–14, 21–22, 25–27, 29, 32, 37–39, 51–54, 61, 67, 69–70, 77, 83–84, 95, 119, 129–152, 159–160, 174, 182–183, 188, 193, 200, 206, 208, 211, 217, 219, 224, 226–227, 231, 241, 252, 313, 337–338, 342, 359–360, 368
nature 5, 7, 8–10, 12–13, 20–22, 24, 27, 30, 37, 39–40, 43, 53–54, 60, 75–80, 83–84, 86–91, 93–98, 100–101, 111, 113–115, 115, 123, 126, 129, 130–132, 135–136, 139, 143–144, 146–152, 156, 158–159, 161, 163–165, 168–174, 178, 183, 185, 196, 214, 217–219, 224–226, 231, 234, 239–241, 245–246, 250–251, 259, 261, 262, 266, 269, 274–280, 285, 288–295, 299–302, 304–305, 308–309, 312–316, 318–319, 322, 324, 326, 328–

329, 331, 333–335, 337–338, 340–341, 344, 346, 351–352, 355–356, 363, 365, 366–367, 370
Newman, John Henry 16, 171, 240, 370
nuptial meaning of the body 97, 123, 274, 284–286, 293, 306, 316, 320, 328, 339, 347, 353

Ockham, William 68, 158, 162–163
order of salvation 184–185
original innocence 125, 276–278, 284, 286–291, 293, 297, 319, 329, 331, 332, 363, 371
original nakedness 287, 289, 293
original sin 23, 159, 289, 297, 323, 363, 365
original solitude 281–284, 287, 289, 293, 308
original unity 281–283, 289, 293

Parmenides 365
passions 54, 58, 60, 116, 125, 134–135, 159–160, 165, 200, 210, 249–251, 256, 258–259, 266, 316, 319, 329
Paul VI 144, 359
persistent vegetative state 86
personalism 5, 8–10, 16, 19, 22, 32–34, 44, 57, 98, 101–103, 108, 115, 117, 124, 128, 272–273, 277, 306, 336, 339, 341, 344, 348, 359; contemporary personalism 102–128; false personalism 93–94, 344
personalist principle 36, 81, 147
person as gift 95, 98, 123, 284
person as relation 95, 98
phenomenology 51, 102, 104–105, 109, 149
physicalism 13, 143–146, 148, 182, 219, 350–352, 360
Pinckaers, Servais 6, 20, 31, 162–163, 166, 190, 205–206, 239, 243, 263
Plato 131, 133, 364, 366
practical reason 28–29, 41, 45–53, 57, 61–62, 67, 122, 129, 135–138, 148, 151, 207, 267–268
pre-moral good and evil 191–192, 208, 210
procreation 20, 37, 69, 87, 95, 146, 178, 219, 221, 275, 292, 313, 315–316, 336–337, 339–344, 347–351, 356, 358–360, 367
proportionalism 6, 14, 16, 61, 70, 145, 151, 155, 170, 182, 186, 188, 193, 194, 204

prudence 46–48, 51–52, 135, 137, 207, 239, 251, 252–258, 260–261, 267, 354

Rahner, Karl 183, 201, 253
rationalism 40, 88, 304–305, 311
Ratzinger, Joseph 131, 246, 366. *See also* Benedict XVI
re-christianization 362
reason 5–7, 9, 13, 15, 19, 21–26, 28–30, 32, 38–42, 45–55, 58, 60, 62, 65–68, 70–72, 76, 79, 83–84, 86, 90, 94–95, 118–120, 129–143, 145–152, 156, 158–159, 161–167, 169–171, 173, 178, 184, 187–188, 193, 205, 210–211, 214–217, 219, 221, 224, 226–227, 229, 231, 234, 241, 243, 249, 251, 257, 261, 266–268, 270, 279, 307, 311, 313–314, 318–319, 337–338, 343, 345, 349, 353, 355, 364–367, 370, 372. *See also* practical reason and creative reason
(scope of) 133–136
Reconciliatio et Paenitentia 202–203
redemption of the body 277, 281, 289–290, 293, 331–332, 335, 354
Redemptor Hominis 23, 127, 225
relativism 6–9, 13–15, 19, 24–25, 40, 42–43, 68, 82, 90, 101, 106, 147, 178, 227, 364–366
(ethical) 21, 26–28, 32, 71, 164, 204
renewal 5–6, 8, 14–16, 19–20, 23, 27–28, 31–32, 44, 224, 233, 271, 285, 313, 329
Rhonheimer, Martin 134–135, 209, 212, 215, 219

sacrament of creation 275, 310, 329, 349, 371
sacrament of redemption 277, 290–291, 329, 371
Scheler, Max 51, 102, 201
secularism 6–8, 8, 14, 19, 28, 157, 292
self-consciousness 34–35, 76, 99, 103, 105, 107–108, 111, 116, 123, 166, 282
self-defence 154–155, 189, 191, 211, 219
self-determination 22, 34–36, 38, 56–57, 76, 78, 80, 94, 97, 100, 102, 104, 107–113, 108, 116, 119, 123, 125–126, 149–150, 156, 158, 164, 166, 197–198, 281–283, 317
self-gift (and self-giving) 10, 21, 47, 62–63, 95–98, 104, 116, 123–126, 160, 235, 260, 262, 278–279, 284–287, 293–294, 305–308, 313, 315–318, 320–321,

325, 327, 329, 331, 333–334, 345–350, 353–355
self-mastery 36–37, 78, 116, 166, 251, 286, 288, 307, 315, 322, 346, 353–356
self-possession 38, 78, 91, 107, 111, 115, 123–124, 166
self and selfhood 22, 86, 103, 105, 112–114, 117, 121, 123, 133, 140, 230, 274, 276, 306, 346, 355
Sermon on the Mount 8, 29, 30, 128, 235, 242, 248, 262–265
sexual intercourse 193, 352, 357
sexuality 10–12, 37, 77, 87, 89, 92, 140, 144–147, 272, 279, 283, 285
sexuality/gender distinction 300–301
shame 287, 293
sin 27, 31, 63, 125, 132, 160, 164, 175–177, 195, 202–204, 224–225, 229–231, 244, 246, 259, 262–263, 277–278, 281, 287–290, 293, 326, 332, 335, 353. *See also* mortal sin, original sin, venial sin
slavery 152–153, 158, 160, 194, 335, 369
Sophists 365
Stein, St Edith 128, 273, 298–300
stem-cell research 11, 15, 23, 25, 26, 33, 37, 88, 115, 157, 169, 291, 361
subjectivity (of the person) 5, 10–11, 22, 32, 34–37, 44–45, 53, 57, 62, 76, 87, 92, 94, 98–103, 106, 108–114, 116–117, 123, 130, 249, 253, 281–283, 305, 307, 314–315, 339–341, 355
substance 10, 34, 75–79, 85–86, 113, 126, 128, 149, 274, 305
suppositum 10, 34, 78, 99–100, 103, 111

teleological (teleological ethics) 39, 204–205
theological virtues 224, 239, 255, 259–261
Theology of the Body 6, 9, 11–12, 32, 102, 117, 272, 274–275, 280, 290–294, 314, 337, 339, 345, 362, 367
theonomy (participated theonomy) 150, 161, 243
tolerance 21, 175–176
trans-gender operations 169
transcendence 21, 84, 109, 121, 125–128, 288
transcendental norms 28, 184, 187
truth 5, 8–10, 13, 15–17, 19–21, 23–30, 32, 36, 38–39, 42–43, 45–46, 48, 50, 52–55, 57, 60, 62–63, 65–67, 73, 75, 77, 82, 84–85, 88–90, 94, 101–102, 108, 111–112, 118–122, 125, 127–128, 130, 132–139, 143, 146, 148–150, 156–179, 185, 192–194, 199, 201–202, 206, 225, 227, 242–243, 249, 253, 268, 272, 274–276, 278, 285–286, 289, 294, 297, 300–302, 305, 307–309, 310–312, 314–316, 322–323, 325, 327, 329–330, 332, 335, 339–342, 344–345, 348–349, 353–355, 358–359, 362–368, 370–371

ultimate good of the person 35, 45, 47, 167–168, 195, 197, 204, 224
utilitarianism 9, 17, 25, 36, 38, 41, 61, 64, 67, 68–72, 82–83, 133, 188, 204–205, 209, 302, 322, 327, 333, 360

Vatican II 5, 8, 19–23, 28, 31–32, 36, 39, 89, 96, 111, 123, 160, 171, 175, 196, 205, 260, 272, 290
venial sin 196–197, 201–203
Veritatis Splendor 5, 6, 10, 14, 17, 27, 31, 32, 52–53, 64, 72, 83, 84, 85, 89, 90, 112, 130, 136, 142–143, 146–147, 151–152, 159, 162, 167, 168–170, 174, 184–186, 198, 200–202, 204, 205, 208–209, 213–214, 216, 226, 229, 233, 235–237, 244, 253–255, 263, 265, 338, 363
virtues 8, 17, 25, 27–31, 37, 44–45, 48, 50–51, 59–63, 67, 72, 124, 128, 131–132, 135, 138, 163, 166, 169, 182, 205, 207, 224, 232, 234, 239–243, 247–263, 267–269, 299–300, 309, 354–355, 363
voluntarism 13, 54, 62, 158, 164, 337–338
von Hildebrand, Dietrich 337, 341

Warnock, Mary 93
West, Christopher 342, 354, 357
Wittgenstein, Ludwig 117
Wojtyla, Karol 11–12, 15–16, 25, 33–38, 45, 49, 51, 56–57, 62, 67, 74, 76, 80–83, 87, 98–110, 112–113, 115–123, 126, 128, 149, 272–274, 277, 319, 322, 357. *See also* John Paul II
Wolfenden Report 12, 177

www.ingramcontent.com/pod-product-compliance
Lightning Source LLC
Chambersburg PA
CBHW032015230426
43671CB00005B/92